Developing Business Knowledge

Developing Business Knowledge

Second Edition

Charles Booth
Jane Harrington

Los Angeles | London | New Delhi
Singapore | Washington DC

First edition first published 2005
Reprinted 2010

SAGE Publications Ltd
1 Oliver's Yard
55 City Road
London EC1Y 1SP

SAGE Publications Inc.
2455 Teller Road
Thousand Oaks, California 91320

SAGE Publications India Pvt Ltd
B 1/I 1 Mohan Cooperative Industrial Area
Mathura Road, Post Bag 7
New Delhi 110 044

SAGE Publications Asia-Pacific Pte Ltd
33 Pekin Street #02-01
Far East Square
Singapore 048763

Library of Congress Control Number: 2008933845

British Library Cataloguing in Publication data

A catalogue record for this book is available from the British Library

ISBN 978-1-84860-437-7 (pbk)

Typeset by C & M Digital (P) Ltd., Chennai, India
Printed and bound in Great Britain by Ashford Colour Press Ltd
Printed on paper from sustainable resources

Contents

Introduction

Introduction

Welcome to the second edition of the customised textbook for the Developing Business Knowledge course (DBK for short). This custom textbook is a reader developed collaboratively by ourselves and SAGE Publications, the leading publisher of English language social science research methods titles. It contains chapters, articles and other material specifically chosen by us from a range of SAGE books and journals, to support your learning on the DBK module. It is essential reading for the course and should be read alongside the module booklet and the seminar readers we will provide separately.

Visit any well-stocked academic library or bookshop and you will find a number of books on business and management research methods. Almost all of them will be aimed at people learning how to carry out empirical research, often as part of a substantial project leading to an academic qualification of some kind. Thus, these books are concerned almost exclusively with equipping students and other researchers with the knowledge and skills deemed necessary to become knowledge producers, albeit often as novices. Our approach is different. Rather than focusing on the methods and techniques of empirical investigation, we are concerned to enable the critical appreciation of published management research: in other words, to help you to read and understand academic research about management that is already in the public domain. In this respect, we try to shift attention from the production of management knowledge towards its consumption.

Although most students who study management research methods do so as part of a primary research project for a thesis or dissertation, this is by no means exclusively the case. Many students carry out research projects based entirely on secondary or tertiary sources. In addition, almost everybody carrying out a major research project, at whatever level, is required to engage in a substantial review of the relevant academic literature. In typical research methods texts, however, the literature review is dealt with in a single chapter – if that – and the discussion often pays little attention to developing readers' understandings of the multiple contexts in which management research is embedded. When literature reviews *are* discussed, emphasis tends to be placed on the mechanics of literature search-ing rather than on the detailed critical evaluation of published research studies.

Similarly, where philosophical or theoretical issues in management research are explored, this tends to be in either rather a detached way or is aimed towards the selection of a methodology for the students' own research, rather than being linked to the evaluation of published research which is itself pro-duced, disseminated and consumed within a complex set of philosophical, the-oretical and disciplinary contexts.

It follows from this, though, that we do not *exclusively* focus on the consump-tion of published research. Indeed, at the risk of contradicting what we said a few paragraphs ago, we would resist the temptation to draw a very strong dis-tinction between the production and consumption of knowledge. In the case of academic management research, producers of knowledge (that is, researchers) are also consumers. In reviewing the academic literature on an issue in order to frame a research question to pursue, or in order to develop a conceptual frame-work, one is simultaneously consuming and producing knowledge. We would go further than this, and say that the production of management knowledge is inevitably shaped by its modes of consumption, and vice versa.

For example, much academic management research is disseminated and con-sumed through the medium of the refereed paper in a scholarly journal, rather than, say, through monographs and other sorts of books. The reward and career structures in management academe – among many other things – influence and are strongly influenced by scholars' abilities to publish this kind of work. It is therefore to be expected that the organization and management of research groups, systems of research funding, the everyday professional and academic practices of researchers, the type of research pursued (in short, the nature and form of knowledge produced) will be profoundly shaped by the specific demands of publication in this medium.

These connections persist throughout the course, and through the activities with which this book is intended to assist you. In order to make sense of an aca-demic paper, for example, it is also important to appreciate the contexts, sys-tems and practices that shaped the study, its publication and dissemination, its critical reception, and so on. Why was the particular research topic chosen? What led to the use of particular methods to investigate the topic? Why is the paper structured in the way it is? Why have the authors chosen to highlight cer-tain evidence to support their claims? Why was it published in this journal rather than that one? Why might it have aroused such controversy? Critical appreciation, or sense-making, in this respect goes well beyond the evaluation of the argument or findings of a piece of research. Context and process are crucial to understanding, not just content.

It is probably important, at this stage, to clarify what we mean by management research, and to begin to explore some of the implications of our framing the sub-ject of the course in this way. Firstly, although we believe that not all research about management is *academic* research, that is the kind of enterprise that we will be focusing on in the course. We follow the position of John Ziman (2000) in distinguishing, not between the sciences and the humanities, for example, but between academic and non-academic science. This is, admittedly, a somewhat problematic viewpoint; when we come to discuss different 'Modes' of knowledge production – including what Ziman calls 'post-academic' science – it will become clear that the distinction cannot be made, in practice, as clearly as we have it here. Similarly, some students may object to the implication that management research is specifically a *scientific* activity (and some may object to any views that it is not!). Some will prefer to think of research as a craft, the skills of which are formed through the development of tacit knowledge over time. Others will protest at the apparent privilege accorded to science as a human endeavour. In a sense, we are using the word 'science' as a kind of shorthand. We readily admit the worth (though would point to the difficulty) of making distinctions between the physical, biological, social and human sciences, for example. But what is at the heart of our position is the view that there is more in common between academic researchers in a business school, a physics research team, and a philosophy department, for example, than there is between an academic management researcher, a management consultant, and a practising manager.

We are not making any claims or judgements about whether this is a good thing or not (although we explore such claims later in the course); many influential people, both within and outside management education and research, have certainly argued that this is one of the reasons management research is in a critical condition. In any case, what Ziman argues – and we endorse here – is that academic science possesses a distinctive culture, history, and set of practices and principles that distinguish it rather fundamentally from other kinds of research about management. For reasons of space, convenience and coherence, we have chosen largely to focus on this type of research.

One of the things we try to do on the course, then, is to explore the modern development of management research, and how it is framed by structures and institutions associated with dominant conceptions of science, including academic disciplines, university departments, learned societies and scholarly journals. The DBK course is therefore intended to enable you to develop an understanding of the multiple contexts in which management research is produced and consumed and the practices through which its production (etc) is accomplished. In DBK those contexts are historical, philosophical and institutional. By *historical* we mean that the systems, structures and practices of academic knowledge production, evaluation and consumption (let us call this *the knowledge system*) have developed over time and that this historical evolution has implications for the nature and organization of the knowledge system as we understand it today. This development (related to the various arguments for 'scientific exceptionalism' discussed in Reading 5) forms the background for the readings in the text.

As far as the *philosophical* context is concerned, Readings 10 and 11 demonstrate that many commentators argue that research is governed by more than value-free observation. There are different ways of knowing, different ways of being-in-the-world – it is argued – that underpin different approaches to research. These ideas are introduced briefly in Reading 2, before being developed in more detail in Reading 7 and 9, and particularly in 10, 11, 13 and 14. These readings are partly oriented towards helping you to interpret and evaluate research from these different perspectives, and partly towards helping you to reflect upon the perspectives themselves and their implications for the knowledge system.

Management research also, of course, takes place within and around a particular *institutional* context. This context is disciplinary (in as much as management and the organizational sciences are an academic discipline or group of disciplines), organizational (much of this research takes place around such organizations as business schools), and disseminational (research is communicated and disseminated through various means, foremost among which is the scholarly publication system). These different sub-contexts each helps shape the knowledge system, in both subtle and more obvious ways. Key readings here are 5, 6, 12, 15, and 16.

The book is organized so that the readings very broadly map onto the topics covered in the DBK course as it evolves over the year. Reading 1, which is a chapter from Locke, Silvermann & Spirduso's book on reading and understanding research, is an introduction to how to read academic research. It should be read alongside the first lecture and seminar. It will help you orient yourself towards the range of skills and values that we aim to help you develop on the programme. Reading 2 is another chapter from the same book and it is an introduction to different types of social research: again, this should be read to orient yourself at the beginning of the course and to begin to gain an awareness of the different ways research can be evaluated, as well as carried out. Reading 3 is a checklist published in Ann Huff's book on writing for scholarly publication. Once more, it will be helpful in orientation as well as giving you a very detailed set of criteria you can use in evaluating the research you read for this and other courses. The final piece of introductory reading is Reading 4, which is a chapter on how to carry out a literature review, from a recent textbook by Nick Lee.

The nature of the management knowledge system is introduced in the next few lectures. Readings 5 and 6 (as well as 12 and 14–16 inclusive, which you will read later in the programme) will be helpful in revising and developing your knowledge of these issues. At the centre of the knowledge system is scholarly publication. Reading 6, by Frost and Taylor, is an essential background paper for this topic. Read it to reinforce your understanding of the lecture and to support the seminar activity (your discussion of Nord's paper and of the data on the publication system).

The next major topic introduced on the course is interpreting and evaluating published research. The readings you will have done at the start of the programme will provide a solid underpinning here. If you have not yet read them, do so before the lecture on 'Introduction to Evaluating Research'. Following this, Reading 7 by Gill and Johnson and Reading 9 by Cresswell are summaries of different types of research and their relationship to management theories. Reading 8, by Teddlie and Tashakkori specifically focuses on mixed methods research. These issues will be explored in much greater depth a bit later on when we encounter the topic of research paradigms. If you want, you can delve a bit further into these issues now by skimming Readings 10 and 11, or you may prefer to save them until later. Before we move to the next major topic (and the core of the course) there is one lecture (on 'Theories and Theorising') which attempts to link together the interpreting/evaluating material and the work which you are doing on the literature review. This lecture is again supported by Reading 9 which sheds light on different approaches to building theories and models in social research.

We now come to the material on research paradigms, which is conceptually enormously important, both in its own right and because it links so many other parts of the course together. We start with Reading 11, Guba and Lincoln's comprehensive overview of the different paradigms. This chapter is a summative overview of different paradigms in qualitative research and should help you to develop a clear understanding of the similarities and differences between the different philosophical approaches to social research. It is supported by the inclusion of various short, definitional, entries from *The SAGE Encyclopedia of Social Science Research Methods* (Reading 10). These readings are essential background reading to support the paradigms lectures. The final reading on this part of the course is the paper by Lewis and Kelemen on multiparadigm inquiry (Reading 13). In contrast to other perspectives, which often argue that different approaches to research can or should be seen as mutually exclusive, Lewis and Kelemen argue for a research strategy which is consciously multi-perspectival. This of course has strong links to the earlier lecture on 'Evaluating Mixed Methodologies' and this paper can be read at the earlier stage of the course if required.

The final topic on the course we have labelled policy issues. It has very clear links back to the material on the knowledge system, as well as to that on paradigms. The first sub-topic is unitarism vs pluralism, which raises the question as to whether management research is better off with a multiplicity of research perspectives or whether the discipline would make more progress by going back to basics and adopting a single perspective. This debate is reviewed in the paper by Hassard and Kelemen (Reading 14). The second sub-topic tackles the thorny question of rigour and relevance in management research – that is, should research be more 'practical' or more 'scientific' in orientation? One perspective on this debate is taken by Michael Goldberg (Reading 15). These issues are also discussed in the series of 'snapshots' we have included (as Reading 12) from the very recent *SAGE Handbook of New Approaches in Management and Organization* Finally, in Reading 16, Ken Starkey and Sue Tempest review and extend these controversial debates in their paper on the future of the business school.

Overall, then, this reader includes material which we believe is essential to supporting your learning on the course. There is rather a large amount of orientation material (Readings 1–4) to get you started, with the main topics up until the beginning of the Easter term covered in Readings 5–9. The material on research paradigms crops up in a number of readings, but is the prime focus of Readings 10, 11 and 13. The final readings (14–16, plus Reading 12) support the final group of lectures/seminars on policy issues and management research. Taken as a whole, the readings should help you navigate your way through the major course topics and provide strong thematic links that help you understand the connections between these various aspects of management research.

A book of this format necessarily presents both advantages and disadvantages compared to more standard textbooks. Because some of the readings are taken from more extended texts, the 'flow' of the book might appear a little jerky and disconnected at times, and in some cases you will not be able to follow up references very easily because we have not always had space to reproduce the bibliographies from all the source texts (if you do want to follow up one of these 'missing' references, email the details to Charles at charles.booth@uwe.ac.uk). The book lacks an index, so it may be that tracking ideas across the different readings is more difficult than with a standard textbook. On the other hand, this is a text that has been designed with specific reference to the structure and content of the DBK module. Without it, there would be no course textbook for DBK. Because we chose the readings with the other course material specifically in mind, you can be sure that each reading, and the collection as a whole, is intended to help you work with ideas and concepts concerning the DBK course.

A final word: we realise that the DBK module, and the materials we provide to support it here and elsewhere, might appear both rather daunting and of limited practical relevance to you as you stand on the threshold of what we hope will be a successful and rewarding career. This book and the other materials we provide are intended to help you cope with the complexity of the course, and to help you in achieving the highest possible level of performance on the module and in the final year of your degree. And as for relevance? Well, it seems obvious that a critical and appreciative engagement with management research should be helpful to you in *all* your final year modules, not just this one. In addition, consider that what you are about to embark on is a study of a large, complex, international organizational system – that of management academe – with radically different systems, structures, values and cultures from the organizational systems you may be familiar with. In a rapidly globalising political economy, developing a competence in understanding and working with difference is becoming part of the demands placed on all managers: and in this respect, DBK is as practically relevant as you can hope for.

Charles Booth
Jane Harrington

July 2008

Reference

Ziman, J. 2000. *Real Science: What It Is, and What it Means.* Cambridge: Cambridge University Press.

How to Select and Read Research Reports

LAWRENCE F. LOCKE, STEPHEN J. SILVERMAN
and WANEEN W. SPIRDUSO

This chapter has two major sections. The first deals with how to select research reports from which you can study and learn, and the second addresses how to read them after you have found them. The latter section involves a discussion of the language of research, the value of working with others as you begin, and how to approach the reading task itself.

❖ GETTING STARTED: SELECTING RESEARCH REPORTS

Looking for the Right Read

If you are using this guide in conjunction with a college course or training program, the selection of reports with which to begin will probably be determined by your instructor. For those of you who are working alone or with an informal study group, we have some advice about picking research reports for practice reading (advice that applies, of course, to those of you in college classes after your instructor turns you loose to find your own readings in the library): *Until you have gained some skill and confidence, select studies dealing with topics about which you have some familiarity.*

That recommendation sounds like simple common sense, but we want to expand on what is obvious by addressing some misunderstandings about how (and for whom) research reports are written. Here are some other reasons for our suggestion to initially select studies in areas for which you have at least basic competence. Researchers write reports in the systematic language that is particular to the area of scholarship represented in the study. That fact adds some complexity to the task of locating reports appropriate for the beginning reader in terms of both language and content.

The languages of research. Based on the common language of everyday speech, research languages (sometimes called *system languages*) add a combination of both technical vocabulary and the conventions (style and format) of scientific writing. Because they are highly formal languages, they allow much less latitude for individual expression and, correspondingly, a great capacity for precision and parsimony. The end result is a dense style of prose containing many unfamiliar words. There is little waste of ink in getting to the point, and each sentence is crammed with important meaning. In our ordinary experience, only specialized documents such as technical manuals and insurance policies present anything like this kind of daunting reading task.

As you might guess, system languages are used because they provide reliability in communication. After a system language is mastered, the words in that language mean one thing (and only one thing) to both reader and writer. The problem is that these languages also serve to limit the access of nonspecialists.

The audience for reports. If you are an outsider, some research reports in the social sciences might just as well have been written in a foreign language, which raises a familiar question: "Why don't researchers write their reports in common language so everyone can understand them?" In answer, the virtue of standardization for reliable communication has already been noted, but the issue of economy bears even more directly on the matter of how reports are written.

If reports were written in a common language that was intended to have the same degree of precision and reliability, most research reports would balloon to many times their present length and still might present significant risk of misunderstanding. Beyond that problem, however, lies an even more fundamental explanation for why authors of research reports do not write in a language intelligible to the layperson.

Researchers write for other researchers (or, at least, for people who are insiders to the area of inquiry), and they have little motive to make themselves understood by outsiders. The reports they write are the primary (although not the only) vehicle for a continuing conversation among active scholars in an area of investigation. When their research is published, what they have learned from a study is both added to the archive of knowledge and made available for assimilation (and critique) by their scientific colleagues. As an outsider, reading research reports allows you to listen in on that conversation, but you must understand that you are not the authors' primary audience.

It is not a matter of hostility to nonresearchers. The point is that you just were not the imagined audience for the report. Being understood by fellow researchers is absolutely critical to personal success as a scholar and, of course, to the wider goals of science. Put bluntly, however, research reports are not intended to be intelligible to the rest of us.

Nevertheless, research reports are in the public domain, and it is fully understood by all that many different kinds of people will read them. In consequence, crashing this party involves none of the social sanctions we reserve for uninvited guests at other gatherings. Besides, in many instances, you will not be a complete outsider, a fact that makes eavesdropping on the conversations of researchers a lot easier.

Because part of a research report's language is drawn from the author's area of scholarship (usually circumscribed by the discipline in which he or she was trained), you should be able to follow at least the broad outline of a study if you have an introductory level of familiarity with concepts in that field. Exceptions lie in the area of specialized research terminology—words that deal with investigative processes themselves and words that are consequent to more advanced (or simply more recent) knowledge than your own. For those words that are completely unfamiliar, some new learning—the learning of the terms and the constructs they represent—is required as part of the reading process.

No guide can make all reports transparent for your inspection. Outside the social sciences, where system languages often have evolved into shorthand symbol systems (e.g., mathematics, chemistry, genetics, dance, physics, astronomy, and statistics), anything short of a solid grounding in the subject matter leaves you forever outside most published reports. Other areas of inquiry, however, make much less heroic demands on the reader.

Although they do have indigenous system languages, professional fields such as education, public health, counseling, nursing, and business administration, as well as some of the disciplines in the social and behavioral sciences (e.g., social psychology, anthropology, communication studies, and political science), are much less impenetrable for the novice. This is largely because they use less cryptic shorthand and more carefully selected common language.

We now go back to the matter of selecting studies for your first efforts. It should now be obvious that, given any choice, you should pick studies from an area in which you have some academic credentials. Beyond that point, however, three considerations will further ease the difficulty of getting started. First, studies of professional practice that employ research methods borrowed from the social sciences (education and nursing are good examples here) offer reports that are often perfect for the novice reader. Second, as a general rule, applied studies dealing with practical problems are easier to decipher than those dealing with basic inquiry into the nature of things. Third, and finally, shorter reports make more sense for the beginner than do lengthy accounts (although page count is not always a reliable indicator of complexity), if only because you can get to the end sooner.

If you are working alone and are particularly nervous about your ability to get off to a good start, we suggest that you retrieve both of the studies for which we have filled out model 12-step forms in Appendix B. Then, as you work your way through the next chapter (5), you can use those reports for your first round of practice. By having our record forms to serve as guides on those first journeys, perhaps you will find yourself less anxious about being out there in foreign territory.

Another strategy for locating reports that are appropriate for beginners to read and understand is to make use of published collections, which reprint carefully selected items from research journals. The editors of such books usually choose reports that are high quality, relatively short, easily deciphered by students in introductory courses, and conveniently grouped into categories according to design, method, or paradigm. Here are good examples in several disciplines: social sciences: Lomand (2002); education: Lyne (1999); qualitative research: Milinki (1999); educational psychology: Patten (2002a); and nursing: Peteva (2003).

Reading Research Cooperatively

If at all possible, find a fellow traveler who can share the work of puzzling through your first reports. In a college research class or topical seminar, the instructor's support almost guarantees that you will not end up completely confused or, worse, completely wrong in your understanding. When you are working alone, those are genuine risks. Having one or several partners, however, not only reduces the perceived hazards, it substantially lowers the possibility of getting hung up. It is our experience that the interactive social effects of exchanging understandings—and misunderstandings—have a powerful and positive influence on the process of deciphering research reports. Two or three people working together can puzzle through difficult passages that any one of them, working alone, would never fathom.

As you will see in Chapter 5, much of our advice is based on the supposition that you are not working alone. If going solo is unavoidable, however, there is help (beyond our suggestion that you begin with reports that have been subject to some form of analysis in this text). A good-quality introductory research textbook can answer many of your questions and provide support while you read.

Any of the textbooks annotated in Appendix A can serve that purpose. We urge you to obtain one of those reference sources, particularly if you are not going to be working with others. You should familiarize yourself with both the content of the opening chapter and the topics that are covered in the main text and appendixes. A glossary of research terminology and a detailed index will serve you well as you confront the exotic tongues in which reports are written. If you need only a brief overview of the methods used in quantitative and qualitative studies, an inexpensive (paperbound) and very effective choice would be Patten (2002b). In that text, the author provides no more than basic literacy in research—including the language and fundamental constructs—but does so with crisp authority and tight focus on the essentials.

Finally, whether working alone or in a college class, before you begin reading that maiden study, we urge you to complete a first reading of the next chapter. In it, we provide several sets of special survival tools that have been field tested with hundreds of novice research readers. The evidence shows that these strategies work for almost everyone who uses them to try to master the craft of reading research.

The first set of survival tools includes three 12-step record forms that provide a simple format for mapping your progress and not getting lost (or overwhelmed). The second set includes a number of exercises that require you to explain research reports to other people. The latter serves to test and expand your understanding of what you have read—perhaps much more rapidly than you would ever have expected. With the help of both of these supporting procedures, most travelers can do more than simply survive their first encounter with the wily research report—they can begin to tame the beast. Before you read about these tools in the next chapter, however, we want to pass on some general advice about how to approach the reading of research reports with an attitude that will maximize the benefits you gain from the endeavor.

❖ HOW TO READ RESEARCH REPORTS

This guide contains a great deal of advice concerning how to approach and actually do the work of reading research reports. Later in this chapter, we provide specific strategies, often in the form of alternative ways of doing tasks, so that readers with different needs and capabilities can find procedures that fit them as individuals. This brief section, however, offers some general advice that we have found useful in helping anyone read research in ways that are fruitful and satisfying.

If you have read this far, it will not surprise you to find that we begin our advice about reading research with some issues that are personal rather than technical. By this point, it should be clear that we regard the most fundamental difficulties in reading reports to be matters of attitudes, values, and confidence.

The technical impediments to understanding research are real enough, but they also represent problems that have straightforward solutions. Getting your attitude adjusted about research, however, is more than a matter of learning a new vocabulary or mastering the arcane conventions of research strategy. Laying the foundations for good readership is intensely personal. It often requires some hard work and persistence, and it has to be accomplished before reading can yield full benefits.

Researchers as Writers: Style and Substance

Like everyone else, researchers come in all shapes, sizes, and personalities. Some produce reports that you will find distant and austere—because that is precisely what the authors are like as people. Other researchers would fit comfortably into your living room for an evening of easy and congenial conversation, and that is exactly how they write.

Beyond qualities of personality, however, are the elements of the writing craft itself. Some investigators obviously have mastered the required skills: They are firm and lucid in their discussion of complex issues and adroit in laying out a clear line of history for their study. Others, just as obviously, are beginners at both formal inquiry and its accompanying demand for writing accounts of what they did. They are uncomfortably tentative and in many ways make it difficult for the reader to follow the story of what was done and what it might mean. In that wide range of expository skills, researchers are no different from the rest of us. If you ask them to explain their work, some produce accounts that are easy to follow, and others present pieces of communication that strain your capacity for attention and convey garbled or incomplete images.

Notwithstanding the commonsense observation that reports differ in their style and intelligibility, the enormous variety in research reports, as prose writing, invariably surprises the beginning reader. The fact that researchers are working within the dual constraints of elaborate scientific conventions and a formal language system leads people to expect that reports will be homogeneous in style and organization, and somehow free from the print of the individual investigator. Nothing could be further from the truth.

Writing technical reports is, nevertheless, writing. Nothing in the prescriptions of format and style can insulate readers as people from authors as people. Accordingly, you should be reassured that having a personal response to what you read is perfectly normal and quite appropriate because, in the end, research reports are personal stories. They are not written by robots, and, although they might be written on computers, they certainly cannot be written by computers.

You should always appreciate graceful writing wherever you encounter it. With research reports, however, pragmatism makes clarity, precision, and thoroughness the elements that matter most. There is no requirement that you enjoy an author's expository style or appreciate the elegance of his or her illustrations. If those happen to be your reactions, so much the better. When they are not, what alternative do you have?

Put directly, you are reading research reports because you are looking for facts and ideas, not because you are seeking entertainment. Within reasonable limits, you must put up with whatever is on the page as long as it yields the substance that you seek.

Researchers as Workers: The Matter of Respect

If you persevere in your efforts to read research as a resource, one particular disposition toward the authors will serve you well. You will have to cultivate this attitude as you practice the skills of consuming research, and you might need to sustain it at some personal cost in the face of serious challenge. It is the attitude of respect—basic respect for the person who did the work.

Let us reduce this matter to its simplest terms. The authors of research reports did the work, took time out of their lives, struggled with ideas, labored over writing the report, and, in the end, took the very real risk of going public, laying their work out in print where everyone can read and judge. That does not make them paragons and certainly does not make inferior science or poor reporting into anything better than it is. What it does do, however, is give you an obligation to take them seriously and to show respect for their intentions.

Whatever your investment as a reader, you owe the author respect for his or her investment as a scholar. You will naturally adopt this attitude when reading strong studies reported in clear, well-organized prose. Unless you are unusually fortunate in your selection of reports to read, however, most will fall somewhat short of that optimum standard.

As you read, it is vital to remember that the vast majority of studies, particularly those in the social sciences, are compromises between perfection and the practicalities of time and money with which the researcher, just like the rest of us, must live. Furthermore, you should keep in mind that it is exceedingly difficult to write a completely transparent historical report of complex technical operations, given the space limits imposed by most research journals.

To the extent, then, that research reports can be problematic documents, all research consumers have to invest some serious effort in reading them. Effort alone, however, will not make it possible to understand every report, and certainly not every report in its entirety. Some reports simply make demands that are beyond the beginning reader's capabilities. This problem, of course, is precisely why this guide was written. What you are doing now is learning how to apply your reading efforts (just trying hard will not be enough). You must "work smart" if you are to get as much as possible from accounts of studies that were (necessarily) less than ideal, that were described through the limited medium of the journal report, and that contain some elements you do not (perfectly) understand. That is simply the way things are.

We trust that most of you can tolerate these limitations and that many of you can find ways to thrive within them.

Belief in the author's good intentions, if not always in his or her good execution, will sustain you through the difficult patches in most reports. If you presume that researchers are honestly trying to inform you, it is easier to work at the task of trying to understand what they have written.

The Reader as Consumer: Burdens to Leave Behind

Disrespectful attitudes toward research authors are not just violations of a humane ethic, they are burdens that become handicaps in learning what reports have to teach. Disrespect often is characterized by a readiness to find fault (which, as we will explain, is not the same thing as reading with caution and a critical eye) and a sense of suspicion about the author's motives. The idea, for example, that academics grind out volumes of second-rate studies on trivial topics for the sole purpose of winning financial rewards, status, or job security is not uncommon among both college students and the lay public. Prejudices like that do not enable readers to be attentive and respectful.

In the social and behavioral sciences, we have observed that some readers approach each study with the assumption that it represents a polemical device intended to promote an ideology dear to the author rather than an honest accounting of inquiry. Accordingly, those readers expend a good deal of energy in searching out flaws or refuting assertions rather than trying (first) to understand what is said.

Another destructive attitude held by some readers is the suspicion that the author is playing games with them. They see the report as the playing field for a lopsided contest in which meanings are deliberately obscured, and the reader is challenged to penetrate the maze of jargon and convoluted argument to discover what happened in the study. Inevitably, the result is anger and resentment over every difficulty encountered in the text.

As you can imagine, when burdened with negative expectations like these, people seldom are able to persevere in their efforts to consume research. After initial attempts that are distracted or aborted by suspicion and hostility, some readers retreat into a state of learned helplessness: "I just can't understand all that strange terminology and stuffy writing." Others simply dismiss any study that is not immediately transparent: "The study was a jumbled mess, just completely confusing."

There is no quick therapy for those negative views and their unhappy consequences. If your own thoughts are troubled by nagging doubts about researchers and their intentions, we offer for your consideration a lesson from our own experience. *We have never encountered a researcher who we honestly thought did not want his or her readers to understand and appreciate his or her work.* Furthermore, we have found most researchers to be people of enormous integrity who have thought long and hard about the ethical issues of doing and reporting their work. They intend to do good research, and they intend that work to be understood.

If you can accept these simple observations as a starting point for your own efforts, in most cases, you and the author will connect. Communicating about complex matters through the medium of ink and paper is full of hazards, especially because it is a one-way process. What is required to avoid these impediments is respect on both sides: the author's respect for the reader's desire and need to understand, and the reader's respect for the author's intention to make that understanding possible.

Reading Research as Puzzle Solving

Understanding research reports is not so much a function of reading as it is of studying. We have encountered very few people who can assimilate a report by starting at the beginning and reading continuously through to the end. If you are like our students (and like us), you will have to flip pages forward and back, underline and highlight, write in the margins (if you have your own copy), make notes, draw diagrams, and take breaks to think about what you have read. In other words, you will have to study the report, not just read it.

The myth that reading research is naturally easy for some people because they are smart or good at science is not supported by our experience. Some readers do learn to "read smart" and persist when the going is tough, but the task is never easy for anyone. When you are struggling with a report, you might find it helpful to remember the following story about people who make things look easy.

Ted Williams was arguably the greatest hitter in baseball history. Stories about his prodigious "natural" abilities are legion, but he was far more than just a marvelous collection of perfect nerve and muscle. He was a student of his art and a product of his work ethic. He summed that up with wonderful simplicity when a reporter once asked him why he bothered to take such long sessions of batting practice every day. Sensing the implications behind that inquiry, he looked hard at the scribe and said, "Don't you know how hard this all is?" (Will, 1990).

In a similar sense, an expert investigator doing research is the same kind of performance that, from the outside, appears easy. In fact, it involves a distinctly uncommon kind of intellectual application—close, disciplined reasoning combined with dogged care in procedure. It follows that reading research calls for a parallel effort, in kind if not in degree. There is no easy way to do the *New York Times* crossword puzzle. There is no easy way to read research reports. We hope we are successful in helping you to find the latter as satisfying to finish as the former—but you will come to understand "how hard this all is."

Communication in Reports: It Takes Two to Tango

Write this down and pin it up in front of your desk: *It takes two people to communicate about research.* In the case of reports, there are (at least) two people involved: the reader and the writer. Each bears some responsibility for doing the work of clear transmission and reception.

Whenever you find yourself confused or frustrated by a report, remember that there are two people involved. It is our experience that many of the problems encountered by beginning readers are caused by inadequate writing. In other words, not all of the problems in understanding are yours. Often, the difficulty lies with the authors' problem in explaining what they thought they meant.

That being true—and we assure you that it is—do not get discouraged. Particularly, do not blame yourself. When you cannot puzzle out what something means, take a deep breath, skip over the offending part (perhaps to return later), and try to pick up the story where it again becomes intelligible.

Like any other intellectual task, reading research involves skills that improve with practice, feedback, and assistance. You will get better at reading, just as researchers get better at writing. Neither of you has to feel uniquely at fault when communication breaks down. All of us are in this together.

Graphic Tools: Most Travelers Need a Map

People differ considerably in the way they represent ideas in their minds. However, we find that virtually all who are just beginning to read research profit from the process of making a map of the events reported in a study. By "making a map," we do not mean anything highly technical and certainly not anything particularly artistic—we mean only a rough flowchart on which are displayed the major steps of the study in temporal sequence. An example is shown in Figure 4.1.

Although drawing little boxes and connecting arrows might feel a bit too mechanical for some readers, we urge you to at least give it a try. Some of our students are more comfortable leaving out the graphics and just listing key words as reminders of the order of events. If that is how your mind works, please be our guest. The important thing is to create some sort of map that locates each operation within a study.

Examples of such flowcharts accompany each of the research examples in Appendix B, and a map of the report is one of the items on the 12-step record forms presented in Chapter 5. Just remember that the point is to help you keep track of what the author is describing. Style is of no consequence. If it works for you, do it.

In mapping the history of a study, the most common fault among beginning readers is a compulsion to transfer every detail in the story to the chart and to get every relationship exactly correct. *Don't try to do that!* Include on your map only what seem to be major steps, and make corrections or additions as the story (and your understanding) unfolds.

The advantage of a box-and-arrow-type diagram is that it easily accommodates events and ideas that are not part of a linear sequence. You can just write things in as connected items wherever they fit into your own thinking. Using the comic-strip artist's convention of the text balloon is a nice way to distinguish such reminders and comments as attachments to your map of the main elements in the study design, as shown in Figure 4.2.

On Getting Hung Up: Do Not Get Stuck on the Wrong Things

It is perfectly natural for beginners to be unclear about what is essential and what is peripheral for understanding a report. Some things just do not matter if your purpose is to ferret out facts and useful ideas. Other things do matter, but finding their exact meaning can be put off until a broad understanding of the study has been acquired. Here are four ways to avoid getting hung up on things that do not

Figure 4.1 Flowchart ("Stress management workshops as workplace interventions: Impact of periodic refresher follow-ups")

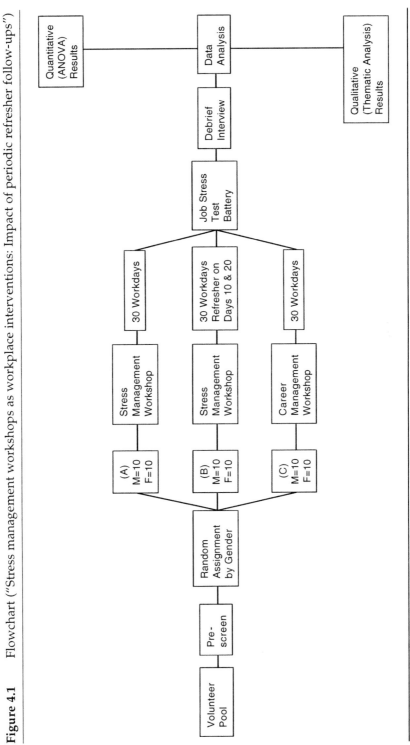

unfamiliar, *look in the text and not in the table!* In any sound report, somewhere will be found a plain-language description of anything found in the analysis that really mattered (in the investigator's mind, at least). In many cases, that bit of text should allow you to proceed with intelligent reading—even if not with full appreciation of the elegance (or appropriateness) of the researcher's statistical analysis.

Where there are plain numbers reported (sometimes as raw data and sometimes as descriptive statistics, such as totals, averages, ranges, and frequencies), it is sometimes quite possible to puzzle out the logic of the analysis even without an understanding of the technicalities involved. Ready assistance is available in some excellent books about statistics that were written for nonstatisticians (several of these are listed in Appendix A; among them, we have found Dodge, 2003, and Pyrczak, 2001, to be particularly helpful for beginning students). Also, the data analysis chapter(s) of an introductory-level research text can often serve to get you past a stumbling block. If you are still stuck, however, after looking for raw numbers, searching out the author's plain-language description of important findings, and using whatever reference aids you have at hand, your only option is to use a time-honored convention—*skip over the statistics and keep on reading.*

Don't let skipping something like statistics panic you, and certainly do not let it make you feel guilty or inadequate. Statistics have a practical purpose, but they are not magical incantations that hold mysterious power. They are just tools.

Trust our reassurance here. The basic purpose of most statistical operations can be figured out with the help of a beginner-level textbook or the help of a friend or mentor. If you encounter any form of quantitative analysis that is more obscure than that, it can safely be skipped over in your reading. Perfect understanding of any analytic technique is rarely essential to finding what you want—good ideas and useful information.

4. *Don't get stuck on* the question, "Is this good research?" Of course, you want to learn how to make better judgments about the adequacy of the studies you read. A sure and unerring hand with that skill, however, is not easy to acquire. To be honest, it takes years of experience to quickly discern flaws of logic and imperfections of analysis in complicated investigation. You must trust the integrity of the journal in which the report appears (and the adequacy of its review procedures) and keep the proverbial grain of salt close at hand.

Fortunately, even the novice will be able to spot the difference between simple forms of sense and nonsense. When you do come upon something that seems improbable in terms of your own knowledge and experience, what do you do? Our advice is firm and simple. Make a note to yourself to look into the matter later, and keep right on reading. Good ideas turn up regularly in studies that contain obvious (and not so obvious) defects.

Torturing yourself with the question, "Is this good research?" will soon short-circuit your ability to attend closely to the author's explanations. Quality in research is always a matter of degree, and perfect studies are rare (it can be argued, as we did in Chapter 3, that they are impossible). Hold off making a summative judgment about the quality of the investigation until you have read the whole report. Formative judgments about particular procedures used, or specific assertions made, by the author are perfectly appropriate and useful observations—just do not let them hold you up.

Yes, there are studies in print that contain such egregious errors that they are not worth the effort of reading. It is our experience that such publications are so rare that they represent little serious risk to the novice reader. In any case, people with extensive experience in doing, writing, and reading research invariably come to believe that the distinction between good and bad research is not easily drawn. Our advice is to use your own common sense about commonsense points and to leave the technical arguments and grand judgments to the experts. Get on with the work of finding interesting or useful knowledge and ideas.

The Limits of Respect: Healthy Skepticism

To close this section, we want to offer another caution. There is a difference between respecting the author of a research report and believing everything you are told. First, researchers do make mistakes when writing up their studies (and you would be astonished to learn how often the processes of publication introduce errors for which the author is not responsible). Second, by their nature, reports are incomplete records, and selective history provides a rich opportunity for all kinds of errors (of omission and commission). Therefore, a little skepticism provides healthy protection against the mistakes that do reach print.

As you read, make it a habit to do a few simple checks. Add up important columns of numbers and see if your sum agrees with that of the author. Be sure you are using figures that truly go together (and beware of discrepancies due to rounding), but when problems persist, mark your marginal flag in red! Arithmetic errors are danger signals.

A number of simple error checks require little time to perform and yield confidence in the report. Is the full citation for an important quotation actually given in the reference list? Is every question that the author formally posed at the outset actually addressed and discussed? Does the size of the subject groups remain the same each time they are referenced in text or tables—and, if not, does the author explain why? If the author says there is a statistically significant difference between the test scores of two groups, look at the actual size of the numerical gap and ask yourself, "Is a performance difference of that size likely to be as important as he or she seems to think it is?" Finally, the irreverent question "So what?" is perfectly legitimate, and, in good reports, the author will raise the question for you. If he or she does not, you have the right to wonder why.

None of these small exercises in healthy skepticism requires the skills of rocket science, but what you can learn from them might be important and sometimes sobering. Careless researchers are often betrayed by their inattention to getting small things exactly right. Their credibility in your eyes must suffer accordingly. Where errors are few, finding them (and here we must be painfully honest) does give the novice a heady sense of power. It is innocent fun to catch the researcher occasionally off base in small details, and, we say, go right ahead and do it, if you can.

However, always keep in mind the honest limits of your ability to critique complex investigations. It is likely that there are many judgments you are not yet competent to make. You have no recourse except to have faith in the skills and integrity of the researcher and the journal. Doing so should not make you uneasy, because all of us have to accept the necessity of trusting the expertise of others—no less in research than in matters of medicine or law. We can assure you that in the vast majority of reports published in refereed journals, such confidence is not misplaced.

You can safely navigate the world of research without falling victim to serious deceptions as long as you maintain an attitude of respectful skepticism. The Romans said it in the Latin phrase *caveat emptor*—buyer beware! We say it in less elegant English—"be respectful but always a little cautious."

2 Types of Research

An Overview

LAWRENCE F. LOCKE, STEPHEN J. SILVERMAN
and WANEEN W. SPIRDUSO

B ecause we suggested in the Preface that this chapter could be used when puzzling through your first attempts at reading reports, you might have arrived here without completing all of the previous chapters. That is perfectly appropriate, and you should find that most of what is contained here is intelligible. As you continue to work through the book and try out our suggested strategies for reading, it might be helpful to return to this chapter occasionally as a way of refreshing your ability to recognize the different types of research encountered.

Previous chapters of this book contain repeated references to the idea that there are different types (or kinds) of research. We have used the generic word *type* to indicate that studies *can* differ from each other in several ways: (a) the initial assumptions they make about the nature of the world (producing paradigmatic differences, such as qualitative and quantitative research), (b) the organization of the study (producing design difference, such as experimental and correlational research), and (c) the procedures used to collect data (producing methodological differences, such as psychometric and interview research).

As you probably will have surmised, the types just mentioned are neither discrete categories (they overlap in all kinds of untidy ways), nor are they an exhaustive list of all the distinctions that account for typological variety in research studies. The three sources of variety noted here, however, contain the most basic elements that characterize alternative ways of doing research—the basic types of inquiry that beginning readers will notice from the outset.

For example, in Chapters 4 and 5, we discussed strategies for reading research reports that, by necessity, required you to distinguish between qualitative and quantitative studies—two types of research that are shaped by different *paradigms* (different sets of assumptions about the nature of reality). Accordingly, you will have noticed on the two 12-step recording forms for research reports that, although the general topics covered at each step do run in parallel, the actual phrasing of the questions sometimes does not. These differences, of course, reflect distinctive elements within the two approaches to inquiry.

Beyond that source of variation lies the fact that each paradigm has spawned a family of alternative types of research (they could be considered paradigmatic subspecies). In quantitative research, distinctly different designs reflect different pragmatic purposes (for example, to create descriptions or to detect associations). Likewise, in qualitative research, strategic variations in design serve different research intentions (for example, production of theory, discovery of participants' perspectives, or social empowerment of participants).

In addition, however, under the qualitative umbrella are types of research that differ for reasons that go beyond the straightforward demands of research strategy. These types reflect different understandings of what constitutes data, how researchers should relate to participants, and what represent acceptable rationales for engaging in social research. Little of that complexity need concern you at this point. For now it is quite sufficient to recognize several of the types you are most likely to encounter in the first tour through the research literature in your own area of interest.

For several reasons, however, the task of dealing with different types of inquiry will not be as daunting as you might anticipate. It is true that different types of research do sometimes produce distinctively different organizations in the reports, and thus pose different demands (and reading problems) for the beginner. As you will discover in this chapter, however, a more direct examination of differences among types of research reveals the paradoxical fact that there also are pervasive similarities. Many variations in research strategy represent different ways of confronting a common set of underlying problems. The nomenclature might differ but, in the midst of variety, you will encounter many familiar ideas.

Before surveying concerns that are generic to many types of inquiry, however, we want to remind you of a point made repeatedly in this text. Although technical knowledge can be helpful in deciphering research reports, you do not need to become an expert in research methodology and design to extract useful information from them. Because we feel strongly about that point, we selected the content of this chapter to provide no more than a simple framework for categorizing studies, as well as the conceptual basis for recognizing a small, basic set of issues pertaining to the conduct of research. If you want more detailed information, the books annotated in Appendix A should provide a helpful place to begin.

❖ GENERIC ISSUES IN RESEARCH

Planning research requires many decisions that ultimately will bear on the quality of the data collected and the credibility of the findings. First among those is the choice of study procedures that relate to the twin characteristics of *validity* and *reliability.* Although those two terms are used in a variety of ways in the scientific community (and synonyms are often substituted in particular research traditions), we will ignore those complexities and define them here in the way that is the most prevalent and that most closely relates to your task of reading reports.

Although the word *validity* generally denotes the condition of being true, researchers use it with regard to two aspects of their investigations. One set of validity issues is internal to a study and concerns whether the research has been designed so that it truly deals with what is being examined. Can the data collected, for example, actually be used to answer the question being asked?

The other validity issue concerns the external question of whether or not the results will remain truthful when subsequently applied to people, situations, or objects outside the original investigation (from our discussion of sampling in Chapter 3, you will recognize that question as the familiar problem of whether or not a study's findings can be *generalized*). The two kinds of veracity are referred to respectively as *internal validity* (Do the findings tell the truth about the question posed in the study?) and *external validity* (Do the findings tell the truth about these questions when they are situated outside the study?). Because it is somewhat less complex, we will begin with the research problems raised by the latter.

The most common circumstance in which external validity becomes an issue occurs when one group of people is examined in the study, but the results and conclusions are applied to another group. What is true for the particular sample of people in the study simply might not be valid for (that is, might not tell the truth about) another group of people—particularly if that group differs in some substantial way.

Medical research commonly presents such problems of external validity. Because studies of this kind are so expensive and consume so much precious time, it can be tempting to extend hard-won knowledge about medicines or medical procedures to people not included in the samples of early investigations. It can also be unfair, misleading, wasteful, or dangerous.

For example, because of the differences between men and women, the National Institutes of Health created the Women's Health Initiative. This broad research program is a response to the fact that many important medical studies in the past used exclusively male samples—with consequent problems of external validity when applications were made to female populations. Using women in medical study samples ensures that problems of external validity that are related to gender do not put women at a disadvantage in obtaining sound health care.

In contrast, internal validity is not concerned with generalizability but with the integrity of the study itself. Internal validity issues range from simple and perfectly obvious to arcane and exceedingly obscure, but, in the end, they all have to do with whether the study has been designed to yield truthful results. To start with an obvious example, if we wish to know whether taking supplemental vitamins increases intelligence, we would not put our subjects on a regimen of multivitamin pills and then weigh them to check for improvement in cognitive function. Weight is not a valid measure of intelligence, although it is perfectly valid as an index of mass (for objects weighed at the same location). The data gathered have to match the question. An intelligence test would serve our study better, although correct selection of a measurement is rarely so obvious.

Four decades ago, Campbell and Stanley (1963) wrote a marvelously lucid monograph that explained many of the problems with internal validity that are possible in experimental studies (and in a number of other closely related designs for research). That little book still is available (an abstract appears in Appendix A), and we recommend it as an economical and pleasurable means not only for surveying the mysteries of internal validity but for learning a great deal about alternative ways of setting up experiments.

A simple example of the many issues of validity discussed by Campbell and Stanley is that of "experimental mortality." That graphic name applies to the fascinating question, "What happens to results when some of the people in a study sample decide to drop out before all of the data are collected?" The answer involves (at least) further questions about the particular people who defect. If all or most of them share a particular characteristic (bored quickly, fatigued easily, and so on), that fact might well influence what is found with regard to the remaining people. In turn, the investigator is left with the question, "Are the subjects completing the study still representative of the population from which they were selected as a sample?" As you can see, issues that deal with internal and external validity create complex problems for researchers.

Experiments, of course, are not the only types of research. The problems of internal and external validity are ubiquitous and must be confronted by researchers in study formats as disparate as questionnaire surveys and field ethnographies. As you read reports from studies with different research designs, you should notice not only the kinds of validity issues that arise but how the investigators attempt to deal with them.

The techniques used by a researcher to collect data—what Campbell and Stanley (1963) call the "instrumentation" of a study—present some of the most common problems of internal validity. Data collection takes a variety of forms, including machines that use computer programs to direct the monitoring of biological processes, survey forms filled out by door-to-door interviewers, psychological tests completed by subjects, field notes from investigators watching children on a playground, and systematic examination of cultural phenomena through the recording of words used in books, television, or movies. All of these are very different methodologies but are subject to the same question: "Do these data provide a truthful reflection of what the study is intended to examine?"

A second question has to be asked about any instrumentation: "Does it collect data in a consistent manner?" That question deals with the second of the two concerns with which we started this discussion—*reliability*. If you take your body temperature with an oral thermometer and get three completely different readings for three consecutive 1-minute stays under your tongue, your instrument probably has a problem with reliability. Of course, it might have shown three identical readings (perfect reliability), but they all might have been incorrect (an issue of validity, because your thermometer does not tell the truth—it *is* consistent, but also a consistent *liar*).

If you consider that example, you will discover a valuable and easy-to-remember rule. If the thermometer produces reliable readings, it still might not be a valid indicator of body temperature. If it provides valid readings, however, then we know that it also must be reliable. That relationship of reliability and validity holds true for all measuring instruments because reliability is a component of validity. In plain language, you cannot tell the truth unless you are consistent, but you can be consistent and not tell the truth.

Clearly, researchers must establish ways of collecting data that are both valid and reliable. A particularly thorough discussion of strategies for achieving those twin goals can be found in Carmines and Zeller (1979).

In many cases, instruments for collecting data can be checked for validity and reliability before they are actually put to use in a study. This is true, for example, of written tests, electronic and mechanical hardware, and rating scales. Often, reports contain descriptions of such verification, including figures that display precisely how close the research tools come to theoretically perfect validity and reliability.

A simple reliability test, for example, is the test-retest procedure that often is used to establish the stability of test results over time. As its name suggests, the same test is given to the same people on two occasions. If the scores for each individual are roughly the same, that can be taken as evidence of the test's reliability. If the scores change substantially (and in apparently random ways) from the first to the second testing, there almost certainly is a reliability problem with the test. Something about the instrument or procedure causes or invites the individual to respond differently at each encounter. The test might yield numbers, but those numbers will be of no use in finding a truthful answer to the research question.

In the case of written tests, another way to check reliability employs alternate forms of the same instrument. Two separate forms of a test are constructed by writing similar, but not identical, questions (they must cover exactly the same constructs and require the same kind of response, but do so in slightly different words). People who score high on one form should score high on the other. If they do not, the investigator will suspect that something is encouraging subjects to respond inconsistently. The cause might lie in the format of the test, the means by which it is administered, the nature of the content, or (most likely) some combination of these factors. Whatever the case, if you cannot rely on subjects to give the same response to questions that differ in only trivial ways, the data will make no sense, and the study itself will become nonsense.

In some forms of research, reliability cannot be tested in advance because there simply is too much variability in the conditions under which data will be collected. Open-ended interviews and field studies of complex human behavior often do not employ instrumentation that can be pretested for reliability (in such cases, the investigator *is* the instrument). Instead, exceedingly careful attention to consistency of procedures across people, contexts, and time; ongoing inspection of recorded data for evidence of unexplained or unexpected content; and persistent effort to maintain high accuracy must provide the support for claims about the reliability of what is captured in the data record.

Validity and reliability are elusive qualities, and few studies are designed in ways that resolve all possible threats to consistent truth. What the reader of a research report has a right to expect, however, is that investigators show awareness of such issues, report what they have done to control the problems, and be frank about the degree of their success in so doing.

As a beginning reader, of course, you will have to depend on the processes of peer review to catch problems with validity or reliability before manuscripts reach print. It should be reassuring to know that suggestions for clarifying such issues are among the most frequent comments that authors receive from reviewers and that inadequate attention to validity and reliability are among the most common reasons for denying publication.

You must remember, however, that standards for validity and reliability cannot be applied as simple absolutes. Given the complex nature of many research questions, reviewers often must ask, "How much lack of confidence in the consistent truthfulness of this study is tolerable?" The answer will be determined by many factors, but everyone—reviewers, editors, researchers, and readers—knows what is ideal. Research should come as close to producing reliably valid results as human skill and effort can devise.

❖   TYPES OF RESEARCH

Research is conducted in many ways. Scholars in each academic and professional area typically make wider use of some methods than others; develop local ground rules for dealing with concerns about reliability and validity; and, quite often, invent technical jargon for the use of insiders. Nevertheless, many of the basic problems in conducting sound investigations are common to all types of research. It is human inventiveness in response to those fundamental difficulties that works constantly to alter the face of the research enterprise.

In the past three decades, the number (and complexity) of research methods has increased sharply, particularly in the social sciences. Where once only a few forms of inquiry were available (and acceptable within the scientific community), many options now exist. This proliferation offers more than just greater freedom for the investigator; it makes possible a better matching of research tools to the demands of each particular question—and that is an enormous advantage.

However, when we hear our students ask the question, "What is the best type of research?" we always know that they as learners and we as teachers still have important work to do. A particular strategy for inquiry is not good or bad in an absolute sense; rather, a type of research is good or bad to the exact degree that it fits well or poorly with the question at hand. You can find our opinions about this subject discussed at some length (Locke, Spirduso, & Silverman, 2000), but a quick review here will serve to ensure that we are all starting with the same assumptions about types of research.

Questions must guide the selection and use of research methods. Although this sounds like common sense, it is not always easy to remember. All of the elegant technical accoutrements of design and method can distract people from the simple fact that it is researchers' sense of what they want to learn, carefully thought out and clearly defined, that, when coupled with appropriate design and methods, becomes the engine that drives everything else. Is this point really important? Our unequivocal answer is "Yes."

It is not at all unusual to encounter studies that have been weakened by the investigator's inadequate attention to carefully thinking through what he or she wants to learn. Such studies are at least as common as those with the opposite sort of problem—soundly crafted questions that are inadequately served by carelessly selected research methods.

The combination of sound questions with appropriate methods separates the powerful from the merely pedestrian in research. There is no "best type of research"—there are only good questions matched with procedures for inquiry that can yield reliable answers. That dictum holds true even in qualitative studies, wherein the starting point for inquiry can be anything in the range between explicit hypotheses at one extreme to nothing more specific than hazy foreshadows of what might be worthy of exploration at the other. Nevertheless, in every study, all of the components must be compatible with the nature of what the investigator seeks to learn.

We will now introduce you to a framework for identifying different types of research. Our system is intended to be utilitarian and certainly is not intended to be definitive. A number of excellent sources provide far greater depth (e.g., Bailey, 1994; Creswell, 2003; Gall, Gall, & Borg, 2003; Krathwohl, 1998; Robson, 2002; Thomas & Nelson, 2001), in some cases devoting entire chapters to research designs that we can only name here. We again urge you to avail yourself of such help when you encounter unfamiliar forms of inquiry. We have abstracted some of these more specialized texts in Appendix A for your reference.

We categorize types of research into three broad divisions: quantitative, qualitative, and mixed method. Figure 6.1 provides a simple map of those divisions and some of their subcategories. This framework was not designed to include all research types or to be an elegant taxonomy. It contains the easily recognizable types that novice readers are most likely to encounter. As soon as you can recognize its various limitations as a classification scheme, you will not need it any longer anyway. As you read research reports, it will be helpful for you to pencil in the new subcategories (or subdivisions of existing subcategories) that you encounter.

Quantitative Research

As we present each type and subcategory, we will discuss the kinds of questions commonly asked, the data collection methods used, and where you can obtain more information about that kind of research. In addition, we will cite a study that provides a sound example. It is not difficult, however, to imagine the kinds of questions that are best answered (and most commonly asked) by investigators using quantitative designs.

Figure 6.1   Organization of Empirical Research

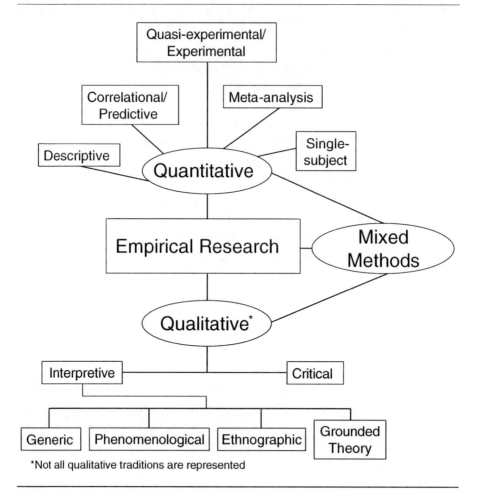

*Not all qualitative traditions are represented

For the central portion of the 20th century, quantitative designs represented by far the dominant type of research in the social sciences. Although other types of inquiry are now in common use, the capacity of quantitative research to describe, predict, and explain social and psychological phenomena has provided a significant part of the foundation on which the modern social sciences have been erected. We begin with a brief discussion of the statistics used in quantitative research. This ordering is convenient because it is the management of quantities that provides hallmark distinctions among the main branches of the quantitative family: descriptive; correlational/predictive;

quasi-experimental/experimental; single-subject; and the recent addition, meta-analysis.

Statistics in quantitative research. Statistics are mathematical tools for manipulating and analyzing numeric data. They range in complexity from the simple average of a group of scores to procedures that require sequences of operations based on esoteric forms of linear algebra before an answer can be derived for the original question.

As you would anticipate, you would need special training to understand the more complicated statistical tools—what they accomplish and how they do it—but, for a surprisingly small investment of study time, you can learn enough about basic statistics to read the "Results" section of many reports and understand what the analysis says about the data. Accordingly, in Appendix C, we provide a user-friendly introduction to some of the most commonly encountered research statistics. How they function in a report is described in terms that make no demand on previous background in mathematics and presume no familiarity with research technology. At the very least, our beginner's guide serves as a valuable supplement to this chapter, a useful introduction to the skills necessary for reading quantitative reports with a critical eye (see Chapter 7), and a guide for selecting additional references.

Most college bookstores have a variety of inexpensive self-study guides, computer-based learning programs, and paperbacks in the "statistics for dummies" genre. Many of these texts provide highly effective ways to obtain a general background for a minimum investment of time. In the more traditional textbook format, however, we think that Pyrczak (1999, 2001, 2002), Dodge (2003), and Holcomb (1998, 2002) are particularly sound and entirely accessible for novice readers (and all six of these references are available in modestly priced paperbound editions). More advanced texts such as Kirk (1995); Pedhazur (1997); Stevens (2002); and Winer, Brown, and Michels (1991) ordinarily are best used in conjunction with statistics courses (or tutorial instruction).

Statistical tools can be categorized by the purposes for which they are commonly employed. As Table 6.1 indicates (in the columns), the function of some statistics is to describe a given set of data (*descriptive* statistics), others are used to examine the relations between or among sets of numeric data (*association* or *correlational* statistics), and still others are employed to detect whether differences between or among groups of data are more than meaningless accidents (*mean difference* statistics).

Table 6.1 provides only the names of various statistical procedures; you will have to obtain explanations of their uses from other sources. When a particular statistic is identified in a report, however, you can use the table to quickly identify the functional family to which it belongs. That, in turn, will reveal something about the type of research involved.

Because the names of statistical procedures are, in some cases, the same as the names of particular research designs (e.g., correlational statistics—which are also called statistics of association, but you are more likely to encounter the term *correlational*—are used in correlational studies to answer questions that inquire about the correlation of variables), people lose track of the distinctions involved. We suggest that you not let that happen. Shaping the question comes first, then the selection of research design, and, finally, decisions about tools for managing and analyzing data. In good research, the three operations must be related by an intrinsic logic, but they are no more the same than are apples and oranges—even when given identical names.

As you examine Table 6.1, notice that it is divided horizontally into univariate and multivariate sections. Analysis of data concerning the single variable factor of intelligence would require a *univariate* (one variable) statistic. If you wanted to examine the impact of nutritional supplements on intelligence and strength, you would have two variables (e.g., IQ test scores and dynamometer readings) and would need a *multivariate* statistic to examine the data. As research has become more sophisticated, this distinction has become more important, and it is one you should begin to notice from the outset.

The following five subsections provide an overview of quantitative research. Table 6.2 presents the purposes and names of some commonly encountered formats associated with three broad categories of quantitative research: descriptive, correlational, and quasi-experimental/ experimental. Because they represent special cases, single-subject research and meta-analysis are not included in the table; they are discussed briefly in the final subsections of this section.

Descriptive research. This form of research captures and displays a graphic picture of some aspect(s) of a situation—expressed in numbers. "What is the reading level of 10th-grade students in a rural school district?" "How long does it take for scholarship athletes to complete an undergraduate degree?" "What kinds of magazines are read by adolescent girls in urban areas?" These are the kinds of questions that call for descriptive studies. Although the relationship between or among groups certainly can be described, you will find it conceptually useful

Table 6.1   Names of Common Statistical Procedures

	Description	Correlation (Association)	Differences in Means
Univariate	Mean $(\mu, \bar{x})$	Pearson's Product Moment Correlation (ρ, r)	t test
	Median (Md)	Coefficient of determination (r^2, R^2)	Analysis of variance (ANOVA)
	Mode	Partial correlation $(r_{ab.c})$	Analysis of covariance (ANCOVA)
	Variance (σ^2, s^2)	Semipartial (part) correlation $(r_{a(b.c)})$	Trend analysis
	Standard deviation (σ, s)	Rank order correlation $(r_s \text{ or } \tau)$	Sign test
	Standard error	Point-biserial correlation (r_{pb})	Mann-Whitney U
	Range	Chi-square (χ^2)	Kruskal-Wallis one-way ANOVA
	Confidence intervals		Friedman two-way ANOVA
	Skewness (γ_1)		Effect size
	Kurtosis (γ_2)		
	Standard scores (z, T)		
	Percentiles		
	Percentile ranks		
Multivariate		Multiple regression	Hotelling's T^2
		Logistic regression	Multivariate analysis of variance (MANOVA)
		Discriminant function analysis	Multivariate analysis of covariance (MANCOVA)
		Cluster analysis	
		Principal components analysis	
		Factor analysis	
		Canonical correlation	
		Path analysis	
		Structural equation modeling	
		Hierarchical linear modeling	

Table 6.2   Purpose, Names, and Examples of Research Techniques Used in Quantitative Research

	Descriptive	Correlational	Quasi-Experimental/ Experimental
Purpose	To describe a sample on a specific variable. Can also describe subsamples on the same variable.	To describe relationships among variables, to predict a criterion variable, or to test a model of the interrelationships among variables used to predict a variable.	To test differences in group means for one or more independent variables.
Names of Commonly Used Research Formats	• Survey research • Political polling • Delphi surveys	• Predictive • Multiple regression • Causal modeling • Structured equation modeling • Path analysis	• Causal comparative • Repeated measures design • Within and between design • Randomize block design • ANOVA or MANOVA
Examples of Research Techniques (for all three research types)		• Data collection with instrumentation for specific variables (e.g., electronic monitoring of brain waves, blood alcohol testing) • Paper-and-pencil inventories • Attitude measures • Surveys • Use of statistics to analyze data	

to assign studies that focus primarily on the analysis of relationships to the following section on correlational research. The statistics used in descriptive research include such tools as measures of central tendency (e.g., mean, mode, and median—these yield descriptions of what is "typical" in a set of numbers, or where the middle is when a set is listed from highest to lowest) or measures of dispersion (e.g., range and standard deviation—describing such characteristics as the number of steps between highest and lowest numbers, or how tightly numbers in a set cluster around a central value).

An example of descriptive research is a report by Coward, Duncan, and Uttaro (1996). They made use of data from a national census of more than 13,000 rural nursing homes. They described nine types of facilities in terms of such variables as availability, size, cost, and the character of long-term care. They drew conclusions about the adequacy of facilities within each type and discussed the implications of their findings for the future of rural nursing homes.

Correlational research. This type of research examines the nature of the relationship between or among variables. Three types will be discussed here: simple, predictive, and modeling. The *simple* form of correlational study employs a statistic that yields a single number (called a *correlation coefficient*) that expresses the extent to which a pair of variables (two sets of numbers) are related—that is, the degree to which we can predict that when measures of one variable produce numbers that are larger or smaller, the numbers for some other measured variable will be similarly larger or smaller. For example, when two sets of test scores shadow each other closely in the same direction, the coefficient will be larger and positive in nature (closer to +1.0). When the numbers closely shadow each other as mirror images (that is, they run in opposite directions), the coefficient will be larger and have a negative sign (closer to −1.0). When the numbers show no particular pattern of association, the coefficient simply will be small (whatever its sign), indicating little relationship (closer to a correlation coefficient of 0.0, the statistical indication that two variables have no relationship whatsoever).

Simple correlational studies are used for questions such as these: "What is the relationship between the number of nurse home visits and outpatient adherence to postoperative routines?" "How do hours invested in practice relate to playing errors in Little League baseball?" "To what extent does educational level relate to the rate of unemployment for men and women?" In each case, one or several forms of correlational statistics could be used to reveal the answer.

As these examples suggest, one of the particularly useful powers of correlational research is that it allows the examination of relationships among variables measured in different units (e.g., pounds and inches, minutes and errors, course credits and months employed). What matters in correlational research is not the actual units of measure but how the relative sizes of scores in different distributions relate to each other (a *distribution* is a list that shows not only the rank order of scores but also the magnitude of difference between adjacent figures).

As an example, Keefe and Berndt (1996) examined the relationship between friendship quality and self-esteem within a sample of seventh- and eighth-grade schoolchildren. They administered tests (with known reliability and validity) for the two variables during the fall and spring semesters. By examining how the relationships (correlation coefficients) changed over time, they were able to make interesting hypotheses about how the availability and quality of friendships might relate to a child's regard for him- or herself.

The second type of correlational design, *predictive research,* is used to improve our capacity to anticipate events. By examining the patterns of association between some set of variables and something that the investigator wishes to predict (usually called the *criterion variable*), it is possible to identify the best possible set of variables to use. Here, an example will serve better than a lengthy explanation.

If you want to know which set of variables best predicts the 5-year survivability of a cancer patient after surgery (choosing from, for example, age, health status, gender, type of malignancy, extent of cancer spread, and postoperative care), a correlation statistic called *multiple regression* would yield the answer. It might well be that all six of those variables used together predict no better than just age and gender when used alone. Whatever the case, the answer can be very important in determining medical procedures and hospital policies governing care for cancer patients.

Prediction research can be particularly valuable when it is necessary to establish priorities for the distribution of scarce resources. Questions such as "For children, which demographic, educational, and home environment factors contribute the most to their reading ability as adults?" allow findings (when properly replicated) to influence educational policy. When available, tax dollars can be invested in programs that are likely to produce the largest improvements in literacy, even though many factors contribute to the development of reading skills.

Vitaro, Ladouceur, and Bujold (1996) published an example of predictive research. They examined the relationships between a number of variables and gambling in young boys. It was not entirely surprising when they discovered that gambling was related to both delinquency and substance abuse. Thus, in practical terms, the results confirmed that social workers should anticipate greater risks associated with gambling among delinquent boys with a record of substance abuse. However, the same statistical analysis revealed that certain measures of anxiety also predicted gambling behaviors—a new and important insight. In addition, when the investigators examined groups of gambling and nongambling boys, they found a number of variables that appeared to discriminate between the two. This combination of correlational study with group comparisons allowed the investigators to inspect their sample from several angles, an approach that can yield rich and sometimes unexpected results.

The third kind of correlational study, *modeling research* (which includes such techniques as path analysis and structural equation modeling), maps in graphic form (often in the familiar format of boxes with connecting arrows) the relationships among a number of variables, displaying the degree to which any one of them can be used to predict one or more of the others. Interlocking questions such as "What is the best set of factors for predicting whether or not a student will graduate from college?" "When placed in a diagrammatic model, how are those contributing factors most logically arranged?" and "How much predictive power is exerted by the various lines of influence drawn among the factors?" illustrate the wonderfully complex sort of problem that can be addressed through the correlational procedures used in modeling research.

The model shown in Figure 6.2 displays a hypothetical set of factors that influences the extent to which adults volunteer their assistance to service organizations. The lines drawn between factors show the direction of influence (what can be predicted by knowledge about a given factor), and the number given for each line (called a *path coefficient*) indicates the degree of influence exerted. In effect, the path coefficients show the power of prediction on a scale from −1.0 to +1.0.

Translated into a set of plain-language statements, the model asserts that how much time people have available is a primary predictor of their volunteer behavior (whether they offer to help at all and, if so, to what extent). The path coefficient of .74 indicates a robust and positive prediction—the more time we have to expend (or believe we

Figure 6.2   Example of a Structural Equation Model

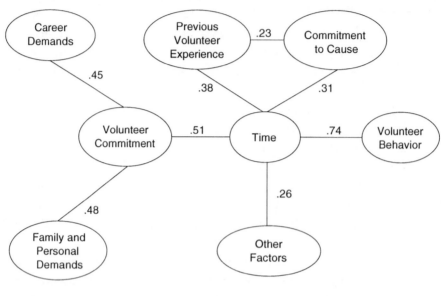

have), the more time we are likely to invest in voluntary service activities.

Note, however, that both the realities of available time and the perceptions of that availability are influenced by other factors, as displayed in the six related latent variables (in the ovals) that directly or indirectly impact time. For example, how much time people believe they have available for such activities as community or charitable service is partly a function of their degree of commitment to the idea that voluntary service to others is an obligation (.51). That commitment, however, is modulated by the very real constraints of career (.45) and family (.48) obligations.

The sense of how much time is available is also influenced by personal commitment to the particular cause at hand (.31). Among the influences that determine our commitment to a service activity is previous experience as a volunteer (the path coefficient of .23 indicates a relatively small, but nevertheless positive, relationship). Did volunteering produce a satisfying sense of accomplishment? Were work conditions acceptable and demands reasonable? If you examine Figure 6.2 closely, you will see that a good experience might exert its influence indirectly by increasing commitment to the particular cause involved, with that, in turn, serving to increase the time devoted.

Alternatively, past experience could have a more direct influence by leading the participant to raise the estimate of time available for any form of service (.38).

Unhappy encounters with volunteering, of course, could have the reverse effect, and the path correlations might have negative signs (bad experiences predicting both lowered commitment and a decrease in the time perceived to be available). As you can see from all of this, statistical modeling can provide useful (and sometimes unexpected) insights into the complexities of how things work—insights that are invisible or only dimly glimpsed from our surface view of relationships.

Modeling research has found a growing number of useful applications in recent years. As an example, Etezadi-Amoli and Farhoomand (1996) used structural equations to develop a model of computer users' satisfaction and performance. They developed a survey form, with appropriate validity and reliability demonstrations, to measure six dimensions of attitude toward computer use. When entered into the equation used for analysis, survey data from a sample of users generated a graphic model that not only arranged the variables in a manner consistent with their interrelationships but highlighted connections that might otherwise have been lost in a swamp of statistics. The model makes graphically clear, for example, that how people feel about computers plays a large role in determining how well they learn to use them. That insight is useful because, absent such evidence, the more likely assumption would be that competence in use is a predictor for positive attitudes—not the reverse.

Quasi-experimental/experimental research. This is a large family of related research designs, and a full explanation of even one would demand far more space than we have available in this introductory text. The feature that ties all of them together is the inspection of data to determine whether two or more groups differ on some variable. The most familiar format is the classic experiment in which the investigator provides some treatment (often called the *intervention)* to one group (the *experimental group)* but not the other (the *control group).* The two levels of treatment (some and none) together constitute the independent variable being manipulated in the study. The two groups are then compared for their status on some variable (usually called the *outcome* or *dependent variable)* that might have been influenced by the treatment.

As you might imagine, the questions being asked, the study design, the statistical analysis employed, and the findings produced can become very complex. For example, many experiments have multiple dependent or independent variables. It is one thing to examine the therapeutic impact of a cold medicine given to a particular sample of afflicted patients, but it is quite another to ask whether there are differences in attitude toward crime, education, and the economy among urban, suburban, and rural voters, when data are divided by gender. There are, however, experimental designs that can juggle the two independent variables (residence and gender) and the three dependent variables (attitudes toward crime, education, and the economy) with precision and elegance.

The family of designs for which the generic term *experiment* is applied in common speech actually consists of two branches that researchers carefully recognize as distinct. The difference between what scholars call *true experiments* and the large subspecies of studies referred to as *quasi-experiments* lies in the degree of control that the investigator exercises over the study. In true experiments, researchers not only choose the treatment, but they also select subjects, assign subjects to groups, and, finally, assign treatments to groups. In its purest form, the true experiment requires that these three manipulations be done through use of random procedures (allowing chance to control selection and assignment).

For example, if an investigator had determined that it would be appropriate to conduct a true experiment to find out whether small, daily doses of aspirin would lower the incidence of heart attacks in a population of older men, he or she would take the following steps. First, the researcher would randomly select a large number of men between the ages of 60 and 65. Next, that sample would be divided by random procedures into two groups. Then, again by a random operation (perhaps the flip of a coin), one group would be designated as experimental (treatment), and members of that group would take one-half of an aspirin every day. The remaining group would be designated as control, and members of that group would take daily dummy tablets (called a *placebo treatment*) made of some pharmacologically inert substance. (If this were a variant of the true experiment called a *double blind*, neither the investigator nor the subjects would know which group was receiving the treatment and which the placebo until all the data had been collected.) Finally, 10 years later, the investigator would count the number of men in each group who had suffered cardiac incidents. The investigator would have had control of each manipulation and would have obtained strong evidence concerning the presence or absence of a causal relationship between the treatment (aspirin) and the variable of interest (heart attacks).

In contrast, quasi-experiments involve conditions under which the investigator does not control one or more of the critical variables and might be unable to use random procedures to select or assign all subjects and treatments. For example, a common form of quasi-experiment is used when it is necessary to study intact groups created by events or natural processes (voters in a rural county of Illinois, people who have been in automobile accidents, or all the students in Ms. Smith's third-grade class). The researcher does not have control over who is selected for study, who is assigned to groups, or, in some cases, which group receives the experimental treatment. Given the logistical difficulty in controlling all of these factors (at least outside the laboratory), it is not surprising that the vast majority of experiments in the social and behavioral sciences are quasi-experiments.

The distinction between the two kinds of experiments is not trivial. In particular, the use of randomization in selecting subjects or assigning treatments has powerful consequences for what can be learned from a study. We will leave to you the thrill of discovering more about this topic from another source at another time (for example, Kirk, 1995; Winer, Brown, & Michels, 1991). We must add, however, that this is a case of the sooner learned, the better served.

Experiments and quasi-experiments are appropriate for the same sorts of research questions; often, the availability of time, subjects, resources, and technology for collection of data determines the choice between the two. A simple question such as "Do employees who receive on-the-job safety training have better safety records than a control group of otherwise equivalent employees without such training?" could be addressed by any of several kinds of experimental or quasi-experimental designs. We would be remiss, however, if we did not note that the complexity of the design selected is not an indicator of research quality. It is far better to use a simple design that fits a simple question than to adopt an unnecessarily complex strategy that yields the same answer. Complexity is costly and multiplies the opportunities to make fatal errors.

An example of a quasi-experiment was reported by Brice, Gorey, Hall, and Angelino (1996). They examined the impact of an eight-session health-promotion program on the subjects' health-related beliefs and subsequent behaviors. Subjects in the treatment group were not selected by random procedures. They were chosen simply because they were available for the program, completed it, and were willing to undergo the 9-month follow-up procedure. The treatment group's scores for the dependent variables of belief and behavior were compared with those of subjects who were on the program waiting list. Careful examination of the two groups revealed few obvious differences in their characteristics, and, given the substantial superiority of outcome scores for the treatment group, the authors seemed justified in concluding that the program had a positive effect.

As we suggested, when contrasting true and quasi-experiments, tight control over subjects, environments, and treatments is often a luxury reserved for laboratory studies. It is singularly difficult to establish the level of control required for a true experiment in the more open and unpredictable conditions of the real world, which is why such investigations are relatively rare. That they are not impossible, however, was demonstrated by Barber and Gilbertson (1996).

In that study, the subjects were partners of people who were both dependent on alcohol and resistant to any change in their behavior. The partners were randomly selected from a larger population and then randomly assigned to four conditions. The treatments were (a) an intervention designed to help the partner, provided on an individual basis; (b) the same intervention for the partner, provided in a group setting; (c) no intervention; and (d) participation by the partner in Al-Anon (a support group for people who are friends, relatives, or partners of alcoholics). Dependent variables included measures of change in drinking behavior, status of other personal problems, and degree of marital consensus. The study found that the various treatment conditions had different effects on different dependent variables (not an uncommon result in multivariate studies). For example, Treatment (a) was the only one to produce positive change in marital consensus.

Single-subject research. This type of research is often categorized as experimental by those who use it to study human behavior. We have listed it here as a separate form of inquiry because it does have distinguishing features that will immediately be apparent to the beginning reader. That the underlying structure and assumptions might match those of an experiment seem less important here than pursuing our purpose—to ease you through the early stages of reading research reports.

Researchers using single-subject designs (a number of alternatives are available) usually are interested in examining the contingencies that shape human behavior. As the name implies, observations are made of a single subject (or of one subject at a time). Typically, the investigator collects data that establish how the subject behaves under normal conditions (called *baseline behavior*), before any treatment is implemented or any change in the situation occurs. Then, the investigator introduces change, adding or removing something that might influence the subject's behavior and recording data that reflect the consequences.

Unlike other forms of quantitative research, it is rare to find statistics used to analyze data in single-subject studies. More typically, the frequency of behavior is graphed across time so that changes such as shifts from baseline, attenuation of effects, and reversal of effects (with removal of treatment) can be noted easily. If data are collected concurrently for a number of such individual graphs, the display of results for even a small set of subjects can be very persuasive. Books by Sidman (1960) and Johnson and Pennypacker (1993) are the standard references for anyone interested in this type of research.

Within the social sciences, there is a virtually endless array of variations on the basic strategy represented in single-subject research. Some of these are widely used to evaluate various methods of modifying human behavior. For example, Maguire, Lange, Scherling, and Grow (1996) conducted a study to examine results produced by an intervention designed to reduce the uncooperative behavior of mentally retarded patients when they have dental work performed. Four adult males who were mildly to severely mentally retarded were the subjects in the study.

A behavioral baseline was established for each of the four participants by recording and graphing the frequency of their resistant behaviors during regularly scheduled appointments (including expressing physical aggression, shouting, refusing to open the mouth, and turning the head away from the dentist). Then, the investigators implemented a treatment for the subjects. The intervention consisted of a number of elements, including having the dentist give an explanation of all parts of the dental procedure, letting the patient touch the tools and ask questions, providing frequent positive reinforcements designed to counteract the negative aspects of the experience, and incorporating breaks to help the subjects manage discomfort. During subsequent appointments at which the treatment was applied, the levels of resistant behaviors decreased sharply from those observed during collection of baseline data. Although the frequency of patient resistance for both baselines and subsequent treatments did show some fluctuation across visits, such a uniform and persistent deflection of rates (coinciding exactly with implementation of the treatment) could not reasonably be attributed to natural variation in the subjects' behavior. The authors concluded that the treatment had been effective in reducing uncooperative behavior in the dentist's chair.

There are a number of interesting variations on the design used in the study just described. In one, called a *reversal design,* the next step would be to remove treatment and to inspect the behavior graphs for a change in frequency, moving back in the direction of the original baseline levels. If that were observed, it would add weight to the argument that the intervention had been the true cause of the patients' change in resistant behavior. Another variation involves the timing of the intervention. If the initiation of the treatment had been spaced across appointments so that Subject 1 received the intervention on the first visit, but Subject 2 not until the second visit, and so on, and each of the behavior graphs deflected downward only as the treatment was introduced (having retained baseline levels until that point), additional weight would have been added to the argument that it was the treatment and not some other condition that was causing the improvement in cooperation. From these examples, it should be clear that for certain kinds of research problems, single-subject designs offer attractive alternatives to more traditional forms of experimentation.

Meta-analysis. In recent years, new methods have been created that allow researchers to combine studies that have the same focus to derive a single result—one that allows for conclusions with considerably more persuasive power than could be provided by any single study. This technique for combining the results from independent studies is called *meta-analysis.* Researchers do not collect original data but aggregate findings from previous studies through the use of special statistical formulae.

Although the statistics might seem mysterious, the basics of the underlying logic are not. In experimental and quasi-experimental studies, the investigator is interested in whether the experimental group, which he or she has "treated" with something (such as special reading instruction, a relaxation program, or a drug), is significantly different from a control group that was not treated. (Researchers use the word *significant* not in the usual sense of *important,* but as the label for differences that are unlikely to be due to chance—i.e., differences probably caused by a treatment.) In the simplest sense, for the difference to be statistically significant, it has to be larger than the average differences among subjects in the control group. That comparison of between-group differences and within-group differences produces a resulting number called the *effect size*, which is the statistical construct on which meta-analysis is based. As we indicate in Appendix C, in the context of experimental research, effect size is an indicator of the strength of the treatment.

In meta-analysis, researchers treat the effect size as a datum—that is, as a score representing the study from which it is derived. The effect sizes from a number of studies are analyzed in ways similar to the standard statistical analysis of data from individuals in a single experiment. If the topic under examination has attracted a substantial amount of interest, it will have produced many studies; if enough of those studies are of high quality, the meta-analysis can determine the average effect size of all the studies taken together. That it can do so regardless of differences in the individual studies (such as sample sizes and methods of data collection) makes meta-analysis a powerful tool.

In some areas of inquiry, for example, a group of studies that has produced only modest results might be concealing the fact that the findings actually are substantial as well as persistent—a fact that can become apparent only through the magnifying power of meta-analysis. If you are interested in learning more, references such as Hedges (1998), Hunter and Schmidt (1995) and Lipsey and Wilson (2000) provide the essential details.

Nichol et al. (1996) conducted a meta-analysis using studies of emergency medical systems (EMSs) for treatment of out-of-hospital cardiac arrests. After carefully selecting the reports to include, they combined results for response time until EMS personnel arrived, bystander application of cardiopulmonary resuscitation, and various types of interventions provided by EMSs. They found that several critical factors influenced survival rates, not all of which were obvious from a reading of the contributory studies when considered individually. Such findings show that we have much to learn by doing research on research, which is the function of meta-analysis.

Qualitative Research

At this point, we have completed our brief overview of issues that are generic to all types of research and our survey of the five basic formats for inquiry within the quantitative domain. We turn now to a different type of inquiry—qualitative research. Before you read the next section, however, it might be helpful to be reminded of three points made in previous chapters.

First, if you arrived here from Chapter 5 (or any other point in the text) because we suggested this section as a resource providing greater detail about qualitative research, you have done exactly the right thing. You should be able to read what follows without difficulty and then return to the earlier point in the text armed with some useful insights into qualitative research.

Second, the general problems of doing good qualitative research will sound familiar. The persistent issues already discussed in this chapter have not been left behind in the world of numbers and statistics. Formulating good questions, matching questions with the appropriate methodology, collecting high-quality data that are valid and reliable, and interpreting those data with thoughtful care still are the name of the game, even when the names given to those problems change.

Third, the change to qualitative research involves more than a change in methods of data collection and more than a change in the form of data from numbers to words. Quantitative and qualitative research reflect different paradigms—that is, they start with different assumptions about the nature of the world, truth, and the functions of research. We will not discuss the philosophic roots of those differences, but we do assert one proposition concerning them. Until you have read and thought about the differing philosophic perspectives that operate in the two worldviews (Denzin & Lincoln, 2000, provides a good place to start), you will not have a full appreciation of either quantitative or qualitative research.

Qualitative research is now represented in many fields of study, and its influence in the social sciences has been growing steadily. In addition, this form of inquiry has been going through a recent period of rapid diversification, with the creation of a number of distinctive research traditions. As illustration, Table 6.3 presents an overview of purposes, commonly used nomenclature, and specific techniques associated with qualitative research. The two traditions, or subcategories, of qualitative research shown in the table will be introduced here in some detail: interpretive and critical research.

Studies broadly categorized as interpretive have found wide use, and, indeed, much of our previous discussion of qualitative research in Chapter 5 pertained primarily to studies that would be classified in that group. The other tradition we will introduce, *critical research,* is less

Table 6.3   Purpose, Names, and Examples of Research Techniques Used in Qualitative Research

	Interpretive	*Critical Theory*
Purpose	To understand a situation from the perspective of the participant.	To understand and critique power within society.
Common Forms	• Ethnographic • Constructivism • Phenomenological • Grounded theory • Participant observation • Interpretive interactionism • Hermeneutics • Case study	• Feminist • Marxist • Critical ethnography • Deconstruction • Postmodernism • Poststructuralism • Foucauldian
Examples of Research Techniques	• Observation and use of field notes • Examination of documents • Interviews	• Analysis of print materials, popular culture, and social structures • Documentation of empowerment activities, often using interpretive research techniques

common, particularly in some disciplines. Its visibility is growing, however, and you are likely to encounter at least one report based on critical theory when exploring the literature on almost any topic of current interest in the social sciences.

Good references are available for all forms of qualitative research. A comprehensive treatment of the qualitative paradigm and its various methodological traditions is available in Denzin and Lincoln (2000). For introductions to interpretive research, we have found Bogdan and Biklen (2003), Creswell (2003), Flick (2002), Maxwell (1996), Merriam (1998), Morse and Richards (2002), and Rossman and Rallis (2003) to be both sound and popular with our students. Truly accessible, introductory-level texts on critical research are more difficult to find, but Thomas (1993) is quite suitable for most purposes.

For readers who are new to the world of research, Robson (2002) might be one of the best resources for beginning their explorations. The author unfolds both qualitative and quantitative approaches to social science in a parallel fashion that clarifies differences and similarities. In its second edition, the book is comprehensive in coverage, strongly oriented toward practical use in designing studies, and persistently understanding about the needs of the novice.

Finally, by now it will be apparent to you that we could not possibly describe all of the variant forms assumed by qualitative research. To meet that need, you must have a true compendium—and, fortunately, there is one. For any short-term purpose, you should locate a library copy of the *Dictionary of Qualitative Inquiry* (Schwandt, 2001). If you have longer-term interests in research, however, purchase of this volume might be unavoidable (priced well under $50.00, the cost of a paperbound edition is not excessive). The book is devoted exclusively to defining the language conventions (a kind label for jargon) of qualitative research. With suggested readings and cross-references given for most entries, this might be one instance when you actually find yourself sitting down to read a dictionary.

Interpretive research. In this kind of study, by acting as the primary instrument for data collection, the investigator builds an extensive collection of *thick description* (detailed records concerning context, people, actions, and the perceptions of participants) as the basis for inductive generation of an understanding of what is going on or how things work (an *explanatory theory*). Often, the purpose of interpretive research is to understand the setting for social action from the perspective of the participants.

Reports can contain richly detailed narratives that are grounded in the data of the participants' own words, as selectively extracted from transcriptions of interviews. Descriptions of context and events are often developed directly from notes (commonly called *field notes*) made in the course of observations at the actual site of interest in the study (a research strategy generally referred to as *fieldwork*). Questions that might be asked in an interpretive study include "How do Native Americans view the criminal justice system?" "How do teachers implement a new state-mandated curriculum in their classroom?" and "What is the experience of teenage runaways when they become homeless?"

Among the methods commonly used by interpretive researchers are interviews, systematic observation of the setting or events under investigation, and analysis of documentary materials (lesson plans, police reports, hospital records, news stories, and diaries). Typically, collection and analysis of data takes place concurrently, with preliminary insights and new questions being used to inform and guide subsequent data collection. Some interpretive research takes the form of case studies (see Merriam, 1998, or Stake, 1995) in which a single participant or site is investigated both in depth and over considerable time. In contrast, research teams, multiple sites, and numerous forms of data collection can make some interpretive studies logistically complex and truly heroic undertakings.

Trustworthiness of data is as vital an issue here as it is in any other form of inquiry. The means used to confront the threats to validity and reliability necessarily take different forms (and have different names) in this research tradition. As you read reports, however, you will have little difficulty in recognizing those familiar concerns.

Results from interpretive studies are reported differently than are those from quantitative research. Prose text rather than tables and graphs give a very different feel to qualitative reports. The similarity to newspaper reporting and historical novels is often striking, and it is in some respects quite genuine because it arises from the author's desire to create a credible and engaging story. The less obvious dissimilarities, however, are what make one research and the others journalism or fictional literature.

Among those differences is the fact that journalists rarely are constrained to make their personal biases and investments in a report a matter of public record, whereas, in many interpretive studies, that obligation is observed with scrupulous care. Journalists are rarely trained in the social sciences and tend simply to describe rather than to analyze what they have observed. For the same reason, they cannot make use of powerful theories in framing and explaining their findings. Also, deadlines play a much more prominent role in reporting than in research and have the inevitable effect of limiting the collection of information. Finally, newsworthy elements (the events and issues that make a good story) often are not the items that have the greatest power to help us understand how and why things happen. Investigative reporters and interpretive researchers share many of the same skills and at their best have much to teach each other. The products of their inquiry are not better or worse than each other, they simply are different—done for different purposes, addressed to different audiences, and shaped by different contingencies.

Here are some examples from a variety of research traditions that have evolved from or been influenced by the qualitative paradigm. We have selected types that are among the most commonly encountered in the social science research literature for applied professional fields such as nursing, social work, education, occupational and physical therapy, public administration, and counseling. The home disciplines of the investigators include psychology, sociology, anthropology, communication, and education.

Generic studies. The term *generic,* used here to indicate a basic or standard form of interpretive research (a nomenclature suggested by Merriam, 1998), refers to qualitative studies with characteristics such as those discussed in this and previous chapters—but without a particular perspective that would immediately mark them as members of a specific tradition. Investigators who do studies like these are seeking to describe and to understand something. In most cases they follow these steps: (a) identify a conceptual model or theoretical framework for thinking about the research problem (usually drawn from one of the disciplines), (b) collect data through interviews, observations, or document analysis, (c) analyze the data through a process that identifies recurring patterns and thematic regularities, and (d) present conclusions in terms that use concepts from the initial framework.

Studies of this sort represent by far the largest number of published reports. Other than the presence of potentially interesting features in design or provocative qualities in the findings, there was little to recommend one selection over any other. Accordingly, we simply drew the generic specimen—Dowson and McInerney (2001)—by lot.

Note, however, that the annotation for this study (as well as those used to illustrate other types of qualitative research) is lengthier by several paragraphs than the preceding examples for designs in quantitative research. That change reflects the more discursive content of qualitative reports (both the use of numbers rather than words and the use of tables for economical presentation serve to keep most quantitative reports lean). In addition, we want readers to grasp the complex notion that in any qualitative study, the investigator is using a more flexible and broadly defined set of tactical possibilities after research is under way. Therefore, it takes a little more space to recount the story— a tale that typically has a few more twists, turns, and subplots than are provided by a tightly designed and faithfully executed experiment.

In a study of 86 male and female pupils at six Australian middle schools, Dowson and McInerney (2001) focused their efforts on identifying and describing the academic achievement goals espoused by the students. The goal descriptions included components in three areas: *cognitive* (what the participants said they thought about their goals), *affective* (what they reported feeling about their goals), and *behavioral* (what they actually were observed doing in relation to their goals). The theoretical framework for the study drew from both achievement and social goal theories.

To establish an initial sense of the range of achievement goals, students first participated in individual conversational interviews. Then, using data from that first cycle of conversations, a subsample of students was interviewed with a more direct focus on particular goals (those involving work avoidance and several forms of social motivation). Finally, two kinds of field observations were undertaken in the classes attended by the participants: (a) structured observations using a schedule based on what had been revealed about student goals during the interviews and (b) unstructured classroom observations that involved taking field notes and engaging in informal conversations with participants.

All data were transcribed into hard copy and then coded for easy retrieval. By inductive analysis (moving from the data to hypotheses or theories), students' statements and investigators' field notes were sorted into categories reflecting similarities in content and context. The categories were refined and then organized according to their relationships with each other. The result was four primary clusters called *goal orientations:* (a) work avoidance—the goal of minimizing effort on academic tasks, (b) social affiliation—the goal of wanting to work together with other students, (c) social responsibility—the goal of living up to perceived expectations, and (d) social concerns—the goal of helping other students.

The resulting description of what students want to achieve in middle school was complex, richly illustrated, and full of surprises. Aside from avoiding work, a persistently maladaptive goal from the adult vantage point, the participants espoused and enacted social goals that clearly constituted important reasons for engagement in learning. Among the conclusions that will catch the attention of any reader was the assertion that social motives, rather than being peripheral to performance of academic tasks, might be salient and highly predictive of school achievement.

Phenomenological studies. Phenomenology is a philosophic perspective that underlies all qualitative research traditions but, when used to examine the meaning of something (an event, role, process, status, or context) from the vantage point of someone (or some group) who actually experiences that phenomenon, both the study and the methodology are likely to be called *phenomenological*. Here you see represented a point we have repeatedly made about the way qualitative researchers think about the world—that reality exists only in the eyes and minds of beholders. In other words, the meaning of "loneliness" can be constructed only out of an understanding of what lonely people say it means. What the researcher thinks something might mean has to be put aside so that he or she can listen attentively to the reports of participants' subjective experiences. It is out of these data that the elements and structure of the phenomenon can be identified and described.

In a study of single and single-again women, Lewis and Moon (1997) asked, "What is it like to be a single woman today?" and "Are the experiences of women who have always been single different from those who find themselves single again after having been married?" A qualitative methodology was selected because the area of investigation was new and the purpose of the study was exploratory and phenomenological in nature.

The report contains both an extensive review of the research literature on the phenomenon of singleness (including the evolving image of single women in recent history) and a description of the authors' own background and connections to the study (their academic backgrounds, professional careers, experience as single women, and sources of interest in the topic).

The study had two phases: (a) 37 single women between the ages of 30 and 65 who had been recruited as volunteers through a newspaper advertisement were divided into small focus groups in which they responded to a series of open-ended questions (the protocol questions were revised after the authors viewed and analyzed the videotape of each meeting, thus progressively sharpening the nature of the probes); and (b) questionnaire responses were analyzed from 39 similar participants who had not been in the focus group interviews. Four of the focus groups in the first phase consisted of women who had always been single, whereas three groups were composed of women who had become single as a function of death or divorce. The semistructured questionnaire used in the second phase was based on recurring themes derived from the focus group data and was prepared in two forms: one for single women and one for single again women.

All interviews and open-ended questionnaire responses were transcribed and coded to allow tallying and comparison. The investigators wrote preliminary statements describing what the participants said they had experienced about being single. Then, working back and forth between the statements and the data set (in an analytic process called *constant comparison*), they produced a final set of themes that represented their findings. After carefully considering issues of reliability and validity, the researchers asserted a single, "overriding" conclusion: *"Single women have unresolved or unrecognized ambivalences about being single"* (p. 123).

They supported that assertion with illustrations drawn from three regularities that appeared in the full data set: (a) women are aware of both the advantages and drawbacks of being single, (b) women are ambivalent about the reasons for their singleness, and (c) although content with being single, many women experience feelings of loss and grief. The reality of singleness as it was lived by the participants was far more mixed than is commonly portrayed in a society that tends either to glamorize or to stigmatize the single life.

Ethnographic studies. With its origins in anthropology, *ethnography* is both a research process (the researcher "does" ethnography in the field), and a product (the reported study can be called "an ethnography"). It is a form of qualitative research used to examine social units, some as broad as an entire culture and some as narrow as a single social unit or setting (a family, classroom, or rest home). The focus is always on the values, attitudes, and beliefs that determine how members of the group behave in the social setting. These are the dispositions and practices we learn to be members of and participants in various organizations and communities, and, although those rules and structures might change over time, they are passed on to newcomers as the shared dimensions of culture (both explicit and implicit) that they are expected to know (and observe).

In the typical format, the researcher gathers data (most commonly through field notes) by direct presence as an observer (and sometimes participant) in the natural setting. The usual objective is to develop a holistic perspective that will allow an analysis of local culture in its full context. The aspect of sociocultural interpretation (including historic, economic, and demographic factors) is what distinguishes classic ethnographic studies from other on-site-observer approaches that generate descriptions of a problem or setting.

There is no particular set of methods used by all investigators, and data collection tactics often evolve as the study proceeds. It is not uncommon for quantitative data to be accumulated along with extensive information that reflects the understandings of the participants (in that latter sense, ethnographic studies are also phenomenological in nature). There is great emphasis on accuracy, detail, and completeness—the agencies of internal and external validity. The final products are descriptions and explanations that illuminate the meaning and function of human actions within a specified setting or a defined social unit.

It would have been easy to select as an example here a study involving ethnography in an exotic cultural context—a village in Mexico, a farming commune populated by members of a conservative religion, or an urban neighborhood with a predominantly immigrant population. Instead, we used our sense of places that would be familiar to the majority of our readers (hospitals, schools, social agencies, small business organizations, churches, athletic teams) to select a study that illustrates the culture present in a local work setting—a place with visible boundaries and recognizable participants.

Francis (2000) set out to ask a simple question about an agency designed to provide case management for homeless people with mental illness: "What is case management, and what, in their own eyes, do case managers do?" As so often happens in qualitative research, however, the question turned out to be far more complicated than the researcher had anticipated. Moreover, the study actually performed in response to those complexities became itself a case study of the centrality of broad social context in understanding local culture. What happened at the agency on a day-to-day basis proved to be as much a function of resource allocation, state and federal contests for power, bureaucratic regulations, and the politics of social systems in which the agency was embedded as it was of how the participants understood their social and professional roles.

Federally funded as a demonstration project, the research site was an agency charged with providing intensive case management for homeless persons who suffer from mental disorder and substance abuse. Immediate administration, however, was under the jurisdiction of the county community health system. Formed into nontraditional teams of service providers consisting of a case manager, a nurse, an outreach worker, a project manager, and a consumer-member (a person with a history of homelessness and addiction), the agency staff placed special emphasis on sharing information both within and across teams.

Over a 5-month period, the investigator collected field note data through daily on-site observation (attending staff meetings, participating in agency activities, and shadowing team members both in and out of the office), as well as through unstructured interviews with 10 informants selected from various roles within the agency. All data were transcribed, coded, and analyzed through use of HyperResearch, a computer program for text analysis.

As soon as on-site observation began, it was immediately clear that participants wanted to talk about how the conflicting regulations of the state, federal, and county bureaucracies made it difficult to provide effective service and retain clients. Thus, the focal question became, Why is it so difficult for this agency to deliver its intensive case management services, and what are the consequences of this difficulty? Although the question was tied tightly to the immediate circumstances of that particular agency, the answer had to be found in the wider sociopolitical context within which it operated.

The county health system had services set up for people who were homeless *or* mentally ill *or* substance abusers, but not all three. The federal funding mandate, however, presumed services for a population with any two or all three of these problems. In the ensuing contest of political wills, the case managers reported a pervasive sense that neither the county administrative system nor the federal bureaucracy was really concerned about whether their clients were actually getting any help.

What evolved was a set of norms that valued (and encouraged) creative evasion of regulations in ways that would make clients eligible for assistance. When such practices failed, clients were left unserved, often after enormous investments of time and emotional capital by case managers. In turn, the accumulation of fatigue and stress began to produce burnout in members of the staff, and, accordingly, the entire organization began to show signs of instability.

These effects were interpreted by the author in terms of classic role-conflict theory, with consequent recommendations for the design of social service agencies. An ethnographic investigation offered far more than a description of what case managers did in a modern social service agency; it provided a demonstration of how an environment made hostile by regulatory conflict can make the most desperately needed, well planned, and adequately funded program go awry.

Grounded theory studies. Although it is employed in studies that reflect a general qualitative orientation (the investigator is the primary instrument of data collection, reality is assumed to be a subjective construct created or negotiated by people, and inductive processes are employed to derive meaning from the data), grounded theory is, nonetheless, a very specific research methodology. At the outset, we need to prepare our readers for what might be two small disappointments. First, no matter which study we select for our illustration, the methods of data collection are likely to sound generally like some of those you already have encountered. Second, although we will describe its purpose and general form, beyond that overview we will not explain how grounded theory, as a specific method, is used to analyze data. The process is complex, specified in great detail, and full of constructs that would be unfamiliar to most readers (Glaser & Strauss, 1967).

Indeed, the method is also unfamiliar to many researchers who freely use the term to characterize any study they have performed in which a hypothesis was derived to explain or understand the data. In the majority of such attributions, however, it is our judgment that, *yes,* they did have a theory, and, *yes,* that theory was derived (more or less) from their inspection of the data, but, *no,* there is nothing in the report to suggest that they actually employed the procedures specified for grounded theory. Incorrect or not, however, that misappropriation of terminology seems to be with us to stay.

The purpose of genuine grounded theory studies seems clear enough—the production (development) of a theory. The theory emerges from the investigators' intimate association with and manipulation of the data (and hence it is "grounded" in the data), and the theory can be used to help understand why the data are the way they are. More to the functional point, grounded theories offer something beyond a descriptive response to the question "What's going on here?" by providing a systematic explanation for both why and how it does go on.

As powerful as they may be, however, such theories can be elusive. Grounded theories are not just lying around in the data waiting to be discovered; they have to be extracted by a theoretically sensitive researcher who guides the data collection process as useful concepts, linkages, and categories begin to appear. Then, the process of constant comparison (going back and forth between tentative explanations and data, searching for confirmation) commonly is used, first to create descriptive categories (a useful by-product of many grounded theory studies) and then as the basis for theoretical assertions that pull things together.

Thus, grounded theory studies do not start with a theory—they end with one. Invariably, the theory is a new one that did not exist before that particular study, because it came out of that particular study. Also, because the theories produced tend to be very specific to the context studied, they often have strong implications for the design of effective practice. What they lack in terms of grand generalization, they gain in terms of applicability.

The central question for the study we selected to illustrate grounded theory (Ungar, 2000) was, "What role do friends and peer groups play in the lives and psychological development of teenagers?" The author of this study was a Canadian clinical psychologist with a practice that included treatment of high-risk adolescents ages 13 to 18. With each of 41 male and female volunteer participants who met the criteria for being high risk (various combinations of poverty, physical and sexual abuse, family violence, neglect, addictions, and mental disorders), two interviews were conducted lasting one to one-and-one-half hours. Most (37) of the participants were or had been the investigator's clients in individual, group, or family therapy, and, in all cases, full clinical case histories were available for review.

In the first interview, open-ended questions were asked from a protocol designed to cover issues related to adolescence, mental health, relationships, social competencies, coping strategies, and experiences of power and control (or lack thereof). In the second interview, questions were shaped by the results from ongoing analysis of data (transcripts) created by the first session. In addition, as a strategy to ensure that the data were trustworthy, participants were asked to comment on the emerging theoretical statements (a process sometimes called *member-checking*).

The grounded theory approach as just defined was implemented throughout the data collection and analysis processes. The result was a theory describing three developmental stages of power as adolescents progressed toward positive self-definitions. This theory suggested a process that was contrary to the widely accepted adult notion that peer groups exert pressure that is one-way and highly coercive, leading vulnerable adolescents into antisocial behaviors. Peer groups were described by participants as forums in which they enhanced personal power through the assertion of a personal identity. In virtually every case, apparent conformity hid the important power the adolescents had within the peer group to be themselves.

At the first developmental stage, the teenage participants described being *stuck* with an identity (usually one given to them by adults such as parents, police, teachers, or other authorities) such as delinquent, troubled, violent, truant, or suicidal. The participants might have had some small degree of agency in choosing their identity, but there were few alternatives other than those assigned by adults.

At the second developmental stage, the participants tried on new identities as a result of the serendipitous discovery and acquisition of another label, often one provided by the different groups with whom they interacted—most particularly peer groups. These unstuck participants became *chameleons*, using their new identities as coping strategies within their difficult life circumstances, allowing them to appear more powerful than they might really feel.

At the third developmental stage, participants reported that they were able to construct self-definitions of their own choosing, which then were accepted and reinforced by peers—and in some cases by family and community members as well. This stage of *acceptance* allowed them to become more resilient and self-assured, proclaiming to the world: "This is who I am. Accept me."

Each of the stages in the developmental theory was grounded in the data, a fact illustrated by description of specific cases and quotations from their interviews. Further, the theory not only was new, it was counterintuitive, running strongly against our adult predisposition to see peer groups as a negative force that often leads hapless youth into delinquency. The reverse appeared to be true for the participants in this study: They used peer groups as means for searching out and assuming new and more positive self-definitions.

Critical research. Investigators doing critical research begin with a number of assumptions that differ sharply from those made by people working within other qualitative research traditions (or within the quantitative paradigm). Most scholars who work from the perspective of what is commonly called *critical theory* value the production of new knowledge through research (although they would insist on defining *knowledge* in their own terms), but only when it is conducted in a socially responsible manner—as they (individually) understand that moral imperative. Again, most of them would regard it as incumbent on the investigator to be concerned with how knowledge is used and, particularly, how that use relates to inequities in the distribution of power and material resources in our society.

The concern for matters of social justice and equity would be extended to any disadvantaged social subgroup: single-parent families, urban schools, minority-owned businesses, former convicts, people on welfare, illegal immigrants, or girls in a male-dominated physical education class. Research, for *most* critical investigators, either must help us understand the sources of inequity (and the social processes that sustain it) or must go beyond that goal to serve as an agent for remedial change by helping to empower members of an oppressed group (usually as a consequence of being participants in a study).

Those two alternatives for doing socially responsible research *both* imply that critical research must be concerned with making a better society—in the first case, indirectly, through improved understanding of social mechanisms, and, in the second case, directly, through empowerment of participants. Even that observation, however, over-simplifies the subtle varieties of critical research as it exists today.

Our use of the italicized word *most* in the text above was intended to clearly signal the qualifier "not all"—that is, we were being deliberate, not simply overly cautious. Critical research is a tradition very much in the making. It is in a state of wonderful disarray. Spirited disputation fills journals and conference meetings, and a heady sense of new enterprise is everywhere. Thus, most critical researchers would agree with our broad characterization of their perspective on inquiry, *but certainly not all.* If you do some background reading in this area (such as Thomas, 1993, mentioned earlier in this chapter), you soon will discover the truth of that assertion.

As you might expect, critical research does not require the investigator to maintain complete objectivity about the study. Indeed, most critical theorists regard objectivity in social science as no more than a polite fiction. That, however, does not indicate a disregard for care and close attention to detail in the planning and execution of a study. Nor does it suggest that critical researchers are not concerned about the quality of data obtained, the systematic use of analytic techniques, or a full accounting of both method and results in the report. They simply believe that all research is value bound and see it as appropriate that they make their *subjectivity* (personal values about the question and commitments about their role as researchers) explicit and public, for both participants and readers.

The questions addressed in much critical research sound similar to those used in interpretive research, although they might signal something about the investigator's social politics. "How do policies in administration of the parole system influence the recidivism rate of adolescents convicted of first-offense, nonviolent crimes?" is an example of the former, whereas "What are the primary vehicles for social oppression of lesbian teachers in the public schools?" represents the latter. Both studies, however, would be concerned with understanding how dominant groups impose their construction of reality and thereby institutionalize disadvantageous positions for stigmatized people. Investigators in both studies might also be committed to finding ways to use that knowledge to confront the inequity.

Often, critical studies that involve a component of social activism include careful documentation of that process. Recording this information is regarded as a particularly important aspect of being a responsible investigator. Because an analysis of the empowerment process often reveals valuable lessons that can inform others who follow, doing so meets the political obligations assumed in critical research.

Methods of data collection in critical research can be closely similar to those used throughout the qualitative domain: interviews, observation, and document analysis. The relationship of the researcher to the participant might be more egalitarian, even to the point of sharing some of the decisions about the course of the study, but, in such investigations, careful collection of data remains a central task.

On the other hand, in this form of inquiry, scholars are persistently testing the boundaries of tradition—even when what constitutes established practice might be no more than a decade old. In some reports published as studies in the critical tradition, the author assumes a stance so far removed from what we have come to expect that he or she is almost unrecognizable as a scholar. Further, even the definition of what constitutes the basic elements of research (design, data, analysis, results) begins to morph into unexpected forms. In the face of such diversity, we offer two examples, representing types drawn from very different locations in this wonderfully messy domain of human inquiry. We hope you regard them as exotic but truly interesting (or, perhaps, exciting) specimens with which to illustrate this type of research.

The tale told by Papineau and Kiely (1996) is unusual in several respects. Clearly, it is about the uses of critical theory, even though the authors elected not to use that term anywhere in the published report. Further, their writing is entirely free of the arcane jargon and philosophical circumlocutions that frequently appear in the writings of critical theorists. In that sense, this is a research report and not a polemic.

That it also happens to be the report of an evaluation study should not concern you at all. This kind of evaluation is as solidly qualitative research as field ethnography.

The story begins with a grassroots community economic development (CED) organization. One of the many similar groups that sprang up in the latter decades of the 20th century, the CED agency that was the focus of evaluation in this study arose through a coalition of community groups operating in an urban neighborhood. Their mission was to promote social change through educative, economic, and social services to single parents, unemployed youths, immigrants, the homeless, and persons on social assistance. To accomplish those ends, they employed a model of action that involved members of the community (including service recipients) as full participants in the development and implementation of solutions for social and economic problems.

Beyond provision of services, however, the members of the CED organization also saw empowerment as a coequal mission. Whatever they undertook (for example, a new employment program for low-income people, or a loan fund to provide capital for starting small businesses), they intended to leave those who received service more self-confident, more skillful in carrying out activities to attain goals, and more inclined to take collaborative action to effect social change. In brief, the target for CED was assistance provided in a manner that would produce empowerment.

After several years of operation, it was no surprise, therefore, when the members of the coalition decided not only that it was time to evaluate how effective the CED programs were in accomplishing their intended missions but that they wanted the process of evaluation to empower *them* as well! Thus, an accurate title for the report of this study might well have been, "Using participatory evaluation to empower the empowerers." It was reasoned that not only would such a process leave the stakeholders in the organization more committed to their work and savvy about getting it done, it would increase their commitment to evaluation results and their utilization.

An experienced evaluation researcher and group leader was employed, and the following design was laid out: (a) the initial plan would be approved by the several boards of directors from the organizations involved, (b) through a small group meeting with all stakeholders (administrators and staff, volunteers, donors, and service recipients), the questions to be addressed in the evaluation would be specified, (c) through a similar process, the instruments (interview and field observation protocols, questionnaires, rating forms) would be drafted, (d) data would be collected, (e) data would be analyzed and evaluation reports prepared, and (f) strategic planning would proceed throughout the organization. Finally, it was decided that the investigator would also document what was done to empower the stakeholders— and how well that worked.

It all happened as planned—for the most part. Things moved more slowly than the ambitious research plan had proposed, and there were a few unexpected defections along the way. For example, service recipi- ents had no time or inclination to do instrument design and data collection tasks, and coalition leaders had no interest in doing data analysis (seeing that as the proper job of the investigator). Nevertheless, the verbatim transcripts of interviews were coded and subject to con- tent analysis. Numeric data from rating scales were consolidated with descriptive statistics. Reports were written and then presented to the CED stakeholders.

And, what were the results? Was the agency serving the needs of its clients and was it leaving them empowered? Of greater interest for us, did the study leave the participants (the organization's stakehold- ers) feeling empowered—an outcome that is central in critical theory? The answers are "yes" to all of these questions—with very few reser- vations. There were grumblings about the evaluation taking too long, asking too much work from participants, and being cumbersome in design. Yet, everyone also agreed that it was open and comprehensive, which are exactly the qualities that require time and broad-based involvement.

There was consensus that the organization had been strengthened and its members energized. There were specific findings to indicate that stakeholders emerged with new skills (computer use, instrument design technology, evaluation strategies) and a greater sense of self- efficacy. The positive evaluation results were used to promote the agency within the wider community, and the positive evaluation expe- rience became a model for other grassroots development groups. The report tells the story of competent critical theory research—and offers evidence that sometimes those tales have happy endings.

At this point, you should fasten your intellectual seat belt for a sudden leap to a location that is much less familiar. The work of Cole and Hribar (1995), although clearly an example of serious scholarship and solidly located in the tradition of social criticism from Marxist and feminist perspectives, pushes hard against the limits of any envelope containing what we would define as qualitative research.

The absence of systematic procedures designed to produce empirical data (aside from what is derived from other sources) is but one of the features that might puzzle some readers. The lack of an identified set of participants in the immediate context of a study might be a source of disorientation for others. Nevertheless, this is a specimen that shows where some social scientists are taking the tradition of critical theory.

So, you might ask, "Is this a research report?" The fact that you (or we) might be made more comfortable if we could exclude it from the category of "research," or at least provide it with a less confusing label ("social critique" would have an air of elegance, "polemical essay" would be more abusive than deserved, and "critical commentary" would be too bland to honestly reflect the sharp edges intended by the authors), is not really relevant. Report, article, essay, or commentary, this type of research is something you will encounter in journals. Perhaps at this stage it is less important to characterize what it represents than it is to listen to what the authors have to say.

In "Celebrity Feminism: *Nike Style*—Post-Fordism, Transcendence, and Consumer Power," Cole & Hribar (1995) examined the phenomenon of the "Just do it!" advertising campaign sponsored by the Nike athletic shoe company. Part of that process involved close (and skeptical) attention to the fact that the corporation has been widely celebrated for its apparent role in encouraging women to become more physically active—before it was fashionable to do so. Drawing from a wide variety of contemporary literature, the authors provide ample evidence that Nike has been portrayed as a progressive, pro-woman company with socially responsible policies.

It might surprise some readers to find that the authors' critique of that characterization does not center on the fact that, through the artful "Just do it!" campaign, a transnational company captured an enormous segment of the worldwide market for women's athletic footwear, promoted sales to a level previously unimagined, and made untold billions in the process. Nike receives no direct condemnation for the fact that it was not acting entirely on the basis of altruistic motives. Instead, the substance of the critique centers on two quite different points.

First, through a long argument that we are not competent to abstract or to even annotate, Cole and Hribar make a case for the possibility that in the course of making women feel "empowered" to take charge of their own bodies, the marketing minions (who, in this case, were women) have replaced (or co-opted) traditional feminism (with its activist political and social agenda). Instead, the Nike campaign has promoted a kind of "celebrity feminism" that looks inward to the self (as body and attitude) rather than outward to the problematic place of women in society.

One of the most striking pieces of evidence in that regard is inclusion of the full transcript for the now famous "Did you ever wish you were a boy?" advertisement. We can testify that reading it now leaves one with the impression that Nike was saying, "With a hard, slender body encased in spandex, *and a pair of our shoes,* you can run away from the real weight of women's history."

The second direction of social critique leads the authors to argue that in the "Just do it!" campaign, Nike was speaking with a forked tongue. Like many transnational corporations, Nike manufactures absolutely nothing—it is a pure marketing company. All shoes are produced in Third World countries, and, the authors claim, they are produced mostly by women who are paid low wages and who work under dangerous and unhealthy conditions.

We found the evidence presented to sustain that point much thinner (and less persuasive), but events since publication have worked to confirm the authors' judgment, at least for corporate entities that depend on cheap labor in third world countries. In recent years, a host of brand-name companies have been scrambling to retrieve their good names as responsible citizens by showing fits of concern about workers at outsourcing sites abroad. We make no claim that this report triggered that wave of corporate sympathy, but that is precisely the kind of outcome that critical researchers hope to produce.

You now will have to contemplate the question we raised at the outset: "Is this a research report?" The authors have asserted that from the postmodern perspective (their particular philosophical vantage point), their work constitutes research. We will not contest that point. What seems more important here is that you begin to form your own judgment on the matter.

Mixed Methodology Studies

We have to admit that this is an unfortunate name for a type of research, whether qualitative or quantitative. It gives the impression that if a qualitative study happens to employ a methodological step that produces numeric data (for example, a count that yields the frequency with which a certain response is given to an interview question), it has become a different and special type of research, or that if a quantitative study includes use of a method commonly associated with qualitative research (for example, interviewing participants to ascertain whether or not they liked a particular experimental treatment), the investigation is no longer a true experiment—and must be called something else.

In neither case is any change required; an experiment remains an experiment even with all sorts of supplemental information from interviews and observation notes, and an ethnography remains an ethnography no matter how many numbers are included in the report. Many social scientists have freely intermixed data types and data acquisition methods without feeling any necessity to take aboard the philosophical perspective of a paradigm other than that which served as the principal guide for their research.

Mixed method studies are not created simply by mixing methods from two paradigms. We believe the mixed method label is justified, however, when other, more profound changes are made in quantitative or qualitative studies. When, for example, the nature of the research problem makes it necessary to use both qualitative and quantitative data in developing a more thorough answer, when each kind of data is subject to rigorous standards of quality that are appropriate within its paradigm of origin, and when interpretation links data types together in a genuine synthesis—that represents something that (in our cosmology, at least) deserves being called a distinct type of inquiry.

A number of scholars have given attention to possibilities for such integration of qualitative and quantitative research, sometimes referring to it as a strategy of *mixed designs*, which to us is a more satisfactory label. Miles and Huberman (1994) have outlined four such alternatives. Their options involve either simultaneous use of parallel qualitative and quantitative strategies or variations on alternation between the two. Any of these designs could be planned and conducted in a manner that conforms to our characterization of a genuine mixed method design for deserving status as a distinct type of research.

There are entire books devoted to this topic (see, for example, Green & Caracelli, 1997, or Tashakkori & Teddlie, 1998, 2003). Because most of them involve plowing through some fairly dense material, however, we suggest that you begin with either of two alternatives:

Robson (2002), whose own approach as a critical realist leads him to make flexible use of research strategies and tools in combinations that seem to best fit the particular research problem at hand, or Flick (2002), who has published extensively about the use of combined paradigms for the purpose of triangulation (designs in which the strengths of one approach are used to compensate for the weaknesses in the other).

Our example of a mixed methodology study (Walker, 1996) is relatively straightforward, and it has the advantage of dealing with a mundane activity of daily life with which all readers are likely to be familiar—watching television. The purpose of the study was to examine the behavior of couples that watched television together (the dominant recreational activity in the United States today), how they used the remote control device (RCD) to select programs, and what feelings those patterns of use produced. Individuals in 36 highly diverse volunteer couples were interviewed with a protocol that included questions of two distinct types.

The more structured section contained sociodemographic questions (age, length of relationship, etc.), as well as items concerned with number of television sets, frequency of joint viewing, and happiness with the behaviors and interactions that occurred while watching with the partner. The second, more open-ended section contained questions that related to power: how the couple decided on a program to watch together, how partners got each other to watch programs they wanted to watch, and the nature and intensity of their frustrations with watching television together.

A coin toss was used to determine which partner would be interviewed first. Partners were interviewed separately, usually in their own homes. Interviews were audiotaped and transcribed. The Statistical Analysis System computer program was used for statistical analysis of the quantitative data. The transcripts of qualitative data were read and reread to create descriptions of both the range of responses and the primary themes that typified feelings and beliefs concerning joint viewing. Results involved presenting a synthesis of data types, sometimes cross-checking for validity, and at other times using both qualitative and quantitative perspectives to fully develop a rich characterization about viewing behavior.

The central conclusion was that partners in close relationships "do gender" and exercise power even in their ordinary, everyday behavior and, specifically, in their selection of television programming via a remote control device. Men control the RCD more than women, and women are far more frustrated by RCD behaviors than are men. Both genders have means for persuading the other partner to watch what they prefer, but, in that negotiation, women only rarely win. Unnegotiated channel switching by men was a frequent occurrence in the participant group, and men persisted in doing that even when their female partners were obviously frustrated by the behavior.

The confluence of qualitative and quantitative data confirmed that among the participants in this study, leisure was a source of conflict—conflict between their own enjoyment and the enjoyment of their partner. Women often expressed resignation about the state of things—only 4 out of 36 thought they might be successful if they attempted to change the way their partners used the RCD. The author provided an array of qualitative and quantitative data to support the assertion that such resignation reflected a latent form of men's power over women.

The women became less able over time to raise issues of concern, they anticipated the struggles that would occur if their own wishes were made known, and they predicted a negative reaction to their wishes from their male partner. Joint television watching by the couples in this study was hardly an egalitarian experience, and the uses of gendered power appeared to undercut the very notion that it is a recreational leisure-time activity for women.

❖ CONCLUDING COMMENTS ABOUT TYPES OF RESEARCH

We have briefly surveyed the kinds of research you are most likely to encounter as you pursue the retrieval and reading of reports. Some of the studies you read will combine aspects of several formats. For example, a study might include both correlations and descriptive comparisons across groups—techniques normally associated with two quite different members of the quantitative research family. Another study might use statistical operations to categorize subjects' attitudes toward their jobs and then employ interviews to capture their perception of workplace conditions. Knowing which methods of data collection were used is not sufficient to predict how data will be interpreted and results identified. Data are always at the center of any study, but the paradigmatic assumptions of the investigator on which the study is grounded are what will shape how findings are understood.

All of that serves to underscore a fundamental truth about the nature of research: Tidy categories are the creations of textbook authors.

For the most part, they do not exist in the real world, where disorder, if not a state bordering on chaos, is the general condition. So please do not be shocked by the fact that what you find in the research literature sometimes seems rather unlike some of our descriptions. Simplifying, and imposing a degree of order that does not appear in nature, was our intention. We hoped to lure you in by not frightening you away.

3

Appendix C

Reviewing Checklist

KURT HEPPARD

This "Reviewing Checklist" is provided to help you assess the overall quality of a scholarly paper or manuscript. I've constructed it from writing and research classes taken with Anne Huff and Chris Koberg at the University of Colorado, then supplemented it by looking at instructions to reviewers from several journals in my field.

Although this is a relatively mechanistic and simplistic system, it has been effective in helping authors make sure that they have not missed important items that reviewers are likely to look for. It can be used early in the writing process (as an outline is being developed) or much later in critiquing finished drafts and resubmissions.

Because this is a generic checklist, some categories may not be relevant to the paper you are considering and you may have other categories or comments to add. In addition, a low rating may or may not indicate a weak paper. Conversely, a high rating may not indicate a strong paper. You will still have the difficult task of drawing together an overall assessment and considering the paper's contribution.

I use the list to systematically remind myself (as author or reviewer) of potentially important categories of scholarly writing. Then I step back to take a more holistic view of the paper. Rather than overwhelm myself and others with detail, I emphasize the most important strengths and weaknesses of the paper I'm considering, and suggest specific steps for improvement as I complete my review. I also try to do this in a way that supports ongoing community, following the guidelines found in Chapter 1 of this book.

1. Introductory Elements
   - Summarizing the paper
   - Title
   - Abstract
   - Introduction
   - Connection with previous conversation
2. Questions for Quantitative Papers
   - Theoretical framework and development of hypotheses
   - Description and evaluation of methods
   - Results
3. Questions for Qualitative Papers
4. Questions for Theory Development
5. Questions for Case Studies
6. Discussion
7. Conclusion

Use the following categories to rate each question. All nonapplicable questions should be left blank.

1. Not at all.
2. Only to a limited extent.
3. At an acceptable level.
4. To a significant extent.
5. Completely.

Introductory Elements	1	2	3	4	5
Summarizing the paper:					
Can you identify the one or two main points of the paper?					
Is the target journal an appropriate outlet for the paper?					
Title:					
Does the title grab attention and say something important about the paper?					
Does it include important words that will index the paper appropriately?					
Abstract:					
Is the abstract compelling? Does it attract attention?					
Does it provide an accurate overview of the paper?					
Does the abstract summarize major accomplishments?					
Does it identify the central theory or literature stream or "conversation"?					
Does the abstract inform the reader about critical features of the article (methodology, data sources, and so on)?					
Does it use relatively simple words and sentences?					
Can the abstract be understood without reading the paper?					
Does the order of the abstract reflect the order of the paper?					
Introduction:					
Does the introduction entice the reader to read on?					
Does it establish a need for the paper by highlighting gaps or disagreements in the literature?					
Does it organize ideas and material in a logical and meaningful sequence, which is then reflected in the body of the paper?					
Does it introduce key concepts from the paper?					
Does it highlight the key contribution or "value added" by the paper					
Connection with previous conversation:					
Are antecedents of the paper clearly identified?					
Is the discussion of previous work an appropriate length?					
Is the author's intended contribution to previous conversation clearly identified? Are key terms defined?					
Would a significant number of scholars in the field find the paper's subject and approach interesting?					

1 = Not at all 2 = Only to a limited extent 3 = At an acceptable level 4 = To a significant extent
5 = Completely

Questions for Quantitative Papers	1	2	3	4	5
Theoretical framework and development of hyphotheses (if appropriate):					
Are the study's propositions and hypotheses clearly articulated?					
Are the basic arguments of the paper important and interesting?					
Are important premises and assumptions identified?					
Is there a graphic depiction of the relationship between key variables in the paper?					
Are key terms defined?					
Would a significant number of scholars in the field find the paper's subject and approach interesting?					
Description and evaluation of methods (if appropriate):					
Is the methodology of the paper clearly identified?					
Are data collection methods described adequately?					
Are the sampling strategy and sample explained?					
Is the operationalization of variables and constructs plausible (content validity)?					
Are dependent variables identified and described?					
Are independent variables identified and described?					
Are control variables identified and described?					
Do measures theoretically relate independent and dependent variables (construct validity)?					
Are control variables used effectively?					
Are questionnaire or other measurement items identified and described?					
Was the discussion of interview or questionnaire construction and response rates clear and comprehensive?					
Have steps been taken to avoid data collection errors?					
Is there evidence of reliability or internal consistency in the study?					
Results:					
Are the findings adequately and accurately described?					
Are results clearly related back to original propositions, hypotheses, research questions, and data analysis?					
Do tables provide sufficient and accurate data to allow the reader to reach independent conclusions?					
Are figures and appendixes used effectively?					
Is implied causality justified?					
Has the author adequately considered alternative explanations for the results found?					

Questions for Quantitative Papers	1	2	3	4	5
Is the purpose of the research adequately established?					
Are the duration and intensity of observation clear?					
Are the nature of the site, and key players, adequately discussed?					
Are methods of collecting and analyzing data adequately described?					
Does the writer convince the reader that he or she was able to gather information about key events from appropriate sources?					
Is there evidence that informants trusted the researcher and were likely to honestly share information with the researcher?					
Has the author adequately considered alternative interpretations of the data presented?					
Is there evidence of systematically considering evidence that contradicts the author's interpretations?					
Is the author adequately considered alternative interpretations of the data presented?					
Is there evidence of systematically considering evidence that contradicts the author's interpretations?					
Questions for Theory Development	1	2	3	4	5
Is the purpose of the research adequately established?					
Is the need for (or purpose of) theory development well established?					
Is previous theory adequately summarized?					
Is the author's contribution to theory significant?					
[s it well organized and clear?					
Is it adequately linked back to the literature?					
Questions for Case Studies	1	2	3	4	5
Is the "story" intrinsically interesting?					
Is sufficient background information provided?					
Are key issues clearly stated?					
Is there enough information to develop alternative scenarios about future development?					
Is there enough information to allow reader to recommend an action and discuss possible consequences of that action?					

1 = Not at all 2 = Only to a limited extent 3 = At an acceptable level 4 = To a significant extent
5 = Completely

Introductory Elements	*1*	*2*	*3*	*4*	*5*
Is there enough information to develop relatively detailed implementation plans for the recommended action or decision?					
Is there enough information to allow the recommended action and its implementation plan to be discussed and analyzed?					
Discussion	*1*	*2*	*3*	*4*	*5*
Does the discussion section introduce new and relevant topics? (It should not simply restate findings.)					
Does the discussion section use consistent terminology that is understandable in the context of the entire paper?					
Are limitations of the study clearly stated?					
Are logical extensions of this study and avenues of additional research provided?					
Conclusion	*1*	*2*	*3*	*4*	*5*
Does the conclusion retain the reader's interest in the subject and the paper itself?					
Are the most important components and contributions of the study highlighted?					
Is there something new in the conclusion that has not appeared elsewhere in this paper?					
Would the busy reader looking only at the introduction and conclusion understand the contribution of the paper?					

1 = Not at all 2 = Only to a limited extent 3 = At an acceptable level 4 = To a significant extent 5 = Completely

4

Reviewing Existing Literature

IAN LINGS

SUPERVISOR'S VIEW: DR ANNE SOUCHON

Many research students approach their study with some degree of anxiety over data collection and/or analysis, blissfully unaware that what will cause them grief is, in fact, the rather innocuous-sounding '*literature review*'. There are two reasons why the literature review is often a major stumbling block.

First, it is a common belief that the literature should be thoroughly reviewed in a bid to identify a suitable topic (and by suitable, of course, I mean one which will make a contribution to knowledge and be deserving of a Ph.D.). Your supervisor may insist on it, even if this process takes you well over a year; even if it delays your study so much that your funding runs out before you've completed your thesis; even if after reviewing 'your' literature, you decide that there is no theoretical gap there after all, and want to start reviewing an entirely different research stream.

Second, intimate knowledge of the literature is essential in order to position the study within its broader area (otherwise, researchers would forever be reinventing the wheel), develop propositions or hypotheses if this is what the study requires, and explain the findings uncovered in the empirical phase of the project. Thus, as Ian Lings explains below, the literature review is the backbone of the project; it supports the entire study. Its importance is so ingrained that I battle on a daily basis with Doctoral students who are so paralysed by the fear of not knowing the literature well enough that they are stuck at reviewing literature and refuse to move on.

So, here are a few hints to reduce your literature review stress:

(A) Choose a *supervisor*, not a topic. A good supervisor will know the literature already and could (I want to say should) steer you towards a worthy topic.

(B) Learn to let go of the literature. Do not get trapped into thinking that you need to keep collecting/reading/assimilating more and more papers *before* you start conceptualising and/or collecting data yourself. If you do, you are simply procrastinating and using the literature as a security blanket, not as a means-to-an-end. And you run the risk of losing focus and getting lost.

(C) Start multi-tasking: keep abreast of new papers coming out *as you embark on other stages of your research.*

And remember that the literature review is an ongoing activity. It is only finished when the thesis has been successfully defended, hard leather-bound (at some considerable expense), and distributed (for free) to friends and family who will never read it!

VIEW FROM THE TRENCHES: JOOBEE YEOW

If there are two words that would appear in the worst nightmares of the perfectionists of this world, especially the perfectionist researchers, they would be *literature review!* I am in the third year of my Ph.D. and even now one of my greatest fears is that I do not know anything and everything regarding my research topic. What if my supervisors ask me this? Or what if my peers ask me that? Or worse, what if someone in the audience when I am presenting my research asks me: 'Why is the moon round in shape'? Shouldn't I know that too? My research is supposed to earth-shattering, it is supposed to solve all the problems of the world! With this in mind, at the start of my research, I combed through every journal paper and book – in fact, anything that was readable, anything that bore even the slightest resemblance to the keywords of my topic. To my bitter discovery, it was not only resource inefficient, but I ended up *lost in reviewing,* torn in all directions.

If I were to offer some advice from my own experience; first and foremost, structure is *very important* in literature review. Secondly, a crucial point is to have structure, and thirdly, you must have guessed, is **structure**. Start by identifying the most relevant authors, journals, databases and other sources that publish work that is most relevant to your topic. By doing this groundwork, you begin to create a boundary in your mind for your literature review, preventing the temptation to go astray – bear in mind that one needs to actually *complete* the Ph.D. at some stage!

Imagine the literature review is in the shape of a diamond. You start at the tip, broaden your knowledge of the topic and eventually come back again to the tip, where now you have gained your focus and pinpointed the gap in the literature. To know when to stop, when you have exhausted most of the literature relevant to your research, is vital as one needs eventually to derive hypotheses and collect data to be able to produce a piece of work to advance knowledge or inform practice. I am not suggesting that you should limit your literature review, but it is impossible for one to know absolutely everything, thus it is important to know in *depth* what you are doing and in *breath* what is relevant to what you are doing.

Last, but not least, a piece of advice from my supervisor at the beginning of my Ph.D. that I still find very useful: 'Your Ph.D. is not supposed to solve the problems of the world, but to make enough of a significant contribution (even as small as it is in the vast sea of knowledge) that you or future researchers will continue and snowball from it to make greater contributions and *eventually*, change the world of knowledge.'

Many beginning researchers have significant problems with reviewing the literature. This might be due to the fact that there just isn't much information out there on how to do it. In fact, many research students are simply given the instruction to 'go away and review the literature on topic x', closely followed by 'see me in a few months'. Learning how to do a good literature review is therefore often done via trial and error. However, it doesn't have to be that way, and in this chapter I hope to give you a good head-start on doing your literature review, and ensuring you end up with a solid piece of work.

The aims of your literature review are to show that you have studied existing work in your field and to provide insights into this work. An effective review critically analyses material, synthesises it, and will be relevant, appropriate, and useful for the reader. Your literature review presents the case and context for the rest of your thesis. For this reason it is important to demonstrate the relationship of your work to previous research in the area. This chapter is written from a deductive perspective; recommending that you should review the literature *before* starting your project. You will probably have an idea of the domain of the literature that you wish to examine and possibly even a more specific and focused area, however, I am assuming that one of your aims in reviewing the literature is to decide on the specific research that you will undertake. An alternative to this view is presented in Alternative View 9.3 which presents a 'grounded' approach in which the literature is not reviewed until after the project has started.

At the end of this chapter I really hope you have come to terms with these key ideas:

- What literature is.
- Where you can find it.
- What a literature review is, and what it does.

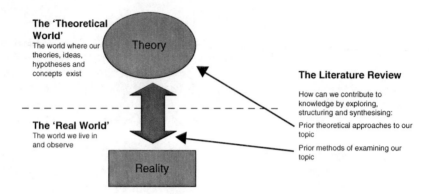

The 'Theoretical World'
The world where our theories, ideas, hypotheses and concepts exist

Theory

The Literature Review

How can we contribute to knowledge by exploring, structuring and synthesising:

Prior theoretical approaches to our topic

The 'Real World'
The world we live in and observe

Prior methods of examining our topic

Reality

Figure 4.1 The place of literature reviewing

- What critiquing the literature means.
- How you can organise your thoughts.
- How you can structure your literature review.
- How you can organise your sources.

Why is it Important to Know This Stuff?

Understanding the basics of reviewing the literature is essential for anyone who wishes to undertake research and contribute to an existing body of knowledge. It's really about uncovering and exploring how prior researchers have explored the theoretical issues in your topic, and also to some extent which methods they have used to collect data and examine those theories, as shown in Figure 4.1. Becoming comfortable with how to locate, understand and critically analyse literature is necessary for you to build your work on top of that which has been done previously. A thorough review of the literature serves several purposes; it helps you to better understand the field in which you are working, it identifies work that has already been conducted and knowledge that has already been developed, it helps you to identify, and often explicitly suggests, areas in which new contributions can be made, and it will illustrate methodologies that have been applied to your particular field of research. In short, the literature review helps you to ensure that you do not simply repeat what has already been done, and to have more confidence that the contribution to knowledge that you wish to make is *indeed* a contribution.

Familiarity with the literature is essential if you are to be able to defend your ideas and arguments in peer-reviewed written work, or even more daunting, when you are standing in front of your peers, be it in front of a class, at a degree viva or at a conference. However, familiarity is not sufficient for a successful literature review, *critical appraisal* is also necessary. Critical evaluation of others' work is a particularly difficult task for many researchers, especially those who feel relatively junior or who are not yet qualified. I have often heard research students and new colleagues comment 'How can I criticise Professor X's work, she is a famous professor and knows so much more than me'. While this is undoubtedly true (professors do usually know more than those just embarking on a research career) the art of the literature review is in the **critique** (not the criticism), and *all work is open to critique*.

As you will see in the following chapters, there are many different ways to approach a given research question. Previous literature will perhaps indicate that different philosophies have been followed, different conceptualisations constructed and different models created. Each of the approaches that you find in published works will present some benefits to answering a particular research question and some inherent limitations to answering the question. It is a discussion of these philosophies, conceptualisations, methods and findings, and their benefits and limitations that forms the basis of the critique of the literature.

Of course, you will also come across some research that is just weak, and can be criticised as being so (sometimes even in the best journals). In order to criticise research as weak, you will need to not only understand how to conduct your review and critique of the literature, you will also need to know about the research designs, methods and analytical techniques discussed in the later chapters of this book.

What is a 'literature review'?

The literature review is literally that, a *re-view* (or look again) at what has already been written about a topic. The literature review is where you demonstrate that you *understand* that which has been done before, and can point to where this existing research is *deficient* in some way. It's important to realise that you are not trying to 'insult' prior research and researchers here, but to point out where existing work needs some supplementing, which maybe because the world has changed since prior work was conducted, or maybe because such work doesn't address important issues that are now relevant – in fact often the authors will indicate this themselves. Further, you need to explain how your work adds to existing knowledge, by overcoming the problems with the existing literature, maybe by bringing together disparate fields of research and extending them, or developing new theory. You also have to show why your work is *important, relevant* and *interesting.* Unfortunately, none of these tasks is easy.

As I mentioned earlier, if you are a research student, it's very likely that one of the first things you will be asked to do on commencing your research degree will be something like 'go away and read the literature' that is relevant to your topic (assuming that you know what your topic will be in more specific terms than just something like 'consumer behaviour' or 'motivation'). Now, it's not that your supervisor doesn't like you and wants to avoid you – although I guess sometimes that's the case. No; at this stage you are actually trying to achieve two simultaneous aims with your reading. You will almost certainly still be trying to tightly define your research problem or thesis (something that you will probably be doing for quite some time in an iterative fashion) and, at the same time, you will be trying to identify, read, understand and assimilate every source of information relevant to your thesis. Therein lies the difficulty. Essentially, you don't know exactly *what* you are going to research until you have read the relevant literature (so everything seems relevant) and you don't know if what you are reading is really relevant until you have decided exactly what you are going to research (which could be many things, as there is more that we don't know than which we do).

If you are in this situation, try to take comfort in two pieces of advice: 'all reading is good',[1] and 'everyone is in the same boat at this stage of their research'. This advice I offer readily, in the knowledge it failed to impress me, assuage my fears and insecurities, or in fact comfort me in any way at all when offered to me by my thesis supervisor. Typically, subsequent experience has shown that he was absolutely right (don't you just hate it when that happens?).

Whatever your situation, one thing is for certain, you have to start somewhere, and, believe it or not, many potential researchers fall at this first hurdle; deciding to start (not deciding *where to* start but just deciding to start *somewhere*). Many of you will have a research topic which is relatively tightly defined. If this is so you will know pretty specifically what you are looking for in relation to unexplained phenomena or theory that is in need of updating or re-examining in the light of a changed world. A **directed** literature review strategy is appropriate in such circumstances. You should write out the research question(s) and analyse it for assumptions (these are what questions you must also answer in order to answer the research question). Write out all of these associated research questions and direct your reading to be able to answers these. IDE 4.1 shows how a research question has assumptions on which it is based, and how further assumptions are made at other stages of the research process. Most often these are not explicitly stated by researchers, but it is useful for you to be aware of the assumptions that you are making in developing your research question and the associated research methods that you wish to adopt to explore your question.

---

[1] Well, this is not strictly always true, but at this point it is a useful rule to live by.

IDE 4.1: Assumptions of a Research Question

A research question is a statement that identifies the phenomenon to be studied. For example, 'What influence do performance bonuses have on employee behaviour?' There are several assumptions that underlie this research question. Firstly, this research question assumes that employee behaviour is something that can be observed by you as a researcher. Underlying this assumption is a realist view of the world, i.e. that there is an observable world to be researched. Depending on the approach that you wish to adopt and the theory on which you base your research, you may have to make further assumptions. If you decide that performance bonuses are one facet of a person's job, along with many other facets, you may wish to adopt a utility framework to analyse the research question. This would require an assumption of 'rational behaviour' and possibly an assumption of utility maximisation by the employee. The question could also be approached using a psychology framework such as the theory of planned behaviour, which also assumes rational behaviour but does not assume utility maximising. Both of these frameworks could direct you to collect quantitative data, which in turn would be based on an assumption that there is a 'real' world and that this can be measured. Further assumptions would then be made in the development of the questionnaire (if one were used) and these will be discussed later in the book. If you were to conduct observational research, then you would make assumptions about the validity and meaning of the observations. You would need to assume that you are observing real behaviour and that your observation is an accurate reflection of what is happening; that you are attributing the correct meaning to the behaviour that you are observing.

If you do not have a very specific research topic, your very first aim should be to try to tightly define your thesis or research question. Most likely, this task will involve coming up with a tentative, working definition. But how on earth do you do this? In this case, an **emergent** literature review strategy works best. Such a strategy involves reading everything, and looking for similarities and contradictions in ideas, methods, theories, assumptions and definitions. From this you can identify interesting research topics that you wish to explore. With the emergent approach, you have the benefit of being able to define the scope of your topic for yourself. Although on the surface this can seem daunting, it has the advantage of allowing you more opportunity to bring your experiences, beliefs and interests to bear on your research. For example, if you are interested in researching 'branding', one starting point is to think about what it is about 'branding' that particularly interests you, and which is not already explained in the literature? Of course, at this point, you don't know if it has already been explained in the literature until you look, but at least you know where to start looking.

Another useful starting point is to think about your observations of the world that suggest to you that existing theory isn't up to explaining the nuances of what you see in the real world. For example, can existing theory explain the fine details of your own experiences of human behaviour, concerning individuals such as customers, employees or managers, or groups such as segments, organisations, industries, or countries? This approach may seem rather 'unscientific' to many (although I hope that reading Chapters 2 and 3 should have given you some pointers on that issue), but it is not a bad place to start developing your research question, provided that you are aware of the purely natural tendency of human beings to confirm our beliefs rather than challenge them; try not to let this bias your readings of the literature.

Furthermore, it is important to remember that you are almost certainly not going to provide a general theory of your field, solve all of the problems that organisations or institutions face and explain all of employee/customer/government or other entities' behaviour (or whatever it is you are interested in). Your research problem will need to be much more focused on a specific issue. Until you have tightly defined your topic, hundreds of sources will seem relevant. However, you cannot define your topic until you read around your research area. Consequently, defining your research question (or thesis) is an iterative process; as you read you refine your thesis, and as you refine your thesis you can decide more easily on what to read and what to ignore.

Finally – and this can be a long and involving process for many – after defining the topic (however tentatively) you are in the position of being able to commence your **directed** reading. But be aware that *directed* is the important adjective here, if you are not directed in your reading you run the risk of becoming lost in the literature, constantly finding exciting avenues to follow but never actually doing anything. You will never complete your research unless you do something. Research requires both *thought* and *action*. Just thinking about your research will not get your thesis written. Please remember that!

Deciding what 'literature' is

It is very common for research students to ask me questions concerning exactly 'what' is literature. It's hard to answer this conclusively, but there are some basic pointers which can help. In general, information for your literature review may be gathered from many sources, and the basic term 'literature' here means the works that you consult to investigate your research problem. That said, while there are many sources of information available, the merits of each must be considered very carefully, and you need to decide how much confidence you wish to place in the information that you find in each of the sources. Should you judge an article from the top journal in your field to be as valuable as one from the local newspaper, or a company report? How do you decide which information is appropriate to include in your literature review? To my mind, there are four main questions that need to be answered for all information in your literature review:

- Is it relevant?
- Does it come from a reputable source?
- Does it present a compelling theoretical argument, and/or rigorous empirical results (i.e. is it any good?)
- What were the motives of the author?

I'll deal with the last question later in the chapter, because it is more concerned with analysing literature, and what you include when you write up your literature review. However, the first two issues are concerned with deciding what types of information to gather for review. To address the question of relevance; there are several decisions that need to be made. Your literature review will need to be sufficiently broad to explain your research area in the context of other research, perhaps in other areas of interest or even other disciplines. Simultaneously, it will have to be focused on your particular research topic, and comprehensive within your own field of enquiry. This means that you will need to be very clear about the definition of your *field* of research; for example, are you doing research in 'marketing' or 'organisational psychology'? Your field should be closely related to your research question or thesis. However, it should not be too close and restrictive, or you run the risk of missing other important literature from adjacent fields, and other disciplines. Actually, you should be adventurous in deciding where contributions to your understanding may come from. Many projects do not restrict themselves to just one body of knowledge, such as marketing, or economics. In fact, some of the best advances in thinking have been as a result of bringing together two or more, apparently disparate, bodies of knowledge to advance in our understanding of the world – which could be termed 'horizontal thinking', as I'll talk about in IDE 4.2.

IDE 4.2: 'Horizontal Thinking'

Horizontal thinking is an interesting term I came across recently when I was reading about creativity, and interestingly enough it recalls a conversation I had with Nick when we were thinking about this book. The idea of horizontal thinking is simply taking ideas and concepts from other fields and disciplines and applying them to your own research problem. It is another great example of how it is useful to read widely and be interested in many different fields. In fact, it's amazing how many ideas you can get from areas which might seem totally unrelated to your own. If you never venture outside your own discipline, you will never be exposed to this kind of thing. There are all kinds of examples of this happening in research, but some of the clearest are the use of Darwinian evolution theory in the social and applied business disciplines, for instance: 'Which automobiles will be here tomorrow?' by Robert J. Holloway, in the *Journal of Marketing*, Vol. 25, Issue 3, p. 35; 'Social Darwinism and the Taylor system: A missing link in the evolution of management?' by Roland E. Kidwell Jr, in the *International Journal of Public Administration*, Vol. 18, Issue 5, p. 767; 'It's Darwinism – survival of the fittest: How markets and reputations shape the ways in which plaintiffs' lawyers obtain clients' by Stephen Daniels and Joanne Martin, in *Law & Policy*, Vol. 21, Issue 4.

Having decided on your topic, and set the scope of your literature search, it is time to start looking for appropriate sources of information. This addresses the second of the two main questions about the confidence of the information and the quality of the source. Where should you get your information about theories, concepts, methods and philosophies that you are interested in? Different types of literature can be grouped in various ways, but for our purposes it is useful to group things according to their intended audience.

Academic literature

Academic (also called 'scholarly') literature can be thought of as work that is written and reported primarily for an academic audience, i.e. scholars who will be using this published work to inform future research in this area. As such, academic literature has certain requirements that are sometimes not met in other types of literature. Academic work should be reported in a scientific manner, such that it is possible for someone reading it to be able to evaluate the theories on which is it based, the research methods used, analyses conducted and conclusions drawn. The need to include lots of information in a very exact manner has the advantage that exactly what the researcher(s) has done should be clear and unambiguous. This means it is easier to identify the limitations of the work, and often this is done for you. However, it can also make academic work dry and tedious to read. The flowery and descriptive language, by its nature often imprecise, which makes normal prose quite interesting to read, often has to be removed to fit to publishing page limits and to make the reporting of the research exact and the work undertaken replicable. Despite the challenge of staying awake while reading academic literature, this is generally the most relevant type of literature for your review. The main sources of academic literature are detailed below, along with some discussion of the usefulness in the critical literature review.

Peer Reviewed Journal articles are works that have been 'refereed' or 'quality assured' by scholars working in the field of inquiry discussed in the paper. If the article is published, then these 'peers' and the journal editor consider that the article has advanced the body of knowledge in some way. In other words, the arguments presented should be well researched and discussed, the research undertaken should have been done in an appropriate manner, the data analysed correctly, and any results should follow logically from the information presented in the article.

As a general rule, peer reviewed articles should be the main source of information for your literature review. Journal articles provide concise information regarding theories, methodologies, applications and interpretations relevant to your thesis. However, not all journals have the same academic standing and it is important to have a feel for the relative importance of each journal in your own field. This is not to say that top-quality work does not appear in lower-standing journals, nor that sometimes average or (frankly) poor work does not appear in top journals. Nevertheless, many people do use the idea of 'journal standing' as a guide to the quality of articles in those journals. Those journals that are the most important tend to have the highest reputation and standing in your field (often called the 'A list'). Many universities have rankings of journals and, although they rarely agree completely, these can be useful in deciding which journals are the most important in your field of study. Table 4.1 is an excerpt from a report which discussed perceptions of different marketing journals, and gives a good example of how different journals are ranked within a field. The *social science citation index* (SSCI) can also be a guide, but not all journals within many fields are ranked by SSCI.

Table 4.1   Example journal quality rankings

Rank	Quality	Name of journal
1	1.867	Journal of Marketing
2	1.837	Journal of Marketing Research
3	1.753	Journal of Consumer Research
4	1.749	Journal of the Academy of Marketing Science
5	1.729	Marketing Science
6	1.608	Journal of Retailing
7	1.587	Journal of Business Research
8	1.544	Journal of Consumer Psychology
9	1.540	International Journal of Research in Marketing
10	1.493	Journal of Advertising
11	1.461	Journal of Advertising Research
12	1.457	European Journal of Marketing
13	1.424	Journal of Service Research
14	1.423	Psychology and Marketing
15	1.380	Marketing Letters

Source: From an unpublished (to date) ranking study, Jordan Louviere, Siggi Gudergan and Ian Lings (University of Technology Sydney).
Note: Quality rankings were determined through a study of marketing academics.

Top-ranking journals can, generally, be thought of as having the most impact in your field, and therefore you can generally have more confidence in the results and findings of any study reported in them. Having said this, it is important not to restrict yourself to just those journals with high quality rankings. There is a whole range of research that is reported in other journals, some are specialist journals and do not always appear high on the list of journal rankings because of their specialist nature, some are journals targeting audiences other than academics. This does not mean that these journals are irrelevant or 'low' quality, just that in the general scheme of things they do not have as much overall impact as others. As Webster and Watson (2002, pp. xiii) report in their discussion of writing a literature review:

> Studies ... have consistently been limited by drawing from a small sample of journals. Even though the [ones] investigated here may have reputations as our top journals, this does not excuse an author from investigating 'all' published articles in a field.

As a final note on journal articles, it is extremely important not to assume that 'just because it is in the journal it must be perfect'. There are many examples of work that has some pretty significant flaws appearing even in top journals. Be aware that time moves on, research standards change, and articles may be published which fall short on some criteria because they are very strong in another. In particular, articles which deal with 'hot topics' may get published even though they are not as strong as they might be. So be careful not to simply assume the quality of the literature, wherever it may appear!

Conference proceedings are articles or abstracts that are published by the organisers of the many academic conferences that occur annually in each field and specialist area. In case you didn't know, academics are always attending conferences (especially those in far-flung locations), and these conferences are ostensibly aimed at disseminating leading-edge research as quickly as possible. They are definitely *not* excuses to visit exotic places and have fun – honest! Many of those who attend conferences go to present their work in front of peers and colleagues, and this work is also generally published in the 'proceedings' of the conference. A lot of conference proceedings are also peer reviewed and have to meet minimum standards of scientific rigour. The main strength of conference proceedings as opposed to peer-reviewed journal articles is that they are often the first place that research is published and tested in front of peer audiences. For this reason, conference proceedings are useful in providing information about the latest research, which often has not yet been published in peer reviewed journals. Conference proceedings are also a useful source of information about who is working in a particular research area, and what they are doing. You can then search to find out what else they have published in other outlets.

Conference proceedings tend not to be a main source of information for a literature review for many reasons. Firstly, there is a general perception in some fields that they are of a 'lower' quality than peer-reviewed journals (although this is not always the case, and not for all conferences in a field either). Further, there is also the idea that most of the high-quality work will eventually reach the journals (academics are rarely happy with 'just' a conference paper). That is not to say that good quality work cannot be expected in a conference paper. Sometimes, conference proceedings can be the only place to get really radical, new, or esoteric work. However, one of the major drawbacks of conference proceedings is the increasing tendency of conference organisers to restrict the size of conference papers to just a few pages. This means that, often, the paper does not provide as rich an indication of the background and scope of the research. Similarly, conference proceedings are often hard to locate and gain access to, unless you know someone who has attended the conference and has the proceedings. Nevertheless, they are a useful resource and are worth pursuing.

Previous research theses and dissertations are also a possible source of information. All UK Ph.D. theses should be published in the British Library and can be requested by inter-library loan. In other countries Ph.Ds may or may not be published; it is often necessary to contact the author to request a copy of their work. However, it is important to remember that they are of uncertain quality (yes, even including mine and Nick's!).[2] For example, you do not know if the student who wrote the thesis did a good job or not; after all, you don't get the examiner's reports on it. Also, most research degrees are seen as an apprenticeship piece, they will often contain mistakes that the researcher would be expected to rectify in subsequent work. As a consequence, you should treat the contents of student theses with some caution. Furthermore, it can be a big task to search through the huge store of theses without any direction. Nevertheless, it's important to realise that they are available to those who are interested.

As a final note, you should be careful about drawing too much from other theses – it can be tempting to use them too much, especially if they are in similar areas. This would seem an opportune moment to mention **plagiarism**: something that should be avoided at all costs. If you don't know what plagiarism is, ask your supervisor or any other academic. They will explain to you what it is, why it is bad and what happens if you get caught[3] – probably at great length.

Teaching literature

Teaching literature is also a type of academic literature; however, its primary purpose is usually to provide a general description of a field, rather than a detailed and scientific description of specific theories and models. This type of literature is generally aimed at students and lecturers who teach or take courses in a field. Teaching literature has many advantages over the academic literature described previously. It is usually much more accessible in

---

[2] Actually, if he ever reads that he might have something to say!

[3] Hint: it's not good!

terms of being easy to read and understand. This makes it a great resource for learning about ideas that are new to you. This accessibility of teaching literature comes at a price though; this type of literature is generally much less comprehensive in its discussion of all aspects of the scientific investigation that underpins what is discussed. This makes it virtually impossible to critique teaching literature in a scientific manner, because essentially what is being presented is '*the accepted wisdom of the day*'. Although teaching literature is a very useful resource to you as a researcher, it should not form a major part of your critical literature review. Two types of teaching literature are discussed below. Hopefully, you will see the merits of both, and also their limitations for inclusion in your literature review.

Textbooks are generally less detailed and less up-to-date than journal articles. By the time that a model or theory has entered the pages of a textbook it is generally seen as the 'accepted wisdom' in a field. This is why it has been included in a book designed for teaching rather than research. Consequently, textbooks are less useful for including in your literature review. But, this does not mean that they are less useful to you. Quite the contrary; as the content of a textbook has been well examined, often simplified and is generally presented in such a way as to facilitate understanding, they make an excellent place to start. This is especially true if the scope of your research takes you into new and unfamiliar disciplines. Textbooks are useful to bring you up to speed on the basic theories quickly and effectively. However, they will not generally provide you with cutting-edge research findings. One thing textbooks are very useful for, though, is for methodology and research techniques (just like this one in fact). The peer-reviewed journal literature on methodology can be a pretty scary place. To write about leading-edge developments in methodology requires that the authors assume those reading the article already know the basics, and often more advanced theories, up to the point at which the paper makes contribution. This may not be the case. It often takes book authors to integrate such material in such a way as to reach a more general research audience.

Finally, as I am becoming aware, the textbook is often the place where authors are able to put down their thoughts without too much censure from reviewers, so you should be aware that not all textbooks have had the same rigorous reviewing as a typical scholarly journal article. Of course, this particular one has.

Case studies

There are two common types of case study that you will come across. These are: (1) Journal articles that describe and report on 'case study research' and which belong in the academic literature category; and (2) Case studies used in teaching, that describe a company situation and provide (or require) some degree of analysis and interpretation.

Adopting a scientific view, the case study can be thought of as a neutral description of a situation, subject to objective analysis. From an artistic perspective, it can be viewed as an incomplete narrative, open to multiple interpretations. Whichever view is adopted, teaching case studies aim for students to gain depth in both problem-solving and problem-posing skills. Most commonly, the scientific view leads you to analyse the facts and to propose a specific answer to a real business problem. The literary view leads you to consider the interpretation of words, to select evidence based on values, and to reflect on the case as a parable. Both of these are laudable aims but they do not address the needs of your research literature review.

Practitioner-oriented literature

We use the term 'practitioner-oriented' to refer to literature who's primary target is those who actually have 'real' jobs in the field you study, if you see what I mean. For example, if you are a marketing researcher, 'practitioner-oriented' literature includes trade journals aimed at retail store managers, advertising executives, human resource managers, rather than journals aimed at academics studying those fields. Several types of practitioner oriented journals are available and some are discussed below.

Magazines and trade journals. The definition of magazines for our purposes is somewhat ambiguous. The Oxford Dictionary lists a magazine as 'a periodical publication containing articles and illustrations'. However, it should be clear at this point that we do not mean magazines like *Woman's Weekly, Hot Celebrity Gossip,* or the *NME* (although we know many academics who do read such august publications[4] for non-research purposes in general). We are assuming that the type of magazine you may consider reading for your research would address issues relevant to your research. Among academic circles I have heard the term '*magazine*' used to describe non-peer-reviewed publications and publications intended for a more managerial audience. These could be quite specialist, such as *The Economist, Marketing Week* or *New Scientist;* or they may be more general in nature, such as *Newsweek, National Interest* or *Time.* These publications can also provide a good starting point for justifying your research and demonstrating that it is both current and topical. General information about new discoveries, policies, etc. can provide a useful way to explain to your reader the impact of your work on the business environment.

As are textbooks, magazines are unlikely to be useful for inclusion in your literature review. However, like textbooks they can be a great resource to help you to understand your research domain. They can also be brilliant to 'set the scene' of your research in the real world, and give it a nice foundation. Typically, articles written in this type of publication are less technically difficult than peer reviewed articles and so can aid in developing your understanding of a particular area, prior to getting into more technical content in peer reviewed journal. It is worth remembering, though, that these articles are often journalistic and may be politically motivated, so it is always worth taking the time to try to understand the motives of the author before using information from them.

---

[4]And many others far too embarrassing to list here!

Government reports and business reports are also a good source of general information. The government and many businesses undertake research into areas of particular importance for them. These published reports can be a useful source of secondary information, depending on your field of study. However, many business reports are confidential, or at least embargoed for a period of time, so those that paid for them can get the best advantage. If you are lucky enough to get hold of one of these before it is released to the public domain, you should be careful about how you use it – or you could get someone (including yourself) into a lot of trouble. However, all publicly listed companies have to produce a public report at the end of each financial year, and these can be very useful for research purposes. A cautionary note with government reports is to remember that there is the potential for them to contain political bias, which may result in reporting of selective 'facts' to support a particular view; they should be interpreted with care!

Newspapers are not usually that useful. Information in newspapers is often only of note as 'background'. For example you may want to refer to particular pieces to illustrate trends, discoveries or changes, in much the same way as you might refer to general magazines, discussed above. Nevertheless, they can give an indication of what the public considers important at the time, which in some fields (especially those which are policy-related) is very important. As with magazines, trade journals, government and business reports, newspaper articles are subject to bias, both from the journalistic nature of the piece and the political affiliations of the source. Depending on the publication, they may also only have a passing acquaintance with the truth, and so caution is advised when using them.

The Internet

The Internet is the fastest-growing source of information on the planet, and it has revolutionised the life of an academic. For example I can't even imagine what it must have been like to have to physically search through hard copies of journals to find an article of use. But while the Internet is a great resource to connect you directly to the sources of literature I have just talked about, what about the information you can also get from the Internet such as on websites and the like? Do not be fooled into thinking that just because information is available on the Internet that it will be useful to you, or should be included in your research. My personal feeling is that you should avoid using the Internet as a direct source of information about theories, models, methodologies and such like. This information will also be available in peer reviewed journals and this should be your first port of call. Anyone with access to a computer can post information on the Internet (I could give you some examples, but the Internet changes so fast that they would be out–of–date immediately).

When you find information on the Internet, you have no way of knowing if this information is true, scientific or motivated by things other than the advancement of knowledge. For example, many individuals have grudges against some corporations, and they have Internet sites as a forum for their bitterness.

If you do search the Internet and find useful models and theories, try to confirm what you have found in scientific publications to see if the theory has been tested. As a great professor (who shall remain anonymous) once said to me 'theory without evidence is just opinion, and opinions are like a★★★holes,[5] everybody has one'.

As a general rule, if you find useful information on the Internet, make sure a reputable source is cited, and then find that study for yourself. If you intend to cite this source, make sure that you have, and can, read the original source yourself.

In suggesting that you avoid using information from the Internet I do not mean avoiding accessing peer reviewed journals available on, or via the Internet. Most academic libraries now have fantastic sets of electronic resources, and there are many databases which collate and index journal articles. These databases are constantly growing, and it is good advice to consult with your librarians to see what you have access to. You may even be able to help out your supervisor – who, if they are anything like me, have no idea of the full range of resources! Furthermore, some academic journals are what can be called 'e-journals', meaning they are published solely on the Internet, and not in hard copy at all. If an e-journal is peer reviewed the quality should be just as rigorous as a typical 'off-line' peer-reviewed journal (depending on the reputation of the journal).

Evaluating the 'quality' of literature

Once you have found the literature, you need to make some kind of 'first-cut' to work out what is worth spending more time on, and what can be discarded immediately. As shown above, there are many different sources of literature and it is easy to get overwhelmed and confused. The following checklist can be used to help you to decide the 'quality' of the research that you have found:

- *Provenance:* What are the author's credentials, qualifications and affiliations? Affiliations can point to alternative motives and so are important. Are the author's arguments supported by some kind of evidence?
- *Objectivity:* Is the author's perspective unbiased or prejudiced? Are contrary views and data considered in the piece or is certain pertinent information ignored to prove the author's point? Typically, journalistic reports do not consider alternative perspectives; often government reports also fail to incorporate alternative views.
- *Persuasiveness:* Which of the author's arguments are the most and least compelling? The peer review process should identify incorrect arguments, but subsequent work may challenge some assumptions and may invalidate the arguments on which the work is based.
- *Value:* Are the author's conclusions convincing? Does the work ultimately contribute in any significant way to an understanding of the subject? Many papers present replications of previous work in new contexts; although this is important to establish the generalisability of a theory, many

---

[5] If you're American, please remove one star.

journals will not publish straight-forward replications. This has the disadvantage that theories may go unchallenged or unconfirmed as replication studies may not get published.

However, remember that there is far more to analysing and reviewing a piece of work than just these few pointers (I'll discuss this soon). In particular, the last two points can be quite a difficult task, and if you are unsure of them at this early stage, it's best to keep the literature for now and make your mind up later, when you come back to read it again (which you will do many times).

Remember that when you are conducting your literature search, you have access to some great resources. Most librarians are also skilled researchers; they can help you identify reputable sources. They have more experience of searching for, and within, these sources and so can save you a lot of time by showing you how it is done most effectively. Your supervisor should be able to guide you towards journal rankings and provide you with a feeling for which are the better journals in your field of enquiry, other research students will have developed research strategies that you could consider adopting, they may have accessed journal databases that you are unaware of, and will almost certainly have made many of the mistakes that you are about to make. Try to minimise your effort by learning from their experiences.

How do you turn 'literature' into a 'literature review'?

As stated earlier, the aims of the literature review are to demonstrate that you understand that which has been done before, explain why your work is important, relevant and interesting, and how it adds to existing knowledge, either by bringing together disparate fields of research and extending them or developing new theory. Before describing what a literature review is, it is worth mentioning the most commonly encountered examples of what a literature review is *not*. The following issues are all very common with new researchers, so you shouldn't feel bad about them. However, if you do find yourself prone to these problems, you should make strenuous efforts to overcome them – and the best way of doing this is to write, write, and write some more. Then get your supervisor to read it. Then write again (and so on …). If you are a research student, one point worth making here is that your supervisor is a useful resource for you,[6] but one which may quickly wear out. Supervisors have many conflicting demands on their time; teaching, writing and reviewing articles and books, administration, supervising other research students. If you put poor work to your supervisors they will be unhappy, and may well tell you so (never a nice experience). If you ask your supervisor to comment on your work, please make sure that it is as good as you can make it. Most importantly, don't be afraid to get feedback, but also please

---

[6]If you are not a research student, your academic colleagues can often perform the same function.

do your utmost to *learn* from that feedback for next time. Most supervisors don't expect fantastic work at first, but it rapidly grates when students repeat the same mistakes over and over.

How not to do it

First, a literature review is not a list or summary of one piece of literature followed by another. It's usually a bad sign to find a series of paragraphs beginning with the name of a researcher, describing what they did and then moving on to the next researcher on the list. The aim of the literature review is not to simply list all the material published, without any consideration regarding how it fits together and how it can be synthesised into your research question. If all you are providing is a list of information then the reader has to do all the work. They have to interpret, synthesise and come to a conclusion about what they have read. They will soon tire and – worse – may come to a conclusion different from the one you hold. After putting in all that mental effort to come to their own conclusions they are unlikely to change their mind just because you wish them to, and you may then experience resistance to your views, making it harder to convince the reader of the 'worth' of your work. IDE 4.3 presents a *laundry list* of relevant facts regarding strategy, resources and capabilities. This example (and IDE 4.4) are not meant to reflect the work of the authors cited, just some inappropriate ways of presenting their work in the context of a literature review. Although the information itself is OK, there is no attempt to *interpret* the information presented and the reader is left to work out for themselves what is important and what is not; also the reader has to try to work out how these different pieces of information fit together. This is really the job of the author, not the reader.

IDE 4.3: A 'Laundry List'

Topic: 'Dynamic capabilities and organisational strategy'
Strategy is a pattern in a stream of decisions that gives guidance to organisations when dealing with its environment, it shapes internal policies and procedures (Hambrick, 1983; Mintzberg, 1978). It is a relative phenomenon; business level strategy can only be analysed substantively in relation to competitors' strategies (Hambrick, 1983).

Porter (1985) states that there are two main strategies that companies can follow in order to increase performance and gain competitive advantage: cost leadership or differentiation. Both strategic options are applicable to a mass market or segmented market approach. In an alternative framework, Miles and Snow (1986) identify four strategic types: Prospectors, defenders, analysers, and reactors.

Gruber and Harhoff (2001) consider resources to be the starting point of strategic deliberations and argue that resources are the main drivers of organisational performance. This view can be traced back to Penrose (1959) who stated that 'The business firm [...] is both an administrative organisation and a collection of productive resources; its general purpose is to organise the use of its "own" resources together with other resources acquired from outside the firm.'

Organisational capabilities are intangible assets or resources, based on skills, learning, and knowledge in deploying resources (Amit and Schoemaker, 1993; Combe and Greenley, 2004). Helfat and Peteraf (2003) differentiate between operational and dynamic capabilities. Operational capabilities are high-level routines (or collections of routines) that offer management a set of decision alternatives for the production of significant outputs. Routines represent repetitive patterns of activities (Nelson and Winter, 1982). Dynamic capabilities do not directly aim at the production of a product or a service (Helfat and Peteraf, 2003; Teece *et al.*, 1997); they build, integrate, or reconfigure operational capabilities and concern change (Helfat *et al.*, 2007).

Eisenhardt and Martin (2000) describe dynamic capabilities as specific organisational and strategic processes that contribute to the value creation of the organisation. They define dynamic capabilities as: 'The firm's processes that use resources – specifically the processes to integrate, reconfigure, gain and release resources – to match and even create market change. Dynamic capabilities thus are the organisational and strategic routines by which firms achieve new resource configurations as markets emerge, collide, split, evolve, and die' (p. 1107).

Teece *et al.*(1997) emphasise the development of management capabilities and combinations of organisational, functional, and technological resources, and define dynamic capabilities as 'the firm's ability to integrate, build, and reconfigure internal and external competences to address rapidly changing environments. Dynamic capabilities thus reflect an organisation's ability to achieve new and innovative forms of competitive advantage given path dependencies and market positions' (p. 516).

Secondly, a literature review is not the same as a *literary* review. The purpose of your review is not to identify the merits and weaknesses of the literary style of the article (whatever you may think about how well it is written or otherwise). Unlike a literary review, which is typically concerned with poems, plays, short stories, novels, or books as a finished piece of writing, a literature review is an extensive search of the information available on a topic and its evaluation. IDE 4.4 shows how a literary review of the literature may look, based on similar content to that in the previous example. You can see that, although a conclusion is

IDE 4.4: A 'Literary Review'

Topic: Dynamic capabilities and organisational strategy

Mintzberg (1978) discussed strategy as a pattern in a stream of decisions that gives guidance to organisations when dealing with its environment, it shapes internal policies and procedures. The article is somewhat technical and the logic of the conclusions was not clear to me, consequently, it is difficult to establish if the definition of strategy is appropriate or not. In contrast, the work of Hambrick (1983) is much easier to read and the suggestion that strategy is a relative phenomenon because any strategy at the business level can only be analysed in relation to competitors' strategies seems reasonable based on the information in the article.

When looking at different types of strategy two main views were available via ABI Inform. One article by Porter (1985) discusses the possibility of two main strategies that companies can follow in order to increase performance and gain competitive advantage. These are cost leadership and differentiation. Porter's suggestion that these options are equally applicable to segmented or mass markets is an elegant solution to the generalisability problem that plagues so much work of this type. An alternative view is discussed by Miles and Snow (1986), but this article was much more technical and did not communicate the basic ideas as well as Porter's work. Consequently, the dual strategy framework proposed by Porter will be used in my study.

presented about the best framework to use, this is based on the literary merit of the article and not the theoretical soundness of the work.

Reading the literature

Let's not make any bones about this, reading academic articles, especially when you are starting your research career, and the area is new to you, is difficult. Not only is it difficult, it's boring a lot of the time. Space in academic publications is expensive, so journal articles have to make maximum contribution for minimum words. This, and the need to be clear and unambiguous, gives rise to a dense, and very exact writing style, with much of the padding which we take for granted removed. This style can be difficult to read because it is generally not entertaining; every sentence contains relevant information that should be important. Don't worry though, reading academic writings should become easier the more you read in your area. From the outset it is worth being purposeful in your reading (and writing).

This will help you to avoid becoming too bogged down with trivia, or by being distracted by new 'shiny' ideas that you will regularly come across.

1. In your reading, remember that you want to précis the work you read, but you have to decide: (a) what information is important to your research, and emphasise it, and (b) what is peripheral, and can be omitted from your review. One way of doing this is to focus on the major concepts, conclusions, theories, arguments, etc. in the article you are reading and look for similarities and differences with other related work, including your own. Before you can do this though, you need to know exactly what problem or research question you are looking at. Try asking yourself: 'What is the *specific thesis, problem, or research question* that my literature review helps to define?' Can you answer it? Once you can, you can then work out which parts of the papers you are reading are important and which are peripheral to your literature review.

2. Related to deciding what is important or not are questions regarding the area of your literature review that you are focusing on. It is unlikely that you will read the papers that form your literature only once; typically, you will need to read them many times, each time looking for something specific and different. Your literature review may have sections looking at issues of theory, methodological issues, quantitative studies and evidence, qualitative studies and evidence, and more. In most cases it is not possible to examine all of these issues at once. Typically at the start of a research project or degree, you don't have the know-how in the area to analyse the literature for methodological issues. If you are a student, training in philosophy and methodology will help you to develop these skills, but you will probably have to wait until you have completed these classes before you can fully analyse the literature for these issues. Try not to worry about this; most people are in the same boat, and don't let them tell you that they are not.

3. Initially you will probably want to review the literature to identify themes, theories, patterns and ideas related to your central thesis. There are many ways of organising information that you find in the literature to help you to identify patterns that arise. For a thematic structure (which is one of the most common structures found in academic wiring of this type) I prefer to use a kind of mind map (see Figure 4.2 overleaf).

Other people use different techniques to organise their thinking; there is no right and wrong way, just the one that suits you the best. Some other techniques for organising information include spider maps, clustering organisers, interaction outline organisers and Venn diagrams. There is some quite sophisticated software available to help you to do this, but I have always found that a piece of flip chart paper and some coloured pens work just as well (but perhaps this is a function of my age and technological ability).

Structure and synthesis: Adding something to what's there

It's important to realise that the literature review should have its own value and intellectual contribution to your research project. As I have already stated, simply listing something does not provide anything that the reader could not do themselves, if they could be bothered. You need to provide some kind of added value to the literature, which proves you know

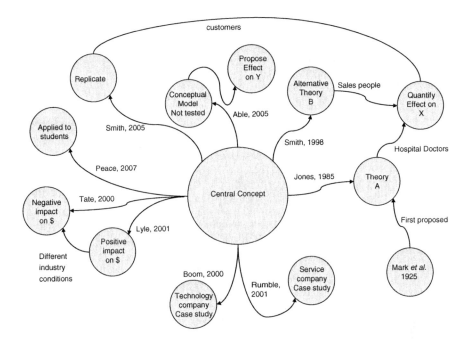

Figure 4.2 A mind map of literature
Note: References are fictitious

the field, as well as have added something. I find that considering the literature review as another component of your theoretical contribution really helps you clarify what you need to do. There are two main ways which a literature review could contribute to our existing knowledge. First is by organising the wide-ranging body of literature in such a way that new perspectives are given, leading to your own research questions. Second is by synthesising and drawing from the literature to create a new and original theory about your topic area. I'll discuss both of these as the chapter moves on.

Structuring your literature review

Rather than simply listing works that have been conducted in your research area, as shown in IDE 4.4, your literature review should be structured around your thesis or research question. The literature should be evaluated and its contribution to your research identified. You will need to consolidate this literature into meaningful 'themes', explaining what is known and what is not, what is controversial and what has already been identified as interesting areas for future research. You will then need to synthesise all this into a new/advanced/modified theory, which I'll discuss in Chapter 5.

Chronological structure: For some studies, organising your literature review chronologically is an appropriate structure. Such chronological literature reviews may be useful if you wish to explore the evolution of a particular theory or body of knowledge. Typically though, a purely chorological structure to your literature review is not appropriate. It is more commonly used to structure sections of the literature review that are organised along other lines. An example of a chronological structure is given in Table 4.2.

Table 4.2   Example of chronological structure

Time period 1	Time period 2	Time period 3
Concepts discussed in this time period. Qualitative work regarding these concepts. Quantitative work examining constructs and their nomological network.	Concepts discussed in this time period – how they evolved from those in the previous time period. Qualitative work regarding these concepts – how does it confirm or challenge previous work? Quantitative work examining constructs and their nomological network – how does it confirm or challenge previous work?	Concepts discussed in this time period – how they evolved from those in the previous time period. Qualitative work regarding these concepts – how does it confirm or challenge previous work? Quantitative work examining constructs and their nomological network – how does it confirm or challenge previous work?

Conceptual and thematic structures: Many literature reviews are organised by the concepts studied. This can be a useful way to organise your writing. Once this broad structure has been adopted, a different structure can be adopted for the discussion of each of the concepts in your review (such as chronological, methodological or contextual.) Organising your literature into meaningful 'themes', and developing an appropriate structure for your literature review can be achieved in many ways. Thematic reviews of the literature are organised around the topic under investigation, rather than chronologically, although the chronology of the literature may also be important. The choice of how to organise your literature review will ultimately depend on your preference, the literature that you are reviewing and the research question that you are addressing. Whatever the structure of your literature review, you will have to illustrate how previous research relates to your research question and how it relates to other works which you include in your review. (Remember, these must also be clearly relevant to your research question.) An example of a thematic structure is given in Table 4.3.

Methodological structure: A methodological review of the literature differs from the above in that the focus usually is not the content of the material; rather it is the 'methods' of the researcher. Typically for first research projects a methodological literature review is not appropriate, as the aim here is generally to understand the concepts, models and

Table 4.3 Example of thematic structure

Construct 1	Construct 2	Construct 3
Definitions of the construct, commonalities and differences in conceptualisations.	Definitions of the construct, commonalities and differences in conceptualisations.	Definitions of the construct, commonalities and differences in conceptualisations.
How it evolved and how it has been applied.	How it is related to Construct 1.	How it is related to Construct 1 and 2.
Empirical studies (qualitative and quantitative) explaining the role of the construct in a nomological network.	Theories that explain these relationships.	Theories that explain these relationships.
Operationalisations of the construct in previous work, strengths and weaknesses of these, etc.	Empirical studies (qualitative and quantitative) examining the relationships between Construct 1 and 2.	Empirical studies (qualitative and quantitative) examining the relationships between Construct 1, 2 and 3.
	Operationalisations of Construct 2 in previous work, strengths and weaknesses of these, etc.	Operationalisations of Construct 3 in previous work, strengths and weaknesses of these, etc.

frameworks used to describe and explore your area of interests. A methodological review of the literature may come later in your project, when you better understand and can critique the methods used by various researchers. At this stage you may wish to revisit your draft literature review and discuss methodology in more detail. This will be dealt with later in the book when methods are discussed. Unless absolutely necessary for your research, I would recommend using a methodological structure only as a sub-structure for a conceptual or thematically organised literature review. In this way, previous research examining the concepts in your conceptual model can be organised according to the methods that were used to conduct the research, but the overall arguments in your literature review remain centred around the relationships between the constructs of interest to you.

Writing within your structure

Once you've decided on how to organise your review, the sections you need to include in the chapter should be easy to figure out. They should arise out of your organisation. In other words, a chronological review would have subsections for each vital time period. A thematic review would have subtopics based upon factors that relate to the theme or issue and a methodological review would have sections reviewing the various methods. However, other sections may be necessary for your literature review but may not fit in the organisation of your work. You will have to decide what other sections to include in your literature review, but remember, put in *only what is necessary*.

In the following discussion, I am assuming a conceptual or thematic structure as this appears to be the most prevalent in social science research. When examining your concepts, you will need to address some common areas that an informed reader will be looking for:

- What do we know about the key concepts or variables?
- What are their characteristics?
- What are the potential relationships between concepts (researchable hypotheses)?
- What existing theories explain the relationships between these key concepts or variables?
- What research has been conducted to explore all of the above?
- Where is this research inconsistent, are variables always viewed as the same thing, or do some authors call different things by the same name, or the same thing by different names?
- What are the overriding characteristics of the concepts?
- Is empirical evidence available to confirm the existence of the concepts, and the relationships between them? If so, how have researchers defined and measured key concepts?
- Is the empirical evidence consistent, inconclusive, contradictory or limited in some way? If so, Why?
- What methodologies have been used?
- Where have data been collected?
- Are these satisfactory?
- How are they similar to what you propose? How are they different?
- Are there views in the literature that need to be examined in more detail?
- Why study (further) the research problem?
- What contribution can the present study be expected to make?

Once you have decided your central research question or thesis, and have identified appropriate sources of information and have started to organise the ideas in these sources of information into some coherent structure, you can start to communicate your *story*.

Remember (and this is a hugely important point), *you are not writing a literature review just to tell your reader what other researchers have done.* Your aim should be to show why your research needs to be carried out, how you came to choose certain methodologies or theories to work with, how your work adds to the research already carried out, and that sort of thing. I always say to students that the literature review is not a history of everything they read, it is an argument.

This raises another, and often painful, point. You have to *edit out information that is not relevant to your argument.* I know that this may be painful for you. After all, you have read the information, internalised it, made notes on it, typed it up and incorporated it into your document – it must be relevant, you took weeks to do all that! Don't delude yourself, examine every sentence critically and ask yourself how does it contribute to the argument that you literature review presents. If it doesn't then cut it out, be ruthless and your review will be much more focused and relevant.

Some final thoughts and tips

Your literature review should aim to critically evaluate previous research, comparing and contrasting what has been done and what hasn't, showing relationships between published works (e.g. is Smith's theory more convincing than Jones'? Why? Did Smith build on the work of Jones?), and demonstrating how this relates to your research. Some tips to help you achieve this are:

- Follow through a set of concepts and questions, comparing papers to each other in the ways they deal with these concepts and questions.
- Among other things you can look at are:
  - What research questions do the authors pose?
  - Do authors define the concepts in the same way?
  - Do they use the same underlying rationale or theory to discuss the concepts? (The next chapter may help you to decide this.)
  - If comparing quantitative research papers; do different authors operationalise constructs in the same way?
  - Are data drawn from similar or different contexts?
  - How are the data analysed?
  - Are the data and analysis appropriate for the study? Can they answer the research question?
  - What are the major conclusions made by the authors in terms of the research questions that the authors pose?
  - Are the data sufficient to draw the conclusions that the authors present?
  - Do authors come to similar conclusions about the nature and impact of the constructs that you are interested in?
  - If not, why not? (The previous questions should allow you to answer this.)
  - What limitations does each of these authors present about their own work?
  - Do they also give you insights into the limitations of previous work? (Often this forms part of the justification that is presented for their work.)

Also, it is vitally important to *keep all your bibliographic information* in an easily retrievable format. One day, possibly quite a long way into in the future, you will have to write your references pages (whether you are writing a thesis, or an article). You do not want to find that you didn't keep the information you need to do this, and consequently have to spend days or weeks finding the references for the citations in your thesis.[7] You will spend a lot of time in the library or on the Internet tracking down the sources that you read, going through your writing to find which information came from which source. Most likely, you will not be able to find all your sources and will then have to remove the ones that you can't find, hoping that they are not critical to your argument. If they are, there is nothing for it but to continue to search for them or a replacement. It is far better to avoid this by keeping

---

[7] As Nick did, and still does! In fact, I bet he is doing it when writing this very book!

this information in your notes from the outset. Always put citations into your writing and immediately into the reference list for your work. Software packages such as Endnote and ProCite can help greatly in this process. However, they don't do it for you; you will have to develop the discipline to remember for each citation to make sure there is a reference. Do you have a piece of work that you are writing at the moment? How many times have you written 'insert ref here' or something similar? If you have, make sure you go back now to find out and insert that reference, you will thank me later (well actually if you do it you will probably not even think about it, if you don't, you may just remember me telling you to and regret ignoring me).

Some things to avoid

Perhaps just as important as the tips about things you need to *do* to help you be successful, are the things you need to *avoid* in order to make a good job of the literature review. So here are a few which may help your cause when you are conducting your review.

Using only those papers that support your view: A common weakness of a literature review is one-sided reporting. It is tempting to report only those studies that support your view of the world and how the constructs within it should relate to each other. This is unscientific and should be avoided. You need to ensure that you review and present papers that both support your view and contradict it (if they exist).

Trying to read everything: If you try this you will never be able to finish reading. The idea of the literature review is to provide a survey of the most relevant and significant work, not to provide a census of all the published work that relates even in the tiniest way to your research. There will also come a time when you have to **stop reading**. This does not mean stop completely but stop for the moment and consolidate your knowledge. Typically, once you have conceptualised your theoretical framework, tested it mentally against your peers, supervisors and perhaps at a presentation, the time has come to nail your colours to the mast and adopt your model as the one that you will use and test further. Stop adding new information from more extensive reading, this will just continue to confuse you and prevent you from progressing. It's time to move on the next stage of your research.

Reading without writing: Even given the often intractable nature of academic journals, it's much easier to read than to write. Not writing is one of the most common mistakes that research students fall into. Many excuses abound, and I have heard a lot of them: 'It's all in my head and I am sorting it out before writing it down', 'I don't need to write because I am much more of a thinker than a writer', 'I'm going to write it all down when I have finished reviewing the relevant literature'. Interestingly enough, Nick used all of these, and still does in fact.

It's all just excuses for putting off what we don't want to do. As a supervisor, no matter how inventive the excuse, I can generally tell when a student is procrastinating for some reason, maybe because they do not understand what they are doing, and are avoiding challenging their understanding by refusing to commit what they know to paper. The discipline of writing helps you to understand what you have read, and highlights what you do and don't know for you and your supervisor. It will help you to identify relationships between the works that you have reviewed, and highlight inconsistencies in the literature and a whole range of other important stuff. By refusing to write you are denying yourself the chance to learn what you know and what you don't. In my experience, persistent refusal to write generally leads to disaster. The student either does not progress their thinking, or the supervisor gives up and decides that the student is not working and cannot meet the research deadlines imposed on them. Either way, a common consequence of failure to write regularly is failure to complete the research project.

It's very important to recognise that what you write will *not* be a final or near-final version, and you should not expect it to be. It will evolve and change as your understanding grows, as you discover new things, as your writing style becomes more 'academic' and as you incorporate your methodology, results and conclusions. Writing is a way of thinking, so allow yourself to write as many drafts as you need, change your ideas and information as you learn more about your research problem. If you are passing these drafts to a supervisor, or colleague, remember my earlier comments and please make sure you don't wear out your supervisors' patience by passing interminable rough drafts to them for comment.

Summary

Remember that the aim of your literature review is to show that you have studied existing work in your field and provide insights into this work. An effective review analyses and synthesises material, and will be relevant, appropriate, and useful for the reader. Your literature review presents the case and context for the rest of your research. For this reason it is important to demonstrate the relationship of your work to previous research in the area. Without a good literature review, your work will never be able to assure the reader that it makes a solid contribution to knowledge, so you should *never* ignore the importance of the literature review stage. Key points to take from this chapter:

- The most important stage in a literature review is **starting**. Do not spend an age agonising over *where* to start, just start somewhere. The path will become clear after a while.
- The second most important stage of the literature review is **stopping**. Eventually you will need to decide that it is time to move onto the next stage of your research, even though you may have missed one or two articles that may be relevant to your research question. If you don't stop you won't progress and consequently won't finish. Don't worry about the one or two articles that you may have missed. If you have conducted a thorough review, there is a vanishing small chance that one or two missed articles will answer your research question for you and spoil your thesis.
- The aims of your research and the research question are important; they help to focus and direct your reading.
- Reviewing academic literature is an iterative process; you will need to read papers several times, each time focusing on different aspects of the paper.

- You will use the literature to explain what is known in the field in which you are working and what is not known.
- What is not known forms part of the rationale for your thesis and motivates the work that you will be doing in your research project.
- Critiquing literature is not the same as criticising it, and in fact authors often critique their own work when they discuss the limitations of their research.
- Your literature can be organised in several different ways, although thematic organisation is often used.

Further reading

There aren't too many sources for information on reviewing the literature, but in more recent times a few interesting pieces of work have arrived.

- *Doing a Literature Review: Releasing the Social Science Research Imagination* by Chris Hart: One of the very few books entirely dedicated to the literature review. As such it is a vital source of information for beginning researchers, and even those more experienced are likely to pick up a few useful tips.
- *Critical Reading and Writing for Postgraduates* by Mike Wallace and Alison Wray: A good introduction for the actual process of reading and critiquing academic literature.
- *Doing Your Research Project: A Guide for First-Time Researchers in Education, Health and Social Science* by Judith Bell: This book is highly rated by many of my students, and gives some good information on how to get out there and review the literature.

Recent work on systematic literature reviewing in the social sciences (drawing from evidence-based medical research) also provides a useful starting point. For an introduction you can check out a 2003 paper in the *British Journal of Management* by David Tranfield *et al.* entitled 'Towards a methodology for developing evidence-informed management knowledge by means of systematic review'.

---

1. Write down your area or field of research.
   - Is it too broad? Can you narrow it down?
   - What *specifically* do you want to look at?
2. List the constructs that you are interested in.
   - Which of these is the central construct of your thesis?
3. Create a mind map with your central construct taking the dominant position and other constructs surrounding it.
   - What does the literature tell you about the relationships between your central construct and the other constructs in your mind map?
   - Does the literature tell you anything about relationships among the other constructs in you mind map?

EXERCISES

4. Look in your literature and identify several different definitions for each of your constructs. (There will be more than one, even if they are somewhat similar.)
    -   How do these definitions differ? Are the differences important?
5. For each of the definitions can you identify different operationalisations of the construct?
    -   If you identified three different definitions in Q4 and three different operationalisations for these definitions in Q5 you now have nine operationalisations of the same thing. This is where it gets interesting. Now you can start to put together a bit of a critique of the literature.
6. How have these operationalisations (or operational definitions) been used? Are they applied qualitatively or quantitatively? Why were they applied in this way and what has the author used them for?
7. Comment on the suitability of the research using the information that you have collected in the previous exercises.
8. Do you have a bibliographic database? If not, set one up today. Go on, just do it. If you already have one, is it up to date?

5 Just What Makes Science Special?

S. YEARLEY

INTRODUCTION

As we saw in the introductory chapter, it is hard to deny that science is special. Science is the exemplar and the measure of knowledge in the contemporary industrialised world. Where religion once set the standard for sure knowledge, and logic was later elevated to the apex of human understanding, in the West science has now secured top position. Science tells us how the world operates. More than this, through its precision and mathematical form, science offers us a tight grasp on the workings of the world; and because of its energetic growth it offers to tell us ever more and more. These are all reasonable bases for thinking very well of science but, compared to the other exemplary forms of knowledge that have been revered in the past, a question hangs over the grounds for the special character of science.

Given the assumed greatness of God or gods, it was not hard to see why knowledge of the deity was assumed to be special and privileged. Societies devoted huge resources to institutions and projects associated with religious insights. If God, or His appointed spokespersons, said that something was the case, then it generally seemed safe to assume that it was indeed the case. Being God, He was not going to be wrong. In practice this did not always work out as straightforwardly as one might suppose. Even within the Christian tradition, for example, there have been frequent disputes over the status of religious knowledge. Alongside the idea of revealed truth coming from God, there has often been the accompanying thought that the true believer needs to have faith rather than the certainty that would come from direct evidence of God's intervention. Other

Christian thinkers turned the argument on its head, claiming that the marvel of the world is evidence of God's existence; some even tried to argue that one can get to the idea of God's existence through the business of reasoning alone. But the core conviction was that what we did know of God and of His views, on sin or redemption, say, we knew for sure. The specialness of the knowledge lay precisely in its certainty, its unquestionable nature. Logic seems to share God's transcendent quality. What was logical for Aristotle is logical for us. Logic may become more refined but things that were once logical do not become illogical overnight. The knowledge that logic offers us is exemplary because of its consistency and certainty. By contrast, scientific knowledge is often changeable and fallible. Even the best scientific ideas of a generation get overturned and most scientists agree that one of the exciting things about science is that it can alter so radically. It seems odd to venerate something so fickle.

Given that scientific knowledge is so changeable, its correctness cannot be the thing which makes it exceptional (unlike the idealised cases of religion and logic). Thus, when people have turned their thoughts to identifying the reasons for the exceptionalness of science they have come up with four kinds of ideas about how precisely its special character manifests itself. Within each of these four approaches there are important and fascinating internal differences but let us consider them in turn before making an assessment of attempts to specify what precisely is distinctive about science. It will be seen later that these fundamental approaches to the special character of science have spread far beyond philosophical and sociological discourse, for example to the worlds of the courts and of political debate, so that time spent on them now is a sound investment.

THE EMPIRICAL FOUNDATIONS OF SCIENCE

The empiricist version of science's special quality claims that scientific knowledge is special because it depends on systematic observation and measurement. Though no longer very popular with philosophers of science, this claim has enduring 'everyday' appeal. Empirical evidence is of course very important to science, as it is to art appreciation, train-spotting and picking the form of race horses. The important question is whether there is anything about the empirical foundations of science which sets it apart from other kinds of endeavour. There are several reasons for thinking not. In part, this is because observation in science is not just a matter of seeing clearly, even if scientific demonstrations are often set up to allow the audience to simply 'see' the truths of science. One sees many things on country walks but people need to be trained to 'see' the geology of the countryside, to observe the evidence of the last ice age in mounds of fractured rock, to see faults and discontinuities in the strata. Scientific observation requires interpretation rather than simply taking images in. But, the position of empiricists is further worsened by the realisation that contemporary science is overwhelmingly based on detection by machines and not by 'seeing' in any common-sense manner. Evidence of early life is found by using electron microscopes. The date of extinction events is observed by using isotopic dating techniques. Sub-atomic particles are observed using traces in cloud chambers. In a sense, each of these things is an observation but the seeing in each case depends on theoretical ideas embedded in, and taken for granted by, the techniques and equipment.

Although these points appear to be serious setbacks for advocates of the idea that science is special because it depends on observation, a worse problem arises when one examines the process by which scientific knowledge grows. In many cases, observations are at odds with other observations or with theoretical ideas. For example, at the end of the nineteenth century most geologists and many biologists believed that the earth was very old indeed, most likely many millions of years. They devised various methods for trying to get a figure for this age observationally, for example by trying to work out how much salt is added to the oceans annually and therefore how long the oceans must have been receiving eroded salts in order to become as salty as they are (on these efforts see Burchfield, 1990). At the same time, physicists were convinced that the sun could not conceivably be that old since it would have grown cold by now. Observation ran up against deduction from accepted theoretical beliefs but did not overturn it. There was always sufficient uncertainty surrounding any of the geologists' indirect 'observations' that they could be disregarded by at least many of the physicists. Other cases have come up with similar findings. Closer to the present, physicists are interested in radiation coming from the sun for what it may tell us about the reactions going on there. A leading component of that radiation is made up of solar neutrinos: curious virtually mass-less and non-electrically charged entities.[1] When scientists have sought to measure the flow of neutrinos these are claimed to be significantly more numerous than calculations from theory would lead one to expect. Someone who stressed the importance of observation might expect the scientific community to be overwhelmingly impressed by the measurements. But they are not (Pinch, 1980: 92). This is in part because the calculations are believed to be soundly based, but also because the measurements are technically so hard to carry out. It is hard to detect things which are almost mass-less. A complicated and costly experiment has to be devised to attempt to observe these neutrinos, and a whole chain of inferences needs to link the arrival of neutrinos with the ultimate print-out from the detector. The power of the observation is tied to the strength of each of those inferential steps, and there is no other source of firm evidence about the strength of those inferences. Worse still, the experimental set-up is so complex and costly that it cannot easily be checked or replicated.

The fourth difficulty with a reliance on observation is a point beloved of philosophers. Observations are of single things. Thus an astronomer interested in the development of stars has to base her or his claims on only certain observations. No astronomer can observe all the stars; there is not enough time. And, in any case, some past stars are now unobservable since we believe them to have ceased to exist already. Equally, the stellar-astronomer cannot observe future stars. Given that general statements cannot, for these reasons, be based strictly on observation, it turns out that there appears to be something undeniably theoretical even about general observation statements. It appears that a basis in observation falls short of justifying the enthusiast's claims for this being the key to the special nature of scientific knowledge. Scientific knowledge *is* based on observation but it cannot be exhaustively justified by observation alone. Apparently, therefore, science cannot be definitively separated from other cultural beliefs which also boast an observational basis.

THE SCIENTIFIC METHOD

Philosophers who wanted to retain the special character of science but who were aware of the flaws in an observation-based defence, looked for their salvation to other aspects of science. Most famously, Popper turned the last-mentioned difficulty on its head and tried to make it the characteristic strength of science. He realised that no amount of positive evidence for a generalisation really helped in the face of the enormity of potential negative observations. What one observed of the collapse of stars of a certain size, for instance, could be confirmed over and over by new observations, but these did not hold any weight against the enormous number of possibly disconfirming cases. However, the finding of one disconfirming case is, logically speaking, enough to demonstrate that one's generalisation is invalid. The sighting of just one black swan (in Popper's celebrated example) shows that the proposition 'all swans are white' is false. Popper accordingly shifted his emphasis from finding confirmatory evidence to the search for falsifications. Even if one could not prove the correctness of a generalisation by observation alone, he claimed that one could definitively falsify such a generalisation. Popper asserted that the distinctive character of science, therefore, was not observation (though observation is indispensable) but a commitment to falsificationism.

This analytical move paid dividends for Popper in several ways. First of all, it allowed him to separate science from various impostors. The truly scientific thinker formulates hypotheses and theories which are open to being falsified. With luck, they will not be. But they must in practice be open to the kind of testing which could falsify them. Charlatan theories, such as – in Popper's view – Freudian psychoanalytical theories and Marxism, provided themselves with alibis and excuses to forestall falsification. Falsificationism thus provided a criterion for demarcating properly scientific from pseudo-scientific theories. The second virtue was that Popper's approach sustained a key role for observation; scientific knowledge was founded in observation but it was not simply the accumulation of observational knowledge. Finally, Popper suggested that his understanding of science provided a methodological guideline for conducting science well: one should make bold conjectures and then be a ruthless falsifier.

There is a strong intuitive appeal to Popper's argument and his fundamental claim is commonly invoked by scientists (see Mulkay and Gilbert, 1981; see also the discussion in Chapter 10 dealing with science and the law). But, sadly for Popper, commentators have been able to point to many problems with his approach. For one thing the logic of falsification is not anything like as clear-cut as he would initially have had one believe. For example, to use the neutrino case again: the mis-match between the expected intensity of neutrinos and the measured amount appears to be a falsification of the theory. But it is quite possible that this has come about because the (fiendishly difficult) experiment is not functioning correctly. Thus, it requires a judgement to decide whether the disconfirmatory 'evidence' really is evidence or whether it is the result of experimental error. It could be that the experiment has been incompetently performed or that the inferential steps in the experiment themselves depend on an assumption which has been falsified. Early reports coming from Australia of the existence of a duck-billed platypus, an egg-laying mammal, were overwhelmingly discounted by Europe-based scientists essentially because it was assumed that it was much likelier that local observers were incompetent than that this apparent challenge to animal classificatory systems could be correct (Dugan, 1987). But, even if no practical doubt attaches to the observation and the assumptions on which it is predicated, one finds that scientists are commonly willing to tolerate anomalous findings. Sometimes they explain them away with after-the-event explanations; in other words they modify the theory in such a way as to accommodate the anomalous observation. On other occasions the scientific community appears simply to decide that it will shelve that objection for the time being. Kuhn, more historian than philosopher of science, noted how frequently this tolerance of exceptions occurred; for him it was a characteristic feature of the way that scientific thinking develops (1970: 18). He considered that anomalies were effectively stored up until a whole catalogue of anomalies could be invoked by challengers to the existing scientific orthodoxy.

Popper was sometimes more 'forgiving' of actual scientists' non-conformity to his principles than at other times (see Popper, 1972a: 33–59 for a rather forgiving version). But, it is clear that if it is at all common for scientists to use after-the-event explanations to account for anomalous findings or just to tolerate them, this makes science much closer to astrology than Popperians would ever be willing to concede and rather undermines the value of the demarcationary aspect of falsification. Moreover, as Popper unenthusiastically acknowledged, Darwin's theory appears to violate his falsificatory principles precisely because the notion of evolutionary benefit is so hard to confine. Darwinian field studies tend to accept that any apparently inexplicable feature of animal or plant design does have some evolutionary advantage. It's simply that it often takes a long while to work out what those advantages are. Even when possible advantages are identified, it is hard to work out a balance of costs and benefits. The peacock's lavish tail may win it more mates but tail-maintenance exacts a biological toll on the bird. Darwinians typically assume that the benefits must outweigh the costs; if not the tail would not be there. But this line of reasoning, present in field biology for over a century and thus apparently acceptable to the scientific community, threatens to become rather circular and thus (in a strict sense) unfalsifiable. Rather than treat any feature of plant or animal design as a potential falsifier of Darwinian theory, all anomalies are set aside until they can be fitted into the evolutionary paradigm.

In light of all these problems with his approach, Popper's supporters did not reject his theory but sought (in a rather non-falsificationist way) to amend it. The most ingenious revision was conducted by Lakatos (see 1978: 8–93). Lakatos proposed that the distinctiveness of science was revealed in the way scientists chose not between competing single theories but in their selection of groupings of theories; these he termed research programmes. He thereby introduced two key revisions to Popper's original scheme. He suggested first of all that it was not reasonable to give up a theory simply because it had been falsified; rather one adopted a new research programme only when its superiority over a preceding one had been shown. That is, one did not jettison one's theory in the light of counter-evidence; one only traded in a theoretical outlook for a superior one. Second, he accepted that it was inevitable that research programmes would produce after-the-event explanations for anomalous findings. Lakatos offered a spatial metaphor for his view of research programmes. They consist of a core of central theoretical commitments surrounded by a protective belt of more dispensable assertions. In his terms, it is rational for scientists to make changes in the protective belt to save the core from falsification. But in the end, the advance of science is still progressive and reasoned because there is a methodology for choosing between research programmes. A research programme can be pronounced to be degenerating when it is constantly responding to new evidence by having to make alterations in the protective belt. By contrast, a progressive research programme is where predictions derived from the theory are not being falsified by the evidence and where surprising predictions are being confirmed. Lakatos himself styles his approach sophisticated falsificationism, and its comparative sophistication is easy to see.[2]

However, there remain two problems with his approach. First, by acknowledging that it is reasonable to retain a theory even in the light of apparent falsifications and numerous anomalies, Lakatos robs himself of a clear methodological guideline. At some point, it appears, the reasonability of a theory/research programme must evaporate and it should become rational to switch out of the degenerating programme into a progressive one. But his theory cannot specify that moment. Popper's unsophisticated approach at least had the benefit of a definite cut-off point. It was irrational to adhere to a theory after it had been falsified. Lakatos can make no such claim. Secondly, Lakatos finds himself struggling to explain how his own theory matches the relevant empirical data. At times he appears to want to say that the best theory of the methodology of science is the one which makes most of the history of science look rational (1978: 121–38). One can understand his rationalist's fondness for that option but it is not at all clear that the version of 'the scientific method' which is most compatible with actual history is necessarily the one which would have been best.

Subsequent authors have taken up Lakatos' mantle – including his direct followers such as Zahar (1973), as well as Laudan (1977) and much more recently Kitcher (1993) – but each has had the difficulty of showing that their account of what is rational for scientists to do accords with what scientists actually do. Each has also struggled to identify the point at which it becomes rational to switch from one theory to another. In outline, the more elaborate and detailed the grounds for switching from one theory/research programme to another (the more sophisticated in Lakatos' sense), the harder it is to eliminate the scope for individual scientists to exercise judgement and thus to disagree with each other about which is the 'rational' path to take. These philosophers have usefully drawn attention to the constituents of scientific theories (the idea of a core and protective belt), and their exhaustive attempts to separate science from non-science turn out to have importance outside this apparently narrow, technical dispute (as will be seen in Chapter 10). But they have not achieved what they set out to do, to specify in close detail what makes science special.

LOOKING TO SCIENTIFIC CONDUCT

If the specialness or exceptional quality of science cannot be located in its method, perhaps it can be located in the social norms which govern conduct within the scientific community. This idea is associated with the earliest systematic analyses in the sociology of science and is particularly identified with the work of Merton who first elaborated this perspective in the 1940s. It was he who argued that there were norms generally accepted in the scientific community which 'possess a methodologic rationale but they are binding, not only because they are procedurally efficient, but because they are believed right and good. They are moral as well as technical prescriptions' (1973: 270). Such norms are thus important on two levels: they describe the normative atmosphere which in fact reigns within the community, and they operate in concert to make the scientific community effective in the production of sound scientific knowledge. As is well known, Merton principally suggested four candidate norms:

> *Universalism*: the belief that ideas should be evaluated according to impersonal criteria irrespective of their source. This norm should make considerations of gender or ethnic background or nationality, for example, unimportant to the assessment of contributions to science.
>
> *Communalism*: the principle that knowledge should be regarded as a common heritage and shared in the scientific community. Thus, scientists receive no payment for their publications in leading journals; indeed there is often a submission fee.
>
> *Disinterestedness*: the idea here is that scientists should not seek personal advancement in the scientific domain through questionable means nor should they advance vested interests through the medium of science. They should avoid 'eclipsing rivals through illicit means' (1973: 276) and ought not to promote the theories of their friends in the hope of back-scratching in return.
>
> *Organised scepticism*: the idea that scientists should not be credulous, not jump to conclusions, but weigh evidence in a considered manner.

The interesting and clever thing about these norms is that they govern the professional conduct of scientists and say little in detail about what one might think of as the 'scientific' aspects of their behaviour, the experimental protocols or what they choose to do in the lab or the field. But these norms none the less have implications for the growth of scientific ideas. For example, the norm of universalism suggests that scientists should, and will generally feel they should, take seriously all contributions to the scientific literature, whether authored by women or men, by gay or straight scientists, by those based in East Asia, Africa or the West. In this case one can quite readily see what Merton is getting at. Reports about, say, measurements of changing rainfall or ocean temperatures from Latin America – maybe as a result of climate change – could be just as important as those from Britain or France. Thus the norms allegedly describe how scientists conduct themselves and explain how such conduct collectively results in the growth of knowledge.

When this line of thinking was advanced by Merton and elaborated by his colleagues, they were able to offer various forms of support for the idea. At one level the proposal had an initial plausibility and seemed to describe how scientists in fact typically behave. Sharing ideas by being communitarian would seem to be inevitably beneficial to science. And the fact that scientists typically do publish their ideas freely and without payment seemed to suggest that there was something distinctive about the professional ethic of science. Secondly, Mertonian sociologists of science could point to cases where broader social trends which overrode the norms had caused disruption to science. To a considerable degree in Nazi Germany and to some extent in the Stalinist Soviet Union, scientific ideas were not treated in a universalistic manner. In one case, the ideas of Jewish scientists were held up to ridicule while, in the other, key ideas emanating from capitalist, imperialist countries were rejected. Mertonians argued that the pace of scientific and technical development slowed in both countries, at least relative to the comparatively universalistic USA, apparently demonstrating the utility of the norms for promoting scientific advancement. Finally, there were cases in the history of science where maverick scientists who had not adhered to the normatively prescribed patterns of behaviour had been subject to criticism. Perhaps most famously, the non-conforming eighteenth-century British chemist Priestley neglected to publish his path-breaking results. Mertonians offered evidence that other scientists responded with indignation to this improper conduct; other scientists' reactions seemed to support Merton's claim that communalism was experienced as a normative commitment. In summary, one can see how the norms should promote the growth of science; one can see that scientists commonly behave in accordance with the norms even at some cost to themselves (for example by publishing openly in journals even if there is a submission fee); one can see how deviation from the norms caused by the imposition of contrasting values (such as racist rejection of 'Jewish science') slows this growth; and one can find evidence that members of the scientific community respond with something like moral outrage to infractions of this normative code. The norms thus seem to govern how scientists conduct themselves and how they judge each other. In their community, scientists are rewarded for adhering to the norms and sanctioned for violating them. This social structure reproduces itself and speeds scientific development.

However, things have not worked out quite as straightforwardly as this view would suggest. For one thing, sociologists working within the Mertonian framework arrived at disconcerting findings. Mitroff conducted a study of scientists working on the origin and nature of the moon, using data from the US space programme. He conducted extensive interviews with members of the scientific community and looked for evidence of normative orientation in their remarks (1974: 27–46). He found statements supporting Merton's norms. But he also found support for contrasting behaviour which his respondents appeared to justify in puzzlingly similar terms. For example, scientists pointed out that, given the sheer amount of information potentially available, one had to limit the sources to which one paid attention. The work stemming from people located in well-known research groups could reasonably be given more attention than people who seemed to spring out of nowhere. Rather than acting universalistically, there were good functional grounds for doing exactly the opposite, being particularistic. Similarly, in order to get new ideas noticed, one had to champion one's innovative proposals. There were good grounds for not being disinterested. To give one's own novel suggestions a chance, one had to promote them above the opposition. In this way Mitroff argued that he had managed to find evidence for the existence of a corresponding set of counter-norms concerning conduct which was regarded as appropriate in the scientific community; he was also able to derive a functional justification for these counter-norms. Sharing and being communalistic are all very well, but there are sometimes grounds for being secretive. One wants to develop an idea to the state that it is reasonably robust before wasting other people's time by presenting it in the scientific literature. Similarly, if scientists took seriously all contributions to the literature and tried to check out the implications of every idea published, they would simply run out of time and scientific advance would grind to a halt.

Mitroff appears to argue that both sets of norms are operative simultaneously. There is a normative push towards universalism *and* towards particularism. He does not elaborate on how this state of affairs can be maintained. On the face of it, having both norms and counter-norms would seem to imply that there can be little normative control at all since more or less any course of action could be justified in the light of one set of norms or the other (Mulkay, 1980). The situation is not as grave as all that, however, since both the putative sets of norms focus on certain dimensions of scientific conduct. They could be read as indicating that, in the scientific community, there are particular sensitivities around issues of universality and of control over one's intellectual product.

This more relaxed interpretation of Mitroff's findings appears attractive in the light of the subsequent argument by Mulkay that Merton's supposed norms do not seem very well reinforced or rewarded in the scientific enterprise. Mulkay points out that there are some bits of scientific behaviour which are closely policed, rules for referencing in publications for example (1976: 641–3). Compared to those activities, conformity with the alleged Mertonian norms is barely policed at all. Rewards, in terms of prestigious jobs and research grants, flow to those renowned for good work and with long lists of highly cited publications. But these positive attributes seem to be the important things, not one's adherence to the behavioural norms. It is only an assumption (by Merton and his colleagues) that the two things – conformity to the norms and academic success – go together. But given Mitroff's findings and the fact that there appear to be so few institutional mechanisms for checking whether scientists do actually behave according to the norms, this assumption seems poorly supported by evidence.

These empirical difficulties for the Mertonian scheme suggest that the case for the four norms seemed convincing for several decades not because of the sociological accuracy of the norms alone but because, at a philosophical level, it appeared that these are the kinds of behavioural regularity that 'must' be enforced if science is to progress. Merton himself claimed that these norms are 'procedurally efficient'. For someone who approaches science as a straightforward empiricist, that is with an almost exclusive emphasis on observation, they would seem to be efficient behavioural characteristics. Of course, Mitroff already argued that, in practice, they might not be as efficient as all that. But from a post-Popperian perspective, their supposed efficiency looks even more suspect. Scientists have to decide which observations to count as 'real' observations and which to dismiss; beyond a certain point, being universalistic is a liability under these conditions. Similarly, as Lakatos' work indicated, scientists must judge whether a research programme is progressive or not and different scientists are likely to come to different conclusions. The injunction to be disinterested and to exercise organised scepticism will not be decisively helpful in making that judgement.

Merton's suggestion of founding the special character of science in the ethos of the scientific community was attractively novel. However, it appears that the evidence for the existence and institutionalisation of the norms is rather less robust than Mertonians had supposed. Worse still, it is not even clear that it would be good for the advance of science to have those norms institutionalised. Merton appears to be correct that certain dimensions of scientific conduct do have a moral or ethical salience to them, particularly certain issues which he lists under universalism (to do with equality of opportunity in science) and under communalism (concerning the ownership of scientific information); these matters arise again in connection with legal understandings of science in Chapter 10. But Mulkay's alternative interpretation, that the norms reflect a professional ideology developed by scientists to defend their independence and relative freedom from external scrutiny, seems to be as valid an analysis as that originally proposed by Merton (Mulkay, 1976).

SCIENTIFIC VALUES

If rules do not accomplish the task set out by rationalist authors of setting science apart from other forms of belief and if the scientific community is not distinguished by its normative ethos, another basis will have to be sought to justify the exceptionality of science. The other popular recourse for philosophical analysts has been to values. Kuhn, whose early work was mentioned above, sought to reduce or overcome the relativistic conse-quences of his earlier studies by suggesting that scientists consistently used a small number of key values for assessing the merits of rival scientific theories or research programmes. He proposed (1977: 322) that scientists prize highly the following five 'standard criteria for evaluating the ade-quacy of a theory': accuracy, consistency, scope, simplicity and fruitfulness. In assessing theories scientists will, on this view (1977: 321–2), evaluate them along the following dimensions:

1. the 'consequences deducible from a theory should be in demonstrated agreement with the results of existing experiments and observations';
2. the theory ought to be consistent internally and 'also with other cur-rently accepted theories applicable to related aspects of nature';
3. the 'theory's consequences should extend far beyond the particular observations, laws, or subtheories it was initially designed to explain';
4. it ought to bring 'order to phenomena that in its absence would be individually isolated and, as a set, confused';
5. the 'theory should be fruitful of new research findings'.

Kuhn argues that scientists recognise that these features are desirable in scientific knowledge. In the language of advertising competitions, scientists use their 'skill and judgement' to assess the relative merits of contending theories or research programmes in the light of these values. The scientific community is the sole authority on the comparative standing of scientific ideas; the values which guide the growth of science are those which scientists collectively decide on. There is no other authority to which appeal can be made. As Kuhn states later in the same paragraph, these values 'provide *the shared basis* for theory choice' (1977: 322, emphasis added). These criteria are just a distillation of what scientists are found to do. One could, in an equivalent way, set out criteria encapsulating the activities of post-expressionist painters, successful romantic poets or leading exponents of dressage.

In Kuhn's statements, however, there remains an uncertainty about the precise nature, source and status of these criteria. For one thing, he accepts that the above is not a comprehensive listing; of these five values he says: 'I select five, not because they are exhaustive, but because they are individually important and collectively sufficiently varied to indicate what is at stake' (1977: 321). However, unless all the values could be listed it is hard to understand in what sense the values can be said to direct scientific decisions. Second, the status of the individual values is unclear. There is a tension between the view that they are simply generalisations about the values which scientists happen to honour – just as one might record the values recognised by followers of an artistic movement – and the suggestion that they have some intrinsic logic or that they derive from some transcendental standard. Third, as Bergström has helpfully pointed out in a thorough review of these arguments, such cognitive values are actually of different sorts, sorts which he labels as 'ultimate, evidential and strategic' (1996: 190).[3] While ultimate values directly reflect the underlying goal of science, evidential and strategic values act more as pointers towards that ultimate goal. Thus, the fifth criterion (fruitfulness) is not necessarily an ultimate value at all; rather one might select fruitful theories for strategic reasons (they allow the scientific community to identify new themes to work on) or on evidential grounds (one feels that a fruitful theory is likely to turn out also to be an accurate one). In Bergström's opinion Kuhn and related authors are unclear about exactly what makes the 'values' valuable.

Partly in response to these ambiguities Newton-Smith (1981) sought to provide a fuller defence of the use of values to preserve the rationality of science. His initial approach to the question differed from Kuhn's in that he began with a realist interpretation of science (for more on the meaning of 'realism', see the next section). Newton-Smith is cautious in his realism. He claims that science is distinguished from most other forms of knowledge because it tends to get truer as it goes along. Still, we cannot accept that our beliefs about the natural world at any particular time are the truth. Rather, we must accept the 'pessimistic induction' (1981: 14) that we will sooner or later abandon our current beliefs as untrue for, judging by the history of science, everything which we now believe true is likely to turn out to be false in some regard. We can, though, pick out criteria which have been used in assessing scientific ideas and which we have good reasons for thinking are linked to an increase in truthfulness or, as he terms it, verisimilitude. However, even though Newton-Smith is clearer about his identification of the ultimate justification for his values, several of the criteria he proposes are similar to those put forward by Kuhn. He lists a series of eight 'good-making features' of scientific theories (1981: 226–32). These are:

1. That a theory should 'preserve the observational successes of its predecessors'.
2. That a theory should be fertile in producing ideas for further inquiry.
3. That a theory should have a good track record to date.
4. That a theory should mesh with and support existing, neighbouring theories.
5. That theories should be 'smooth'; meaning that it should be possible to adjust the theory easily in the light of anomalies which are bound to emerge.
6. That a theory should be internally consistent.
7. That theories should be compatible 'with well-grounded metaphysical beliefs': that is, theories should accord with the same metaphysical assumptions as sustain the rest of science.
8. Although hesitant because of the ambiguity of this criterion, it is probably beneficial for theories to be simple.

What is significant about this list of criteria is not just the individual recommendations but the claim that the values each has a double justification. Newton-Smith asserts that they are both the criteria by which scientists do judge and criteria which can be shown to be rational for scientists to adopt in the light of the assumed goal of science, namely to become truer and truer. Thus, theories should be compatible with widely adopted metaphysical assumptions because it is very hard to see how science could be becoming more correct if major sections of it depended on conflicting metaphysics. If a new physical theory, for example, meant that while biology required the universe to be one way, physics entailed another ordering, that would be a retrograde movement.

Newton-Smith thus seeks to tackle Kuhn's problem head on: his theory is avowedly empirical and normative. It is an account of the values which scientists as a matter of fact generally do take into account and it is a demonstration of why scientists are right to honour those values. It is this latter aspect which would potentially allow Newton-Smith to claim that science is rational and that scientific knowledge is uniquely authoritative. But how satisfactory is this normative element? As Newton-Smith himself makes clear, none of the criteria is inviolable. On occasions some values may have to be subordinated to others. For example, a theory (T1) with a poor track record may be preferable to some other theory (T2) because of T1's assessment on the other values even though T2 has a better track record. In the great majority of scientific decisions, therefore, a judgement will have to be made about the merits of different theories' 'scores' on the eight values. And with these eight criteria to be taken into account the scores can be totted up in very many different ways. Just using the criteria will thus demand a huge exercise of judgement by scientists.

But the situation is even more complex than this for the criteria are not automatic in their application. Take criterion four for instance: meshing with and supporting neighbouring theories is a far from simple require-ment. Which are the neighbouring theories? Looking back to the dispute outlined earlier about the age of the Earth, it would be evident for sup-porters of the geological position that the study of the growth of biologi-cal diversity was a field neighbouring the study of the Earth's age. For physicists, however, the study of biological phenomena would be only very remotely connected to the issue of the probable antiquity of the Earth. But even if neighbours could be uncontentiously identified it would still be unclear how to evaluate the degree of support given to those neighbouring theories. Is it better to lend a great deal of support to a few neighbouring theories or to lend some support to a lot of neighbours? When viewed in this way it appears that Newton-Smith's approach is subject to the same practical limitations as those Kuhn (1977: 324) admitted for his own since:

> When scientists must choose between competing theories, two men fully committed to the same list of criteria for choice may neverthe-less reach different conclusions. ... With respect to divergences of this sort, no set of choice criteria yet proposed is of any use. One can explain, as the historian characteristically does, why particular men made particular choices at particular times. But for that purpose one must go beyond the list of shared criteria to characteristics of the individuals who make the choice.

Later on in the same text Kuhn reinforces this point, acknowledging that 'little knowledge of history is required to suggest that both the application of these values and, more obviously, the relative weights attached to them have varied markedly with time and also with the field of [science in which they are applied]' (1977: 335).

Newton-Smith took Kuhn to task (1981: 122–4) for not rooting his pro-posed values in the rational requirements of science. For him, Kuhn was making too weak a case for science by implying that the five Kuhnian values were just a statement of how scientists happened to conduct them-selves. As a realist, Newton-Smith cannot allow that science comprises a set of values or criteria one can choose to follow or not. The values must not just be a convention; they have to be the real values for getting on best in describing the world. But, as we have seen, the practical normative force of the proposed eight values is much less than Newton-Smith would seem to require.

One may accept that there is a certain plausibility to the values. They may describe the kinds of considerations which scientists appear to have in mind when selecting theories; they may even strike us as the kind of consideration which scientists ought to have in mind. But, unless we have good reasons for thinking that the values direct scientific choices in a strong sense, this normative force is of limited consequence. Providing a list of values which scientists should honour but which, in practice, does not constrain scientific choice at all closely, does rather little to revitalise the authority of any specific scientific judgements. Newton-Smith supplies us with general grounds for thinking that science as a whole is a reasoned undertaking but he does not reassure us that any particular scientific judgement could not reasonably have come out differently. By listing his suggested criteria in a chapter entitled 'Scientific Method', Newton-Smith might be seen as implying that the criteria can be used as something like a recipe for demonstrating the exceptionalness of scientific progress. It should now be clear that they cannot serve in this capacity.

REALISM

Though philosophers such as Popper, Kitcher and Kuhn have engaged in their different ways with the issue of how it is that science secures its position of special authority, a rather different line of argument has been developed by other philosophical analysts (including, to some degree, Newton-Smith). Their position is commonly termed realism. They are much less concerned with the mechanics of scientific advancement than with considering the status of the entities (particularly theoretical entities such as scientific 'laws') posited by scientists. The realist position maintains that the things disclosed by science are among the real constituents and the real mechanisms of the natural world; they are – in the philosophical cliché – the furniture of the universe. Given that realists believe that science tells us about the real fabric of the world, it is in some sense quite unnecessary to worry about how exactly science manages to be progressive. For realists, the important thing is that the scientific endeavour tells us how the world is; the fact that it does this is far more important than the secondary issue of how it does it. And even if we cannot at present specify in detail how science does it, that will not stop realists claiming both that it does do it and that we know that it does.

Some philosophers had seen the 'how' question as the route to demonstrating the superiority of science. But realists typically use different arguments. They commonly concentrate on figuring out the way the world must be if we humans are to have knowledge of it. That is to say, realists use transcendental arguments to work out what the fact of human knowledge tells us about the relationship between humans and the natural world. Bhaskar has stated this as clearly as any of the realists:

> It is not necessary that science occurs. But given that it does, it is necessary that the world is a certain way. It is contingent that the world is such that science is possible. And, given that it is possible, it is contingent upon the satisfaction of certain social conditions that science in fact occurs. But given that science does or could occur, the world *must* be a certain way. Thus, the transcendental realist asserts, that the world is structured and differentiated can be established by philosophical argument; though the particular structures it contains and the ways in which it is differentiated are matters for substantive scientific investigation. (1978: 29 original emphasis)

The realist argues that, for science to exist, the world must have certain properties or characteristics. And humans, as part of that world, must have certain characteristics as well. It is important to see that the claim here is not a narrowly factual or empirical one. Realist philosophers move from the fact of science's existence to deduce what the world must be like, in general terms, for science to be possible at all. Their main appeal is to reason – to pure thinking – not to detailed claims about the actual behaviours of scientists.

Given this orientation, it goes almost without saying that realists are not primarily interested in trying to demonstrate how it is that scientists' activities or procedures are able to produce a special kind of knowledge. They tend to take it as a given that science is successful, and then aim to work out what this implies about the nature of the world and our relationship to it. For example, Bhaskar's argument is not intended to convince people who believe that science is unsuccessful. He is trying to show that analysts of science who think – as an extreme follower of Popper might – that science is composed only of competing, alternative hypotheses are mistaken. He proposes that the practice of science makes no sense without two separate presuppositions. The first is that the objects of scientific knowledge are independent of the activity of science itself. The second is that scientific knowledge can only be produced by a community of knowers; it is not the spontaneous product of individual observers' perceptions. Thus, for example, his retort to the Popperian is that 'To be fallibilist about knowledge is to be realist about the world' (1978: 43). The very idea of falsifying hypotheses makes no sense unless one assumes that there is an independent natural world with the capability of falsifying our proposals; to be a Popperian is thus (says Bhaskar) implicitly to endorse realism.

For this reason, the realist's best argument is that, if we think about it, the very business of engaging in science presupposes realist assumptions. They believe that any other position is untenable; scientists' actions would be at odds with those alternative claims. Even if people deny that they are realists, their very conceptualisation of science belies their words. Realists' claims for the special character of science are a consequence of this argument; science is special because it tells us about the real causal structures of the world. Quite reasonably, realists view this as no mean feat and thus as considerable evidence of special-ness.

As indicated in the quote above, realists such as Bhaskar acknowledge that their philosophical arguments are limited to establishing that 'the world is structured and differentiated' but can tell us nothing substantive about how the world is, since that is the business of science. Given this limited objective, one might wonder what use realists suppose their arguments are. The prime answer is two-fold. In part, their arguments are intended to put a stop to misunderstandings about what science and the scientific community must be like; Bhaskar believes that Popper and Kuhn and many others are barking up the wrong tree, thus wasting time and perpetuating mistakes about the status of science's discoveries. Secondly, he appears to believe that the practice of knowledge-making sometimes goes wrong because it is allied to a false philosophy. In Bhaskar's case, he wishes to reform social science (in a neo-Marxist direction) and wishes to outlaw other schools of social-scientific thinking by showing that those schools are philosophically untenable.

Proponents of the other arguments I have reviewed may or may not explicitly identify themselves as realists; of course, Bhaskar would wish to claim them all as realists, at least at an implicit level. Thus Newton-Smith claims to be a temperate realist and bolstered his claims about the good-making features of science with arguments from realism. He argues that the conceptual values are compatible with transcendental arguments about how scientific knowledge and the real world must be. Popper was apparently much more impressed with the fallibility of science. Too much realism about any existing conception was likely to be misplaced since scientific development entails a constant challenging and overthrow of existing ideas. In Newton-Smith's words, Popper was struck by the pessimistic induction that all current science is likely to turn out to be wrong. In this regard, it should also be noted that realists, while typically realist about the empirical and experimental sciences, are also often realist about arithmetic, geometry and other forms of abstract knowledge too, as will be seen in the next chapter.

The kind of arguments advanced by Bhaskar and other realists have clearly exercised a strong appeal, but in important ways they are both too strong and too weak. They are too weak in the sense that, even if one accepted them, that acceptance would very often have few consequences. In a controversy in the scientific community, realism will not generally help one decide which position to favour since, as Bhaskar acknowledges above, 'the particular structures [the world] contains and the ways in which it is differentiated are matters for substantive scientific investigation'. Similarly, realism will not typically help policy-makers decide which scientists' advice to heed or help a court decide to which expert witness it should pay most attention. At the same time, the argument is too strong because it appears to use transcendental arguments to demonstrate the existence of a real world when the only thing knowable about this world is that it is real. It seems to solve the problem of the exceptional character of science but only does so by inferring the existence of a real world about which we can know nothing except those things which scientists have already told us. In that sense, it is a little like transcendental arguments for the existence of God: arguments that purport to tell us that God exists but which leave everything else important about God to the sources which previously informed us. In this way, the argument seems perilously close to circularity. This issue of the status of realist arguments will be considered again in Chapter 2.

CONCLUDING DISCUSSION

This chapter has been concerned with trying to pin down precisely the source of science's exceptionalism. If scientific knowledge is to stand apart from other forms of knowledge in contemporary society then one would presume there would be an identifiable basis for that distinctiveness. Analysts of science have identified four main routes for attaining this Grail. However, though each of these approaches is partly persuasive, none achieves its initial goal. The only philosophical approach (realism) which comes close to making science stand out and be truly exceptional pulls off this trick by claiming that the practice of science *necessarily* implies that the world is real and that science gives us access to that real world. Realism insists that science is exceptional but the only evidence is the existence of science itself.

While the reviews conducted in this chapter largely point to dead-ends if one's interest is in proving how exactly science is exceptional, that does not mean that the approaches have been futile. For one thing, many of the arguments considered here turn out to be important later on when we come to analyse the standing of science in court or the role played by scientists in advising on policy. On top of this, the analysts whose work has been considered have made useful contributions to the study of science, even if they haven't achieved all they set out to do. Popper's observation about the importance of falsification and falsifiability will crop up again several times. Lakatos' distinction between the central core and the protective belt provides an important way of describing the structure of many scientific theories. Merton's emphasis on universalism has continued to play a key role in the study of controversies involving science while the kinds of concern raised by realists turn out, perhaps surprisingly, to be critical to many schools in the sociology of science including the ethnomethodologists. Finally, it will be seen that the cognitive values emphasised by Kuhn and Newton-Smith mirror in an interesting way the manner in which a sociological analysis of science has most successfully been developed. It is to that programme of studies in the sociology of science that we turn in the next chapter.

---

[1] Relating back to the introduction and my discussion of the search for WIMPs, it should be pointed out that neutrinos themselves are thought by some to be part of the dark matter. But for neutrinos to make up any substantial proportion of the missing masses, they would have to be found to have more mass than is generally reckoned to be the case. It is possible that there are different kinds of neutrinos, some being WIMPy, others not.

[2] Even though Popper was sometimes less naïve a falsificationist than at other times, he was never this sophisticated.

[3] My thanks to Alan Weir of the School of Philosophical Studies at Queen's University Belfast for alerting me to Bergström's analysis.

6

Partisan Perspective

A Multiple-Level Interpretation of the Manuscript Review Process in Social Science Journals

PETER J. FROST and RONALD N. TAYLOR

One powerful source of influence on the direction of a scientific field is the academic journal. Knowledge in a field is disseminated in large measure through manuscripts published in journals; the careers of scholars, their visibility in a field, and their mobility in and across academic institutions are significantly influenced by the degree to which their work is published in the respected journals of their profession. At the same time, the potential for game playing in the review process is made explicit in prescriptions for manuscript publication given, somewhat tongue in cheek, by Chambers and Herzberg (1968) and by Mahoney (1978). Tactics they prescribe to authors for "winning" the refereeing game include use of obscure references, flattery, a barrage of submissions to an editor, footnotes acknowledging powerful friends, the highlighting of successful results, anticipating reviewer problems in the manuscript, and frequent citation of their own works.

Such influence and criticisms should be carefully studied to understand the nature of the influence and its relationship to the development of a scientific field. Despite numerous studies of how social science journals work (see Lindsey, 1978, for a comprehensive review of research), no conceptual or analytic framework exists for examining these phenomena. At the core of our publication systems is the manuscript publishability decision. Systematic studies of manuscript publishability decisions are needed to increase our awareness of what we say and what we do as scientists. Such reflexivity by social scientists has been called for by writers such as Gouldner (1976) and Habermas (1973) but is rarely attended to in practice.

We believe that academic journals and the publishability decisions that occur within them are organizational phenomena that are amenable to study through applications of organizational science knowledge. Despite the existence of theories and empirical research methodologies that organizational scientists have developed and applied enthusiastically to a wide variety of topics and situations, there has been little attempt to apply these same resources to look inward, critically, at our own institutions in an attempt to increase understanding of the very nature and development of a field itself (Nord, 1980). Application of organizational science knowledge to the academic journal represents a step in this direction.

In this chapter we analyze the manuscript review process in social science journals, and particularly the manuscript publishability decision, by applying a number of conceptual lenses or frameworks that have been developed in the organizational science field. The analysis is conducted at three levels: societal, organizational, and individual. First we apply an ideological influence perspective or model, which focuses on journal decision making in the broad context of scientific communities within which journal decision making takes place. Then, to the manuscript review process we apply perspectives derived from Allison's (1971) framework of decision making (the governmental politics, organizational processes, and rational actor models).

Based on our analysis of the journal decision-making process from the vantage points provided by these four models, we discuss possible avenues for further research on the publishability decisions of journals and possible improvements to the process.

Criticisms of journals and the decisions about what manuscripts to publish are discussed in several places in the relevant literature (e.g., Bedeian, Downey, Price, & Salancik, 1980; Frost, Taylor, & Cummings, 1981; Latané, 1979a, 1979b; Lindsey, 1978; Peters, 1976). Major sources of irritation and disaffection for dissatisfied readers tend to be the lack of quality in journal content, sterile journal material, and irrelevance of articles. Authors identify high rejection rates for their manuscripts (for example, four out of five submissions), excessive publication lags of accepted manuscripts, and unclear criteria used by editors and reviewers to accept or reject manuscripts. Journal editors sometimes express frustration with the poor quality of manuscripts and identify their own concerns as being high workloads, increasing production costs, publication deadlines, and authors' and institutions' demands for quick and/or favorable decisions to aid pending promotion and tenure decisions. Reviewers are often dissatisfied with high workloads and relatively low extrinsic rewards.

The central issues that underlie these and other concerns about the review process may relate to four major dimensions of decision making. The first dimension is *efficiency* of the decision process: that is, speed of decisions, rapidity of knowledge dissemination, cost control, and the editors', reviewers', and authors' use of time. A second dimension is *innovation:* openness to publishing material on new paradigms, new ideas, new methodologies, controversial issues, or material that excites, informs, or even challenges existing theories and practice. The third dimension concerns *quality,* which relates to the nature of knowledge produced: adequacy of arguments, methodology, and analysis contained in manuscripts (essentially a concern with preventing Type I or Type II decision errors). Quality also relates to decisions about the initial correctness of questions asked (a concern with preventing Type III errors). The fourth dimension deals with the *fairness* of decisions made: It is assumed that all scientists and their ideas have an equal chance to be published in journals. Fairness is the degree to which this ideal is fulfilled.

These dimensions are interrelated and interact so that improvements on one may involve improvements or declines on one or more of the other dimensions. Wade, for example, expresses the trade-off between the dimensions of innovation and quality as the "accept is to reject paradox" (Wade, 1979, p. 487). He explains that, while openness to manuscripts with variable content increases clutter and reduces overall quality, being closed to such material may cut off promising material. The unselective editor, on the other hand, may produce a journal containing too much worthless material. If too selective, however, the editor may create a sterile journal. Similarly, editors who increase efficiency through reducing decision turnaround time cause reviewers to rush to meet decision deadlines, thereby reducing the competence of reviews and review decisions.

Our analyses and our prescriptions for researching and operating the review process have an intended bias. Our approach is primarily that which represents the *author.* As such, the predominant emphasis of the research issues we identify and the prescriptions we propose has to do with innovation and fairness, although we do not ignore questions of efficiency and quality. Our perspective is likely to be different in some respects than those of other partisans—editors and reviewers, for example. We believe that discussion based upon the values, experiences, questions, and empirical answers that each partisan brings to the debate will greatly enhance our understanding and management of the publishing process, so that it serves well individual authors and the community of scholars in which they work.

TOWARD UNDERSTANDING
THE MANUSCRIPT REVIEW PROCESS

In this section we provide a conceptual framework for analysis of the manuscript review process, review some of the relevant research, discuss questions that need to be researched to better understand these processes, and identify appropriate research methodologies. We examine journal decision making in the larger context of society and then apply Allison's framework to the decision process. This framework integrates a diversity of research literatures that are not typically juxtaposed to examine a phenomenon in the field. Allison's governmental politics model emphasizes coalitions, power, and political behavior; his organizational processes model uses organizational theory, in particular that which deals with formal organizational structure and design; and his rational actor model harnesses decision theory literature. Each of the four models we use draws upon a particular set of assumptions, variables, and relationships. Each model brings into focus aspects and issues concerning the decision that are ignored by others but that appear to have a bearing on understanding decision making in journals.

Ideological Influence and the Manuscript Review Process

Ideology represents what a society defines as reality; it comprises beliefs about how the world operates, and articulates the values, expectations, standards, and so forth that are intended to inform and orient people's behavior (Berger & Luckmann, 1966; Wilson, 1973). Decision making, given this perspective, is influenced by the values, expectations, and standards of the society in which it is embedded (Clegg, 1975; Edelman, 1977; Gouldner, 1976; Habermas, 1973). This perspective brings into focus the ways a body of people—a profession, a school of thought, a community of scientists—sees, behaves, and acts.

The characteristics of an ideology are frequently "taken for granted" by most members of a society so that the ideology's impact on behavior is not immediately apparent unless made explicit in some way (Edelman, 1977). Nevertheless, an ideology is created, interpreted, maintained, and defended by the actions and attitudes of members of a society who have a vested interest in the ideology and its perpetuation. Such individuals constitute a dominant coalition within the society. The impact of ideology on decision making is assumed to be upon the very definition of social reality—including the "game" and "the rules of the game"— within which decisions are made (Legge, 1978). The ideological influence perspective on decision making is concerned with the societal values, expectations, and standards that surround the choice of a decision maker and what that choice reveals about what is legitimately included in the decision maker's domain (and about what is excluded from that domain).

Competing definitions of acceptable or legitimate scientific endeavor and notions of dominating ideologies, which shape the nature, focus, and content of scientific communication, are brought into focus when the manuscript review process is examined in terms of ideological influence (Clark, 1973; Edelman, 1977; Gouldner, 1976; Kuhn, 1970). Given this perspective, decisions to publish or reject manuscripts reflect editorial attention to a value system—frequently taken for granted—that governs the scientific research process. This value system may determine, in large measure, what is included in, or excluded from, the content of academic journals. Clark (1973), speaking as a black researcher and editor, articulated the ideological influence on scientific endeavors in his critique of psychology in which he argued psychology excluded discussion, research, and publication in areas of study such as exploitation, imperialism, and oppression—areas that are defined as important by black thinkers. Instead, Clark pointed out, psychology legitimated areas such as behavior control, deviance, criminality, and so forth. Editors, from Clark's perspective, are selected and then act to preserve the status quo of a dominant ideology of science. Editors attempting to legitimate knowledge that does not fit the prevailing social reality of the field in which the journal is published may not survive in the role. In the extreme case, the journal itself may not survive.

Ideologies are formulated or interpreted and are maintained by those in a group who have a vested interest in the values and practices inherent in particular ideologies. Given this assumption, selection of editors becomes an important choice for a dominant elite given that editorial choices of manuscripts for publication reflect and shape what is believed to be valid scientific knowledge. Selection of editors for journals as a reflection of ideological influence has been reported in the literature (e.g., Crane, 1967; Lewin &

Duchan, 1971; Mitchell, 1951; Teghtsoonian, 1974; White, 1970; Yoels, 1971,1974). Yoels (1971,1974) studied the pattern of appointments of editor-in-chief to the *American Sociological Review* and other social science journals during the period 1948 to 1971. He reported that doctoral graduates of Columbia and Harvard who were editors-in-chief of social science journals were significantly more likely than other editors-in-chief to select their own university doctoral graduates for editorial appointments. Yoels suggested the existence of a relationship between the power structure of social science disciplines and the appointment of editors and the resultant dissemination of information (Yoels, 1974).

The virtual absence of women as editors of social science journals may also reflect a dominating value system. In APA journals during the period 1929 to 1949, Mitchell (1951) found that women accounted for only 1 journal editor year out of 187 journal editor years. During this same time period, 20% of APA Fellows were women. Teghtsoonian (1974) documents more recent evidence suggesting underrepresentation of women as editors of psychology journals. She used two samples of journals: (a) 11 journals in 1970-1972 and (b) APA journals in 1972. She observed that women were represented as published authors at a level consistent with their division membership in APA. However, in sample A, 5% of editors were women while 15% were authors. In sample B, 7% of editors were women, while 14% were authors. She examines several competing explanations for her findings, including lower publication rates and lower research quality for women researchers. Despite some sex-based differences in the sample, such as lower publication rates, the magnitude of the difference between women as editors and as authors suggests that editor selection in the journals studied was biased in favor of males. We suspect that this bias may be less marked in the present era, but we lack systematic empirical evidence to confirm this view.

Researching the Review Process. The ideological influence perspective on journal decision making suggests other issues that concern defining, maintaining, and communicating a social reality. Specifically, it appears useful to develop and test hypotheses about the mechanisms and dynamics through which the editors (and reviewers) of journals in a field are selected and monitored (including an examination of selection criteria), about the content that is included and excluded in journals as a result of the manuscripts that are accepted and rejected by editors (and reviewers), and about the likely roles that dominant coalitions might play in determining, interpreting, and maintaining ideology through their relationship to the manuscript review process. This perspective also directs us to a concern with the selection, training, and reward systems used to find, prepare, monitor, and motivate scholars in the various fields of science.

Focus on social class, on institutional, sex-structured, and other stratification patterns of scholars who research, edit, and publish in a field, is important. Equally important is an examination of the historical development of journals to attempt to understand the process of ideological influence on editorial decision making. If biased selection of editors occurs in journals, how does it occur? Are certain research groups excluded by virtue of inbreeding within research communities or covert networks of scholars? Lewin and Duchan (1971) and White (1970) suggest that bias against selection of women as journal editors may occur because men are reluctant to sponsor women in professions and are also reluctant to include them in informal networks of information and association that might serve to increase the visibility of women in the research communities from which editors are drawn. It is possible that influences such as social class may operate differentially in different subfields in a scientific community. For example, editorial boards of journals in some subfields of social science have a high representation of women and of minority groups, while this is not so in journals of other subfields.

One criticism of scholars in social science fields is that their research efforts are frequently opportunistic and entrepreneurial. Critics argue that topics chosen are faddish, research findings are published piecemeal, studies are rarely longitudinal, and systematic programs of research are rare (Dunnette, 1963; Nord, 1978,1980). Examinations of the existence, extent, and effects of these practices in the context of the selection, training, and reward systems of a field may well prove fruitful.

The issues identified above are likely to be amenable to research techniques such as content analysis, interviewing, documentary analysis, and participant observation. Application of techniques and orientation from fields such as her-meneutics and literary criticism should also prove useful in seeking answers to questions about ideological influences and the publication of research (Burke, 1966; Edelman, 1971, 1977; Gusfield, 1976; Huff, 1983; Toulmin, 1958).

Ideological Influence Applications to the Manuscript Review Process

Our major concern when analyzing the manuscript review process from a societal perspective is with ideologies and with domination. Strategies intended to reduce the communicative distortion inherent in such domination (Habermas, 1973, 1975), and to encourage innovativeness of actors in the review process, ought to emphasize minimization of dominance—through actions on system-wide variables—linked to manuscript review decisions.

From this societal perspective, reducing power differentials may require voluntary or institutionalized action. Voluntary power sharing can be facilitated by the creation of a community of organizational scientists who can and will choose to encourage the development of diverse approaches to the assessment of knowledge. The content and intent of selection, training, and reward systems in the field ought to emphasize and support risk taking in decision making; tolerance for alternative interpretations of reality; ease and skill in use of power-sharing tactics; efforts to invent, rather than imitate, in developing and disseminating knowledge; and an orientation toward problems and situations that favor diversity rather than uniformity (Frost, 1980; Weick, 1979).

At this macro-societal level of influence, actors impinging on the review process include ruling elites and various publics, most notably the professional readership in the field. Providing structured avenues to shared power and thus greater flexibility and innovativeness in the process involves increasing the options and reducing the dependencies that actors have on other actors engaged in the decision process. Funding and other resources provided to authors, editors, and reviewers ought to be free from constraints intended to influence choices of topics, and recommendations and decisions on manuscript publication. Funding ought to allow actors the flexibility to go elsewhere for decisions and actions, to initiate new ideas, to start new journals, or to bypass the journal altogether through books or other media forms.

A different strategy for minimizing communicative distortion and for increasing innovativeness involves establishing or facilitating informal and formal avenues for the exercise of countervailing power in a scientific system. Formal countervailing power can be created by establishing boards of appeal to whom people can take grievances relating to the production and publication of scientific knowledge (Newman, 1966). An author who feels intimidated or wronged in the review process could appeal a review decision and have the manuscript subjected to independent assessment. Readers who perceive censorship of ideas and methodologies could have recourse to the same device. Another strategy for opening the journal system to new ideas involves representation of different paradigms to key decision-making committees in a field.

Informal countervailing power can be established through legitimation and encouragement of lobbying behavior by people who perceive inequalities and abuses of power in the review process of journals in their field. A norm for scientists that stresses collective action to press for change would likely stimulate diversity and awareness of alternatives in the process.

A more radical strategy with implications for avoiding dysfunctions in the field has been advocated by Nord (1978). He suggested that the manuscript review process in academic journals be eliminated. This has the obvious advantage of saving a number of the costs associated with the review process. The costs saved are reviewers' time, the opportunity costs incurred by rejecting valuable manuscripts, and the loss of manuscripts containing at least some sound original ideas. In addition to these cost savings, the "open gate" policy produces the benefits of deemphasizing the importance of publications in career development and professional status and, we hope, its adoption would lead to less gamesmanship and more emphasis upon publication quality rather than quantity. This is important where publications have become ends in themselves rather than means for reporting and advancing knowledge.

Nord's prescription has its costs, some of which he acknowledges. He speculated that in the short run the journals would be plagued by a glut of low-quality articles and that the number of pages would be costly to publish. However, he suggested that the use of a researcher's number of publications to evaluate his or her career progress would be less attractive and researchers might become more concerned with presenting a complete development of their work rather than rushing into print with its dissected parts. Nevertheless, abolition of editorial review as a basis for publication of manuscripts remains a high-risk venture, which is unlikely to be embraced by journals, in which editors perceive a need for control of costs, publication time, and quality. Nord's proposed strategy is intended as a jolt to scientists, to generate thought and discussion about extremes in the operation of academic journals on a field.

THE GOVERNMENTAL POLITICS
MODEL OF MANUSCRIPT REVIEW

The governmental politics perspective views decision making as the political result of bargaining among organizational actors. This model focuses attention on the perceptions, motivations, power, and maneuvers of players in a political game. Decisions are made by pulling and hauling among the organizational actors—the impact of these actors is depicted in terms of their access to the game and to the regularized channels of action in the organization, to their power and skill, and to their desire to use this power. Power is assumed to be influenced by variables such as position (in the game), expertise, control over information, ability to influence other players' objectives, access to others with information, and so forth. Actors take stands and act in the bargaining exchange in terms of their power, their perspectives on the problem, their stakes in the issue, and the deadlines that are attached to decisions.

Manuscript review decisions are seen as the outcomes of bargaining among key actors. Evidence of the political nature of the review process comes from several sources. Pfeffer, Leong, and Strehl (1977) have pointed out that the assessment of the worth of social science research output is far more subjective and more political than is the case with physical science research. They observed greater use of particularistic standards of evaluation (assessments influenced by nepotism, friendship, professional affiliation, and so forth) in social than in physical science fields. Mahoney (1977), in a controlled experiment, reported reviewer bias against manuscripts containing results contrary to reviewers' theoretical perspectives. Similarly, Abramowitz, Gomes, and Abramowitz (1975) observed that reviewers with leftist leanings provided more generous evaluations of manuscripts containing data supporting proactivism of students than those containing data supporting antiactivism students. Mahoney, Kazdin, and Kenigsberg (1978) found a correlation between self-citation by authors and reviewers' acceptance of manuscripts. In a study of editorial decisions in management and social science journals, Kerr, Tolliver, and Petree (1977) reported author reputation as being positively correlated with manuscript acceptance. Sil-verman (1976), drawing on his experience as an editor of the *Journal of Higher Education,* described the boundary spanning covert roles an editor plays as a means of accomplishing goals and of getting things done. The editor, in Silver-man's experience, is sometimes a methodologist, sometimes a scholar. On occasions, he is an organizational man (Silverman's terms) and, at other times, a social being; each role is a response to different organizational actors and issues.

Frost et al. (1981), in a preliminary report of interviews with organizational science journal editors, observed that an important source of editors' perceived power resides in their conscious choice of reviewers. Publication of controversial or marginal manuscripts, in this sense, depends on the choice of potentially sympathetic or hostile reviewers.

Rodman and Mancini (1977) identify three areas of editorial decision making that are not open equally to all actors in the review system. These are submissions by authors who are sponsored by individuals of special status, inside track submissions that come from authors having a special relationship with editors, and background communications between some—but not all—parties to a review decision (e.g., confidential reviewer comments to editors or telephone, luncheon, and other informal discussions between editors and reviewers about an author's submission, and so on). Rodman and Mancini report that editors acknowledge a high incidence of each of these three events. While their findings do not reveal what editors do in response to such submissions, in combination with the research cited above, they do provide a sense of the political nature of at least some aspects of the review process.

Given the lack of agreement among social scientists as to what constitutes valuable research and what a given manuscript contributes to a field, and given the prevailing uncertainty as to causes and effects in prevailing models and theories in social science, it is perhaps reasonable to predict that the review decision outcome will involve judgment and/or compromise among the various actors in the process (Thompson, 1967).

Decision-making strategies involving judgment and compromise have been depicted and discussed within the context of organizational choice by several authors (Baldridge, 1971; Cyert & March, 1963; Frost & Hayes, 1979; Pettigrew, 1973; Pfeffer, 1981; Pfeffer & Salancik, 1978). Such strategies include an important role for power and political behavior as determinants of decision outcomes. The power available to actors in the decision process appears to reside in organizational and individual sources. Hickson, Hinings, Lee, Schneck, and Pennings (1971) and Pfeffer (1981) identify some organizational sources such as level of formal authority, degree of control over resources, accessibility to information, and ability to reduce uncertainty for other organizational members. French and Raven (1960) identify some individual sources (frequently linked to organizational sources) such as level of expertise and personal charisma.

Researching the Review Process.   The manuscript review decision perceived as a political game or process brings into focus several actors, the most important ones being, perhaps, the editor, the reviewer, and the author. These three actors can be depicted as a triad as well as in various dyadic combinations (editor-author, editor-reviewer, author-reviewer). Each of these actors brings to such interactions various resources and personal characteristics that provide him or her with power bases from which to influence the manuscript review decision. The bases include formal authority or position power (perhaps most applicable to the editor), control over information (for example, ground rules for manuscript acceptability), access to audiences and legitimation of ideas (a gate-keeping role available to editors and reviewers), availability of alternative manuscripts and of outlets for manuscripts, as well as the actor's status (often institutionally linked), and technical expertise.

Research that examines power differences and relationships among these key actors should prove of considerable value in understanding how manuscript decisions are made. It should be possible to identify conditions in which actors are relatively equal in power in the triad or in a given dyad as well as those in which actors are relatively unequal in power. Different behaviors by respective actors and different outcomes would be expected under each of these two conditions. We should expect, under conditions of relatively equal power, for example, that behavior of the actors would approximate a negotiated or bargained outcome involving extensive dialogue between the actors.

We should expect, under conditions of unequal power, that the behavior of actors would be different. The high-power actor will perhaps attempt to define and impose a reality on the low-power actors. Actors with high power relative to other actors in an exchange relationship have considerable discretion to influence the outcomes of that exchange. What they do with this discretion will likely be a function of their values and intentions and of the consequences of their actions once implemented. Intentions and values apart, power has the capacity to corrupt the power holder, particularly in the sense that powerful actors may treat less powerful actors in demeaning ways, devaluing the worth of the latter's work and treating the low-power actor as an object—as a means to an end— rather than as another human being or as a colleague in the research enterprise (Nord, 1977). Under such conditions, low-power actors become alienated from the process (Israel, 1971).

Studies of married couples, employer-servant, and manager-subordinate relationships in which power differences between actors were either large or small lend support to this view (Kipnis, 1972; Kipnis, Castell, Gergen, & Mauch, 1976). Kipnis and his colleagues, in field and laboratory studies, observed that people with power frequently attempted to influence those without power. They believe that they control the less powerful person's behavior and performance and think poorly of the latter and of his or her original contribution to any outcomes in the relationship. They observed also that individuals with high power tend to distance themselves psychologically and socially from those with low power.

Research is necessary into the potential existence, level, and nature of alienation among editors, authors, and reviewers who have low power in a review relationship. Some possible scenarios for low-power actors in this process are sketched below.

The low-power actor, if alienated by a relationship with an actor of high power, may simply disengage, ending the process. Alienated editors, reviewers, or authors may withdraw from the process and may simply cease contributing to the production and assessment of scientific knowledge. (Latane, 1979b, ascribes a decline in manuscripts submitted to the *Journal of Personality and Social Psychology* during 1977 to the dissatisfaction that authors felt with editorial policies introduced at that time.)

Alternatively, authors can choose to withdraw from the spirit and intention of the scientific process while giving it lip service, contributing only in a mechanical sense. For example, an alienated author who desires visibility and recognition in his or her field may give up attempts to contribute original creative work, including the pursuit of interesting and researchable ideas, and attend to research that has already been defined and assessed as real and valuable by the more powerful editors or reviewers. Alienation in this case is reflected in a channeling of research efforts toward "playing the game"—to "making it"—in the system. Such alienated behavior among actors is likely to produce mindless, bureaucratic, uncreative research and to encourage unimaginative, conservative reviewing, and is likely to yield editorial actions on manuscripts that reinforce the status quo.

Powerful editors can also influence the content of a manuscript revision, perhaps unduly. For example, the terms an editor lays out for revision of a manuscript may be such that an author is faced with having to give up the essence of his or her style and substance to ensure that it is published in the journal.

Alienated behavior may include falsification of data to make it acceptable for publication, tapping more powerful individuals to influence the review process, accepting manuscripts to repay or incur favors or to keep material from competing journals, and self-interested recommendations of flawed manuscripts that support the recommender's own research. These are not easy behaviors to document empirically, yet researchers such as Snell (1973) and Ceci and Peters (Holden, 1980), who falsified previously published manuscripts by changing author names and some minor manuscript content, found that the falsifications went largely undetected in the review process. Ceci and Peters rewrote abstracts, altered the opening sentences and inserted fake names and institutional affiliations on 10 articles published in 10 widely read psychological journals. These papers were resubmitted to the journals in which they had previously been accepted. Only three of the journals detected the deception. Snell submitted previously published manuscripts containing minor modifications of content and his own, rather than the actual author's, name to five journals. None of the journals spotted the changes. Snell points out that more subtle plagiarisms and falsifications are likely to succeed if the author presents impressive, though false, evidence in a manuscript.

Wolins (1962) encountered the data falsification issue in a study in which he reanalyzed the data supplied to him by five authors. In seven reanalyses, he found errors of sufficient magnitude to change the results of the studies involved. Twenty-one other authors who replied to Wolins's request for data from their recently published works indicated that their data were either lost, misplaced, or accidentally destroyed.

Alienated actors may resist rather than withdraw from the review process. They may attempt to overthrow the existing system so as to redress the power imbalance, or they may attempt to create new journals that provide them with more power and a different outlet for their manuscripts. Examples of both actions are likely to be found among scientific journals and are amenable to research that would test these and other hypotheses.

Viewing manuscript decisions as a political process involving the use and perhaps the abuse of power by key actors in the process identifies aspects of decision making that are very different than those that emerge when the decision is looked at as a rational action or as the outcome of interacting organizational routines. It highlights negotiated as well as possibly covert manipulative aspects of the publishability decision.

Governmental Politics Applications to the Manuscript Review Process

Modifying the balance of power between and among actors in the review process can be accomplished by *intervention,* by altering the power differential in a specific review situation, in effect by managing power differentials, or by *design,* by institutionalizing power-sharing structures that are intended to apply to all review decisions. Power in each case may be given to, or taken from, others.

Managing Power Differentials—Cooperative Strategies. Actors in a power relationship have both latent and actual (used) power (Bachrach & Baratz, 1962; Heydebrand, 1978; Nord, 1976). Efforts to manage high power differentials require that actors with high power act to reduce the differential in a given situation by using less than their full power, or that they harness the differential in ways beneficial to other actors in the exchange (Deutsch, 1949, 1962). Laboratory studies of behavioral and attitudinal outcomes when power is used in cooperative rather than competitive contexts support the notion that actors with high power can work productively with low-power actors provided the context is congenial (Tjosvold, 1982; Tjosvold & Deemer, 1980). In Tjosvold's studies, highland low-power actors in a competitive context were suspicious of each other, withheld resources, and developed negative attitudes toward one another. Low-power actors reported high insecurity about the relationship. Opposite outcomes were observed in a cooperative context. High- and low-power actors developed a liking and trust for each other and a willingness to work toward common goals.

Strategies that incorporate two-way communication between actors, integrative problem solving rather than competitive (win-lose) responses, and coaching rather than judgmental/critical behavior provide opportunities for minimizing existing power differentials (Blake & Mouton, 1961; Filley, 1975; Meyer, Kay, & French, 1965).

Actions by editors pertinent to manuscript review decisions include use of additional reviewers for controversial manuscripts, author selection of reviewer pools for editors to choose from, author-referee dialogues prior to editorial decisions on manuscripts (Glenn, 1976), choice of sympathetic rather than critical reviewers, editors acting as referees on manuscript assessment where the content requires special attention, and editor/referee coaching of authors for manuscript revision.

Strategies such as those outlined above emphasize greater power sharing between editor and author through greater participation on the part of the author in the decision process. However, participation is not a sufficient condition for equalizing power (Locke & Schweiger, 1979; Mulder & Wilke, 1970). The crucial action appears to be use of participation by the high-power actor to increase the expertise, the expert power base of other actors in the exchange. For example, the editor may provide, through communication of extensive feedback from reviewers and him- or herself, insights into the manuscript material that allow the author to improve the quality of the manuscript substantially (whether for resubmission to the journal or to be sent elsewhere). Editors of several organizational science journals do this with some or all author submissions.

Managing Power Differentials—Conflict Strategies.   Actors with high power may intervene in particular situations to modify the power balance. Editors with high relative power may choose to overrule referees whose actions or recommendations (e.g., cursory reviews, personal attacks) contravene the spirit of fair assessment. Editors can threaten to reveal a reviewer's name to an author if a tardy review is not forthcoming. Rodman (1970) has reported success with this strategy. Reviewers with high relative power can threaten resignation if they perceive an editorial decision to be manipulative.

Conflict strategies also provide an opportunity for intervention attempts by actors with low relative power toward modifying the power balance. For example, referees with low relative power can petition or create a lobby of reviewers to confront editors or authors perceived to be abusing the decision process.

Authors with low relative power can move to multiple submissions of their manuscript to journals to gain leverage (Peters, 1976). Authors can also intervene by persisting, by reasserting the case for a paper with an editor/referee when it has been rejected (Kosinski, 1979).

Strategies such as coaching or intervention are not cost-free, of course. They involve considerable investments of time and effort by both high- and low-power actors and may extensively delay the decision time for a manuscript. Applied to many authors and manuscripts, the strategies may lead to serious publication delays. Cooperative, coaching strategies may also create conditions in which the author, if overly compliant and trusting, yields his or her ideas in the manuscript to the judgments and recommendations of the editor or the reviewer (the high-power actor). The resulting manuscript may be an improved product but it may cost the author's integrity. This is perhaps particularly a danger when manuscript acceptance is tied to institutional decisions in promotion or tenure affecting an author. The benefits of coaching low-power actors likely outweigh the costs, nevertheless.

Conflict strategies such as multiple submissions will probably overload journals already burdened with high submissions. It is not inevitable that an author will take the first manuscript acceptance he or she gets from a journal (Turner, 1976). However, given the orientation of minimizing power differences between actors such as editor and author, ground rules can no doubt be worked out. Authors could be asked to specify to which journals a manuscript has been sent and agree, in return for speedier reviews, to a deadline for accepting or rejecting a journal's acceptance of a manuscript (Turk, 1976).

Institutionalizing the Equalization of Power. Strategies discussed above reflect acceptance of existing power differentials between actors and emphasis is upon strategies for managing power imbalance in specific situations. Other strategies can be focused on designing systems to equalize power across situations in a journal. Research on communication and information networks suggests that power equalization and effective decision making for complex tasks is best accomplished by establishing all channel rather than star or chain networks (Bavelas, 1950). Review situations in which one actor has high formal power relative to other actors facilitate and sustain the differential when one actor receives all the inputs and controls the flow of information to each of the other actors. This is perhaps the pervasive structure for most review processes in prestigious scientific journals. The powerful editor is at the center of the process and is the only actor dealing directly with other actors in the process. The restricted communication network also facilitates increased power of reviewers relative to authors because the latter must proceed in relative ignorance of how the reviewer evaluates manuscripts. The power potential of the reviewer is particularly high in blind reviews. The reviewer can make recommendations with relative impunity because he or she does not have to confront the author. Glenn (1976) has suggested that critiques by reviewers be submitted to authors for response before the editor makes a decision on whether to accept or reject the papers. The author would be allowed to respond only to major points and factual errors made by the reviewer.

The network can be altered to equalize power among actors by opening channels, thereby increasing the chances of redistributing expertise and authority, which are the bases of expert and formal power (Mulder & Wilke, 1970). Multiple exchanges between editor, reviewer, and author are feasible in an era of conference call technology and professional association meetings, both national and international. In addition, viewing the review board or panel as part of the network suggests that editors, authors, and reviewers can call for activation of additional channels and interactions to further reduce power inequalities. Policy on all channel networks can include membership of panels as negotiated outcomes, that is, members are proposed and selected by editors, authors, and referees. The *Personality and Social Psychology Bulletin,* a journal perceived to be both innovative and efficient, requests as standard policy that authors nominate three potential reviewers of their manuscript at the time of submission. The journal also instituted a system for evaluating journal functioning on an ongoing basis but dismantled it due to lack of interest (Latane', 1979a).

The primary disadvantages or costs of structural changes are the potential for time delays in the review and publication decision outcomes and, perhaps more substantively, the protection of reviewer and author from biases that may be associated with removing the "blind" character of a review, which is intended to minimize recommendations and decisions linked to personal likes and dislikes between actors. Nevertheless, the identity of authors can frequently be detected in blind reviews—especially in very specialized research areas where the community of researchers is small. To ensure a truly blind review, the process should include the editor. Only administrative personnel really need to see the name of the author to correspond with the author. However, if the editor is not blind to the author's identity, then negotiated, shared communication channels may prove beneficial to author and journal.

Institutionalizing power equalization in journals may yield a new set of biasing factors. We anticipate that it would slow the review process. Given an emphasis on negotiation and on two-way communication, it is also possible that it would favor strong personalities with high interpersonal competence.

THE ORGANIZATIONAL
PROCESSES MODEL OF MANUSCRIPT REVIEW

This perspective depicts decisions as outcomes of organizations operating in regular, systematic ways, the unit of analysis being organizational action. The model assumes that organizations function according to established procedures, routines, and standard operating procedures (SOPs). It also assumes that these programmed organizational processes establish the context and, to a large degree, constrain the choices open to decision makers at the top of organizations and thus constrain organizational action. It also includes the condition in which the absence of programs and standard operating procedures for dealing with organizational events can constrain choice.

Most editors inherit a system of routines and procedures for selecting and rejecting manuscripts when they take on the job. In addition, there are SOPs and routines that originate outside the journal organization and are acquired by editors and reviewers from the training and indoctrination received during their "apprenticeship" and in subsequent years (Mintzberg, 1979). Thus it is possible to depict two sets of routines: the bureaucratic and the professional. Changing bureaucratic routines can be accomplished by altering the things organizations attend to; changing professional routines requires changes in the actors involved in the process.

The decision to accept or reject or request revision of a manuscript is an organizational action, the result of interacting between the routines and procedures practiced by governing bodies, editorial boards, reviewers, managing and copyediting departments, suppliers, printers, readers, and authors. The editor deciding on the publishability of a given manuscript is constrained by the nature of the journal's mandate (for example, to publish empirical versus conceptual material), by production deadlines, by space and cost limitations, by the quality focus, by the number of manuscript submissions, by the turnaround time of reviewers assessing manuscripts, as well as by the procedures and approaches that reviewers use to make and convey recommendations to the editor.

The existence of routines for processing a manuscript (for example, assessment guidelines to reviewers, deadlines for first decision notification to authors, decision rules for resolving reviewer disagreements, and so on) and the implementation of these routines impinge on and shape the editor's decision. They constrain what the editor can do with a manuscript, and this may be either functional or dysfunctional for dissemination of knowledge in a field. Absence of such routines may also affect the decision outcome. So the nature and speed of decision making varies because of the presence or absence of reviewer routines and procedures. Whitley (1970) observed that a highly institutionalized reviewer system involving a formal review board produced faster editorial decisions on manuscript publishability than did an informal arrangement involving an editor and his immediate colleagues. This suggests that a formal mechanism such as an editorial board may improve the efficiency of the review process.

McNamara and Woods (1977) surveyed published articles in four psychological journals and concluded that an absence of editorial policies and procedures in these and other journals has led to a failure of journal editors to detect and reject unethical studies in social science literature. Rodman (1970) identifies the absence of standardized procedures for reviewers as a prime cause of delays in editorial decisions about manuscripts.

Research into manuscript review as an organizational process has been limited largely to a concern with reviewer routines and procedures. The research has centered on the nature and extent of interreviewer agreement on manuscripts and prescriptions for improving the level of agreement through such approaches as standardized assessment forms, reviewer training, and so forth. Researchers disagree on the level of interreviewer agreement that occurs in the review process. For example, among pairs of reviewers who examined 193 manuscripts, Smigel and Ross (1970) report 72.5% agreement to accept or reject a manuscript. Scott (1974), on the other hand, using decision data from a two-year period as associate editor of the *Journal of Personality and Social Psychology,* reported a correlation of only $r = .26$ between reviewers on the crucial "recommended to accept" decision. McReynolds (1971) found an interreviewer reliability of $r = .45$ among reviewers of conference research papers. Based on a hypothetical model of editorial review as a probabilistic process, Stinchcombe and Ofshe (1969) argued that reviewer assessment of the true worth of manuscripts is highly error prone and that many good papers are likely to be rejected by the typical review process. But, generally, theory and research about organizational processes has not been applied to the manuscript review decision.

Researching the Review Process. Manuscript review decisions and the organizational procedures and routines that constrain them can also be studied in terms of the relative utility of alternative organizational structures and designs for effective decision making. For example, processing manuscripts from submission by authors to final editorial decision and publication or rejection can be examined in terms of structural variables such as centralization, standardization, coordination, and their interrelationships (Blau & Schoenherr, 1971; Mintzberg, 1979). Similarly, journal organizations can be studied as systems (Burns & Stalker, 1961), in terms of the nature of differentiation and integration mechanisms in organizations (Lawrence &

Lorsch, 1967), in terms of information processing (Galbraith, 1973), interdependence of work units (Thompson, 1967), innovation management
(Duncan, 1976), or requisite variety (Weick, 1979). Organizational research
that deals with strategic choice (e.g., Child, 1972) should provide avenues
for the systematic study of the interaction between editors and the organizational routines that they must deal with in review decisions.

Organizational Processes Applications to the
Manuscript Review Process

Some researchers argue that editorial decision making would be improved
if the reviewer procedures were better harnessed. Newman (1966), for example, recommends that editors publish standards and acceptance criteria that
reviewers should adhere to (and that authors can attend to in preparing manuscripts). He also recommends the use of at least three reviewers for each
article. Wolff (1973) urges development of objective checklists and training
programs so that, ideally, manuscripts can be assessed by trained clerks.
Bowen, Perloff, and Jacoby (1972) express similar sentiments. Scott (1974),
however, argues that the editor's decision on suitability of a manuscript is
inherently a judgment call based on reading reviewer comments and recommendations and the manuscript itself. Given the lack of paradigm development in the social sciences and the diversity of orientations in any given
social science field, a low level of interreviewer agreement perhaps accurately reflects the facts of social science research. Scott stresses the need to
develop procedures that will protect the author from arbitrary and narrowly
based decisions on a submitted manuscript rather than developing schemes
and routines that attempt to create a convergence of reviewer assessments.

Scott argues that, while an editor may have to make the final judgment
on manuscripts, the application of some existing decision strategies involving the development of voting procedures and routines may prove to be useful ways of improving reviewer inputs to the editorial decision. For
multiple-attribute decision making, the least demanding procedure for
aggregating preferences regarding manuscript characteristics is, perhaps,
for the reviewer or editor to set preference constraints (Coombes, 1964;
Dawes, 1971), an approach commonly used in cognitive process studies. A
number of such constraints can be set up to operate either conjunctively (all
must be satisfied) or disjunctively (only one needs to be satisfied). The constraints may be set up sequentially and may depend on the results of preceding evaluations. The usual operating mode with these procedures is to
search for an alternative that satisfies the constraints, without trying to

determine whether a better alternative exists. This procedure could be applied appropriately to choice of manuscripts for publications given that manuscripts typically are judged at one time against criteria that exist in the minds of reviewers and editors. It also permits shifts in constraints to reflect experience of reviewers creditors with regard to quality of manuscripts available to the journal.

The procedures discussed above are useful for multiple-person situations because different reviewers can impose different constraints. Hence their preferences can be reflected without trying to aggregate them into a simple social choice function.

One group of voting strategies involves the SPAN technique proposed by MacKinnon and MacKinnon (1969). Each member of a reviewing panel, for example, would be given a fixed number of votes that he or she could allocate directly to manuscripts being reviewed or to other reviewers. The underlying rationale is that reviewers should allocate votes to other reviewers when the former feel they have less knowledge than do other reviewers and when they can identify other reviewers' greater expertise. This process is iterated in SPAN until all votes are distributed to alternatives. The major advantage of SPAN voting as an application to the manuscript review process is that more knowledgeable evaluations would result because the preferences of reviewers would be weighted according to their recognized expertise. A disadvantage may be the concentration of evaluation of manuscripts on certain topics in the hands of a relatively small number of recognized authorities who may tend to resist new ideas. Of course, the SPAN voting strategy would require that all reviewers be known to each other.

In applying the logrolling strategy to manuscript review processes, reviewers would be permitted to trade off votes on manuscripts that they consider relatively unimportant, but that other reviewers may consider very important, in exchange for future votes on manuscripts that they feel are very important (Buchanan & Tullock, 1962; Coleman, 1966). By use of this method, even a relatively non-influential single reviewer (not aligned with a coalition) can express some of his or her preferences. This process may operate in manuscript review procedures at present through reviewers informing the editor, for example, that, "after all, I have not accepted many of the manuscripts I have reviewed, therefore this one that I feel strongly about should be accepted." The advantage of formalizing the procedure is to ensure that many neutral votes will not mask the strong preferences that are expressed by a few reviewers. If no reviewer feels strongly about a manuscript, it will not be accepted.

Attention to design of the journal organization should improve the conditions under which the editor decides the fate of a manuscript. The review decision (the outcome of organizational processes) may be improved by the establishment of routines and systems that coordinate and sequence the movement of the manuscript through its various phases, while preserving flexibility to attract and assess content that is innovative and requires special treatment in some way. To attain optimum flexibility and consistency in organizations, Hedberg, Nystrom, and Starbuck (1976) invoke the metaphor of organizations as tents and prescribe minimum levels of organizational elements such as consensus, consistency, and rationality. Duncan (1976) suggests an ambidextrous organization to accomplish these objectives. Weick (1977) suggests the development of self-designing systems to increase efficiency and innovation in organizations.

Duncan's prescription of an ambidextrous organization is informative and illustrates the application of organizational processes ideas to journal design. The editor seeking to produce, in a timely fashion, manuscripts that contribute significantly to the field, needs an organization that processes innovative submissions efficiently. Organizational goals, rules, and procedures that clarify and distinguish what is needed by each organizational unit and actor (e.g., reviewers, managing editors, copy editors, authors, and so on) and that coordinate their activities ought to facilitate an efficient process of translating manuscripts into published acceptances or redirected rejections. On the other hand, handling and assessing the innovative content of manuscript submissions requires, in Duncan's terms, a more flexible organizational component and ways to harness the reviewing and editorial functions that allow for flexibility and creativity of operations. Editors may need to establish a pool of reviewers, with greater diversity of characteristics in terms of age, minority representation, area of expertise, professional training or orientation, and so on, who can be retained to operate as a task force or a team, reporting to the editor in ways independent of the editor's regular reviewing board. They may be given a special mandate to seek out and help authors develop challenging or stimulating aspects of manuscripts that might otherwise be rejected, or to act as devil's advocates by responding to the review recommendations of other individuals who have a different mandate in the process.

Editors may recruit a project team of reviewers, perhaps appoint a project manager editor, and charge that group to develop and shape a special issue devoted to a particular research theme. This might permit an infusion into the journal organization of new ideas about the substantive content of the journal as well as the processes whereby manuscripts are selected.

The Duncan organizational process model applied to academic journals would require development of a broad policy and organizational structuring to allow one phase and one set of organization actors to pursue the review decision with a minimum of formality and centralized decision making and a high degree of complexity (in the sense of diverse, highly professional occupational specialties) so as to diagnose and assess innovative submissions. It would require a second phase and set of organizational actors to process the manuscripts to completion in the journal. This second phase would emphasize formalized rules and procedures, centralized decision making, and a low level of complexity. Integration of the two phases would be in the hands of the editor or of a team of editors, depending upon the extent to which the journal has been, or needs to be, differentiated (Lawrence & Lorsch, 1967). Duncan's ambidextrous organization may serve to make the constraints on editorial decisions due to organizational processes more manageable. Considerations of cost and availability of reviewers may make it unwieldy for some journals, however.

Other prescriptions for managing organizational processes include development of computerized listings of experts in a variety of fields as is used in the *Human Organization* journal. This allows an easily retrievable, diverse pool of potential reviewers for an editor to use. The potential costs of such an approach include installation and maintenance of the system and the potential unevenness in reviewer reports to an editor relative to those from a smaller board of regular reviewers. Latané (1979a) describes routines introduced into the operation of the journal *Personality and Social Psychology Bulletin,* which, in only five years, emerged as a major journal in its field. Successful routines included limitation of articles to four pages whenever possible; assessment of submission fees to share quality control costs with authors (this fee was discontinued when a new publisher, Sage, absorbed the production cost of the journal); instructions to authors to provide camera-ready copy of their manuscripts to save time and money (also discontinued because of adequate funding under Sage); and appointment of category or topic editors to spread the editorial workload more efficiently.

Increasing the requisite variety of a journal organization to match a complex and changing environment may be accomplished by creating diversity of representation in the editorial and reviewer roles on a journal. The recently founded journal *Organization Studies,* for example, has its publisher's main office in Berlin, an editor-in-chief located in Britain, a book review editor from the Netherlands, and an editorial board representing several schools of thought and several different nations. The editor-in-chief position is expected to rotate over the years and will include incumbents from different countries and institutions.

THE RATIONAL ACTOR MODEL
OF THE MANUSCRIPT REVIEW PROCESS

The rational actor perspective, one person or many persons acting in consort, depicts governmental decision making in terms of choice among alternatives made by a single, consistently purposeful actor. If an action occurs, it is assumed that there must be a goal or objective that may be expressed in terms of a "payoff or "preference" function. Understanding decisions made by this unitary actor involves vicariously putting oneself in the decision maker's place in a particular situation so as to understand the actor's goals, objectives, alternatives particular to the situation, and consequences attached to each alternative. Given the constraints of the situation, the actor's choice among alternatives is predicted in terms of optimizing some value of the actor.

The rational actor resembles Merton's (1973) normative scientist who applies objective standards to research. The normative scientist is emotionally detached and consciously disinterested in the outcomes of such research and is objective and detached when assessing research output from any source, including his or her own work. The model can apply to authors preparing manuscripts for submission to journals or to reviewers assessing such submissions because it is assumed they act rationally in making decisions. In terms of the rational actor, the decision to publish or reject a manuscript is primarily a function of the journal editor's preferences, actions, and objectives.

The editor, as a rational actor, decides the fate of a manuscript in terms of one or more purposes, such as to publish manuscripts that contribute significantly to the field or to create or maintain a particular level of prestige or excellence for the journal in the field. The editor's preferences may include emphasis on empirical rather than theoretical work; his or her alternatives may include publication frequency, or the journal size, use of reviewer recommendations, or availability of comparable manuscripts.

Some researchers have studied editors' objectives and preferences in manuscript assessment. Chase (1970) reported "logical rigor" in a research manuscript as the criterion ranked of primary importance to editors in a sample of editors from natural and social science journals. However, she observed differences in criteria rankings between editors of physical (hard) science and those of social (soft) science journals. Natural scientists' high-ranked criteria were "replicability of research techniques," "originality," "mathematical precision," and "coverage of the literature." Social scientists' high-ranked criteria were "logical rigor," "theoretical significance," and "applied significance."

More recently, Lindsey (1978) analyzed responses of 265 editorial board members of psychology, sociology, and social work journals to an inventory of research values comprising 12 items designed to reflect the essential criteria of scientific inquiry. The most important criterion for publication as judged by editors in this study was the "value of an author's findings to the field." Other important criteria included "grasp of design," "sophistication of methodology," "theoretical relevance of material," and "creativity of ideas." These results reflect self-report responses to prespecified sets of publishability criteria and are informative.

Whitley (1970) describes a case study of editorial decision making in two social science journals, one interdisciplinary and one purely disciplinary in focus. He examined the manuscript acceptability decision in terms of reviewer and author characteristics such as professional age and number of publications. Differences were observed between reviewers of the two journals in terms of decision-making characteristics. High-publishing reviewers for the interdisciplinary journal accepted more manuscripts than did low-publishing reviewers. No such distinction was observed among reviewers for the "pure" discipline journal.

Little is known of the ways editors actually choose and order their decision preferences or their purposes or goals. The research cited above only gives an indication of editors' purposes, but this research requires augmentation through modeling what editors actually do in reaching their decisions.

Researching the Review Process. From a rational actor perspective, several existing decision models appear applicable to a study of the editors' decision-making process. In situations where a number of similar decisions are made over time by a decision maker, as is the case with journal editors, it is possible to build a simple model of these behaviors (Slovic & Lichtenstein, 1971). For example, on manuscript review decisions, the accept/reject assignments can be the dependent variable and the characteristics of manuscripts reviewed can be independent variables. A linear regression model can then yield coefficients describing the decision maker's behavior. Using this approach, insights into decision rules can also be obtained for individual reviewers and for editorial boards. Given a sufficient number of manuscript choices over time, shifts in decision rules can be identified or decision rules used by different editors can be compared.

Another approach for aggregating preferences regarding manuscripts is to apply a subjective weighting model. Regression procedures, based on actual choices or ratings of an editor, can be used. Alternatively, decision makers can be asked directly for their preferences and these figures can be used to obtain a coefficient. In such cases, it is usual to separate the scaling of intra-attribute values from the interattribute weighting of importance. This allows for curvilinear relationships reflecting the worth of various attribute values to decision makers (Miller, 1970).

The weighting of importance of attributes can be related to higher order objectives of journals; the instrumentality of attributes in reaching ends higher in some goal hierarchy (such as significant contribution to a field) determines the weighting (Sayeki & Vesper, 1973). Direct assessment models are common to many areas of decision making and have a long history, being represented, for example, in Benjamin Franklin's (1772/1956) "moral algebra."

An alternative rational analytic approach to the study of manuscript review is suggested by research into opinion revision by individuals processing information. Rather than attempting to analyze the processes involved in reviewing manuscripts (attributes of manuscripts, criteria, and so on), one could describe manuscript decisions in terms of the extent to which the opinions of editors (or reviewers) are revised when they consider hypotheses investigated in the manuscript under review with regard to the findings reported. Lykken (1968) develops this approach as a means of determining theory corroboration and conclusiveness of research reports. The value and publishability of manuscripts is assessed, therefore, in terms of the extent of opinion revision, given the nature and outcome of the hypothesis testing process. While authors implicitly or explicitly confirm or revise their opinions on the hypotheses tested, and such considerations no doubt influence decisions on what they will do with the material, it is the nature and extent of opinion revision by editors and reviewers that is most relevant here.

Systematic application of the rational actor perspective to the review process should provide useful insights into how editors (as well as authors and reviewers) make decisions about manuscripts and their publishability. It is unlikely that the perspective will explain all or perhaps even a sizable proportion of variance in the decision process, however. Editors make decisions in the context of organizational constraints. Other variables and processes require consideration if we are to more fully understand the review process. Furthermore, the rational actor perspective as a model of the behavior of scientists has been subject to criticism. For example, Mitroff (1974) observed and described the passionate pursuit of theories by moon scientists and the strong personal bias that scientists displayed in assessing the worth of their own and others' research.

Manuscript review described as an opinion revision process based on overall contribution to knowledge has limitations. Among these are the following: (a) It requires that hypotheses be explicitly stated; (b) relatively large opinion revision is necessary to justify publishing a manuscript; (c) replications, either direct or systematic, are not encouraged; and (d) inputs must be combined if more than one person's opinion (e.g., a panel of reviewers) is involved.

Rational Actor Applications to the Manuscript Review Process

Making explicit to authors the preferences of reviewers and of editors, establishing clearly for authors the ground rules for acceptance or rejection of manuscripts, should aid them in deciding whether and in what way their manuscripts ought to be submitted to any given journal. Moreover, clarification of goals and preferences permits an examination of journal operational policies in the light of objectives of related professions. Clarification of the variables in the rational actor's decision-making process should help make explicit, also, the risk-taking propensity of the decision maker. A particular stance by an editor (conservative or risky) toward publishing manuscripts can be more easily reinforced or altered once it has been clearly articulated. Another way of clarifying the rational actor's decision process would be to publish from time to time shortened versions of "rejected" manuscripts along with comments of reviewers (Nord, 1978). Erickson (1977) describes publication of a manuscript in a criminology journal with accompanying reviewer comments and author responses. Such practices ought to prove valuable to authors and to students of the review process.

THE MANUSCRIPT REVIEW PROCESS RECONSIDERED

In this chapter we have viewed the manuscript review process used by scientific journals from four perspectives and have explored ways to advance understanding and practice of this aspect of journal functioning. The ideological influence, governmental politics, organizational process, and rational actor approaches to decision making offer many concepts and techniques relevant to such an analysis. In addition, our multiple-lens analysis of the manuscript review process suggests a variety of strategies and tactics that might be applied to improve the process. If the accumulated social science knowledge concerning the manuscript review process is to effectively advance journal functioning, it will be necessary for us, as a community of scholars, to examine the quality of our journals, their efficiency, the innovativeness of their content, and the fairness of journal procedures for members of a scientific community. We also need to demonstrate a readiness to implement changes in the manuscript review processes of journals where needed. Before academic journal policies and practices can be modified, individuals in established positions of power in a field must be willing to bear much of the risk inherent in initiating and sustaining changes. Such concerns, issues, and changes appear to us to pose major challenges to scientific fields such as our own in the years ahead. We are hopeful that our professional journals will fulfill their potential for advancing the social sciences.

REFERENCES

Abramowitz, S. I., Gomes, B., & Abramowitz, C. V. (1975). Publish or politic: Referee bias in manuscript review. *Journal of Applied Social Psychology, 5*(3), 187-200.

Allison, G. T. (1971). *The essence of decision.* Boston: Little, Brown.

Bachrach, P., & Baratz, M. S. (1962). The two faces of power. *American Political Science Review, 16*(4), 947-952.

Baldridge, J. F. (1971). *Power and conflict in the university.* New York: John Wiley.

Bavelas, A. (1950). Communication patterns in task oriented groups. *Journal of Accoustical Society of America, 22,* 725-730.

Bedeian, A., Downey, H. K., Price, K. E., & Salancik, O. R. (1980). *Strategies for maximizing acceptance of your research by journals.* Unpublished transcript of symposium presented at the Academy of Management national meetings, Detroit.

Berger, P., & Luckmann, T. (1966). *The social construction of reality.* New York: Doubleday.

Blake, R. R., & Mouton, J. S. (1961). Reactions to intergroup competition under win-lose conditions. *Management Science, 7,* 420-425.

Blau, P. M., & Schoenherr, R. A. (1971). *The structure of organizations.* New York: Basic Books.

Bowen, D. D., Perloff, R., & Jacoby, J. (1972). Improving manuscript evaluation procedures. *American Psychologist, 27,* 221-225.

Buchanan, J. M., & Tullock, C. (1962). *The calculus of consent.* Ann Arbor: University of Michigan Press.

Burke, K. (1966). *Language as symbolic action.* Berkeley: University of California Press.

Burns, T., & Stalker, G. M. (1961). *The management of innovation.* London: Tavistock.

Chambers, J. M., & Herzberg, A. M. (1968). A note on the game of refereeing. *Applied Statistics, 17,* 260-263.

Chase, J. M. (1970). Normative criteria for scientific publication. *American Sociologist, 5,* 262-265.

Child, J. (1972). Organization structure, environment, and performance: The role of strategic choice. *Sociology, 6,* 1-22.

Clark, C. X. (1973). Introduction: Some reflexive comments on the role of editor. *Journal of Social Issues, 29*(1), 1-9.

Clegg, S. (1975). *Power, rule and domination.* London: Routledge & Kegan Paul.

Coleman, J. S. (1966). The possibility of a social welfare function. *The American Economics Review, 56,* 1105-1122.

Coombes, C. H. (1964). *A theory of data.* New York: John Wiley.

Crane, D. (1967). The gatekeepers of science: Some factors affecting the selection of articles for scientific journals. *American Sociologist, 2,* 195-201.

Cyert, R., & March, J. G. (1963). *A behavioral theory of the firm.* Englewood Cliffs, NJ: Prentice Hall.

Dawes, R. M. (1971). A case study of graduate admissions: Applications of three principles of human decision making. *American Psychologist, 26*(2), 180-188.

Deutsch, M. (1949). An experimental study of the effects of cooperation and completion upon group process. *Human Relations, 2,* 199-231.

Deutsch, M. (1962, November). Cooperation and trust: Some theoretical notes. In *Nebraska Symposium on Motivation.* Lincoln: University of Nebraska Press.

Duncan, R. B. (1976). The ambidextrous organization: Designing dual structures for innovation. In R. Kilmann, L. R. Pondy, & D. Slevin (Eds.), *The management of organization design, research, and methodology* (Vol. 1, pp. 167-188). New York: North Holland.

Dunnette, M. D. (1963). Fads, fashions and folderol. *American Psychologist, 21,* 343-352.

Edelman, M. (1971). *Politics as symbolic action.* Chicago: Markham.

Edelman, M. (1977). *Political language: Words that succeed and policies that fail.* New York: Academic Press.

Erickson, R. V. (1977). From social theory to penal practice: The liberal demise of criminological causes. *Canadian Journal of Criminology and Corrections, 19*(2), 170-191.

Filley, A. C. (1975). *Interpersonal conflict resolution.* Glenview, IL: Scott, Foresman.

Franklin, B. (1952). Letter to Joseph Priestley. Reprinted in *The Benjamin Franklin sampler.* New York: Fawcett. (Original work published 1772)

French, J. R. P., & Raven, B. (1960). The bases of social power. In D. Cartwright & A. F. Zander (Eds.), *Group dynamics* (2nd ed., pp. 607-623). Evanston, IL: Row Peterson.

Frost, P. J. (1980). Blindspots in the study of organizations: Implications for teaching and application. *Group and Organizational Studies, 5*(2), 169-177.

Frost, P. J., & Hayes, D. C. (1979). An exploration in two cultures of political behavior in organizations. In A. Negandhi & G. W. England (Eds.), *Cross-cultural studies in organization functions.* Kent, OH: Kent State University Press.

Frost, P. J., Taylor, R. N., & Cummings, L. L. (1981). *Editorial and review processes.* Unpublished paper presented at plenary session, Administrative Sciences Association of Canada, Halifax, Nova Scotia.

Galbraith, J. R. (1973). *Designing complex organizations.* Reading, MA: Addison-Wesley.

Glenn, N. D. (1976). The journal article review process: Some proposals for change. *American Sociologist, 11,* 179-185.

Gouldner, A. W. (1976). *The dialectic of ideology and technology.* New York: Seabury.

Gusfield, J. R. (1976, February). Literary rhetoric of science: Comedy and pathos in drinking driver research. *American Sociological Review, 41,* 16-34.

Habermas, J. (1973). *Theory and practice* (J. Viertel, Trans.). Boston: Beacon.

Habermas, J. (1975). *Legitimation crisis* (T. McCarthy, Trans.). Boston: Beacon.

Hedberg, B. L., Nystrom, P. C., & Starbuck, W. H. (1976). Camping on seesaws: Prescriptions for a self-designing organization. *Administrative Science Quarterly, 21*(1), 41-65.

Heydebrand, W. (1978). Book review of critical issues in organizations. In S. Clegg & D. Dunkerley (Eds.), *Administrative Science Quarterly, 23*(4), 640-645.

Hickson, D. J., Hinings, C. R., Lee, C. A., Schneck, R. C., & Pennings, J. M. (1971). A strategic contingencies theory of intra-organizational power. *Administrative Science Quarterly, 16,* 216–224.

Holden, C. (1980, September). Not what you know but where you're from. *Science, 209,* 1097.

Huff, A. S. (1983). A rhetorical examination of strategic change. In L. R. Pondy, P. J. Frost, G. Morgan, & T. C. Dandridge (Eds.), *Organizational symbolism.* Greenwich, CT: JAI Press.

Israel, J. (1971). *Alienation: From Marx to modem sociology.* Boston: Allyn & Bacon.

Kerr, S., Tolliver, J., & Petree, D. (1977). Manuscript characteristics which influence acceptance for management and social science journals. *Academy of Management Journal, 20,* 132-141.

Kipnis, D. (1972). Does power corrupt? *Journal of Personality and Social Psychology, 24,* 33-41.

Kipnis, D., Castell, P. J., Gergen, M., & Mauch, D. (1976). Metamorphic effects of power. *Journal of Applied Psychology, 61,* 127-135.

Kosinski, J. (1979, February 19). Polish joke: How the publishers got stung. *Tune.*

Kuhn, T. S. (1970). *The structure of scientific revolutions* (2nd ed.). Chicago: University of Chicago Press.

Latané, B. (1979a). *Journal of Personality and Social Psychology:* Problem, perspective, prospect. *Personality and Social Psychology Bulletin, 5*(1), 19-31.

Latané B. (1979b). *Personality and Social Psychology Bulletin:* Five year summary. *Personality and Social Psychology Bulletin, 5*(4), 418-419.

Lawrence, P. R., & Lorsch, J. W. (1967). *Organization and environment.* Cambridge, MA: Harvard Graduate School of Business Administration.

Legge, K. (1978). *Power, innovation and problem-solving in personnel management,* London: McGraw-Hill.

Lewin, A. Y., & Duchan, L. (1971). Women in academia. *Science, 173,* 892-895.

Lindsey, D. (1978). *The scientific publication system in social science.* San Francisco: Jossey-Bass.

Locke, E. A., & Schweiger, D. M. (1979). Participation in decision-making: One more look. In B. M. Staw (Ed.), *Research in Organizational Behavior, 1,* 265-339.

Lykken, D. T. (1968). Statistical significance in psychological research. *Psychological Bulletin, 70,* 151-159.

MacKinnon, W. J., & MacKinnon, M. J.. (1969). Computers: The decisional design and cyclic computation of SPAN. *Behavioral Science, 14.*

Mahoney, M. J. (1977). Publication prejudices: An experimental study of confirmatory bias in the peer review system. *Cognitive Therapy and Research, 1,* 161-175.

Mahoney, M. J. (1978). Publish and perish. *Human Behavior, 2,* 38-41.

Mahoney, M. J., Kazdin, A. E., & Kenigsberg, M. (1978). Getting published. *Cognitive Therapy and Research, 2*(1), 69-70.

McNamara, J. R., & Woods, K. M. (1977). Ethical considerations in psychological research: A comparative review. *Behavior Therapy, 8,* 703-708.

McReynolds, P. (1971). Reliability of ratings of research papers. *American Psychologist, 25,* 400–401.

Merton, R. K. (1973). *The sociology of science: Theoretical and empirical investigations,* Chicago: University of Chicago Press.

Meyer, H. H., Kay, E., & French, J. R. P., Jr. (1965). Split roles in performance appraisal. *Harvard Business Review, 43,* 123-129.

Miller, J. R., III. (1970). *Professional decision making.* New York: Praeger.

Mintzberg, H. (1979). *The structuring of organizations.* Englewood Cliffs, NJ: Prentice Hall.

Mitchell, M. B. (1951). Status of women in the American Psychological Association. *American Psychologist, 6,* 193-201.

Mitroff, I.I. (1974). *The subjective side of science.* Amsterdam: Elsevier.

Mulder, M., & Wilke, H. (1970). Participation and power equalization. *Organizational Behavior and Human Performance, 5,* 430-448.

Newman, S. H. (1966). Improving the evaluation of submitted manuscripts. *American Psychologist, 21,* 980-981.

Nord, W. R. (1976). Developments in the study of power. In W. R. Nord (Ed.), *Concepts and controversy in organizational behavior* (pp. 437-450). Pacific Palisades, CA: Goodyear.

Nord, W. R. (1977). Job satisfaction reconsidered. *American Psychologist, 1026-1035.

Nord, W. R. (1978). Comparison and extensions on Frost's and Weick's analysis of blindspots. *Group and Organizational Studies, 5*(2), 189-197.

Nord, W. R. (1980). Toward an organizational psychology for organizational psychology. *Professional Psychology, 11*(3), 531-542.

Peters, C. B. (1976). Multiple submissions: Why not? *American Sociologist, 11,* 165-179.

Pettigrew, A. M. (1973). *The politics of organizational decision making,* London: Tavistock.

Pfeffer, J. (1981). *Power in organizations.* Marshfield, MA: Pitman.

Pfeffer, J., Leong, A., & Strehl, K. (1977). Paradigm development and particularism: Journal publication in three scientific disciplines. *Social Forces, 55,* 938-951.

Pfeffer, J., & Salancik, G. R. (1978). *The external control of organizations.* New York: Harper & Row.

Rodman, H. (1970). The moral responsibility of journal editors and referees. *American Sociologist, 5,* 351-357.

Rodman, H., & Mancini, J. A. (1977). Editors, manuscripts and equal treatment. *Research in Higher Education, 7,* 369-374.

Sayeki, Y., & Vesper, K. H. (1973). Allocation of importance in a hierarchical goal structure. *Management Science, 19,* 667-675.

Scott, W. A. (1974). Interreferee agreement on some characteristics of manuscripts submitted to the *Journal of Personality and Social Psychology. American Psychologist, 29*(9), 689-702.

Silverman, R. J. (1976). The education editor as futurist. *Teachers College Record, 77,* 473-493.

Slovic, P., & Lichtenstein, S. (1971). Comparison of Bayesian and regression approaches to the study of information processing in judgements. *Organizational Behavior and Human Performance, 6.* 649-744.

Smigel, E., & Ross, H. L. (1970). Factors in editorial decision. *American Sociologist, 5,* 19-21.

Snell, J. C. (1973, May). Editorial standards and authenticity of manuscripts: An earlier generation revisited. *The American Sociologist, 8,* 90-91.

Stinchcombe, A. L., & Ofshe, R. (1969). On journal editing as a probabilistic process. *American Sociologist, 4,* 116-117.

Teghtsoonian, M. (1974). Distribution by sex of authors and editors of psychological journals 1970-1972: Are there enough women editors? *American Psychologist, 29,* 262-269.

Thompson, J. D. (1967). *Organizations in action.* New York: McGraw-Hill.

Tjosvold, D. (1982). Effects of approach to controversy on superior's incorporation of subordinates' information and decision making. *Journal of Applied Psychology, 67*(2), 189-193.

Tjosvold, D., & Deemer, D. K. (1980). Effects of controversy within a cooperative or competitive context on organizational decision making. *Journal of Applied Psychology, 65*(5), 590-595.

Toulmin, S. E. (1958). *The uses of argument.* Cambridge: Cambridge University Press.

Turk, A. T. (1976). Replies to Calvin Peters. *The American Sociologist, 11,* 169-170.

Turner, R. H. (1976). Replies to Calvin Peters. *The American Sociologist, 11,* 168-169.

Wade, N. (1979, May). To accept is to reject: The publishing paradox. *Science, 487.*

Weick, K. E. (1977, Autumn). Organization design: Organizations as self-designing systems. *Organizational Dynamics,* pp. 31-46.

Weick, K. E. (1979). *The social psychology of organizing* (2nd ed.). Reading, MA: Addison-Wesley.

White, M. S. (1970). Psychological and social barriers to women in science. *Science, 170,* 413-416.

Whitley, R. D. (1970). The formal communications system of science: A study of the organization of British social science journals. *Sociological Review, 16,* 163-179.

Wilson, J. (1973). *Introduction to social movements.* New York: Basic Books.

Wolff, W. M. (1973). Publication problems in psychology and an explicit evaluation scheme for manuscripts. *American Psychologist, 28*(3), 257-261.

Wolins, L. (1962). Responsibility for raw data. *American Psychologist, 17,* 657-658.

Yoels, W. C. (1971). Destiny or dynasty: Doctoral origins and appointment patterns of editors of *The American Sociological Review,* 1948-1968 (*&. American Sociologist, 6,* 134-139.

Yoels, W. C. (1974). The structure of scientific fields and the allocation of editorships on scientific journals: Some observations on the politics of knowledge. *Sociological Quarterly, 15,* 264-276.

7 The Role of Theory in Research Methods

J. GILL AND P. JOHNSON

A n attempt is made to introduce the essential, largely philosophical, issues underpinning much of the remaining chapters. This chapter first briefly explores the inter-relationship between theory and practice making the point that there is nothing so practical as a good theory. It then covers the theoretical foundations of inductive and deductive approaches to research and finally compares them.

Theory and Practice

Although we might not be immediately aware of it, our everyday lives are fundamentally interwoven with theory. One important aspect of this 'theory-dependent' character relates to the way in which the various practical activities in which we routinely engage might be seen as involving regular attempts to create, apply and evaluate theory.

Our use of the term 'theory-dependent' must not be confused with the term 'theory-laden'. Although the two are related, the latter specifically refers to the way in which the prior theories and values of the observer influence what he or she 'sees'; that is, as Hanson (1958, p. 7) claims, 'there is more to seeing than meets the eyeball'. Thus the issue of how observation is 'theory-laden' raises the problem that there is no independent or neutral point from which an observer might occupy and objectively observe the world and thus all knowledge is knowledge from particular points of view or paradigms (see Burrell and Morgan, 1979). The methodological implications of the 'theory-laden' nature of observation are considered later; meanwhile, we shall use the term 'theory-dependent' to refer to the way in which human practical activities entail the application of theory in various ways.

To many readers, particularly those who might perceive themselves as 'practical people', this might seem an absurd assertion. Often such a view is expressed in the lament of vocationally orientated management and business students, to which we referred in Chapter 1, that particular courses are too 'theoretical' or 'academic' and hence irrelevant to the 'real' world of their chosen careers. Intriguingly this lament, which is an example of what Grey and Mitev call management *technicism* (1995, pp. 77–8), resonates with the archaic Platonic–Aristotelian view that theoretical knowledge was knowledge acquired for its own sake, rather than for some use.

Both Plato and Aristotle severed theory from practice in the sense that they distinguished between *episteme* (genuine theoretical knowledge that was an end in itself) and *doxa* (opinions or beliefs suitable only for the conduct of practical affairs). For many commentators such a view tended to endow a passivity and submissiveness on the part of people to nature's vagaries. However, to some extent this view of knowledge and science lost its dominance during the seventeenth and eighteenth centuries with the arrival of a new version of the scientific enterprise articulated by people such as Francis Bacon (Johnson and Duberley, 2000; Tiles, 1987). This emphasized the necessity for science to provide knowledge and theory for the control of nature through the discovery of physical regularities which allowed for the prediction of, intervention into and manipulation of nature.

Moreover, as we shall try to demonstrate, the conception of theory as being divorced from practice is grounded in a misunderstanding of the nature and purposes of theory.

During our everyday lives we all regularly attempt to understand the events that occur around us. For instance, in regard to the social behaviour of the people with whom we have regular contact, whether colleagues at work or friends and neighbours, we routinely have expectations about the way they will behave in particular circumstances. These expectations are closely tied to explanations of why they behave in the ways that they do. These expectations and explanations might concern rather mundane events such as a friend's change in mood or the behaviour of particular groups of colleagues at work, or even more personally distant events such as the performance of the national cricket team or the apparent nationwide increase in the incidence of particular types of criminal

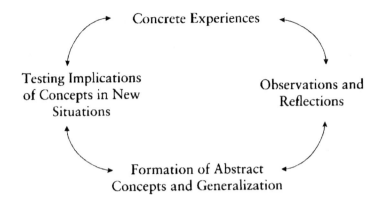

Figure 3.1 Kolb's experiential learning cycle (Kolb, Rubin and McIntyre, *Organization Psychology: An Experiential Approach*, 1979, p. 38. Reprinted by permission of Prentice-Hall Inc., Englewood Cliffs, NJ

behaviour. Regardless of the particular focus of these expectations and explanations, when the former are not fulfilled or when the latter appear to be wrong, we will often reflect upon recent events and experiences and thereby begin to generate new webs of explanations and expectations that help us understand and cope with the events that impinge upon us (Law and Lodge, 1984, p. 125). This process might result in our changing the way in which we do things, such as how we relate to friends or communicate with colleagues at work.

For Kolb, Rubin and McIntyre (1979), although their terminology is somewhat different, the above processes are linked to how human beings learn and might be diagrammatically represented by the model in Figure 3.1.

According to Kolb, learning might start with the experience of an event or stimulus, which the individual then reflects upon in trying to make sense of it. This might lead to the generation of explanations of how or why something happened the way it did – explanations that can then be used to form an abstract rule or guiding principle that can be extrapolated (or generalized) to new events and stimuli of a similar type to that already experienced. Indeed, for Kolb, learning can start at this point where such a rule is merely received from others by the learner, along with its web of explanations and expectations, and is subsequently applied by that learner and thereby tested out. In either case, whether the rule is received or generated out of the prior experience and reflection, its testing in new situations creates new experiences which enable consequent reflection, observation and ultimately new rules. Kolb, Rubin and McIntyre (1979) suggest that particular individuals might emphasize particular elements of the learning cycle due to the presence of particular predilections into which they have been socialized.

For our purposes here, what is very significant about the processes described above is that they might be seen as attempts at constructing and evaluating explanatory statements, or theories, about what is going on around us. As Friedman (1953) puts it, such theories might be seen as 'filing systems' which allow observations to be used for predicting (i.e. they create expectations) and explaining events. For instance, consider the following statements/views:

1. The notion that a friend's evident irritability is due to his or her inability to get sufficient sleep the previous night.
2. The proposition that capital punishment deters would-be murderers.
3. The claim that the demise of English test-match cricket is due to too many one-day matches being played in county cricket.
4. The idea that improved training provision will create a more productive, reliable and satisfied workforce.

These four statements are all theories. They are all characterized by an attempt at explaining observations and, from those explanations, predictions or expectations might be generated. In this they reveal an important aspect of a theory – that it can be used to guide our practical actions, e.g. if we do A then B will happen, if we don't do A then C will happen. Taking theory 4 above, we could thus claim that if we improve a workforce's training we should expect an increase in employee productivity, reliability and satisfaction. By actually attempting to do this, and then by observing what happens, we can evaluate the accuracy of that theory; an outcome of that evaluation may be a retrospective change in the nature of theory 4 so as to make it more accurate.

Indeed, it is this latter process of the evaluation and change of theory, which is so often haphazard and imprecise, that for some commentators (e.g. Kidder and Judd, 1986, p. 5) separates science from common sense. Basically, it is claimed that 'science' entails deliberate and rigorous searches for bias and invalidity – processes which a range of commentators have noted to be remarkably lacking when it comes to management's appropriation of organizational recipes deriving from 'management gurus' (Huczynski, 1993) or copied from other institutions (Cappelli, *et al.*, 1997; Scott and Meyer, 1994).

Theories and hypotheses

Now, to elaborate upon the above, it is necessary to consider more closely what a theory is and attempts to do. Although the terms 'theory' and 'hypothesis' are often used interchangeably, in its narrowest sense a theory is a network of hypotheses advanced so as to conceptualize and explain a particular social or natural phenomenon. In this, each hypothesis presents an assertion about the relationship between two or more concepts in an explanatory fashion. Concepts are the building blocks of theories and hypotheses in that they are 'abstract ideas which are used to classify together things sharing one or more common properties' (Krausz and Miller, 1974, p. 4).

For instance, in theory 4, or more accurately hypothesis 4 above, 'improved training', 'productive', 'reliable' and 'satisfied' are all concepts. Moreover, we can see that theory 4 links together these concepts in an explanatory way. Such explanations are usually causal – that is, they state that one aspect of our world causes, or leads to another (see Pratt, 1978, pp. 65–7, for an elaboration of what is meant by 'cause' and its importance); that A causes or leads to B (i.e. in theory 4, improved training causes or leads to a more productive, reliable and satisfied workforce).

An alternative example might be a hypothetical assertion that

1. a participative management style causes or leads to job satisfaction among the manager's subordinates; and
2. job satisfaction causes or leads to increased productivity.

From 1 and 2 we might infer that

3. a participative management style causes or leads to increased productivity among the manager's subordinates.

Obviously this theory would normally state the underlying reasoning behind the postulated associations between management style, job satisfaction and productivity. Although this example seems deceptively simple, hypotheses can be much more complex, not only in terms of being interlinked with other hypotheses but also by bringing in qualifying concepts that limit the causal relationship to particular classes of phenomena, e.g. A causes B only in conditions of C.

For instance, we could rewrite our initial hypothesis that a participative management style causes job satisfaction among subordinates by limiting its applicability to conditions where subordinates are motivated primarily by the desire for intrinsic rewards. By implication, where those conditions do not apply, neither does the hypothesis or eventual theory.

In trying to understand and explain the social and natural phenomena that surround us, and in our attempts at making decisions about what to do in particular circumstances, nobody escapes making or assuming these kinds of theoretical linkages. Every intentional act can be seen as an attempt to produce some desired state of affairs. This implies the belief on the part of the actor that a causal relationship exists between his or her decision, or act, and the state of affairs he or she desires. In this sense much of our everyday social lives and our work activities are in essence theory-dependent activities. Now this clearly illustrates the conjectural and practical aspects of theory, since people act in accordance with their expectations, or prejudices, as to what will happen in particular circumstances – conjectures often derived from impressions regarding what has previously happened in similar circumstances. Thus, even the most mundane activity, such as walking down a street, might be considered in terms of an actor applying theoretical assertions, virtually without thinking about them in a conscious fashion, that are borne out by being able to accomplish that activity. Often it is only when we become aware that our expectations, that are grounded in such tacit or taken-for-granted knowledge, have not been met (perhaps due to the intervention of some capricious circumstances) that we begin consciously to re-evaluate the webs of causal relationships that have previously been used to orientate our action. Out of this re-evaluation we begin to generate a new theory to account for the previously unconsidered anomalies. So, to paraphrase Douglas (1970, pp. 80–103), such tacit knowledge is ordered and reordered according to the ebb and flow of situations.

So it is evident that theories are a means by which we generate expectations about the world; often they are derived from what we have perceived to have happened before and thus they influence (tacitly or otherwise) how we set about future interactions with our world(s). Moreover, it is also evident that if we have the expectation that by doing A, B will happen, then by manipulating the occurrence of A we can begin to predict and influence the occurrence of B. In other words, theory is clearly enmeshed in practice since explanation enables prediction which in turn enables control.

Indeed, one could argue that science has to some degree enabled the explanation and prediction of aspects of nature and thereby has allowed for human beings to exercise increasing control over nature. The advances in medicine, engineering and agriculture, for example, can all be considered in this light.

Theory and management control

However, our concern in this review is with a substantive domain, management, that is essentially dependent upon the social sciences (see Lupton, 1971) in that its concern is primarily with the macro/micro-behaviour and activities of human beings. Moreover, if we were to agree with commentators as varied as Braverman (1974, p. 68), Mant (1977) or Stewart (1982) there appears to be an inextricable relationship between management and the control of the behaviour of subordinates so as to ensure that the latter accomplish particular tasks. If this is so, the importance of theory so as to enable such a control process is only too evident: as Pugh (1971, p. 9) claims, every managerial act rests upon 'assumptions about what has happened and conjectures about what will happen; that is to say it rests on theory'.

As we have implied above, managers in their everyday activities rely upon both theories deriving from their 'common sense' and theories deriving from social science research. Although, as we shall see, the differences between the two are subtle and complex, many social scientists would ostensibly claim that the differences relate primarily to the extent to which social science research incorporates the overt and rigorous search for bias (Cook, 1983, p. 82), while common sense does not. For instance, Kidder and Judd (1986, p. 18) claim that

> social scientists look for biases and pitfalls in the processes used to support and validate hypotheses and submit their conclusions to the scrutiny of other scientists who attempt to find biases that were overlooked. The casual observer or ordinary knower often gathers evidence in support of hypotheses without being aware of or worried about the biases inherent in the process.

As we have already noted, the danger in uncritically and unreflectively acting upon commonsense theories and hypotheses of the casual observer may be that one entraps oneself in the current 'traditions' or 'fads' dominant among the social groups to which we belong or defer to, at work or elsewhere. Although these traditions and fads may at first sight appear plausible as they 'create order out of disorder' (Huczynski, 1993, p. 198), the potential for 'groupthink', so vividly described by Janis (1972), is only too clear.

These issues provide a very useful starting point for considering the processes by which social science theories are constructed, evaluated and justified. In other words, what are the sources of such theories and hypotheses, and how do we set about judging rigorously whether or not these theories and hypotheses are true?

Different answers to these questions enable us to distinguish between different social science research methods: that is, we can differentiate between research methods that are deductive and those that are inductive.

Deduction

A deductive research method entails the development of a conceptual and theoretical structure prior to its testing through empirical observation. As the reader may realize, deduction in this sense corresponds to the left-hand side of Kolb's experiential learning cycle (see Figure 3.1) since it begins with abstract conceptualization and then moves on to testing through the application of theory so as to create new experiences or observations.

To many researchers working within the deductive tradition, the source of one's theory is of little significance (Popper, 1967, pp. 130–43) – it is the creative element in the process of science that is essentially unanalysable. Instead what is important is the logic of deduction and the operationalization process, and how this involves the consequent testing of the theory by its confrontation with the empirical world. Essentially the process of deduction might be divided into the following stages.

Concepts

The researcher decides which concepts represent important aspects of the theory or problem under investigation. As we have seen, concepts are abstractions that allow us to select and order our impressions of the world by enabling us to identify similarities and differences, e.g. 'efficient', 'social class', 'authoritarian', 'satisfied', and so on.

The theory, or hypothesis, of interest links two or more concepts together in a causal chain – a set of untested assertions about the relationship between the concepts.

However, since concepts are abstract they are not readily observable, and therefore the asserted relationships between concepts provided by the theory are not open to empirical testing until these abstractions are translated into observables or indicators – that is, they have to be operationalized.

Rules

Through the operationalization of a concept it becomes defined in such a way that rules are laid down for making observations and determining when an instance of the concept has empirically occurred. For instance, take the concept 'managerial level' – something that is regularly used by some researchers to identify similarities and differences between the people with whom we come into contact, e.g. junior managers, middle managers and senior managers. But when people use this concept to categorize others, they often do so in vague and varied ways. For instance, the term 'middle manager' used by one person may mean something very different when used by another. They may appear to be talking about the same things when in fact they are not: e.g. one person might mean people in a certain income bracket, someone else may identify 'middle manager' with accent or educational background, but not income. Essentially, what these people are doing is operationalizing a concept in different ways and hence creating different meanings.

Operationalization

Therefore by creating rules for making observations we are making a clear definition of what it is we are going to observe. In this we create indicators, or measures, which represent empirically observable instances or occurrences of the concepts under investigation. That is, we overtly link the abstract concept to something that is observable and whose variation is measurable. The linking rules, that is, the rules about when and where an observable instance of the concept has empirically occurred, are called operationalizations (see Figure 3.2). The point of these rules is that, by using the same indicators of a concept, and by standardizing the recording of the results of any observation, it should be possible to have a 'reliable' measure of the relevant concept.

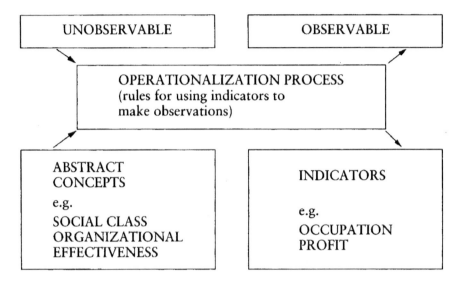

Figure 3.2 Operationalizing concepts

There is a great deal of choice regarding how we operationalize concepts such as 'managerial level' or 'organizational efficiency' and it may be instructive at this point to try Exercise 3.1.

Instructions

The process of operationalization enables the construction of clear and specific instructions about what and how to observe. This enables the testing of hypotheses and theories by confronting them with the empirical data, which is then collected. In this testing, priority is given to what are considered directly observable phenomena and behaviour: things, events or activities which are publicly observable and hence can be corroborated and agreed upon by other observers. This emphasis upon the control of potential bias through replication by others has thus led to attempts to create standardized procedures for undertaking observation that can be followed exactly by those other researchers. This has in turn created the tendency in this approach to dismiss the analysis of the subjective or intangible since these kinds of phenomena, it is often claimed, cannot be directly observed in an unproblematic fashion and hence any findings cannot be corroborated through the replication of the research by other researchers.

Testing by corroboration

The outcome of the above is the process of testing, by which the assertions put forward by the theory or hypothesis are compared with the 'facts' collected by observation. Often, within the deductive tradition, once tested and corroborated the theory is assumed to be established as a valid explanation. Those explanations are often termed 'covering-law explanations' in that the observations or variables to be explained are covered by the assertions about those phenomena contained within the theory. However, since these covering-law explanations posit regular relationships between those variables, which hold across all circumstances, they not only explain past observations but also predict what future observations ought to be like. Take the example: 'water boils when heated to 100° centigrade, at sea level, in an open vessel'. This covering-law not only explains what has happened when water is heated to 100° centigrade in such circumstances but it also predicts what will happen if water is subjected to those conditions. However, in practice it is the statistical version of the covering-law, whereby the relationships asserted by the theory have only some degree of probability of obtaining across all circumstances, that has generally been adopted by social scientists working within this deductive tradition.

Exercise 3.1

1. Identify some alternative ways of operationalizing managerial level and organizational effectiveness with regard to the findings of research.

2. What do you think happens when we operationalize concepts in different ways?

What might this imply about deductive research methodology?

Corroboration problematic

We have used the term 'corroboration' above in a fairly unproblematic fashion; but what is possible in, and what is meant by, corroboration, is open to some dispute. Here we must turn to some of the debates that have taken place, and are continuing, in that branch of philosophy that has a concern with science: the 'philosophy of science'. What we are alluding to here has often been called 'Hume's problem of induction'. This problem arises because the testing of a theory inevitably involves a finite number of observations; and even if every observation that is made confirms the assertions put forward by a theory, logically we can never be certain whether some future observations might demonstrate instances in which the theory does not hold. It was Karl Popper, in perhaps one of his more famous contributions to the philosophy of science, who attempted to avoid the difficulties apparent in attempting to verify, or prove, a theory by a finite number of observations. Popper eschews 'verificationism', in which scientists attempt to prove or justify their theories, by proposing the maxim of 'falsificationism', in which scientists must attempt to refute their theories. At the risk of oversimplifying, what Popper (1967; 1972a; 1972b) proposes is that no theory can ever be proved by a finite number of observations – no matter how many confirmatory instances not yet observed which demonstrate the falsity of the theory. Take an example from Popper – that all swans are white; to Europeans this seemed self-evident, confirmed by millions of observations, until they explored the Australian continent. A further example of the potential problems created by 'induction' is provided by the statement 'one plus one equals two'. Again this appears self-evident, something that has been verified or confirmed by so many observations it would be impossible to count them. But according to the maxim of Popperian falsificationism, despite these numerous (but finite) confirmatory observations, we cannot be sure that some future instance might demonstrate its falsity, or limit its applicability. Indeed, such a consideration is to some extent borne out by the observations made in subatomic physics, that when two subatomic particles collide, their resultant fusion creates a mass that is sometimes more, or less, than their combined masses (Capra, 1975).

So, to summarize, Popper argues that while theories can never be proved true, they can be falsified, since only one contradictory observation is required. For Popper, therefore, the defining features of scientific theories are

1. they are capable of empirical testing;
2. scientists should not try to find confirming instances of their theories but, rather, should make rigorous attempts at falsifying them; and
3. science advances as falsified propositions and theories fall away leaving a core of theory which has not, as yet, been disproved.

For Popper, knowledge grows through the above processes whereby error is removed. It follows that a critical attitude is a fundamental distinguishing feature of both science and rationality. Indeed, for Popper (1967, p. 50), a dogmatic attitude

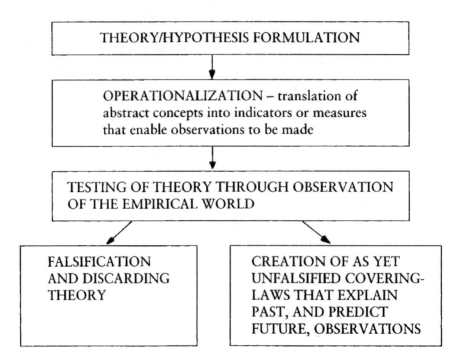

Figure 3.3 The process of deduction

> is clearly related to the tendency to verify our laws and schemata by seeking
> to apply them and confirm them, even to the point of neglecting refutations,
> whereas the critical attitude is one of readiness to change them – to test
> them; to refute them; to falsify them, if possible.

The deductive approach is summarized in Figure 3.3.

Problems with deduction

The deductive tradition in the social sciences (although, as we shall show later,
in Chapter 9, it is by no means unproblematic) clearly specifies what is involved
in being 'scientific knowledge'. Often the approach illustrated in Figure 3.3 is
called the 'hypothetico-deductive method'. It emphasizes that what is important
in 'science' is not the sources of the theories and hypotheses that the scientist
starts out with, rather it is the process by which those ideas are tested and justified that is crucial. Generally, the hypothetico-deductive approach to research is
intimately bound up with what is often termed 'positivism'. Three of the main
characteristics of positivism (there are others, which we shall consider later and
that are elaborated in Keat and Urry, 1975, Chapter 4) are

1. the view that, for the social sciences to advance, they must follow the hypothetico-deductive methodology used, with such evident success, by natural scientists (e.g. physicists) – in a nutshell, the experimental method;
2. the knowledge produced and the explanations used in social science should be the same as those proffered by the natural sciences – e.g. that A causes B; and
3. the above entails social scientists treating their subject-matter, the social world, as if it were the same as the natural world of the natural scientist.

It is from objections to the implications and assumptions of such a conception of social science that particular inductive approaches to research arise.

Induction

The logical ordering of induction is the reverse of deduction as it involves moving from the 'plane' of observation of the empirical world to the construction of explanations and theories about what has been observed. In this sense, induction relates to the right-hand side of Kolb's learning cycle (Figure 3.1), i.e. learning by reflecting upon particular past experiences and through the formulation of abstract concepts, theories and generalizations that explain past, and predict future, experience. In sharp contrast to the deductive tradition, in which a conceptual and theoretical structure is developed prior to empirical research, theory is the outcome of induction.

The debates and rivalry between supporters of induction and supporters of deduction, in both the natural and social sciences, have a long history (Ryan, 1970; Johnson and Duberley, 2000). However, the modern justification for taking an inductive approach in the social sciences tends to revolve around two related arguments.

First, for many researchers working within the inductive tradition, explanations of social phenomena are relatively worthless unless they are grounded in observation and experience. Perhaps the most famous rendition of this view is provided by Glaser and Strauss (1967) in their book *The Discovery of Grounded Theory*. In this they argue that in contrast to the speculative and a priori nature of deductive theory, theory that inductively develops out of systematic empirical research is more likely to fit the data and thus is more likely to be useful, plausible and accessible especially to practising managers (see: Tenbrunsel *et al.*, 1996; Partington, 2000).

Critiques of positivism

The second, and related, rationale articulated in support of an inductive approach arises more overtly out of a critique of some of the philosophical assumptions embraced by positivism. It is to this critique that we shall now turn.

As we have seen, one of the main themes of positivism and of much of the deductive tradition in the social sciences is a conception of scientific method constructed from what is assumed to be the approach in the natural sciences, particularly physics. This entails the construction of covering-laws that explain past and predict future observations, through causal analysis and hypothesis testing. The format of this explanation and prediction is

A causes B

or

Variation in A causes variation in B

that is

Stimulus A causes Response B

Specifically, it is this form of explanation and prediction that provides the initial point of departure for the ensuing critique that justifies much of inductivism in the social sciences.

At the risk of oversimplifying, many supporters of induction in the social sciences reject the causal model illustrated above because they consider that this kind of explanation is inappropriate. Although it may be adequate for the subject-matter of the natural sciences, it is not adequate for the social sciences. This is because there are fundamental differences between the subject-matter of the social sciences (human beings) and the subject-matter of the natural sciences (animals and physical objects) from which the covering-law model came.

This position is illustrated by Laing (1967, p. 53), who points out the error of blindly following the approach of the natural sciences in the study of the social world. 'The error fundamentally is the failure to realise that there is an ontological discontinuity between human beings and it-beings . . . Persons are distinguished from things in that persons experience the world, whereas things behave in the world.'

Here Laing is drawing attention to the following issues:

1. Human action has an internal logic of its own which must be understood in order to make action intelligible. It is the aim of social science to understand this internal logic.

2. The subject-matter of the natural sciences does not have this subjective comprehension of its own behaviour – it does not have an internal logic which the scientist must tap in order to understand its behaviour. Therefore the natural scientist can legitimately, and indeed has to, impose an external logic upon the behaviour of his or her subject-matter in order to explain it. But such methodology is inappropriate and does not explain the actions of human beings, due to their subjectivity. Thus the behaviour of a billiard ball might be adequately understood in terms of necessary responses caused by particular sets of stimuli in certain conditions; but the actions of the billiards players can be adequately explained only through reference to their subjective motives and intentions; their interpretation of the situation and their knowledge of the rules of the game.

3. Therefore, the social world cannot be understood in terms of causal relationships that do not take account of the situation that human actions are based upon the actor's interpretation of events, his or her social meanings, intentions, motives, attitudes and beliefs; i.e. human action is explainable only by understanding this subjective quality. Therefore human action is seen as purposive and becomes intelligible only when we gain access to that subjective dimension.

4. It follows that research in the social sciences must entail emic analyses, in which explanations of human action derive from the meanings and interpretations of those conscious actors who are being studied. Thus the etic analyses embraced by deduction, in which an external frame of reference is imposed upon the behaviour of phenomena, are inappropriate where the phenomena in question have subjective capabilities – it is this internal dimension that is the key to explanation in the social sciences.

Inductivists therefore reject the stimulus–response model of human behaviour that is built into the methodological arguments of positivism. 'Stimulus causes response' is rejected in favour of

(a) stimulus → experience and interpretation → response, *or*
(b) interpretation and meaning → action.

In (a) above, the actor's subjectivity is taken to be an 'intervening variable' that mediates between the stimuli coming from external social reality and subsequent human responses expressed as behaviour or action. In (b), however, the actor's subjectivity is accorded greater 'formative or creative' power in its own right. Thus the interpretation of reality, upon which actions are based, is not merely the medium through which external stimuli act (as in (b)). Rather, it has a projective quality in the sense that such subjective processes create the reality in which action arises (see Berger and Luckmann, 1967; Burr, 1995), and hence the conception that subjectivity mediates external stimuli becomes rather meaningless. All there is is that subjectivity.

Although these differences have resulted in somewhat different methodological traditions, both (a) and (b) above share a commitment to conceiving human action as arising out of actors' subjectivity. Thus the possession by human beings of a mind has freed them from the stimulus–response relationships that dominate the behaviour of 'natural phenomena' (see Mead, 1934). Obviously, this view has created particular methodological commitments:

1. It creates serious objections to the contention of some positivists, that social phenomena might be treated as being analogous to the 'it-beings' or 'things' of nature and thereby are amenable to a similar type of causal analysis in which the subjective or intentional dimension is lost. Instead, it is postulated that the difference between the social and the natural world is

   > that the latter does not constitute itself as 'meaningful': the meanings it has are produced by men in the course of their practical life, and as a consequence of their endeavours to explain it for themselves. Social life – of which these endeavours are part – on the one hand, is produced by its component actors, precisely in terms of their active constitution and reconstitution of frames of meaning whereby they organise their experience. (Giddens, 1976, p. 79)

2. These considerations create the need for social scientists to explain human behaviour adequately, to develop a sympathetic understanding of the frames of reference and meaning out of which that behaviour arises. This sympathetic understanding is sometimes called *verstehen*, and it entails 'fidelity to the phenomena under study' (Hammersley and Atkinson, 1983, p. 7).

3. The methodological implications of this perspective entail the avoidance of the highly structural approaches of deduction; these, it is usually argued, prevent and ignore the penetration of actors' subjectivity. This happens because the deductive researcher, prior to conducting empirical research, formulates a theoretical model of the behaviour of interest, which is then tested. Hence they impose an external logic upon a phenomenon which has an internal logic of its own. It is precisely the discovery of this internal logic, through empirical research, that is the concern of many supporters of induction in the social sciences. To achieve this, what is recommended are unstructured approaches to research that ostensibly allow for access to human subjectivity, without creating distortion, in its natural or everyday setting.

4. Naturally the prescriptions described above have caused the positivist counter-argument that because this kind of inductive research is unstructured, it is unreliable since it is not replicable and therefore bias cannot be ruled out. Indeed, many positivists regard the 'intuitive or empathic grasp of consciousness' as merely a possible source of hypotheses about human conduct and not a method for social science research in its own right (Giddens, 1976, p. 19).

Research Methods Compared

As a heuristic device, it is possible to construct a continuum of research methods that allows us to differentiate between different methods in terms of the various logics they bring to bear in conducting research. That is, we can discriminate between different methods in terms of their relative emphasis upon deduction or induction, their degree of structure, the kinds of data they generate and the forms of explanation they create. At each extreme of the continuum we can distinguish what are known as nomothetic and ideographic methodologies.

Nomothetic methodologies (Burrell and Morgan, 1979, pp. 6–7) have an emphasis on the importance of basing research upon systematic protocol and technique. This is epitomized in the approach and methods employed in the natural sciences, which focus upon the process of testing hypotheses in accordance with the standards of scientific rigour. Standardized research instruments of all kinds are prominent among these methodologies. Emphasis is therefore placed upon covering-law explanations and deduction, using quantified operationalizations of concepts in which the element of motive/purpose/meaning is lost, because of the need for precise models and hypotheses for testing.

Ideographic methodologies (Burrell and Morgan, 1979, pp. 6–7), on the other hand, emphasize the analysis of subjective accounts that one generates by 'getting inside' situations and involving oneself in the everyday flow of life. There is an emphasis upon theory grounded in such empirical observations which takes account of subjects' meaning and interpretational systems in order to gain explanation by understanding.

Any method adopts a position on a continuum according to its relative emphasis upon the above characteristics shown in Table 3.1.

Table 3.1 A comparison of nomothetic and ideographic methods

Nomothetic methods emphasize		Ideographic methods emphasize
1. Deduction	*vs*	Induction
2. Explanation via analysis of causal relationships and explanation by covering-laws (etic)	*vs*	Explanation of subjective meaning systems and explanation by understanding (emic)
3. Generation and use of quantitative data	*vs*	Generation and use of qualitative data
4. Use of various controls, physical or statistical, so as to allow the testing of hypotheses	*vs*	Commitment to research in everyday settings, to allow access to, and minimize reactivity among the subjects of research
5. Highly structured research methodology to ensure replicability of 1, 2, 3, and 4	*vs*	Minimum structure to ensure 2, 3 and 4 (and as a result of 1)

Laboratory experiments, quasi-experiments, surveys, action research, ethnography

◄──►

methodological continuum

It is to the various different methods (laboratory, quasi-experiments, surveys, action research and ethnography), their various commitments and characteristics, together with their use in management research, that we turn in the following chapters. First, however, we consider experimental research design.

Suggested Further Reading

H. Blumer's 'What is wrong with social theory' provides an interesting consideration of the role and nature of theory in social science, as does T. Lupton's *Management and the Social Sciences* with specific reference to management. For an interesting analysis of the interplay between management theory and practice the reader should see D. Tranfield and K. Starkey's *The Nature, Social Organization and Promotion of Management Research: Towards Policy.* Meanwhile for an incisive critique of technicism in management education we recommend C. Grey and N. Mitev's *Management Education: A Polemic.* Also useful for its focus on the world of the manager is P. Checkland's *Systems Thinking, Systems Practice.* Checkland, himself trained as a physical scientist, reviews the systems movement as a scientific endeavour to tackle the ill-structured problems of the managerial world. He comes to the conclusion that 'hard systems' engineering needs to be modified to something more appropriate which he calls 'soft systems' methodology. We have found the book to be particularly useful in helping students from a background in the physical or natural sciences to bridge the gap between 'hard' and 'soft' systems approaches to management research.

W. Wallace's *The Logic of Science in Sociology* elaborates an overview of the various elements in scientific research with particular reference to issues of induction and deduction. M. Lessnoff's *The Structure of Social Science* gives a detailed survey of many of the philosophical issues important in social science research, with an interesting focus upon the relevance of a natural science 'model' for research in the social sciences. P. Johnson and J. Duberley provide an overview of the key epistemological debates which influence management and organizational research in their book *Understanding Management Research.*

For an interesting and and increasingly important perspective on the relationship between theory and data, C. C. Ragin discusses how all social research constructs representations of social life through a dialogue between ideas (theory) and evidence (data) in his book *Constructing Social Research: The Unity and Diversity of Method.* Meanwhile for those who wish to explore the assumptions that underpin different approaches to research and theory in further depth, B. D. Slife and R. N. Williams' *What's Behind the Research? Discovering Hidden Assumptions in the Behavioural Sciences* provides a thorough overview of pyschoanalysis, behaviourism, humanism, cognitivism, eclecticism, structuralism and postmodernism. Assumptions specifically about human behaviour are investigated by P. Ashworth's *Psychology and Human Nature* in which he examines the major contributors to the development of our thinking about consciousness, selfhood, culture and the effects of the physical world on genetic inheritance.

Major Issues and Controversies in the Use of Mixed Methods in the Social and Behavioral Sciences

C. TEDDLIE and A. TASHAKKORI

This chapter answers two basic questions related to the *Handbook of Mixed Methods in Social and Behavioral Research* (hereafter referred to as the handbook):

1. Why do we need a handbook in this field at this point in time?

2. What major issues and controversies does this handbook address?

As the editors of this handbook, it is our opinion that the area of mixed methods research has reached a critical point in its development that allows for the publication of a handbook. We agree that the field is just entering its "adolescence" and that there are many unresolved issues to address before a more mature mixed methods research area can emerge. Nevertheless, we also believe that the handbook, with its explicit recitation of important issues and its presentation of differing points of view regarding these issues, will stimulate greater maturity in the field.

Mixed methods research is still in its adolescence in that scholars do not agree on many basic issues related to the field. It may be that scholars will ultimately agree to disagree on some of these issues; for instance, they may decide that there are several viable ways to categorize mixed methods research designs such that more than one competing typology will be widely recognized and used by scholars in different contexts. It is not the resolution of the basic issues that is important; rather, it is the presentation and discussion of the differing viewpoints that is crucial at this time.

We have identified six major unresolved issues and controversies in the use of mixed methods in the social and behavioral sciences:

1. The nomenclature and basic definitions used in mixed methods research

2. The utility of mixed methods research (why do we do it)

3. The paradigmatic foundations for mixed methods research

4. Design issues in mixed methods research

5. Issues in drawing inferences in mixed methods research

6. The logistics of conducting mixed methods research

These issues are discussed throughout the handbook and serve as one of the major ways in which content is integrated throughout. In each of the sections in this chapter, we (a) define the problem and why it is a major issue in mixed methods research, (b) briefly state our position with regard to the issue, and (c) introduce the positions of others in the handbook.

In their chapter on mixed methods design, Maxwell and Loomis (Chapter 9, this volume) state that they are not taking an adversarial or polemic stand toward other approaches. That is our position

throughout this chapter: We are presenting different points of view on several important issues so as to stimulate further dialog. Ultimately, the better ideas should prevail as the field matures.

◆ *The Evolution of the Research Enterprise in the Social and Behavioral Sciences*

THREE METHODOLOGICAL MOVEMENTS IN THE SOCIAL AND BEHAVIORAL SCIENCES

The historical analysis that follows describes how the field of mixed methods has developed to the point where a handbook is now necessary. Currently, researchers in the social and behavioral sciences can be roughly categorized into three groups: (a) quantitatively oriented researchers (QUANs)[1] working within the postpositivist tradition and primarily interested in numerical analyses, (b) qualitatively oriented researchers (QUALs) working within the constructivist tradition and primarily interested in analysis of narrative data, and (c) mixed methodologists working within other paradigms (e.g., pragmatism, transformative-emancipatory paradigm) and interested in both types of data. (For a discussion of pragmatism, see Maxcy, Chapter 2, this volume. For a discussion of the transformative-emancipatory paradigm, see Mertens, Chapter 5, this volume.)

The first two groups need no introduction to readers. The dominant and relatively unquestioned methodological orientation (with the exception of anthropology and sociology in some cases) during the first half of the 20th century was quantitative methods and the positivist paradigm. This orientation was transformed during the 1950-1970 period as postpositivists responded to some of the more obvious difficulties associated with positivism, yet the methods stayed quantitative. QUALs refer to this as the "received" paradigm.

Qualitatively oriented researchers (e.g., Eisner, Geertz, Lincoln & Guba, Stake, Wolcott) wrote several popular books during the 1970-1985 period that were critical of the positivist orientation and proposed a wide variety of qualitative methods. The most common name given to the paradigm that was associated with the qualitative research position during this period was constructivism. This qualitative research movement gained widespread acceptance, as described by Denzin and Lincoln (1994):

> Over the past two decades, a quiet methodological revolution has been taking place in the social sciences. . . . The extent to which the "qualitative revolution" has overtaken the social sciences and related professional fields has been nothing short of amazing. (p. ix)

Recent theoretical work in the qualitative research movement (e.g., Lincoln & Guba, 2000; Schwandt, 2000) has led to the conclusion that multiple paradigms (and not just constructivism and its variants) are applicable to qualitative research. This point is discussed later in this chapter because it represents an interesting change in perspective from a group that has historically tied particular methods to particular paradigms.

Mixed methodologists need more of an introduction because they have been neither the traditionalists (quantitatively oriented researchers) nor the revolutionaries (qualitatively oriented researchers) over the past 30 years. Despite this, researchers have employed mixed methods through-

out the 20th century and into the 21st century, as described throughout this chapter. Before the paradigm wars, there was no need for mixed methodologists to bring attention to their distinct orientation. Before the incompatibility thesis (i.e., stating that it was inappropriate to mix quantitative and qualitative methods), researchers who used mixed methods to answer their research questions were mostly unaware that they were doing anything out of the ordinary.

These three methodological "movements" continue to evolve simultaneously throughout the social and behavioral sciences. While one may be more in ascendance for some period of time, all three methodological orientations are practiced concurrently. This handbook focuses on the *third methodological movement,* which is just now explicitly developing.

A HISTORICAL ANALYSIS OF THE EMERGENCE OF MIXED METHODS

Denzin and Lincoln (1994) defined five "moments" in the history of qualitative research: the traditional (1900-1950), the modernist or Golden Age (1950-1970), blurred genres (1970-1986), the crisis of representation (1986-1990), and postmodern or present moments (1990-present). These broad historical periods agree to a substantial degree with our previous analysis (Tashakkori & Teddlie, 1998) of the evolution of mixed methods research, although we have divided the periods somewhat differently (1900-1950, 1950-1970, 1970-1990, and 1990-present). This section describes what was happening in mixed methodology research as the qualitative research world was going through its first five moments.[2]

The "traditional" 1900-1950 period actually saw a substantial degree of important mixed methods research ongoing with little methodological controversy. Maxwell and Loomis (Chapter 9, this volume) contend that there was less orthodoxy in methodology during this time period than later in the century. While there had been some debate since the mid-19th century (especially in sociology during the 1920s and 1930s) about the relative merits of quantitative and qualitative research (e.g., Hammersley, 1992), this debate did not have the rancor that accompanied the later paradigm wars.

Classic mixed methods studies from this period are described in this handbook from the field of sociology (Hunter & Brewer, Chapter 22, this volume). These works include the Hawthorne studies (Roethlisberger & Dickson, 1939) and the studies of "Yankee City" (Warner & Lunt, 1941). For example, there was extensive use of both interviews and observations in the overall research program in addition to the famous experimental studies associated with the "Hawthorne" effect.

The time period labeled "modernist" or "Golden Age" (1950-1970) by Denzin and Lincoln was marked in the history of mixed methods research by two major events: (a) the debunking of positivism and (b) the emergence of research designs that began to be called "multimethod" or "mixed." While a distinct field of mixed methods had not emerged by this time, numerous important studies using mixed methodologies occurred, especially in the field of psychology (see the chapters in this volume by Maxwell & Loomis [Chapter 9] and Waszak & Sines [Chapter 21]). These studies included the Festinger, Riecken, and Schachter (1956) research on end-of-the-world cults, the Robber's Cave Experiment by Sherif, Harvey, White, Hood, and Sherif (1961), and Zimbardo's (1969) simulated "prison" studies of deindividuation. For example, Sherif, et al. (1961) made extensive use of qualitative participant observation data to explain quantitative results from the field experiment used in the Robber's Cave Experiment.

Positivism was discredited as a philosophy of science after World War II (e.g., Howe, 1988; Reichardt & Rallis, 1994). Dissatisfaction with the axioms of positivism (e.g., ontology, epistemology, axiology)[3] became increasingly widespread throughout the 1950s and 1960s, giving rise to postpositivism, the intellectual heir to positivism. Landmark works of postpositivism (e.g., Hanson, 1958; Popper, 1935/1959) gained widespread credibility during the late 1950s. Tenets of postpositivism include value-ladenness of inquiry (research is influenced by the values of investigators), theory-ladenness of facts (research is influenced by the theory that an investigator uses), and the nature of reality (our understanding of reality is constructed). These beliefs are widely held by mixed methodologists.

The other important development of this period was the emergence of the first explicit multimethod designs, which inevitably led to studies that mixed quantitative and qualitative methods. Campbell and Fiske (1959) proposed their "multitrait-multimethod matrix," which used more than one quantitative method to measure a psychological trait. They did this to ensure that the variance in their research was accounted for by the trait under study and not by the method that was employed to measure it (e.g., Brewer & Hunter, 1989; Creswell, 1994).

The periods described by Denzin and Lincoln as "blurred genres" (1970-1986) and "crisis of representation" (1986-1990) coincide with what we (Tashakkori & Teddlie, 1998) have called "the ascendance of constructivism, followed by the paradigm wars." Several significant events for mixed methodology occurred during the 1970-1990 period such as (a) qualitative methods and constructivism grew quite rapidly in popularity, (b) the paradigm wars were launched based largely on the incompatibility thesis, (c) mixed methods studies were introduced in conjunction with writings on triangulation, and (d) important mixed methods studies and syntheses appeared.

The discrediting of positivism resulted in the increasing popularity of paradigms more "revolutionary" than postpositivism. These paradigms have several names (e.g., constructivism, interpretivism, naturalism), with constructivism being the most popular.[4] Theorists associated with these paradigms borrowed from postpositivism but then added dimensions of their own (e.g., Denzin, 1992; Gergen, 1985; Hammersley, 1989; Lincoln & Guba, 1985). Some of these theorists argued for the superiority of their own paradigm so as to overcome the biases associated with the deeply embedded traditions of positivism or postpositivism (i.e., the "received" paradigm).

For example, Lincoln and Guba (1985) set up contrasts between positivism and naturalism (constructivism) on basic issues: ontology, epistemology, axiology, the possibility of generalizations, and the possibility of causal linkages. Given such contrasts, it was inevitable that paradigm wars would break out between individuals convinced of what Smith (1994) called the "paradigm purity" of their own position. Paradigm "purists" further posited the incompatibility thesis with regard to research methods: Compatibility between quantitative and qualitative methods is impossible due to the incompatibility of the paradigms underlying the methods. According to these theorists, researchers who combine the two methods are doomed to failure due to the differences in underlying systems.

Scholars criticized the incompatibility thesis by noting that, among other points, mixed methods were already being used in many fields (e.g., Brewer & Hunter, 1989; Greene, Caracelli, & Graham, 1989; Patton, 1990). For example, Greene et al. (1989) presented 57 studies that employed mixed methods and described their design characteristics.

Progress was also made during this period on the explicit specification of mixed methods research designs. Denzin (1978) introduced the term "triangulation," which involved combining data sources to study the same social phenomenon. He discussed four types, including data triangulation (the use of multiple data sources) and methodological triangulation (the use of multiple methods). Jick (1979) discussed triangulation in terms of the weaknesses of one method being offset by the strengths of another method. He also discussed "across methods triangulation," which involved quantitative *and* qualitative approaches.

The period described by Denzin and Lincoln (1994) as "postmodern or present moments" (1990-present) coincides with what we have called the emergence of "pragmatism and the compatibility thesis." Two significant events for mixed methodology that occurred during this period were that (a) the pragmatist position was posited as a counterargument to the incompatibility thesis and (b) several seminal works appeared aimed at establishing mixed methods as a separate field.

On a philosophical level, mixed methodologists had to counter the incompatibility thesis, which was predicated on the link between epistemology and method. To counter this paradigm-method link, Howe (1988) posited the use of a different paradigm: pragmatism. A major tenet of Howe's concept of pragmatism was that quantitative and qualitative methods *are compatible*. Thus, because the paradigm says that these methods are compatible, investigators could make use of both of them in their research. This position has been questioned by several scholars writing within the mixed methods literature, and this debate is discussed in a later section of this chapter.

A short list of influential mixed methods works that appeared during this time period includes Creswell (1994), Greene and Caracelli (1997), Morgan (1998), Morse (1991), Newman and Benz (1998), Patton (1990), Reichardt and Rallis (1994), and Tashakkori and Teddlie (1998). These works include several typologies of mixed methods designs, enumeration of key words with both consistent and inconsistent definitions, different paradigm formulations, and so on.

WHY A HANDBOOK NOW?

The previous historical analysis yields several reasons why this is a good time to produce a handbook:

1. The requisite elements for the field of mixed methods now exist: basic terms and definitions thereof, typologies of research designs, arguments for the use of paradigms, and the like.

2. Many scholars would like to see greater consistency across the terms and definitions.

3. The handbook can be used as another piece of evidence for the overall legitimacy of mixed methodology as a separate methodological movement.

4. That which is unique about mixed methods can be displayed in distinction to purely quantitative or purely qualitative methods.

5. The handbook and specific chapters can be used as a pedagogical tool for professors teaching courses in the area.

6. The handbook presents a third alternative for researchers in the social and behavioral sciences as an overall method for doing research.

◆ *The Nomenclature and Basic Definitions Used in Mixed Methods Research*

The development of a nomenclature that is distinctly associated with mixed methods is both extremely important and overdue. As this book was being produced, we asked the authors to designate and define a few terms, which they considered essential, from their various chapters. In this handbook, we present a Glossary that consists of the terms and definitions that our authors designated to be important.

There are multiple definitions for several of the Glossary terms, and these point out disagreements among the authors. We believe that these alternative definitions are a sign of strength in a field that is still in its adolescence because it indicates that different authors disagree about exactly what a term means but nevertheless think the term is important. Hopefully, these differences of opinion regarding the basic terminology of the field will be resolved over time, and the publication of the Glossary may serve as a catalyst in this resolution.

An interesting distinction exists between the QUAL and QUAN traditions with regard to the issue of common nomenclature and definitions. Traditional quantitative definitions of basic constructs and designs have been long established in classic texts (e.g., Cook & Campbell, 1979) and in the annals of statistics and measurement journals. While there is slow evolution in the QUAN methodological research area,[5] no one expects large changes in the basic paradigm, constructs, or research designs associated with this worldview.

Common definitions of qualitative constructs and designs, on the other hand, have been slow to develop.[6] Part of the reason for this is that many of the leading figures in qualitative research do not believe that such codification is either possible or even productive.

A reasonable question for mixed methodologists at this point in time is "Do we want a common nomenclature with a set of terms and definitions?" We believe that the answer from the majority of authors contributing to this handbook is yes. Part of the reason for this is that the lack of an overall system of terms and definitions has led to confusion and imprecision in the presentation of research findings, as noted by Datta (1994) and others.

This section on nomenclature in mixed methods is concerned with issues related to a common nomenclature for mixed methods research. It is divided into four parts:

1. Commonalities across the definitions of terms associated with mixed methods

2. Inconsistency in basic definitions (using *multimethod* as an example)

3. The choice of bilingual or common nomenclature (using *validity* as an example)

4. Differences across disciplines in terms of nomenclature

COMMONALITIES ACROSS THE DEFINITIONS OF TERMS ASSOCIATED WITH MIXED METHODS

Some of the terms uniquely associated with mixed methods have been defined consistently across a number of authors. These terms are found in the Glossary with no alternative definitions.

An interesting case in point is the term *data transformation* with its two sub-processes that are defined in the Glossary as follows:

- *Qualitized data:* Collected quantitative data types are converted into narratives that can be analyzed qualitatively.

- *Quantitized data:* Collected qualitative data types are converted into numerical codes that can be statistically analyzed.

These definitions were first derived by Miles and Huberman (1994), who coined the term "quantitize" in a sourcebook for qualitative data analysis. We (Tashakkori & Teddlie, 1998) then applied the same process to the transformation of quantitative data (qualitize). These terms are specific enough to be presented consistently in a number of sources (e.g., Boyatzis, 1998), including six chapters of the current handbook (Chapters 1, 12, 13, 14, 21, and 23).

For instance, Sandelowski (Chapter 12, this volume) describes her use of quantitizing techniques in a study where she transformed narrative interview data into numerical data that were then analyzed using Fisher's exact probability test (Sandelowski, Harris, & Holditch-Davis, 1991). In her qualitizing example, she discusses taking quantitatively derived clusters of numerical data and transforming those into distinct qualitatively described "profiles" using grounded theory.

Other examples of terms with widely accepted meanings are some of the basic mixed methods designs such as equivalent status designs, dominant-less dominant designs, sequential designs, and simultaneous or concurrent designs. Creswell, Plano Clark, Gutmann, and Hanson (Chapter 8, this volume) interestingly take some of these basic designs and cross them with other design components to create unique mixed model designs such as the "sequential explanatory" and "concurrent transformative" design types.

Another contribution of the Glossary is the introduction of some innovative new terms to the mixed methods lexicon. For instance, several new terms for mixed methods data analysis are included from Onwuegbuzie and Teddlie (Chapter 13, this volume), including qualitative contrasting case analysis, qualitative residual analysis, qualitative follow-up interaction analyses, and qualitative internal replication analysis. Another example is fused data analysis (an integrated analysis in which the same sources are used in different but interdependent ways) from Bazeley (Chapter 14, this volume).

INCONSISTENCY IN BASIC DEFINITIONS

As the field of mixed methods has evolved, there has been inconsistency in the manner in which certain terms have been defined. The Glossary attests to this in its alternative definitions of some basic terms. For several years, the terms *multimethod design* and *mixed methods design* have been confused with one another. There seems to be a particular issue with the term *multimethod design*, which has been defined quite differently by different authors:

◆ Campbell and Fiske (1959) introduced the term "multitrait-multimethod" matrix to connote the use of more than one quantitative method to measure a personality trait.

◆ Morse (Chapter 7, this volume) defines multimethod design as "qualitative and quantitative projects that are relatively complete but are used together to form essential components of one research program."

◆ Hunter and Brewer (Chapter 22, this volume) define the multimethod strategy as "the use of multiple methods with complementary strengths and different weaknesses in relation to a given set of research problems. But these criteria don't imply that one must always employ a mix of qualitative and quantitative methods in each project. This may sometimes be the case, but some research problems might be better served by combining two different types of quantitative methods . . . or of qualitative methods."

Thus, the term multimethod design has been used to describe the following:

◆ the use of two quantitative methods;

◆ the use of relatively separate quantitative and qualitative methods; and

◆ the use of both QUAN and QUAL methods or the use of two different types of either QUAL or QUAN methods (QUAL/QUAL or QUAN/QUAN).

Throughout this volume, we are more interested in the consistent use of the term *mixed methods*, but this difficult term *multimethod* (research or strategy or design or whatever) must also be addressed to create a common nomenclature. We recently (Tashakkori & Teddlie, in press) proposed a typology of research designs that incorporates both mixed and multimethod designs in a consistent manner. The following is an outline for that typology together with definitions for the key terms:

I. Multiple Method Designs (more than one method or more than one worldview)

  A. Multimethod designs (more than one method but restricted to within worldview [e.g., QUAN/QUAN, QUAL/QUAL])

    1. Multimethod QUAN studies

    2. Multimethod QUAL studies

  B. Mixed methods designs (use of QUAL and QUAN data collection procedures or research methods)

    1. Mixed method research (occurs in the methods stage of a study)

    2. Mixed model research (can occur in several stages of a study)

We (Tashakkori & Teddlie, in press) have defined multiple method designs as research in which more than one method or more than one worldview is used. At least three broad categories of these multiple method designs have been identified in the literature: (a) multimethod research, (b) mixed method research, and (c) mixed model research.

In *multimethod research* studies, the research questions are answered by using two data collection procedures (e.g., participant observation and oral histories) or two research methods (e.g., ethnography and case study), each of which is from the same QUAL or QUAN tradition. This was the type of design first proposed by Campbell and Fiske (1959) for QUAN applications only.

We suggest *mixed methods* (plural) *designs* as a cover term for mixed method and mixed model research. *Mixed method research* studies use qualitative and quantitative data collection and analysis techniques in either parallel or sequential phases. This mixing occurs in the methods

section of a study. For example, this is the type of research in which a qualitative *and* a quantitative data collection procedure (e.g., a personality inventory and a focus group interview) or research method (e.g., an ethnography and a field experiment) are used to answer the research questions. Although mixed method studies use both qualitative and quantitative data collection and analysis, they are often marginally mixed in that they are frequently either qualitative or quantitative in the type of questions they ask and the type of inferences they make at the end of the studies.

Mixed model research (Tashakkori & Teddlie, 1998), by contrast, is mixed in many or *all* stages of the study (questions, research methods, data collection and analysis, and the inference process). It is obvious, from the preceding discussion, that mixed model research has to meet a much more stringent set of assumptions than does multimethod or even mixed method research. For example, mixed model research might have multiple research questions, each rooted in a distinct paradigm (what Greene & Caracelli, 1997, called "dialectic"), and might make multiple inferences corresponding to different worldviews. Therefore, one of the assumptions of such research is that it is indeed possible to have two paradigms, or two worldviews, mixed throughout a single research project.

This typology of multiple method designs is an effort to provide some consistency in the literature, especially with regard to the misuse of the *multimethod* term and the introduction of the mixed model concept. We invite others to refine (or reject and replace with something better) our typology. A later section of this chapter presents much more information on typologies of research designs in mixed methods and how these typologies are similar and different.

THE CHOICE OF BILINGUAL
OR COMMON NOMENCLATURE

One of the major decisions that mixed methodologists have to make concerning nomenclature is whether to

◆ use a bilingual nomenclature that employs the QUAL, QUAN, or a combination of QUAL and QUAN terms for issues such as validity and sampling or

◆ create a new language for mixed methodology that gives a common name for the existing sets of QUAL and QUAN terms.

We believe that mixed methodologists should adopt a common nomenclature transcending the separate QUAL and QUAN orientations when the described processes (QUAL and QUAN) are highly similar and when appropriate terminology exists. Currently, the decision to use either bilingual or common nomenclature must be made separately for each of the large-component parts of research methodology (e.g., sampling, validity) because the terminology in each is so varied.

For instance, although sampling has well-defined and entrenched QUAL and QUAN techniques, it is possible to develop a common terminology. Sampling may be conceptualized on a continuum with probability samples (from QUANs) on one side and purposive samples (from QUALs) on the other (see Tashakkori & Teddlie, 1998). Different sampling strategies may be placed on such a continuum. As an example, in such a classification, QUAN's quota sampling is classified as purposive, next to QUAL's sequential sampling.[7] Kemper, Stringfield, and Teddlie (Chapter 10, this volume) demon-strate numerous ways in which these probability and purposive sampling strategies may be combined in mixed methods studies.

Another reason to develop a common nomenclature pertains to situations in which the existing QUAL and QUAN terms have been overly used or misused. Probably the best example is that of the current use of the term *validity* in the QUAN and QUAL traditions.

Lincoln and Guba (1985) attempted to set up a system in which there were equivalent QUAL terms for existing QUAN validity types. For instance, they equated credibility with internal validity and equated transferability with external validity (p. 300).

This attempt at bilingualism in the QUAN and QUAL communities was criticized by many, including Maxwell (1992). Terms that the critics believed were more appropriate (e.g., understanding, authenticity) were put forth to replace validity, with the result being an explosion in the number of validity (or authenticity) types proposed from the QUAL community over the past 10 years. This increase in the variants of QUAL validity types mirrors an already long list of QUAN validity types that include both design and measurement constructs.

Table 1.1 lists 35 types of validity, and this list is not exhaustive. With so many types of validity, the term has lost meaning. This is a good example of a situation in which mixed methodologists may want to create their own terminology to simplify matters and to give greater meaning to the processes being described.

This section on nomenclature is closely linked with a later section on quality of inferences. In that section, we propose the use of terms associated with "inference" as the mixed methodology equivalent of validity.

**TABLE 1.1   Types of Validity in Qualitative and
               Quantitative Research**

Quantitative	Qualitative
Internal validity (causal, relationship definitions)	Catalytic validity
	Crystalline validity
Statistical conclusion validity	Descriptive validity
External validity	Evaluative validity
Population	Generalizability validity
Ecological	Interpretive validity
Construct validity (causal)	Ironic validity
Consequential validity	Neopragmatic validity
Validity (measurement)	Rhizomic validity
Face	Simultaneous validity
Content	Situated validity
Criterion related	Theoretical validity
Predictive	Voluptuous validity
Concurrent	Plus terms associated with authenticity
Jury	Educative
Predictive	Ontological
Systemic	Catalytic
Construct validity (measurement)	Tactical
Convergent	
Discriminant	
Factorial	

SOURCES: These types of validity were compiled from several sources, including Cook and Campbell (1979); Cohen, Manion, and Morrison (2000); Lincoln and Guba (2000); Lather (1993); Maxwell (1992); Messick (1995); and Tashakkori and Teddlie (1998).

DIFFERENCES ACROSS DISCIPLINES IN TERMS OF NOMENCLATURE

A final nomenclature issue that deserves some attention concerns the fact that several different fields in the social and behavioral sciences have contributed to mixed methods and that they use somewhat different terms. For instance, we have contributions in this handbook from evaluation research (Rallis & Rossman, Chapter 17), management and organizational research (Currall & Towler, Chapter 18), health sciences (Forthofer, Chapter 19), nursing research (Twinn, Chapter 20), psychology (Waszak & Sines, Chapter 21), sociology (Hunter & Brewer, Chapter 22), and education (Rocco & colleagues, Chapter 23). Some obvious differences exist among these chapters in terms of nomenclature.

For instance, Twinn (Chapter 20, this volume) concludes from her review of nursing research that the term *triangulation* was used much more than the terms *mixed methods* and *multimethod design*. Indeed the term *triangulation* is featured highly in two other chapters in this handbook written by authors from the nursing research field: Morse (Chapter 7) and Sandelowski (Chapter 12). Sandelowski (Chapter 12, this volume) concludes that the term *triangulation* has been used so much that it has no meaning at all. The term *triangulation* does occur in each of the other six separate "discipline" chapters noted previously, but primarily as a historical artifact rather than as a currently dominant term.

All of the individual "disciplines" in this handbook also use different typologies to organize the studies in their field except for two that use no typology at all (Forthofer, Chapter 19, and Hunter & Brewer, Chapter 22). This variety in typologies used exemplifies the diversity of approach across the different fields and the fact that all of the reviewers selected typologies close to their own disciplines.

For instance, Rallis and Rossman (Chapter 17, this volume), writing in the field of evaluation research, chose a typology developed by others working in evaluation (Greene & Caracelli, 1997). Currall and Towler (Chapter 18, this volume), writing in the field of management and organizational research, chose a typology developed by Creswell (1994), who has a background in educational psychology. Twinn (Chapter 20, this volume), writing in the field of nursing research, uses a basic nursing research text in evaluating and categorizing mixed methods research in her field (Polit & Hungler, 1999). Waszak and Sines (Chapter 21, this volume), writing in the field of psychology, classify their research studies by type of research design, which is certainly appropriate for

that field of study. Rocco and colleagues (Chapter 23, this volume), writing in the field of education, classify their research studies by paradigmatic orientation (pragmatic or dialectical), which is appropriate for the discipline that spawned the paradigm wars and the incompatibility thesis.

These differences in terminology and typology can be expected at this time in the development of the field. As mixed methods research evolves and more common terms appear, these differences should diminish.

◆ The Utility of Mixed Methods Research

The utility of mixed methods research concerns "why" we do them. With the plethora of research methods associated with either the QUAL or the QUAN tradition, why would we go to the bother of combining them, or of generating new techniques, to do mixed methods research?

The ultimate goal of any research project is to answer the questions that were set forth at the project's beginning. Mixed methods are useful if they provide better opportunities for answering our research questions. Also, mixed methods are useful if they help researchers to meet the criteria for evaluating the "goodness" of their answers (e.g., Tashakkori & Teddlie, 1998) better than do single approach designs.

There appear to be three areas in which mixed methods are superior to single approach designs:

◆ Mixed methods research can answer research questions that the other methodologies cannot.

◆ Mixed methods research provides better (stronger) inferences.

♦ Mixed methods provide the opportunity for presenting a greater diversity of divergent views.

MIXED METHODS RESEARCH CAN ANSWER RESEARCH QUESTIONS THAT THE OTHER METHODOLOGIES CANNOT

One dimension on which quantitative and qualitative research is said to vary is the type of question answered by each approach. Some authors have suggested that QUAL research questions are exploratory, while QUAN research questions are confirmatory. Erzberger and Prein (1997) and Tashakkori and Teddlie (1998, in press) have disagreed with this dichotomization of research questions. Erzberger and Prein (1997) labeled it "a Cinderella position view of qualitative research" (p. 143) in that it "restricts the use of qualitative methods to preliminary phases of social research where quantitative techniques could not (yet) be employed" (p. 142).

Punch (1998) provided another argument against this dichotomization:

> Quantitative research has typically been more directed at theory verification, while qualitative research has typically been more concerned with theory generation. While that correlation is historically valid, it is by no means perfect, and there is no necessary connection between purpose and approach. That is, quantitative research can be used for theory generation (as well as verification), and qualitative research can be used for theory verification (as well as generation). (pp. 16-17)

We agree with this statement, yet we also believe that most QUAN research is confirmatory and involves theory verification, while much QUAL research is exploratory and involves theory generation. What happens when you want to do both? *A major advantage of mixed methods research is that it enables the researcher to simultaneously answer confirmatory and exploratory questions, and therefore verify and generate theory in the same study.*

Many of the research projects that we supervise are doctoral dissertations where the students want to simultaneously accomplish two goals: (a) demonstrate that a particular variable will have a predicted relationship with another variable and (b) answer exploratory questions about how that predicted (or some other related) relationship actually happens.

An example is a recent dissertation by Stevens (2002). In this study, the student wanted to examine and describe the changes that occurred in a set of middle schools as a result of the introduction of an external change agent, a distinguished educator (DE), through a new state school accountability program. It was hypothesized that teachers in schools with the DE would perform better on measures of teacher effectiveness than would teachers in schools without the DE.[8]

The study's quantitative quasi-experimental design confirmed the hypothesis: Teachers in the schools with the DEs had significantly higher rates of effective teaching than did teachers in the schools without the DEs. While this result was important, the doctoral student also wanted to know how this had occurred. Simultaneously to gathering the quantitative data, she conducted case studies in each of the schools using qualitative techniques such as observations, interviews, and document analysis. The DEs were perceived as having a positive influence on teacher collaboration and sharing, on the expectations of both teachers and students for student learning, and on the quality of instruction. These positive school and teacher effectiveness processes led to the higher rates of effective teaching.

This mixed model study could not have been conducted exclusively within either the quantitative or the qualitative tradition. The mixed model design allowed the doctoral student to simultaneously confirm a quantitatively derived hypothesis and explore in greater depth the processes by which the relationship occurred.

MIXED METHODS RESEARCH PROVIDES BETTER (STRONGER) INFERENCES

Several authors (e.g., Brewer & Hunter, 1989; Greene & Caracelli, 1997; see also Creswell et al., Chapter 8, this volume) have postulated that using mixed methods can offset the disadvantages that certain of the methods have by themselves. Johnson and Turner (Chapter 11, this volume) refer to this as the *fundamental principle of mixed methods research:* "Methods should be mixed in a way that has complementary strengths and nonoverlapping weaknesses." A classic case involves using case studies in conjunction with mailed surveys. One method gives greater depth, while the other gives greater breadth; hopefully, together they give results from which one can make better (i.e., more accurate) inferences.

Further support for the usefulness of mixed methods came from Greene et al. (1989), who proposed five functions for such methods: triangulation, complementarity, development, initiation, and expansion. The first two functions of mixed methods (triangulation and complementarity) are related to the fact that mixed methods lead to multiple inferences that confirm or complement each other. The

other three functions (development, initiation, and expansion) are more related to mixed methods studies in which inferences made at the end of one phase (e.g., QUAL) lead to the questions and/or design of a second phase (e.g., QUAN).

Also, complex social phenomena such as the DE intervention described earlier (Stevens, 2002) require different kinds of methods so as to best understand and make inferences about these complexities (Greene & Caracelli, 1997). Such social phenomena cannot be fully understood using either purely qualitative or purely quantitative techniques. We need a variety of data sources and analyses to completely understand complex multifaceted institutions or realities. Mixed methods can provide that.

MIXED METHODS PROVIDE THE OPPORTUNITY FOR PRESENTING A GREATER DIVERSITY OF DIVERGENT VIEWS

One of the agreements against mixed methods is related to the final conclusions or inferences. What happens if the QUAN and QUAL components lead to two totally different (or contradictory) conclusions? Erzberger and Prein (1997) asked and answered the question eloquently:

> What happens if the two perspectives do not fit together . . . ? The idea that qualitative and quantitative findings always relate to different aspects of *one* research object does not automatically mean that a coherent picture can be depicted. It even has to be expected that this type of "peaceful coexistence" between methodological paradigms will be rather infrequent. . . . Research findings can converge, which can be seen as an indicator of their

validity; secondly, they can generate a new comprehension of the phenomenon by forming complementary parts of a jigsaw puzzle, or, thirdly, they can produce unexplainable divergence leading to a falsification of previous theoretical assumptions. (pp. 146-147)

According to this view, divergent findings are valuable in that they lead to a reexamination of the conceptual frameworks and the assumptions underlying each of the two (QUAL and QUAN) components. Johnson and Turner (Chapter 11, this volume) state that one of the major reasons for following the fundamental principle of mixed methods research is to "elucidate the divergent aspects of a phenomenon." Further analyses of the data in the form of possible transformation of data types to each other, internal validity audits (Tashakkori & Teddlie, 1998), and design of a new study or phase for further investigations (Rossman & Wilson, 1985) are three outcomes of such reexamination.

Deacon, Bryman, and Fenton (1998) summarized the advantages of this reexamination:

Whatever short-term inconvenience this may cause, in many cases the reappraisal and re-analysis required can reap long term analytical rewards: alerting the researcher to the possibility that issues are more multifaceted than they may have initially supposed, and offering the opportunity to develop more convincing and robust explanations of the social processes being investigated. (p. 61)

The different inferences from mixed methods research often reflect different voices and perspectives. Such diversity of opinion is welcome in mixed methods research (for an extended discussion of the ramifications of the divergence of qualitative and quantitative findings in mixed methods research, see Erzberger & Kelle, Chapter 16, this volume).

◆ The Paradigmatic Foundations for Mixed Methods Research

A continuing issue in mixed methods research concerns the manner in which paradigms are used in the development of the field. Researchers have had at least six different positions on the issue of how paradigms are to be used in the development of mixed methods research:

1. Some scholars believe that methods and paradigms are independent of one another; therefore, the epistemology-method link is not an issue, and it is permissible to do mixed methods research (a-paradigmatic thesis).

2. Some researchers agree with the tenets of the incompatibility thesis and conclude that mixed methods research is impossible (e.g., Smith & Heshusius, 1986).

3. Some scholars believe that mixed methods are possible but that they must be kept separate so that the strengths of each paradigmatic position (e.g., postpositivism, constructivism) can be realized (Brewer & Hunter, 1989; Morse, 1991; see also Morse, Chapter 7, this volume). We label this point of view the "complementary strengths" thesis.

4. Some researchers believe that a single paradigm should serve as the foundation for mixed methods research.

a. Some advocate that pragmatism serve as the foundation for mixed methods research (e.g., Datta, 1997; Howe, 1988; Patton, 1990; Tashakkori & Teddlie, 1998; see also chapters in this volume by Maxcy [Chapter 2], Bazeley [Chapter 14], Rallis & Rossman [Chapter 18], Forthofer [Chapter 19], and Rocco et al. [Chapter 23]).

b. Some advocate that the transformative-emancipatory paradigm serve as the foundation for mixed methods research (see, e.g., Mertens, Chapter 5, this volume).

Some scholars propose the "dialectic" stance, which does not advocate one paradigm above others but rather sees mixed methods research as intentionally engaging a multiple set of paradigms and their assumptions (e.g., Greene & Caracelli, 1997; see also Greene & Caracelli, Chapter 3, this volume). According to these theorists, all paradigms are valuable, but only partial, worldviews. To think dialectically means to examine the tensions that emerge from the juxtaposition of these multiple diverse perspectives.

Some scholars believe that multiple paradigms may serve as the foundation for doing research in the social and behavioral sciences. This position has been explicitly applied to qualitative research (e.g., Lincoln & Guba, 2000; Schwandt, 2000), but it is also applicable to mixed methods research (see, e.g., Creswell et al., Chapter 8, this volume). A difference between this position and the dialectic stance is that the multiple paradigm theorists believe that one type of paradigm is best used when one is doing one type of study, while another paradigm is best used if one is doing another type of study. Those advocating

the dialectical stance reject the selection of one paradigm over another.

The remainder of this section contains more detailed discussions of these six points of view.[9]

THE A-PARADIGMATIC STANCE

Some scholars see the epistemology-methods link as distracting or unnecessary and simply ignore it, continuing to work as they always have worked, using whatever methods seem appropriate for the question at hand. This is often the stance of scholars working in applied fields such as evaluation, nursing, and the health sciences.

In a book where he also discussed the connection between paradigms and what he called "mixed form" designs, Patton (1990) made the following commonsense statement:

> In short, *in real world practice, methods can be separated from the epistemology out of which they emerged.* One can use statistics in a straightforward way without doing a literature review of logical-positivism. One can make an interpretation without studying hermeneutics. And one can conduct open-ended interviews or make observations without reading treatises on phenomenology. (p. 90, italics in original)

THE INCOMPATIBILITY THESIS AND MIXED METHODS RESEARCH

As noted throughout this chapter, the incompatibility thesis states that compatibility between quantitative and qualitative methods is impossible due to the incompatibility of the paradigms that underlie the methods. This thesis was argued during the time period labeled by some (e.g., Gage, 1989) as the paradigm wars. Theorists writing primarily during the paradigm wars of the 1980s (e.g., Guba, 1987; Smith, 1983; Smith & Heshusius, 1986) indicated that researchers who try to combine the two methods are doomed to failure due to the inherent differences in the philosophies underlying them. For example, Guba (1987) stated that one paradigm precludes the other "just as surely as the belief in a round world precludes belief in a flat one" (p. 31).

Denzin and Lincoln (1994), in the first edition of the *Handbook of Qualitative Research,* were explicit in their description of the separateness of the qualitative and quantitative methodologies:

> The five points of difference described above . . . reflect commitments to different styles of research, different epistemologies, and different forms of representation. Each work tradition is governed by a different set of genres. . . . Qualitative researchers use ethnographic prose, historical narratives, first-person accounts, still photographs, life histories, fictionalized facts, and biographical and autobiographical materials, among others. Quantitative researchers use mathematical models, statistical tables, and graphs. (p. 6)

The incompatibility thesis has now been largely discredited, partially because scholars demonstrated that they had successfully employed mixed methods in their research. Smith (1996) lamented the success of the compatibilists' point of view:

> In 1986 I published an article . . . (Smith & Heshusius, 1986) that, be-

cause of its early reception, I thought would prevent for some time to come a closing down of the conversation about the compatibility-incompatibility of the approaches. . . . I was overly optimistic to say the least, because by 1990 or so the issues were decided in favor of the compatibilists. This happened not because they had the better arguments, but because educational researchers in general lost whatever interest they may have had in the discussion. I remember the editor of a major journal writing to me saying that most researchers had become bored with philosophical discussions and were more interested in getting on with the task of doing their research. (pp. 162-163)

Even though the incompatibility thesis per se is not held by many researchers today, it has influenced some other more popular positions (e.g., the complementary strengths thesis, the dialectical thesis).

THE COMPLEMENTARY STRENGTHS THESIS AND MIXED METHODS RESEARCH

Some researchers believe that mixed methods are possible but that they must be kept as separate as possible so that the strengths of each paradigmatic position (e.g., postpositivism, constructivism) can be realized (Brewer & Hunter, 1989; Morse, 1991; Stern, 1994). For example, Morse (Chapter 7, this volume) reminds readers of "the edict that the researcher must retain the assumptions of each paradigm." She views the "ad hoc" mixing of methods as a serious threat to the validity of mixed methods research.

Similarly, Brewer and Hunter (1989) suggested that a multimethod approach to research is superior to a monomethod approach because it provides grounds for data triangulation. Brewer and Hunter disfavored what they labeled "composite" methods research, which is composed of "elements borrowed from the basic styles" (p. 80). While acknowledging the strengths of composite methods, these authors concluded that the basic methods lose some of their strengths when incorporated into competing methodologies. In addition, they contended that this methodological eclecticism does not provide enough data for proper "cross-method comparison."

On the other hand, Maxwell and Loomis (Chapter 9, this volume) do not believe in uniform purely qualitative and purely quantitative research paradigms. Citing several sources, these authors argue convincingly that each of these two generic positions has a large number of separate and distinct "components." They argue further that these quantitative and qualitative components can be put together in multiple legitimate ways. Because the two research paradigms are not "pure" to begin with, researchers lose little when they mix them up in a variety of often creative ways.

A reading of this handbook indicates that most of its authors are comfortable with mixing their methods and are, in general, not very concerned with the purity of the underlying paradigms being maintained.

THE SINGLE PARADIGM THESIS AND MIXED METHODS RESEARCH

Another result of the paradigm wars was the search by individuals using mixed methods for a paradigm to support their methodological predilection. The single paradigm/methodology link was initiated by Lincoln and Guba (1985) with their equation of the two single links between postpositivism-quantitative methods and constructivism-qualitative methods. Because the qualitative and quantitative positions had their own epistemologies, scholars using mixed methods began looking for a paradigm to support their methodology.

Several scholars (e.g., Howe, 1988) posited a link between pragmatism and mixed methods. Later, other scholars (e.g., Mertens, 1998, 1999) discussed the transformative-emancipatory paradigm as a philosophical underpinning for mixed methods. The remainder of this subsection contains brief presentations of these two philosophical positions and their association with mixed methods.

Pragmatism as the Foundation for Mixed Methods Research. Several authors (e.g., Datta, 1997; Howe, 1988; Patton, 1990; Rossman & Wilson, 1985; Tashakkori & Teddlie, 1998) have proposed that pragmatism is the best paradigm for justifying the use of mixed methods research. For example, Rallis and Rossman (Chapter 17, this volume) present what they call a "pragmatic framework" for the use of mixed methods in evaluation research.

Maxcy (Chapter 2, this volume) presents an extended discussion of the link between pragmatism and the use of mixed methods in the social and behavioral sciences. In his chapter, he traces the development of pragmatism from the early philosophers (e.g., Charles Sanders Peirce, William James, John Dewey, George Herbert Mead, Arthur F. Bentley) through more contemporary voices (e.g., Cleo Cherryholmes, Richard Rorty). The work of Cherryholmes (1992, 1999) is singled out as an example of important current writing in the area of "critical pragmatism."

Tashakkori and Teddlie (1998, pp. 22-30) made a number of points regarding pragmatism and mixed methods:

♦ Pragmatism supports the use of both qualitative and quantitative research methods in the same research study and within multistage research programs. Pragmatism rejects the incompatibility thesis.

♦ Pragmatist researchers consider the research question to be more important than either the method they use or the paradigm that underlies the method. We refer to this as the "dictatorship of the research question."

♦ Pragmatists also reject the forced choice between postpositivism and constructivism with regard to logic, epistemology, and so on. In each case, pragmatism rejects the either/or of the incompatibility thesis and embraces both points of view (or a position between the two opposing viewpoints).[10]

♦ Specific decisions regarding the use of mixed methods or qualitative methods or quantitative methods depend on the research question as it is currently posed and the stage of the research cycle that is ongoing.

♦ Pragmatism avoids the use of metaphysical concepts (e.g., "truth," "reality") that have caused much endless (and often useless) discussion and debate (e.g., Howe, 1988).

♦ Pragmatism presents a very practical and applied research philosophy.

Tashakkori and Teddlie suggested, "Study what interests and is of value to you, study it in the different ways that you deem appropriate, and utilize the results in ways that can bring about positive consequences within your value system" (p. 30).

See our Chapter 26 in this handbook for more discussion of pragmatism and mixed methods.

The Transformative-Emancipatory Paradigm as the Foundation for Mixed Methods Research. In Mertens's chapter in this handbook (Chapter 5; see also Mertens, 1998, 1999), she presents the transformative-emancipatory paradigm as a third alternative to the positivist-postpositivist and interpretive-constructivist paradigms. She concludes that the underlying philosophical assumptions and methodological implications of the transformative-emancipatory paradigm can be used fruitfully within the discussion of mixed methods in research.

Mertens advocates the creation of a more just and democratic society as the ultimate goal for conducting research. She believes that this goal should permeate the entire research process, from problem formulation through the drawing of conclusions and into the use of the results. The following are some tenets of the transformative-emancipatory paradigm, according to Mertens (Chapter 5, this volume):

♦ The paradigm places central importance on the experiences of individuals who suffer from discrimination or oppression.

♦ Researchers working within the transformative-emancipatory paradigm are aware of power differentials in the context of their research and use their research to promote greater social equity and justice.

♦ With regard to ontology, Mertens states that the transformative-emancipatory viewpoint is to describe reality within its multiple contexts (e.g., cultural, political, economic, historical).

◆ With regard to epistemology, Mertens states that interaction between the researcher and the participants is essential and that this interaction requires understanding and trust.

◆ Mertens concludes that from a methodological point of view, mixed methods offer especially promising ways to address the concerns of diverse groups in an appropriate manner.[11]

See our Chapter 26 in this handbook for more discussion of the transformative-emancipatory paradigm and mixed methods.

THE DIALECTICAL THESIS AND MIXED METHODS RESEARCH

The dialectic stance assumes that all paradigms have something to offer and that the use of multiple paradigms contributes to greater understanding of the phenomenon under study. Greene and Caracelli (1997; Chapter 3, this volume) are the foremost proponents of this position, which has also been adopted by other writers in this handbook (e.g., Maxwell & Loomis, Chapter 9).

Greene and Caracelli (1997; Chapter 3, this volume) reject the continued search for the single best paradigm as a relic of the past and the paradigm wars. Instead, they believe that multiple diverse perspectives are important because they are required to explain the complexity of an increasingly pluralistic society.

An important component of this position is the ability to think dialectically. This involves consideration of opposing viewpoints and interaction with the "tensions" caused by their juxtaposition. These tensions come from the differences in the assumptions of the different para-digms. There are several other points about conversations/dialogues in dialectic inquiry, including the following (Greene & Caracelli, Chapter 3, this volume):

◆ These conversations/dialogues are not typically about philosophical issues but rather about the phenomena that are the subject of the research.

◆ Historical dualisms (such as those featured in the paradigm wars) are not of particular importance in dialectical inquiry. There are no endless discussions of induction versus deduction, subjectivity versus objectivity, and so on.

◆ Greene and Caracelli list some dichotomies that are important in dialectical inquiry: value-neutrality and value-commitment, emic and etic, particularity and generality, social constructions and physical traces, and so on.

THE MULTIPLE PARADIGM THESIS AND MIXED METHODS RESEARCH

Some scholars believe that multiple paradigms may serve as the foundation for mixed methods research. For instance, Creswell and colleagues (Chapter 8, this volume) present six advanced mixed methods designs and then argue that no single paradigm applies to all of the designs. Referencing Denzin and Lincoln (2000), Creswell and colleagues conclude that multiple paradigms may be applied to diverse mixed methods designs. Researchers have to decide which paradigm is best given their choice of a particular mixed methods design for a particular study.

Creswell and colleagues give several examples: Postpositivism might be the best paradigm for a sequential-explanatory design using quantitative methods, interpretivism might be the best paradigm for a sequential-exploratory design using qualitative methods, several paradigms may serve as the framework for a triangulation design, and so on.

This multiple paradigm perspective stems at least partially from recent writings in qualitative research methodology. The editors of the second edition of the *Handbook of Qualitative Research* (Denzin & Lincoln, 2000) drew the following conclusion:

> A complex, interconnected family of terms, concepts, and assumptions surround the term *qualitative research*. These include the traditions associated with foundationalism, positivism, post-foundationalism, postpositivism, poststructuralism, and the many qualitative research perspectives and/or methods connected to cultural and interpretive studies. (p. 2)

Later in the same chapter of their book, Denzin and Lincoln (2000) concluded that there are four major paradigms that structure qualitative research: positivist-postpositivist, constructivist-interpretive, critical (e.g., Marxist, emancipatory), and feminist-poststructural (pp. 19-20).

In the same volume, Schwandt (2000) concluded that there were three epistemological stances for qualitative research: interpretivism, hermeneutics, and social constructionism:

> Thus qualitative inquiry is more comprehensible as site or arena for social scientific criticism than as any particular kind of social theory, methodology, or philosophy.... I focus on the site as an arena in which different epistemologies vie for attention as potential justifications for doing qualitative inquiry. (p. 190)

THE EVOLUTION IN THOUGHT REGARDING PARADIGMS AND RESEARCH METHODS

The preceding discussion has presented six different positions on the issue of how paradigms can be used in mixed methods research. Some of these positions are directly related to seminal works in the field of qualitative research, and they represent important aspects in the evolution of thought in that area regarding the paradigm-method link. Consider the following three "snapshots" from that evolution:

1. Lincoln and Guba (1985) presented their paradigm table contrasting the positivist and naturalist positions on five dimensions and arguing for the superiority of the naturalist position. Naturalism was posited as the paradigm that supported qualitative research methods, while positivism underlay the use of quantitative methods. During this time period, the incompatibility thesis was postulated.

2. In the first edition of the *Handbook of Qualitative Research*, the position of the qualitative research theorists softened a bit. Guba and Lincoln (1994) protested the use of the term "paradigm wars" and opened the door to possible reconciliation:

   > The metaphor of paradigm wars described by Gage (1989) is undoubtedly overdrawn. Describing the discussions and altercations of the past decade or two as wars paints the matter as more confrontational than necessary. A resolution of paradigm differences can occur only when a new paradigm emerges that is more informed and sophisticated than any existing one. That is most likely to occur if and when proponents of these

several points of view come together to discuss their differences. (p. 116)

However, in the same volume, Denzin and Lincoln discussed five points of difference between qualitative and quantitative research, indicating that they were "governed by a different set of genres" (p. 6). (See the extended quote earlier in this section.)

3. In the second edition of the *Handbook of Qualitative Research*, the position of the qualitative research theorists changed even more, as indicated by the quotes from both Guba and Lincoln (2000, p. 2) and Schwandt (2000, p. 190). Now, it was determined that multiple paradigms (including positivism-postpositivism) could be used to support qualitative research.

There appear to be three reasons for the evolution in the position of the qualitative research theorists over time:

◆ Initially, the qualitative research theorists believed that they had to demonstrate the supremacy of their ideology and method to that which they called the "received" view of science (positivism-postpositivism). As it turned out, however, the ready acceptance of qualitative research by many in the social and behavioral sciences over the decade from 1985 to 1995 made further attacks on the received tradition unnecessary.

◆ Coincidentally, there was an explosion in the number of paradigms to be discussed. The initial two-column paradigm table (naturalism and positivism) in Lincoln and Guba (1985) became a four-column paradigm table (positivism, postpositivism, critical theory, and constructivism) in Guba and Lincoln (1994), which then became a five-column paradigm table (with the addition of the participatory-cooperative paradigm) in Lincoln and Guba (2000). In addition, there was a particularly large explosion in paradigms associated with qualitative research methods. There are six chapters in the second edition of the *Handbook of Qualitative Research* devoted to different paradigms. With so many paradigms to choose from, it made sense to advocate the multiple paradigm stance as opposed to the single paradigm/methodology viewpoint.

◆ There is evidence that the qualitative research theorists were uncomfortable in their perceived role as originators of the paradigm wars. The previous quote from Guba and Lincoln (1994, p. 116) indicates that they did not like the "confrontational" components of the paradigm debate.[12] The multiple paradigm stance is much less confrontational.

Thus, the increased legitimacy of qualitative research methods, the increase in the number of paradigms that could be associated with qualitative research methods, and the unpopularity of the paradigm wars all were factors that led to the current advocacy of the multiple paradigms perspective.

THE RESIDUES OF THE WARS

So, what does this historical analysis have to do with mixed methods at the current point in time? There are ongoing consequences of the paradigm wars—some positive and some negative. As noted throughout this chapter, the paradigm wars (and particularly the incompatibility thesis) were a major catalyst in the development of the mixed methods as a distinct third methodological movement.

The paradigm wars and the discussions that are still ongoing point out the continuing importance of paradigms to researchers (including mixed methods researchers) today. At least nine of the chapters in this handbook (Chapters 1, 2, 3, 4, 8, 9, 17, 23, and 26) contain lengthy discussions about paradigms and mixed methods. These discussions and debates will continue to help define mixed methodology as a separate research movement.

Nevertheless, there are some negative residuals of the paradigm wars. There are still many graduate programs in various disciplines across the country that consider themselves and their students to be QUALs or QUANs. Students often identify themselves as QUANs or QUALs and never again will (if they ever did before) darken the door of a lecture hall where the opposing methodology is being presented. Therefore, we are raising a generation of scholars, many of whom do not know what a standard deviation is, on the one hand, or what a constant comparative analysis is, on the other.

Schwandt (2000) commented on this issue:

> So the traditional means of coming to grips with one's identity as a researcher by aligning oneself with a particular set of methods (or by being defined in one's department as a student of "qualitative" or "quantitative" methods) is no longer very useful. If we are to go forward, we need to get rid of that distinction. (p. 210)

◆ Design Issues in Mixed Methods Research

Many individuals writing in the field of mixed methods have proposed their own typologies of mixed methods research designs. Indeed, several contributors to this handbook present original or revised typologies (e.g., Morse, Chapter 7; Creswell et al., Chapter 8; Tashakkori & Teddlie, Chapter 26) or have had their typologies described by others in this volume (e.g., Greene & Caracelli, 1997; Greene et al., 1989).

This section describes issues related to typologies of mixed methods research designs that are discussed throughout the handbook. We examine seven of these issues in this chapter:

1. Are typologies of mixed methods designs necessary? Why?

2. Can we expect a typology to be exhaustive?

3. What are the major typologies of mixed methods research designs presented in this handbook?

4. What criteria can a researcher use to select the best mixed methods design for his or her research project?

5. Is there an alternative way to discuss different kinds of mixed methods designs other than using typologies?

6. What are points of agreement regarding design issues in mixed methods research?

7. What are continuing points of controversy regarding design issues in mixed methods research?

ARE TYPOLOGIES OF MIXED METHODS DESIGNS NECESSARY? WHY?

Scholars writing in the field of mixed methods research have presented typologies of mixed designs from the time the field emerged. For instance, Greene et al. (1989) examined a large number of mixed methods studies and developed a typology for the designs used in those studies based on purpose and design characteristics.

Why did Greene et al. (1989) want to develop a typology of mixed methods research designs, and why have so many of their colleagues followed suit? Following are five reasons why typologies have been used in classifying mixed methods designs:

1. Typologies of mixed methods designs help to provide the field with an organizational structure. For instance, the Greene et al. (1989) analysis indicated that there were at least five distinct types of mixed methods designs. At this point in time, given the wide range of typologies, it is more accurate to say that such typologies provide the field with multiple competing organizational structures.

2. Typologies of mixed methods designs help to legitimize the field because they provide examples of research designs that are clearly distinct from either quantitative or qualitative research designs. For instance, the basic mixed methods designs proposed by Morse (1991) were different from the designs found in either quantitative or qualitative research methods. No one before had ever used names such as "simultaneous triangulation" and "sequential triangulation" in describing quantitative or qualitative research designs.

3. Typologies of mixed methods research designs are useful in helping to establish a common language for the field. Again, using the work of Morse (1991; Chapter 7, this handbook) as an example, her typologies of mixed methods research designs included notations and abbreviations that many scholars still use today (e.g., simultaneous design, sequential design).

4. Typologies help researchers to decide how to proceed when designing their mixed methods studies. Typologies pro-vide a variety of paths that may be chosen to accomplish the goals of researchers' studies. They may include particular mixed methods research designs that are most appropriate for the goals of particular research projects.

5. Typologies are useful as a pedagogical tool. Presenting a variety of mixed methods research designs to students helps familiarize them with the criteria underlying the designs and gives them prototypes on which to model their own research. A particularly effective teaching technique is to present competing design typologies and then have the students discuss their strengths and weaknesses.

CAN WE EXPECT A TYPOLOGY TO BE EXHAUSTIVE?

We often expect that a typology will be exhaustive; that is, we expect that the typology will include all of the elements within the universe of elements for that particular quality. This expectation is based on the presumed thoroughness of typologies of elements found in the physical world.

Such an expectation is not reasonable with regard to a typology of mixed methods research designs.[13] Maxwell and Loomis (Chapter 9, this volume) point out the very obvious fact that "the actual diversity in mixed methods studies is far greater than any typology can adequately encompass."

Mixed model designs can be distinguished on a number of different dimensions (e.g., purpose, underlying paradigm), and developing a typology that would encompass all of those dimensions would be impossible. What is more, even if we could list all of the mixed methods designs at one point in time, the types of designs would continue to evolve, thereby making the typology no longer exhaustive.

The best one can expect is to adopt a typology of mixed methods research designs that includes the most important criteria to the individual researcher. Indeed, the best typology of mixed methods designs for a researcher might change later if the context within which the researcher is operating changes.

WHAT ARE THE MAJOR TYPOLOGIES OF MIXED METHODS RESEARCH DESIGNS PRESENTED IN THIS HANDBOOK?

Morse (1991; Chapter 7, this volume) and Morgan (1998) Typologies. Morse (1991), writing in the applied field of nursing, authored an important article on approaches to qualitative-quantitative methodological triangulation. In that article, she presented a notational system that is also found in her chapter in this handbook (Chapter 7). While some of Morse's definitions do not currently agree with those of others writing in the field (see subsection on points of controversy later), her basic terminology and notational system is still widely employed today. Her notational system is the standard currently used in the mixed methods research area.

Components of this system include the following:[14]

♦ Use of the abbreviations QUAN for quantitative and QUAL for qualitative

♦ Use of the plus sign (+) to indicate that data are collected simultaneously (e.g., QUAN + qual)

♦ Use of the arrow to indicate that data collection occurs sequentially (e.g., QUAL → quan)

♦ Use of uppercase to denote more priority given to that orientation (e.g., QUAN)

We discuss the criteria used in developing typologies of mixed methods research designs throughout this chapter. These criteria are used to differentiate between research designs within the typology and to express important underlying assumptions. In Morse's typology, there are two obvious criteria that distinguish between the designs: the sequence in which data are collected and the priority assigned to one orientation or the other (dominant, less dominant).

Following Creswell's (1994) distinction between dominant and less dominant approaches in mixed methods studies, Morgan (1998) presented a "Priority-Sequence Model" consisting of a set of decision rules for combining qualitative and quantitative data collection in a study. Decision rules consist of (a) deciding the priority of either the qualitative or the quantitative method and (b) deciding on the sequence of the two by identifying the order of conducting the complementary method (either a preliminary or a follow-up phase). The four basic designs that result from these two decisions are qualitative preliminary (qual-QUAN), quantitative preliminary (quan-QUAL), qualitative follow-up (QUAN-qual), and quantitative follow-up (QUAL-quan) (p. 367). This typology of designs includes multiphase studies and does not impose any limitation on the order of QUAL and QUAN phases of the study.

Greene and Caracelli (1997; see also Greene et al., 1989) Typologies. Greene et al. (1989) presented a typology of mixed methods designs based on their function or purpose, as noted earlier in this chapter. There were five designs in their initial typology. A later revision

(Greene & Caracelli, 1997) included two types of designs with a total of seven distinct mixed methods designs: component designs (triangulation, complementary, and expansion) and integrated designs (iterative, embedded or nested, holistic, and transformative).

Other scholars (e.g., Creswell, 2002, chap. 17; McMillan & Schumacher, 2001) have developed typologies of mixed methods designs that include some of these functions.

Creswell (2002, chap. 17; see also Creswell et al., Chapter 8, this volume). Incorporating the Greene et al. (1989) purposes, while also taking the sequence of QUAL and QUAN components, Creswell (2002) classified mixed methods designs in three types: triangulation, explanatory, and exploratory. In the triangulation mixed methods design, the investigators "collect both quantitative and qualitative data, merge the data, and use the results to best understand a research problem" (pp. 564-565). The explanatory design consists of "collecting quantitative data and then collecting qualitative data to help explain or elaborate on the quantitative results" (p. 566). The exploratory design has an opposite sequence consisting of "first gathering qualitative data to explore a phenomenon, and then collecting quantitative data to explain relationship found in the qualitative data" (p. 567). The emphasis in this typology is on type of data.

In the triangulation design from Creswell's (2002, chap. 17) typology, the QUAL and QUAN components proceed in a simultaneous or parallel manner (Tashakkori & Teddlie, 1998). The other two designs are sequential. The explanatory design has a QUAN-QUAL sequence, while the exploratory design has a QUAL-QUAN sequence.

By contrast, McMillan and Schumacher (2001) adopted three types from Greene

et al. (1989): complementary, developmental, and expansion designs. Their complementary design is parallel (they use the term *simultaneous*), while the other two are sequential. However, unlike Creswell's sequential designs, the order of the QUAL and QUAN phases are not predetermined (i.e., each might start with a QUAL or a QUAN phase).

The design chapter by Creswell and colleagues in this handbook (Chapter 8) demonstrates both progress toward a convergent model and a divergence of ideas. After an insightful review of the current typologies, Creswell and colleagues identify four criteria (dimensions) for conceptualizing a mixed methods design (see Table 8.3 in their chapter). They then propose six types of mixed methods design: sequential explanatory, sequential exploratory, sequential transformative, concurrent triangulation, concurrent nested, and concurrent transformative. Criteria used in the Creswell and colleagues classification include the sequence in which data are collected, the purpose of the study, and theoretical perspective (transformative or not).

Tashakkori and Teddlie (1998). We (Tashakkori & Teddlie, 1998) developed a typology of mixed method and mixed model designs based on "procedure" or method of study rather than on priority of orientation, purpose of study, theoretical perspective, and so on. In this subsection, we review our 1998 typology, revising it slightly with regard to terminology. In Chapter 26 of this handbook, we extend the typology by expanding on what we called parallel mixed model designs and sequential mixed model designs in the 1998 typology. The following are a series of points that describe our 1998 typology of mixed method and mixed model designs:

◆ First, we distinguished between mixed method and mixed model designs.

Mixed method designs are those that combine the qualitative and quantitative approaches into the research methodology of a single study or a multiphased study. These methods are further subdivided into five specific types of designs: sequential studies, parallel/simultaneous studies, equivalent status designs, dominant-less dominant studies (Creswell, 1994), and "designs with multilevel utilization of approaches in which researchers utilize different types of methods at different levels of data aggregation" (Tashakkori & Teddlie, 1998, p. 18).

♦ Mixed model studies are considerably different. These are studies that "combine the qualitative and quantitative approaches within different [stages] of the research process" (Tashakkori & Teddlie, 1998, p. 19). Extending the work of Patton (1990), we classified three stages of the research process: exploratory versus confirmatory nature of the investigation, quantitative and qualitative data/operations, and statistical analysis/inference and qualitative analysis/inference.[15] Mixed methods relate to the data collection/operations stage only, while mixed model studies concern all three stages.

♦ A shortcoming of this classification is that it does not clearly differentiate between the data analysis stage and the nature of the final inferences that are made on the basis of the data analysis results. The main reason for this lack of differentiation in the typology of designs is that we, like many other writers, believe that all inferences in social/behavioral research have *some* degree of subjectivity and value in them (see Moghaddam, Walker, & Harré, Chapter 4, this volume). Also, regardless of type of analysis, we usually go beyond the "results" by offering more abstract/

general explanations for events/behaviors and the like in the conclusion of a report. In other words, following both types of data analysis, inferences vary in degree of qualitative and quantitative approaches. Instead of being a dichotomy (constructivist/subjectivist vs. objectivist/value-neutral [see Crotty, 1998; Greene & Caracelli, Chapter 3, this volume]), multiple inferences are made at the end of the study, each varying in generality, subjectivity, cultural orientation, political ideology, value orientation, and so on. Therefore, adding type of inference to our proposed typology is not necessary or even possible. Figure 1.1 depicts this relativity of inferences following QUAL and QUAN data analysis.

♦ In an extension of our earlier work, we now distinguish between monostrand and multistrand mixed model studies, using the word *strand* in the sense that Maxwell and Loomis do in this handbook (Chapter 9). A monostrand mixed model design is a study with a single method for answering either QUAL or QUAN research questions. The data may be transformed from QUAL to QUAN (or vice versa) and analyzed to reach either a QUAL or a QUAN inference. The monostrand studies are mixed across stages of the research process such that one stage is different (in QUAL or QUAN orientation) from the other two stages. These monostrand mixed model studies are the building blocks of the more common multistrand mixed model studies.

♦ Eight designs emerge from the combination of the three research stages noted (a graphic presentation of these designs may be found in our Chapter 26 in this volume). They are presented in Table 1.2 (e.g., Mixed Type IV, which is an exploratory investigation, with qualita-

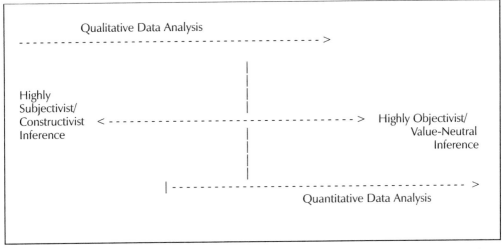

Figure 1.1. Dimensions of Data Analysis and Inference in Tashakkori and Teddlie's Monostrand Mixed Model Typology

tive data collection and operations and statistical analysis/inference). Two are classic single approach designs (pure QUAN and pure QUAL). The other six designs[16] are monostrand mixed model designs in that there is a switching of the approach (e.g., from QUAL to QUAN) in one of the stages of the study. For example, the Mixed Type IV design is a predominantly exploratory study in which the data are quantitized and analyzed statistically.

◆ Multistrand mixed model studies were referred to as parallel mixed model designs (Type VII) and sequential mixed model designs (Type VIII) in the Tashakkori and Teddlie (1998) typology. In a multistrand mixed model design (what Creswell, 1994, called a two-phase design), there are multiple types of questions (QUAL and QUAN) and both types of data and data analysis techniques. The inferences that are made on the basis of the results are both subjectivist/constructivist (QUAL

[Crotty, 1998]) or objectivist (QUAN) in approach. This type of design may be sequential or parallel.

◆ Chapter 26 in this handbook contains an extension of Tashakkori and Teddlie (1998) in that several specific parallel and sequential multistage mixed model designs are presented.

WHAT CRITERIA CAN A RESEARCHER USE TO SELECT THE BEST MIXED METHODS DESIGN FOR HIS OR HER RESEARCH PROJECT?

We have argued that typologies of mixed methods research designs are important for several reasons, including helping the researcher select a particular design for his or her study. The process of selecting the best mixed methods research design for a project is a complex one involving several steps (both assumptions and actions). The details for much of this

TABLE 1.2 Tashakkori and Teddlie's (1998) Classification of Single Strand Mixed Model Designs

	Confirmatory Investigation			Exploratory Investigation			
	Quantitative Data/Operations	*Qualitative Data/Operations*		*Quantitative Data/Operations*		*Qualitative Data/Operations*	
		Statistical analysis and inference	Qualitative analysis and inference	Statistical analysis and inference	Qualitative analysis and inference	Statistical analysis and inference	Qualitative analysis and inference
Statistical analysis and inference	Pure quantitative	Mixed Type I	Mixed Type II	Mixed Type III	Mixed Type VI (rare)	Mixed Type IV	Pure qualitative
Qualitative analysis and inference	Mixed Type V (rare)						

process were derived from Morgan (1998) and Creswell and colleagues (Chapter 8, this volume):

1. There are a number of typologies of mixed methods research designs, as noted previously.

2. None of these typologies is exhaustive, as argued in a previous section.

3. The researcher wants to select the best research design for his or her particular study and assumes that one of the published typologies includes the best design for the project.

4. Typologies may be differentiated by the criteria that are used to distinguish among the research designs within them (Morgan, 1998; Creswell et al., Chapter 8, this volume). These criteria identify the important assumptions of the typology.

5. The criteria that each typology uses may be determined through an analysis of the designs within the typology. We did this for several of the typologies previously described in this section. Both Morgan (1998) and Creswell et al. (Chapter 8, this volume) identified two basic criteria in the designs presented by Morse (1991) and others: These designs vary in terms of the sequence in which the QUAN and QUAL data collection procedures are implemented, and they vary in terms of the priority given to each type of data (QUAN or quan, QUAL or qual).

6. These criteria may be listed by the researcher, who then may select the criteria that are most important to him or her. Creswell and colleagues (Chapter 8, this volume) list four such criteria and then assess their six mixed methods designs according to those criteria. In addition to order of implementation

and priority, Creswell and colleagues distinguish two other criteria: stage of integration and theoretical perspective. The stage of integration criterion comes from Tashakkori and Teddlie's (1998) typology that suggests that integration of the QUAL and QUAN perspectives can occur at different stages of the research process (research question, data collection, data analysis, or data interpretation). The theoretical perspective criterion comes from the writing of Greene and Caracelli (1997), who included a transformational, action-oriented dimension to their research. The presence or absence of this theoretical perspective constituted the fourth of Creswell and colleagues' (Chapter 8, this volume) criteria for distinguishing among research designs. Of course, other criteria may apply. For instance, it is obvious that the purpose of the study plays a large role in the two typologies of Greene and Caracelli (1997; see also Green et al., 1989). Also, number of strands (monostrands or multistrands) is an important criterion in Tashakkori and Teddlie's update of their 1998 typology. Of course, it is up to the researcher to select the particular criteria that are important to him or her.

7. The researcher may then apply the selected criteria to potential designs, ultimately selecting the best research design for his or her study.

8. To do this, the researcher must determine which of the research designs is most in accordance with the desired qualities on the selected criteria. For example, if the researcher believes that qualitative research will play the predominant role in his or her study, then the researcher should select a design in which that is the case.

9. In some cases, the researcher may have to develop a new mixed methods design because no one best design exists for his or her research project. Also, some designs may change over the course of the study. This might occur, for instance, if one type of data becomes more important as the study develops.

IS THERE AN ALTERNATIVE WAY TO DISCUSS DIFFERENT KINDS OF MIXED METHODS DESIGNS OTHER THAN USING TYPOLOGIES?

Some readers may tire of the different typological approaches to mixed methods research designs and seek another, more dynamic point of view. Maxwell and Loomis (Chapter 9, this volume) present an alternative approach to conceptualizing mixed methods designs. Instead of presenting another typology of designs, they introduce what they call an "interactive model" for research design in which the components of research design (purpose, conceptual framework, research question, methods, and validity) are components in a network or web rather than in a linear progression (e.g., from purpose to method to inference). The authors then apply this interactive model to mixed methods research, demonstrating how the different components of real mixed methods studies are integrated. Furthermore, in each of these five components, the investigators use quantitative or qualitative lenses/ approaches for different conceptualizations.

Maxwell and Loomis's conception of the differences between quantitative and qualitative research is also different. Their analysis concerns what they call variance theory and process theory.

Maxwell and Lomis see their approach as complementary to the more typical ty-

pological approaches and suggest that we should combine both strategies when analyzing mixed methods research designs. Their contribution to the handbook (Chapter 9) is highly creative and should generate friendly debate.

WHAT ARE POINTS OF AGREEMENT REGARDING DESIGN ISSUES IN MIXED METHODS RESEARCH?

Creating a systematic and more uniform conceptualization of mixed methods now appears more possible than ever before because the requisite "elements" are largely in place due to the high-quality contributions that have emerged over the past 10 years. These elements are demonstrated throughout this handbook, which we also hope will serve as a stimulus for further development and unification. It is useful to look at the points of commonality that we now have with regard to mixed methods research design:

♦ Scholars agree that it is possible to use both QUAL and QUAN methods to answer objective-value neutral AND subjective-constructivist questions.

♦ Scholars agree, to different degrees, that it is possible to have both inductive/ exploratory questions and deductive/ confirmatory ones in the same study.

♦ Scholars agree, more or less, that different orientations may be mixed in the statement of purposes/questions of the study (e.g., exploration, explanation, confirmation, political/social transformation), methods (e.g., QUAN and QUAL sampling, data collection procedures, data analysis), and/or inferences/ conclusions.

◆ Scholars agree that research questions do not emerge in a vacuum. Rather, they emerge or are influenced by the culture of the investigator as well as through social and political agendas. This point of view is reflected in several chapters in this handbook (Moghaddam et al., Chapter 4; Mertens, Chapter 5; Newman, Ridenour, Newman, & De-Marco, Chapter 6).

◆ There is basic agreement on the terms and notations used in describing mixed methods research designs.

◆ Many scholars recognize that there are many research questions that can be answered only with a mixed methods design.

◆ Most agree with Creswell and colleagues (Chapter 8, this volume) that a mixed methods study involves the collection of both quantitative and qualitative data in a single study, in which the data are collected concurrently or sequentially, and involves the integration of the data at one or more stages in the process of research.

WHAT ARE CONTINUING POINTS OF CONTROVERSY REGARDING DESIGN ISSUES IN MIXED METHODS RESEARCH?

While we are closer than ever before to the development of a uniform and systematic classification of mixed methods design, there is still great divergence of ideas among the scholars in the field, as readers will notice throughout this handbook:

◆ Different criteria are used by different scholars in defining their typologies of mixed methods research designs.

◆ There is confusion between the descriptions of data analysis and the interpretation of the results (what we call "inferences").

◆ There is divergence in nomenclature, with the same design being labeled differently by different scholars (e.g., simultaneous, concurrent, or parallel). This extends to some basic terms such as mixed methods designs (see, e.g., Morse, Chapter 7, this volume).

◆ Triangulation, complementarity, and expansion are used by some scholars to represent types of *design*. As demonstrated by Erzberger and Kelle (Chapter 16, this volume), they are possible outcomes of research; therefore, it is not always possible to predict which of the three might occur at the end of a mixed methods study.

◆ Erzberger and Prein (1997) criticized limiting exploratory designs to a QUAL-QUAN sequence. They argued that is it possible to have an exploratory QUAN study with a QUAL phase to confirm/disconfirm the inferences that were made in the first phase.

◆ Miller (Chapter 15, this volume) argues that researchers should give priority to QUAN inferences in QUAN-QUAL designs. Onwuegbuzie and Teddlie (Chapter 13, this volume) counterargue that the overall research purpose should determine which inference is given primacy.

◆ Issues in Drawing Inferences in Mixed Methods Research

Much of the literature on mixed methods has been devoted to issues of research design or paradigm. Although these discussions have led to the identification of a large variety of design and paradigm issues, they have distracted us from the most important component of any research project: the inference (see Miller, Chapter 15, this volume).

We believe that the ultimate advantage of using mixed methods is in the quality of inferences that are made at the end of a series of phases/strands of study. As such, we differentiate the "results" of a study from the "inferences" that are made from that study. Results are the outcomes of data collection and data analysis (e.g., data reduction by creating themes or numerical indicators, establishing the degree of relationship between two categories). Inferences are based on the investigators' interpretations and expansions of such results. As discussed by Moghaddam and Hare (1995), inferences are always made in the cultural context. Hence, the same results might lead to different interpretations by different investigators in two different cultural contexts.

This section on inferences in mixed methods begins with some basic definitions, including inference, inference quality, design quality, interpretive rigor, and inference transferability. We then discuss three basic challenges related to the issue of inference in mixed methods research, with an emphasis on inference quality. Finally, we discuss issues related to inference transferability.

BASIC DEFINITIONS OF INFERENCE AND INFERENCE-RELATED MATTERS IN MIXED METHODS RESEARCH

The Definition of Inference: One Common Term for QUALs and QUANs. Consistent with the writings of some of the authors in this handbook (e.g., Miller, Chapter 15; Erzberger & Kelle, Chapter 16), we (Tashakkori & Teddlie, in press) defined "inference" elsewhere as

> an umbrella term to refer to a final outcome of a study. The outcome may consist of a conclusion about, an understanding of, or an explanation for an event, [a] behavior, [a] relationship, or a case (e.g. in qualitative research). We use the term "inference" as a mixed methods term because it may take a variety of meanings ranging between a purely qualitative connotation to a purely quantitative connotation. The dictionary definition of "infer" (the root word for inference) is central to our decision to use the term broadly. The definition is as follows: "to bring or carry in; cause; induce" (Webster's New World Dictionary, 3rd Edition, p. 691), or "to draw a conclusion , as by reasoning" (Webster's Universal College Dictionary, 1997, p. 418). Thus, the dictionary definitions for infer include making conclusions, as well as both the term "cause," which is associated with the quantitative orientation, and the term "induce" (the root word for induction), which is associated with the qualitative orientation.

This is also consistent with Angeles's (1981) *Dictionary of Philosophy,* in which inference is defined as "a conclusion reached," a "deduction from premises that are accepted as true," or an "induction" by "deriving a conclusion from factual statements taken as evidence for the conclusion" (p. 133). Therefore, inference is a term that can be used by QUALs and QUANs alike because it refers to the inductively or deductively derived conclusions from a study.

Use of the Term Inference Quality *Rather Than* Validity.[17] We also use the umbrella term *inference quality* to refer to issues such as internal validity (QUAN term) or credibility (QUAL term). Cook and Campbell (1979) defined internal validity as the "approximate validity with which we infer that a relationship between two variables is causal or that the absence of a relationship implies the absence of cause" (p. 37). More recent definitions of internal validity include noncausal relationships. For example, Krathwohl (1993) defined it as "the power of a study to support an inference that certain variables in it are *linked* in a relationship (p. 271, italics in original). According to this expanded definition, internal validity is the degree to which alternative plausible explanations of the results are ruled out, controlled for, or eliminated. Lincoln and Guba (1985) proposed credibility as the QUAL equivalent for internal validity and proposed several techniques to produce it (e.g., prolonged engagement, persistent observation) (p. 300).

Alternatively, we propose the term *inference quality* as the mixed methods term for the accuracy with which we have drawn both our inductively and our deductively derived conclusions from a study. There are two basic reasons for proposing a new mixed methods term to replace the traditional QUAN and QUAL terms. First, we believe that mixed methods researchers should adopt a common nomenclature that transcends the QUAL and QUAN orientations when the described processes are highly similar and when appropriate terminology exists. Second, we especially believe that a common nomenclature is necessary when the existing QUAL and QUAN terms have been overly used or misused.

The concepts of internal validity and credibility appear to be highly similar because both processes involve determining the degree to which a researcher believes that his or her conclusions accurately describe what actually happened in the study. In one case, the researcher rules out alternative explanations through research design and logic. In the other case, the investigator uses a variety of techniques, the most important of which is to ascertain whether the research participants find the investigator's conclusions "credible" (i.e., member checks).

Fortunately, an appropriate alternative term exists for internal validity/credibility in the form of *inference quality*. We have demonstrated how inference takes into consideration both the QUAL (inductively derived) and QUAN (deductively derived) concepts of coming to conclusions. Quality is a straightforward word connoting degree of excellence. Because quality has seldom been used in research methodology, it has not been overly used or misused.

The second reason for proposing a new mixed methods term is when the existing QUAN or QUAL terms have been overly used or misused. As we concluded in a previous section of this chapter on nomenclature, "validity" has been used in such diverse and imprecise ways that it has lost its meaningfulness as a distinct term connoting either internal or external validity, or catalytic or ironic validity, or any of the other 35 types of validity found in Table 1.1.

The pioneers who proposed the original use of the term *validity* in research and measurement (e.g., Campbell & Stanley, 1963; Cook & Campbell, 1979) made seminal contributions to our understanding of design and measurement issues in quantitative research methodology. However, we believe that validity has become a catchall term that is increasingly losing its ability to connote anything. When a term is used with other words to connote so many meanings, it essentially has none. As Lincoln and Guba (2000) concluded, "Radical reconfigurations of validity leave researchers with multiple, sometimes conflicting, mandates for what constitutes rigorous research" (p. 178).

It should be reiterated at this point that we are not suggesting that QUANs stop using the term *internal validity* in their research studies or that QUALs stop using the term *credibility*. Instead, we are suggesting that when researchers use mixed methods, *inference* and *inference quality* are better terms to use when describing the mixed (QUAL and QUAN) results.

Terms Associated With Inference Quality. In determining the authenticity of findings from qualitative research, Lincoln and Guba (2000) suggested that there are two basic criteria: rigor in the application of method and rigor in interpretation. We now apply these concepts with regard to mixed methods and inference quality. We contend that mixed methods nomenclature should include two important aspects of inference quality. The first we call *design quality,* which comprises the standards for the evaluation of the methodological rigor of the mixed methods research, and the second we call *interpretive rigor,* which comprises the standards for the evaluation of the accuracy or authenticity of the conclusions.

With regard to design quality, we can assemble a whole set of criteria from both the quantitative and qualitative orientations to determine whether our study adheres to commonly accepted best practices. If, for example, we coupled a small-scale quasi-experimental study together with extensive interviews and observations of participants, then a variety of criteria could apply such as the following. Were the participants selected in accordance with the best sampling criteria available? Was the treatment consistent with the definition provided in the statement of purpose? Was there prolonged engagement with and persistent observation

of the participants? Was a dependability audit undertaken?

The issue of *interpretive rigor* is more difficult to assess. Lincoln and Guba (2000) defined the concept as follows: "Are we *interpretively* rigorous? Can our cocreated constructions be trusted to provide some purchase on some important human phenomenon?" (p. 179).

How might this interpretive rigor be determined? There have been a number of attempts in qualitative research to further analyze what we are calling interpretive rigor, including the Guba and Lincoln (1989) description of five authenticity criteria (fairness, ontological authenticity, educative authenticity, catalytic authenticity, and tactical authenticity). Indeed, attempts to further refine the "internal validity" of qualitative research findings have led to the further proliferation of different kinds of validity or authenticity.

A more productive manner for handling this issue of interpretive rigor might be to describe a process whereby the accuracy, or authenticity, of our conclusions/interpretations is assessed. We offer such a process in a later subsection of this chapter.

Inference Transferability. While inference quality is emphasized in this chapter, we also need to consider the generalizability of our results—or what the QUANs have called external validity or what the QUALs have called transferability of results. Although the controversies regarding external validity or transferability are easier to deal with than issues of inference quality, they still pose a challenge to mixed methods researchers.

We propose to use the term *inference transferability* as an umbrella term that refers to both the QUAN term *external validity* and the QUAL term *transferability.* As with inference quality, we believe that a common nomenclature should be adopted when the described QUAL and QUAN processes are similar and when appropriate terminology exists.

The concepts of external validity and transferability are similar because both processes involve determining whether our conclusions may be extrapolated beyond the particular conditions of the research study. When introducing transferability as the qualitative equivalent of external validity, Lincoln and Guba (1985) referred to transferability of the results from the sending context to the receiving context. One had to know the characteristics of both contexts to know how transferable the results were. Therefore, thick descriptions of the contexts are required. The quantitative concept of external validity encompasses populations, settings, and times.

Again to avoid some of the confusions surrounding the term *validity,* we propose replacing it with *transferability,* borrowed from qualitative research literature. Like the terms *inference* and *quality,* transferability seems appropriate for use in both the QUAN and QUAL contexts and has not been overly used or misused. *Inference transferability* can be used as an overall umbrella term, while other terms may refer to more specific types of transferability:

♦ Transferability might refer to contexts other than the ones studied (*ecological transferability*).

♦ Transferability might refer to individuals/groups or entities (e.g., texts, artifacts) other than the ones studied (*population transferability*).

♦ Transferability might refer to other time periods (*temporal transferability*).

♦ Transferability might refer to other modes/methods of measuring/observ-

ing the variables/behaviors (*operational transferability*).

Summary of Definitions of Inference-Related Matters in Mixed Methods Research. We used the term *inference* to refer to an outcome of a study, whether it is derived inductively or deductively. We used the term *inference quality* to refer to a process that encompasses both internal validity and credibility. We then defined two aspects of inference quality: design quality and interpretive rigor.

We also defined inference transferability as a term that encompasses external validity and transferability. Other important concepts related to inference transferability include ecological transferability and population transferability.

The labels that we proposed throughout this chapter were constructed through combining what we consider to be the best nomenclature from the current research methodology literature (e.g., inference, quality, transferability) and avoiding overused or misleading terminology. We hope that other mixed methods scholars refine these terms further as we move toward a more unified nomenclature.

THREE BASIC CHALLENGES RELATED TO THE ISSUE OF INFERENCE IN MIXED METHODS RESEARCH

There is much inconsistency between and within the QUAL and QUAN orientations with regard to the issue of inference or what others refer to as validity. Mixed methodologists face at least three challenges with regard to the issue of inference:

1. confusion between the quality of data/observations and the quality of inferences that are made on the basis of the analysis of such data;

2. controversies regarding standards for evaluating inference quality (what we call design quality and interpretive vigor); and

3. creating bridges or superordinate standards for evaluating the quality of inferences in mixed methods research.

In the following subsections, we summarize our positions regarding these three issues.

Confusion Between the Data Quality and the Quality of Inferences Based on That Data. We have noted before (Tashakkori & Teddlie, 1998, in press) that there is a need for differentiating data quality from inference quality. There is no doubt that the quality of *measures/observations* affects the quality of the *inferences* that are made at the end of the study; that is, bad measures/observations will lead to inaccurate conclusions regardless of the design. But assuming acceptable measures/observations, the quality of inferences is largely independent of the quality of data; that is, inaccurate conclusions may be made on the basis of good data. Inference quality has to be evaluated separately from data quality, and the standards for evaluating them are not the same (Tashakkori & Teddlie, 1998).

Obviously, the fundamental principle of data quality in mixed methods research should be the following: "If the data do not represent the theoretical phenomena or the attributes under study, then nothing else in the design of the study matters." In other words, nothing good emerges from bad data. In QUAN research, this is known as the GIGO (garbage in, garbage out) principle. Data quality affects what Cook and Campbell (1979) called the "construct validity of putative causes and effects" (p. 59). In Cook and Campbell's terms,

> For persons interested in theory testing, it is almost as important to show that the variables involved in the research are constructs A and B (construct validity) as it is to show that the relationship is causal and goes from one variable to the other (internal validity). (p.83)

Similarly, a person involved in studying a phenomenon qualitatively must be sure that the data represent the phenomenon of interest. The investigator must follow certain established procedures, such as prolonged engagement, to be sure that he or she is examining the correct phenomenon. As we noted elsewhere,

> It is important that investigators spend an adequate amount of time in the field to build trust, learn the "culture," and test for misinformation either from informants or [from] their own biases. . . . The purpose of prolonged engagement is to provide "scope" for researchers by making them aware of the multiple contextual factors and multiple perspectives of informants at work in any given social scene. (Tashakkori & Teddlie, 1998, p. 90)

Controversies Regarding Standards for Evaluating Inference Quality. One major issue under this challenge is a matter of definition: Sometimes QUAL and QUAN researchers define the same concept differently. If a mixed methodologist wanted to establish that a certain type of validity existed with a research study, then such a conflict in definition would make the establishment of validity impossible. For example, both QUALs and QUANs (e.g., Liebert & Liebert, 1995; Maxwell, 1992) have used the term *theoretical validity*. In QUAL research, it has been used to represent "the degree that a theoretical explanation developed from a research study fits the data" (Johnson & Christensen, 2000, p. 210). In other words, do the inferences of the study (emergent theory) fit the data? By contrast, in QUAN research, *theoretical validity* has been used as the degree to which the interpretation of the findings is consistent with the theories and known knowledge in the field. In other words, does the inference fit the present knowledge and theories outside of the study? Obviously, the two questions asked by the term *theoretical validity* are very different from each other.

Of course, we have suggested that a more global term, *inference quality,* be used to assess the accuracy with which we have drawn both inductively and deductively derived conclusions from a mixed methods study. By using a common term to assess both the internal validity and the credibility of a study, we avoid some of the problems that practitioners of the two orientations have in interacting with one another.

In both traditions, the strategies for evaluation and for improvement of inferences may generally be placed along four evaluation dimensions: consistency within the design of the study, consistency of multiple conclusions with each other, consistency of interpretations across people, and distinctiveness of the interpretations from other plausible ones.[18] These four dimensions lead to four types of criteria for evaluation that are not necessarily exhaustive (there might be others) or mutually exclusive (one does not preclude the others). These four dimensions are (a) within-design consistency, (b) conceptual consistency, (c) interpretive agreement (or consistency), and (d) interpretive distinctness.

The remainder of this subsection provides examples of questions that might be asked in the evaluation of the inference quality of our research, which is a function of both design quality and interpretive rigor. In the examples that follow, the criterion of within-design consistency is related to what we call design quality. What we call interpretive rigor is related to the other three criteria.

1. *Within-design consistency* is the consistency of the procedures/design of the study from which the inferences emerged:

    Is the design consistent with the research questions/purpose?

    Do the observations/measures have demonstrated quality?

    Are data analysis techniques sufficient/appropriate for providing answers to research questions?

    Do the results happen the way the investigator claims they did? Do they have the necessary magnitude/strength or frequency to warrant the conclusions (*demonstrated results* in QUAL research, *magnitude of effect* in QUAN research)?

    Are the inferences (e.g., emergent theory or explanations) consistent with the results of data analysis? Do they strongly "follow" the findings?

    Are the inferences consistent with the research questions/purposes? Are the inferences obtained in each of the two strands (QUAL and QUAN) consistent with the corresponding research questions/purposes?

2. *The conceptual consistency* dimension consists of the degree to which the inferences are consistent with each other and with the known state of knowledge and theory. It incorporates explanation credibility and credible results audits from QUAL research.

2a. Consistency of inferences with each other within a study (cross-inference consistency):

    Are answers to different aspects of the research question/purpose consistent with each other?

Is the final (global) inference consistent with the ones obtained on the basis of QUAL and QUAN strands of the study? As Erzberger and Kelle (Chapter 16, this volume) suggest, inconsistent inferences obtained from phases/strands of a mixed methods study (e.g., dissonance, complementarity) should lead to a different higher order inference than should consistent inferences (e.g., triangulation, expansion).

2b. Consistency of inferences with current state of knowledge and theory (theoretical consistency):

Do the inferences take the current literature into consideration?

Are the inferences consistent with the state of knowledge? If not, do the inferences offer explanations (theory) for the inconsistency?

3. *Interpretive agreement* (or *consistency*) is consistency of interpretations across people (e.g., consistency among scholars, consistency with participants' construction of reality):

Do other scholars agree that the inferences are the most defensible interpretation of the results?

If participants' construction of the events/relationships is important to the researcher, do the interpretations make sense to participants of the study?

4. *Interpretive distinctiveness* includes the degree to which the inferences are distinctively different from other possible interpretations of the results and the rival explanations are ruled out (eliminated):

Are the inferences distinctively superior to other interpretations of the same findings? This is consistent with the criteria for evaluating internal validity in QUAN research where the

final inferences are the strongest and the most defensible to other scholars and are clearly distinct from other plausible interpretations of the results. Also, it is consistent with the "rival explanations eliminated" in QUAL research.

Are there other plausible explanations for the findings?

We believe that in evaluating the quality of inferences in mixed methods research, the issue of dominance or priority of one methodological approach (e.g., QUAL-quan, qual-QUAN) over another is not very important. Therefore, we have not included it in the preceding criteria/questions.

At the end of each strand/phase of the designs, inferences are made that are either qualitative (predominantly inductive, subjective, constructivist, emic, etc.) or quantitative (predominantly deductive, objective, value-neutral, etic, etc). These inferences either (a) follow each other, separated by a study (i.e., an inference points to the necessity of further data collection and analysis, which is followed by new inferences), or (b) are combined/contrasted to achieve a fuller picture of a phenomenon. The first type of inference is achieved in sequential designs, while the second is achieved in concurrent and transformational designs discussed in an earlier section of this chapter.

Strategies for integrating these inferences and the role of each (e.g., exploratory or confirmatory, triangulation or expansion, etc., as discussed by Miller [Chapter 15], Erzberger & Kelle [Chapter 16], and others in this volume) are more crucial than the dominance of one approach over another. One of the difficult tasks facing mixed methodologists has been in the formulation of such strategies. Erzberger and& Prein's (1997) "rules of integration" are expanded and discussed in detail in this handbook by Erzberger and Kelle (Chapter 16). Miller (Chapter 15) skillfully discusses a variety of issues regarding the term *inference* (as a process and as a product), and suggests "rules" for integrating inferences obtained from QUAL and QUAN phases.

Creating Bridges (Superordinate Standards) for Evaluating the Quality of Inferences in Mixed Methods Research. There appear to be four ways to create superordinate standards for evaluating the quality of inferences in mixed methods research:

1. Identify terms that are the same or similar in both traditions.

2. Borrow terms from the QUAL orientation that have potential for representing concepts in both.

3. Borrow terms from the QUAN orientation that have potential for representing both.

4. Construct totally new terms.

We have used all four of these techniques (in some combination) throughout this chapter to create a common nomenclature for inference in mixed methods. For example, the term *inference* means about the same in both traditions because it has been used very rarely (in definitions) in either one. We borrowed the term *transferability* from the QUAL literature to construct *inference transferability* as a common term for *external validity* and *transferability*. We took terms such as *population* from the QUAN literature to help denote certain types of transferability (e.g., population transferability). *Inference quality* is a good example of a constructed term.

SOME FURTHER COMMENTS ON INFERENCE TRANSFERABILITY

We have previously suggested (Tashakkori & Teddlie, 1998) that inference transferability is relative. That is, no research inference in social and behavioral sciences is fully transferable to *all* (or even most) settings, populations (of entities, people, texts, etc.), or time periods. On the other hand, we believe that any inference has *some* degree of transferability to other settings, populations, or times.

How do we determine the range of transferability of mixed methods inferences? A number of the scholars in this handbook (e.g., Kemper et al., Chapter 10; Johnson & Turner, Chapter 11) suggest that mixed methods inferences are more transferable than the inferences of either the QUAL or QUAN component. This assumption is based on the *gestalt principle* that the whole is bigger than the sum of its parts.

Finally, we believe that although inference transferability and quality might be improved by mixed methods, mixing two or more (QUAL and QUAN) strands/phases with poor inferences will not improve the otherwise poor quality of inferences that are made on the basis of each. The literature is littered with QUAN studies in which interpretations are made on the basis of small correlations or small magnitudes of differences between groups. The results of such studies are readily amenable to multiple inferences, some of which are more plausible than the ones made by the investigators (see, e.g., Ratner, 1997, p. 35; Tashakkori & Ropers-Huilman, 2000). On the other hand, the literature also includes QUAL studies in which a collection of isolated observations and personal opinions is used to make inferences that claim to represent others' perceptions and realities. Combining such poor quality inferences into global mixed methods inferences will not improve the rigor of the conclusions.

Our Chapter 26 in this handbook contains more details comparing our position on inferences to those of the authors of two other chapters: Miller (Chapter 15) and Erzberger and Kelle (Chapter 16). This is another of those areas in mixed methods research where there is lively debate but no consensus at this point in time. The discussion in Chapter 26 points out areas of agreement and contention with regard to the use of inferences in mixed methods.

◆ The Logistics of Conducting Mixed Methods Research

The issue of the logistics (i.e., organization and implementation) of mixed methods research is probably the least discussed of the major issues presented in this chapter. From our viewpoint, logistics involves both pedagogy (teaching people how to do mixed methods research) and collaboration (researchers working together in mixed methods research projects). Although little doubt is expressed regarding the usefulness of mixed methods for answering many research questions, it is also widely acknowledged that implementing mixed methods requires more time and effort than does implementing single approach studies (e.g., Creswell, 2002, chap. 17; McMillan & Schumacher, 2001). On the other hand, applied researchers in health, behavioral, and social sciences are increasingly expected to use mixed methods to answer increasingly complex and multifaceted research questions (Tashakkori & Teddlie, in press).

While there has been steady progress in the development of mixed methods over the past 10 to 15 years, there are still very few university courses available that are specifically devoted to mixed methods research (Tashakkori & Teddlie, in press; see also Creswell, Tashakkori, Jensen, & Shapley, Chapter 24, this volume). Part of the reason for this is that the current cohorts of professors teaching research methods never took a course in mixed methods themselves because it was not a recognized research topic when they were in graduate school. This lack of formal courses in the area obviously causes problems for the implementation of mixed methods research projects because all of the researchers involved are essentially self-taught.

Mixed methods research (especially in large-scale projects) is an area that is facilitated by collaboration or the team approach (Shulha & Wilson, Chapter 25, this volume). As suggested by others (Hafernik, Messerschmitt, & Vandrick, 1997; Miller & Crabtree, 2000), collaboration research not only is necessary for answering complex research questions but also enriches the experiences and competencies of the researchers who are involved.

THE FAILURE OF PEDAGOGY

As noted in the paradigm section earlier in this chapter, there are still many professors in graduate programs across the country who consider themselves and their students to be either QUALs or QUANs. These professors might not actively discourage their students from taking courses in the other research tradition, but they certainly do not encourage them. The minimum educational requirement for doing mixed methods research is to have taken courses in both the QUAL and QUAN research traditions or to be self-taught (which requires years of experience).

As Creswell and colleagues (Chapter 24, this volume) conclude, now is the time for attention to be paid to the teaching of mixed methods research courses. Articles and chapters on teaching qualitative methods are readily available (e.g., Stallings, 1995; Webb & Glesne, 1992), but the first two publications (of which we are aware) on teaching mixed methods have just appeared in 2002 (Creswell et al., Chapter 24, this volume; Tashakkori & Teddlie, in press). Fortunately, these two publications both contain a sample syllabus and a listing of a set of modules together with readings for the courses. Creswell and colleagues (Chapter 24, this volume) list more than 20 books, chapters, and articles, thus indicating the wide range of available high-quality sources for a mixed methods course.

It is good that such sources exist because an examination of most current general research methodology textbooks in the social and behavioral sciences would verify that some of them (e.g., psychological research methods) are still lacking even a systematic coverage of qualitative methods. When both approaches to research are presented, they are typically presented in a binary manner, completely separated from each other in different chapters. Currently, there are very few textbooks that cover mixed methods (e.g., Creswell, 2002; McMillan & Schumacher, 2001). The new edition of Johnson & Christensen's (2000) text is also expected to include a chapter on mixed methods.

THREE MODELS FOR PROFESSIONAL COMPETENCY AND COLLABORATION

There are three current models for professional competency and collaboration. According to one model, to find the best answers to research questions, a researcher should be able to fully use methods from both traditions. One of the concerns often expressed in this respect is that it might be impossible for a single researcher to have the necessary competencies in *both* qualitative and quantitative methods.

A second model solves the problem of dual competency by proposing a team approach to research. According to this model, research teams may consist of researchers with competency in one of the two traditions. Such a model is not uncommon in large-scale studies, especially in health sciences. A research team in such projects consists of one or more qualitative and one or more quantitative researchers. How do these team members conceptualize different aspects of the question, plan and implement data collection and analysis, and integrate the obtained inferences in a consistent and fully integrated manner? Mixed methods research is not a simple collection of two strands of data collection and analysis. The strength of the mixed methods designs is in using a systemic approach to integrate multiple types of questions that are answered by multiple types of data and an analysis procedure that ultimately leads to an integrated set of inferences.

A third model (Newman & Benz, 1998; Tashakkori & Teddlie, in press) calls for a *minimum* competency in both qualitative and quantitative designs on the part of all researchers in the project, together with a highly specialized set of competencies in one of the two designs. Large-scale studies and/or those studies that require highly specialized competencies in *both* traditions can achieve this goal by using a team approach consisting of predominantly qualitative and quantitative researchers (see Shulha & Wilson, Chapter 25, this volume).

While the team approach solves the problem of a single researcher having to know both types of research, it also creates new problems. Although this would alleviate the problem of requiring multiple competencies, it does not alleviate the problem in smaller scale studies, or in doctoral dissertations, where only one investigator has to conduct the study from the conceptualization phase to the inference phase. Another problem with the team approach is that, without a minimum competency in *both* types of research, the team members are not able to efficiently communicate and coordinate the research activities. Without some familiarity with *both* traditions, integrating the inferences that are drawn by different team members might be difficult. In our experience, even when a team includes qualitative and quantitative researchers working together, communication between them is hampered by this lack of familiarity with the methods of the other tradition.

For the team members to understand each other, some common language is needed. For this reason, we believe that the third model just presented (the minimum competency model) is a necessary prerequisite for the second one (the team approach). Investigators' "methodological bilingualism" (at least a minimum degree of familiarity with both types of methods) is necessary for effective mixed methods teams. This points to the need for fundamental change in the teaching of research methods in our graduate programs in social, behavioral, and health sciences.

◆ Summary: The Third Methodological Movement

This chapter has reviewed six major issues in the use of mixed methods research in the social and behavioral sciences. These issues are discussed in more detail throughout this handbook and are reexamined in our Chapter 26. It is through the intensive examination and resolution of these (and other) controversial issues that the *third methodological movement* (mixed methods research) will be firmly established alongside the other two.

■ Notes

1. Morse (1991) introduced the abbreviations QUAN and QUAL to stand for the respective quantitative and qualitative stages of a mixed-methods research design. We have extrapolated the terms QUANs and QUALs to apply to researchers who are quantitatively and qualitatively oriented.

2. While two other moments were noted in the second edition of the *Handbook of Qualitative Research* (Denzin & Lincoln, 2000), we believe that the original five moments are more appropriate for this comparison.

3. Ontology refers to the nature of reality, epistemology refers to the relationship of the knower to the known, and axiology refers to the role of values in inquiry.

4. We use the term *postpositivism* to refer to a family of paradigms that also includes positivism and empiricism. We use the term *constructivism* to refer to a family of paradigms that also includes interpretivism and naturalism.

5. Examples include recent criticisms of the abuse of statistical significance (e.g., Thompson, 1998) and the shift toward emphasis on reporting effect sizes in the *Publication Manual of the American Psychological Association* (American Psychological Association, 2001).

6. That is not to say that such sources are unavailable; rather, they are more rare in the QUAL world than in the QUAN world. For example, see Schwandt (1997) for a dictionary of terms used in QUAL inquiry.

7. As another example, probability samples require a random selection of a relatively large number of units. Randomly selecting 5 hospitals from a total of 200 does not provide a probability (cluster) sample. The result of such sampling strategy may be classified somewhere in the middle of the continuum between

probability and purposive sampling (for further discussion, see Tashakkori & Teddlie, 1998, p. 72).

8. All schools had some assistance from the state in the form of a District Assistance Team; the experimental schools in the study also had the DE.

9. Greene and Caracelli (Chapter 3, this volume) describe four stances on mixing methods and mixing paradigms that are similar to the six points of view described in this chapter.

10. See Tashakkori and Teddlie (1998, pp. 20-30) for an extended comparison of pragmatism with positivism, postpositivism, and constructivism.

11. Qualitative or quantitative methods may also be used in research associated with the transformative-emancipatory paradigm so long as the ideological perspective described in this section shapes the research.

12. Guba (1996) expressed being concerned about his colleague Dan Stufflebeam's criticism of the paradigm tables as having "introduced a major schism into the profession" (p. 46).

13. This problem of the exhaustiveness of the typology is not restricted to mixed methods designs. Campbell and Stanley (1963) introduced the nonequivalent control group design as a single design type (i.e., the untreated control group design with pretest and posttest). More than a decade later, Cook and Campbell (1979) presented a family of "generally interpretable nonequivalent control group designs" with eight members. Quasi-experimental work ongoing between these two books had led to the invention or discovery of several new members of the family of designs.

14. Some of the definitions given here are related to current use of the symbols. For instance, the use of uppercase letters to express priority or dominance (see Creswell et al., Chapter 8, this volume) is different from Morse's preferred terms of thrust and drive (see Morse, Chapter 7, this volume).

15. The confirmatory versus exploratory dimension distinguishes between predominantly deductive (hypothesis-testing) questions and predominantly inductive questions. A clear QUAN-QUAL distinction is not offered on this dimension. Instead, it is suggested that QUAN questions are predominantly hypothetico-deductive, while QUAL questions are predominantly inductive. In any study, QUAL or QUAN has elements of both inductive and deductive components.

16. Examples of all six of these designs were taken from the Louisiana School Effectiveness Study (Teddlie & Stringfield, 1993) and presented in Tashakkori and Teddlie (1998).

17. Interestingly, Cronbach (1982) also made extensive use of the terms internal *inference* (conclusion) and external *inference* (extrapolation) in his theory of how to do evaluations of educational and social programs. He used the terms *internal validity* and *external validity* to refer to the "trustworthiness" of the internal or external inferences. His distinctions are similar to our use of the terms *inference* (he also used the term *inference*) and *inference quality* (he instead used the term *validity*).

18. Our conceptualization of these four dimensions was inspired by theories of social perceptions such as Kelley's (1967) attribution theory.

■ *References*

American Psychological Association. (2001). *Publication manual of the American Psychological Association*. Washington, DC: Author.

Angeles, P. A. (1981). *Dictionary of philosophy*. New York: Barnes & Noble.

Boyatzis, R. E. (1998). *Transforming qualitative information: Thematic analysis and code development*. Thousand Oaks, CA: Sage.

Brewer, J., & Hunter, A. (1989). *Multimethod research: A synthesis of styles*. Newbury Park, CA: Sage.

Campbell, D., & Fiske, D. W. (1959). Convergent and discriminant validation by the multitrait-multimethod matrix. *Psychological Bulletin, 54,* 297-312.

Campbell, D. T., & Stanley, J. (1963). *Experimental and quasi-experimental design for research*. Chicago: Rand McNally.

Cherryholmes, C. C. (1992). Notes on pragmatism and scientific realism. *Educational Researcher, 21*(6), 13-17.

Cherryholmes, C. C. (1999). *Reading pragmatism*. New York: Teachers College Press.

Cohen, L., Manion, L., & Morrison, K. (2000). *Research methods in education* (5th ed.). New York: Routledge/Falmer.

Cook, T. D., & Campbell, D. T. (1979). *Quasiexperimentation: Design and analysis issues for field settings*. Boston: Houghton Mifflin.

Creswell, J. W. (1994). *Research design: Qualitative and quantitative approaches*. Thousand Oaks, CA: Sage.

Creswell, J. W. (2002). *Educational research: Planning, conducting, and evaluating quantitative and qualitative research*. Upper Saddle River, NJ: Merrill Prentice Hall.

Cronbach, L. J. (1982). *Designing evaluations of educational and social programs*. San Francisco: Jossey-Bass.

Crotty, M. (1998). *The foundations of social research: Meaning and perspective in the research process*. Thousand Oaks, CA: Sage.

Datta, L. (1994). Paradigm wars: A basis for peaceful coexistence and beyond. In C. S. Reichardt & S. F. Rallis (Eds.), *The qualitative-quantitative debate: New perspectives* (pp. 53-70). San Francisco: Jossey-Bass.

Datta, L. (1997). A pragmatic basis for mixed-method designs. In J. C. Greene & V. J. Caracelli (Eds.), *Advances in mixed-method evaluation: The challenges and benefits of integrating diverse paradigms* (pp. 33-46). San Francisco: Jossey-Bass.

Deacon, D., Bryman, A., & Fenton, N. (1998). Collision or collusion? A discussion of the unplanned triangulation of quantitative and qualitative research methods. *International Journal of Social Research Methodology, Theory, and Practice, 1*, 47-64.

Denzin, N. K. (1978). The logic of naturalistic inquiry. In N. K. Denzin (Ed.), *Sociological methods: A sourcebook*. New York: McGraw-Hill.

Denzin, N. K. (1992). *Symbolic interactionism and cultural studies*. Cambridge, UK: Basil Blackwell.

Denzin, N. K., & Lincoln, Y. S. (1994). Introduction: Entering the field of qualitative research. In N. K. Denzin & Y. S. Lincoln (Eds.), *Handbook of qualitative research* (pp. 1-18). Thousand Oaks, CA: Sage.

Denzin, N. K., & Lincoln, Y. S. (2000). Introduction: The discipline and practice of qualitative research. In N. K. Denzin & Y. S. Lincoln (Eds.), *Handbook of qualitative research* (2nd ed., pp. 1-28). Thousand Oaks, CA: Sage.

Erzberger, C., & Prein, G. (1997). Triangulation: Validity and empirically based hypothesis construction. *Quality & Quantity, 2*, 141-154.

Festinger, L., Riecken, H. W., & Schachter, S. (1956). *When prophecy fails*. Minneapolis: University of Minnesota Press.

Gage, N. (1989). The paradigm wars and their aftermath: A "historical" sketch of research and teaching since 1989. *Educational Researcher, 18*(7), 4-10.

Gergen, K. J. (1985). The social constructionist movement in modern psychology. *American Psychologist, 40*, 266-275.

Greene, J. C., & Caracelli, V. J. (Eds.). (1997). *Advances in mixed-method evaluation: The challenges and benefits of integrating diverse paradigms* (New Directions for Evaluation, No. 74). San Francisco: Jossey-Bass.

Greene, J. C., Caracelli, V. J., & Graham, W. F. (1989). Toward a conceptual framework for mixed-method evaluation designs. *Educational Evaluation and Policy Analysis, 11*, 255-274.

Guba, E. G. (1987). What have we learned about naturalistic evaluation? *Evaluation Practice, 8*, 23-43.

Guba, E. G. (1996). What happened to me on the road to Damascus. In L. Heshusius & K. Ballard (Eds.), *From positivism to interpretivism and beyond: Tales of transformation in educational and social research* (pp. 43-49). New York: Teachers College Press.

Guba, E. G., & Lincoln, Y. S. (1989). *Fourth generation evaluation*. Newbury Park, CA: Sage.

Guba, E. G., & Lincoln, Y. S. (1994). Competing paradigms in qualitative research. In N. K. Denzin & Y. S. Lincoln (Eds.), *Handbook of qualitative research* (pp. 105-117). Thousand Oaks, CA: Sage.

Hafernik, J. J., Messerschmitt, D. S., & Vandrick, S. (1997). Collaborative research: Why and how? *Educational Researcher, 26*(9), 31-35.

Hammersley, M. (1989). *The dilemma of qualitative method: Herbert Blumer and the Chicago tradition.* London: Routledge.

Hammersley, M. (1992). *What's wrong with ethnography.* London: Routledge.

Hanson, N. R. (1958). *Patterns of discovery: An inquiry into the conceptual foundations of science.* Cambridge, UK: Cambridge University Press.

Howe, K. R. (1988). Against the quantitative-qualitative incompatibility thesis or dogmas die hard. *Educational Researcher, 17*(8), 10-16.

Jick, T. D. (1979). Mixing qualitative and quantitative methods: Triangulation in action. *Administrative Science Quarterly, 24,* 602-611.

Johnson, B., & Christensen, L. (2000). *Educational research: Quantitative and qualitative approaches.* Boston: Allyn & Bacon.

Kelley, H. H. (1967). Attribution theory in social psychology. In D. Levine (Ed.), *Nebraska Symposium on Motivation.* Lincoln: University of Nebraska Press.

Krathwohl, D. R. (1993). *Methods of educational and social science research: An integrated approach.* New York: Longman.

Lather, P. (1993). Fertile obsession: Validity after poststructuralism. *Sociological Quarterly, 34,* 673-693.

Liebert, R. M., & Liebert, L. L. (1995). *Science and behavior: An introduction to methods of psychological research.* Englewood Cliffs, NJ: Prentice Hall.

Lincoln, Y. S., & Guba, E. G. (1985). *Naturalistic inquiry.* Beverly Hills, CA: Sage.

Lincoln, Y. S., & Guba, E. G. (2000). Paradigmatic controversies, contradictions, and emerging confluences. In N. K. Denzin & Y. S. Lincoln (Eds.), *Handbook of qualitative research* (2nd ed., pp. 163-188). Thousand Oaks, CA: Sage.

Maxwell, J. A. (1992). Understanding and validity in qualitative research. *Harvard Educational Review, 62,* 279-300.

McMillan, J. H., & Schumacher, S. (2001). *Research in education: A conceptual introduction* (5th ed.). New York: Longman.

Mertens, D. M. (1998). *Research methods in education and psychology: Integrating diversity with quantitative and qualitative approaches.* Thousand Oaks, CA: Sage.

Mertens, D. M. (1999). Inclusive evaluation: Implications of transformative theory for evaluation. *American Journal of Evaluation, 20*(1), 1-14.

Messick, S. (1995). Validity of psychological assessment. *American Psychologist, 50,* 741-749.

Miles, M., & Huberman, M. (1994). *Qualitative data analysis: An expanded sourcebook* (2nd ed.). Thousand Oaks, CA: Sage.

Miller, W. L., & Crabtree, B. J. (2000). Clinical research. In N. K. Denzin & Y. S. Lincoln (Eds.), *Handbook of qualitative research* (2nd ed., pp. 607-631). Thousand Oaks, CA: Sage.

Moghaddam, F. M., & Harre, R. (1995). But is it science? Traditional and alternative approaches to the study of social behavior. *World Psychology, 1,* 47-78.

Morgan, D. (1998). Practical strategies for combining qualitative and quantitative methods: Applications to health research. *Qualitative Health Research, 8,* 362-376.

Morse, J. M. (1991). Approaches to qualitative-quantitative methodological triangulation. *Nursing Research, 40*(2), 120-123.

Newman, I., & Benz, C. R. (1998). *Qualitative-quantitative research methodology: Exploring the interactive continuum.* Carbondale: University of Illinois Press.

Patton, M. Q. (1990). *Qualitative evaluation and research methods* (2nd ed.). Newbury Park, CA: Sage.

Polit, D. F., & Hungler, B. P. (1999). *Nursing research principles and methods* (6th ed.). Philadelphia: J. B. Lippincott.

Popper, K. R. (1959). *The logic of scientific discovery.* New York: Basic Books. (Original work published 1935)

Punch, K. F. (1998). *Introduction to social research: Quantitative and qualitative approaches*. Thousand Oaks, CA: Sage.

Ratner, C. (1997). *Cultural psychology and qualitative methodology: Theoretical and empirical considerations*. New York: Plenum.

Reichardt, C. S., & Rallis, S. F. (1994). Qualitative and quantitative inquiries are not incompatible: A call for a new partnership. In C. S. Reichardt & S. F. Rallis (Eds.), *The qualitative-quantitative debate: New perspectives* (pp. 85-92). San Francisco: Jossey-Bass.

Roethlisberger, F. J., & Dickson, W. J. (1939). *Management and the worker*. Cambridge, MA: Harvard University Press.

Rossman, G. B., & Wilson, B. L. (1985). Numbers and words: Combining quantitative and qualitative methods in a single large scale evaluation study. *Evaluation Review, 9*, 627-643.

Sandelowski, M., Harris, B. G., & Holditch-Davis, D. (1991). Amniocentesis in the context of infertility. *Health Care for Women International, 12*, 167-178.

Schwandt, T. A. (1997). *Qualitative inquiry: A dictionary of terms*. Thousand Oaks, CA: Sage.

Schwandt, T. A. (2000). Three epistemological stances for qualitative inquiry: Interpretivism, hermeneutics, and social constructionism. In N. K. Denzin & Y. S. Lincoln (Eds.), *Handbook of qualitative research* (2nd ed., pp. 189-214). Thousand Oaks, CA: Sage.

Sherif, M., Harvey, O. J., White, B. J., Hood, W. R., & Sherif, C. W. (1961). *Intergroup conflict and cooperation: The Robber's Cave Experiment*. Norman: University of Oklahoma, Institute of Intergroup Relations.

Smith, J. K. (1983). Quantitative versus qualitative research: An attempt to clarify the issue. *Educational Researcher, 12*(2), 6-13.

Smith, J. K. (1996). An opportunity lost? In L. Heshusius & K. Ballard (Eds.), *From positivism to interpretivism and beyond: Tales of transformation in educational and social research* (pp. 161-168). New York: Teachers College Press.

Smith, J. K., & Heshusius, L. (1986). Closing down the conversation: The end of the quantitative-qualitative debate among educational researchers. *Educational Researcher, 15*(4), 4-12.

Smith, M. L. (1994). Qualitative plus/versus quantitative: The last word. In C. S. Reichardt & S. F. Rallis (Eds.), *The quantitative-qualitative debate: New perspectives* (pp. 37-44). San Francisco: Jossey-Bass.

Stallings, W. M. (1995). Confessions of a quantitative educational researcher trying to teach qualitative research. *Educational Researcher, 24*(3), 31-32.

Stern, P. N. (1994). Eroding grounded theory. In J. Morse (Ed.), *Critical issues in qualitative research methods* (pp. 214-215). Thousand Oaks, CA: Sage.

Stevens, J. G. (2002). *Differential modes of external change agent support in diffusion of innovation*. Unpublished doctoral dissertation, Louisiana State University.

Tashakkori, A., & Ropers-Huilman, B. (2000). Methodological and conceptual issues in research on gender and ethnicity [review of *Gender, Culture, and Ethnicity: Current Research About Women and Men*]. *Contemporary Psychology, 45*, 170-174.

Tashakkori, A., & Teddlie, C. (1998). *Mixed methodology: Combining the qualitative and quantitative approaches* (Applied Social Research Methods, No. 46). Thousand Oaks, CA: Sage.

Tashakkori, A., & Teddlie, C. (in press). Issues and dilemmas in teaching research methods courses in social and behavioral sciences: A U.S. perspective. *International Journal of Social Research Methodology*.

Teddlie, C., & Stringfield, S. (1993). *Schools make a difference: Lessons learned from a 1-year study*. New York: Teachers College Press.

Thompson, B. (1998, April). *Five methodology errors in educational research: The pantheon of statistical significance and other faux pas*. Invited address presented at the annual meeting of the American Educational Research Association, San Diego.

Warner, W. L., & Lunt, P. S. (1941). *The social life of a modern community* (Yankee City

Series, Vol. 1). New Haven, CT: Yale University Press.

Webb, R. B., & Glesne, C. (1992). Teaching qualitative research. In M. LeCompte, W. Milroy, & J. Preissle (Eds.), *The handbook of qualitative research in education* (pp. 771-814). San Diego: Academic Press.

Zimbardo, P. G. (1969). The human choice: Individuation, reason, and order versus deindividuation, impulse, and chaos. In W. T. Arnold & D. Levine (Eds.), *Nebraska Symposium on Motivation* (Vol. 17, pp. 237-307). Lincoln: University of Nebraska Press.

9

The Use of Theory

J. CRESWELL

In *quantitative research*, the hypotheses and research questions are often based on theories that the researcher seeks to test. In *qualitative research*, the use of theory is much more varied. Thus, this book introduces the use of theory at this time in the design process because theory provides an explanation for the variables in questions and hypotheses in quantitative research. In contrast, in a quantitative dissertation, an entire section of a research proposal might be devoted to explicating the theory for the study. Alternatively, in a qualitative study, the inquirer may generate a theory during a study and place it at the end of a project, such as in grounded theory. In other qualitative studies, it comes at the beginning and provides a lens that shapes what is looked at and the questions asked, such as in ethnographies or in advocacy research. In *mixed methods research*, researchers may both test theories and generate them. Moreover, mixed methods research may contain a theoretical lens, such as a focus on feminist, racial, or class issues, that guides the entire study.

The chapter begins by focusing on theory-use in a quantitative study. It reviews a definition of a theory, the placement of it in a quantitative study, and the alternative forms it might assume in a written plan. Procedures in identifying a theory are next presented followed by a "script" of a "theoretical perspective" section of a quantitative research proposal. Then the discussion moves to use of theory in a qualitative study. Qualitative inquirers use different terms, such as theories, patterns, and naturalistic generalizations, to describe the understandings developed in their studies. Sometimes these understandings occur at the beginning of a study; at other times, they appear at the end. Examples illustrate the alternatives available to qualitative researchers. Finally, the chapter turns to the use of theories in mixed methods research and the use of theory in a type of strategy of inquiry—the transformative strategy—that emerged recently in the literature.

QUANTITATIVE THEORY-USE

Definition of a Theory

In *quantitative* research, some historical precedent exists for viewing a theory as a scientific prediction or explanation (see G. Thomas, 1997, for different ways of conceptualizing theories and how they might constrain thought). For example, the definition of a theory, such as the one by Kerlinger (1979), is still valid today. A theory is "a set of interrelated constructs (variables), definitions, and propositions that presents a systematic view of phenomena by specifying relations among variables, with the purpose of explaining natural phenomena" (p. 64).

In this definition, a theory is an interrelated set of constructs (or variables) formed into propositions, or hypotheses, that specify the relationship among variables (typically in terms of magnitude or direction). The systematic view might be an argument, a discussion, or a rationale, and it helps to explain (or predict) phenomena that occur in the world. Labovitz and Hagedorn (1971) add to this definition the idea of a *theoretical rationale*, which they define as "specifying how and why the variables and relational statements are interrelated" (p. 17). Why would an independent variable, X, influence or affect a dependent variable, Y? The theory would provide the explanation for this expectation or prediction. A discussion about this theory, then, would appear in a section of a proposal titled a *theory-base*, a *theoretical rationale*, or a *theoretical perspective*. I prefer the term *theoretical perspective* because it has been popularly used as a required section for a proposal for research when one submits an application to present a research paper at the American Educational Research Association conference.

The metaphor of a rainbow can help to visualize how a theory operates. Assume that the rainbow *bridges* the independent and dependent variables (or constructs) in a study. This rainbow, then, ties together the variables and provides an overarching explanation for *how* and *why* one would expect the independent variable to explain or predict the dependent variable.

Theories develop when researchers test a prediction many times. Recall that investigators combine independent, mediating, and dependent variables based on different forms of measures into hypotheses or research questions. These hypotheses or questions provide information about the type of relationship (positive, negative, or unknown) and its magnitude (e.g., high or low). The hypothesis might be written, "The greater the centralization of power in leaders, the greater the disenfranchisement of the followers." When researchers test hypotheses such as this over and over in different settings and with different populations (e.g., the Boy Scouts, a Presbyterian church, the Rotary Club, and a group of high school students), a theory emerges and someone gives it a name (e.g., a theory of attribution). Thus, theory develops as explanation to advance knowledge in particular fields (G. Thomas, 1997).

Another aspect of theories is that they vary in their breadth of coverage. Neuman (2000) reviews theories at three levels: micro-level, meso-level, and macro-level. Micro-level theories provide explanations limited to small slices of time, space, or numbers of people, such as Goffman's theory of "face work" that explains how people engage in rituals during face-to-face interactions. Meso-level theories link the micro and macro levels. These are theories of organizations, social movement, or communities, such as Collins's theory of control in organizations. Macro-level theories explain larger aggregates, such as social institutions, cultural systems, and whole societies. Lenski's macro-level theory of social stratification, for example, explains how the amount of surplus a society produces increases with the development of the society.

Theories are found in the social science disciplines of psychology, sociology, anthropology, education, and economics, as well as within many subfields. To locate and read about these theories requires searching literature databases (e.g., *Psychological Abstracts*, *Sociological Abstracts*) or reviewing guides to the literature about theories (e.g., see Webb, Beals, & White, 1986).

Form of Theories

Researchers state their theories in several ways, such as a series of hypotheses, "if . . . then" logic statements, or visual models. First, some researchers state theories in the form of interconnected hypotheses. For example, Hopkins (1964) conveyed his theory of influence processes as a series of 15 hypotheses (slightly altered to remove all the male-specific pronouns). For any member of a small group, some hypotheses are:

1.   The higher her rank, the greater her centrality.

2.   The greater his centrality, the greater his observability.

3.   The higher her rank, the greater her observability.

4.   The greater his centrality, the greater his conformity.

5.   The higher her rank, the greater her conformity.

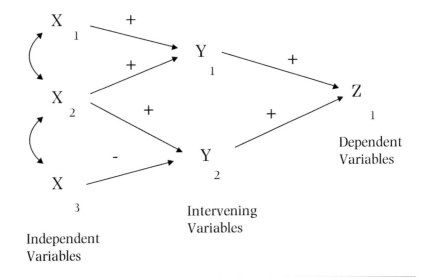

Figure 7.1   Three Independent Variables Influencing a Single Dependent Variable Mediated by Two Intervening Variables

6.   The greater his observability, the greater his conformity.

7.   The greater her conformity, the greater her observability. (p. 51)

A second form is to state a theory as a series of "if . . . then" statements that explain why one would expect the independent variables to influence or cause the dependent variables. For example, Homans (1950) explains a theory of interaction:

> If the frequency of interaction between two or more persons increases, the degree of their liking for one another will increase, and vice versa . . . persons who feel sentiments of liking for one another will express those sentiments in activities over and above the activities of the external system, and these activities may further strengthen the sentiments of liking. The more frequently persons interact with one another, the more alike in some respects both their activities and their sentiments tend to become. (pp. 112, 118, 120)

Third, an author may present a theory as a visual model. It is useful to translate variables into a visual picture. Blalock (1969, 1985, 1991) advocates causal modeling and recasts verbal theories into causal models so that a reader can visualize the interconnections of variables.

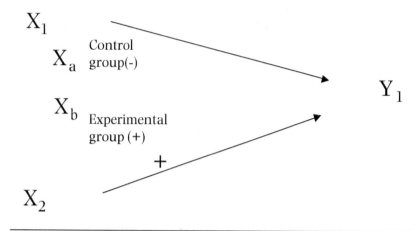

Figure 7.2 Two Groups Given Different Treatments on X_1 Are Compared in Terms of Y_1 Controlling for X_2

Two simplified examples are presented here. As shown in Figure 7.1, three independent variables influence a single dependent variable mediated by the influence of two intervening variables. Setting up a diagram such as this one shows the possible causal sequence among variables, leading to path analytic modeling and more advanced analyses using multiple measures of variables as found in structural equation modeling (see Kline, 1998). At an introductory level, Duncan (1985) provides useful suggestions about the notation for constructing these visual, causal diagrams:

- Position the dependent variables on the right in the diagram and the independent variables on the left.

- Use one-way arrows leading from each determining variable to each variable dependent on it.

- Indicate the "strength" of the relationship among variables by inserting valence signs on the paths. Use positive or negative valences that postulate or infer relationships.

- Use two-headed arrows connected to show unanalyzed relationships between variables not dependent upon other relationships in the model.

Though more complicated causal diagrams can be constructed with additional notation, the model presented here portrays a basic model of limited variables, such as typically found in a survey research study.

Independent   **Dependent**

Exogenous   **Endogenous**

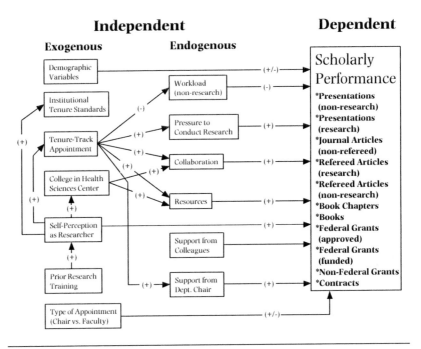

Figure 7.3 A Visual Model of Faculty Scholarly Performance

SOURCE: From P. W. Jungnickel (1990), *Workplace Correlates* and *Scholarly Performance of Pharmacy Clinical Faculty Members*, unpublished proposal, University of Nebraska–Lincoln. Used with permission.

A variation on this theme is to have two independent variables in which one variable compares a control and experimental group and a second variable simply measures an attribute or characteristic. As shown in Figure 7.2, two groups on variable X_1 (X_a and X_b) are compared, along with variable X_2 (a control variable) as they influence Y_1, the dependent variable. This design is a between-groups experimental design. The same rules of notation discussed above apply.

These two visual models are meant only to introduce possibilities for connecting independent and dependent variables to build theories. More complicated designs employ multiple independent and dependent variables in elaborate models of causation (Blalock, 1969, 1985). For example, Jungnickel (1990), in a doctoral dissertation proposal about research productivity among faculty in pharmacy schools, presented a complex visual model as shown in Figure 7.3. Jungnickel asked what factors influence a faculty member's scholarly research performance.

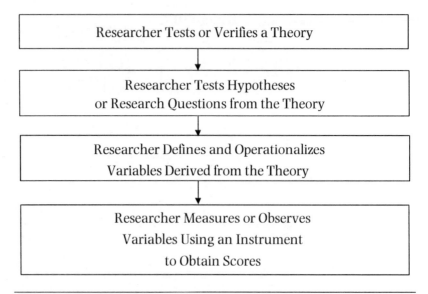

Figure 7.4 The Deductive Approach Typically Used in Quantitative Research

After identifying these factors in the literature, he adapted a theoretical framework found in nursing research (Megel, Langston, & Creswell, 1988). He developed a visual model portraying the relationship among these factors. The model follows the rules for constructing a visual model introduced earlier. He listed the independent variables on the far left, the intervening variables in the middle, and the dependent variables on the right. The direction of influence flowed from the left to the right, and he used "+" and "−" valences to indicate the hypothesized direction.

Placement of Quantitative Theories

In *quantitative* studies, one uses theory deductively and places it toward the beginning of the plan for a study. With the objective of testing or verifying a theory rather than developing it, the researcher advances a theory, collects data to test it, and reflects on the confirmation or disconfirmation of the theory by the results. The theory becomes a framework for the entire study, an organizing model for the research questions or hypotheses and for the data collection procedure. The deductive model of thinking used in a quantitative study is shown in Figure 7.4. The researcher tests or verifies a theory by examining

Table 7.1   Options for Placing Theory in a Quantitative Study

Placement	Advantages	Disadvantages
In the introduction	An approach often found in journal articles, it will be familiar to readers. It conveys a deductive approach	It is difficult for a reader to isolate and separate theory base from other components of the research process
In the literature review	Theories are found in the literature, and their inclusion in a literature review is a logical extension or part of the literature	It is difficult for a reader to see the theory in isolation from the scholarly review of the literature
After hypotheses or research questions	The theory discussion is a logical extension of hypotheses or research questions because it explains how and why variables are related	A writer may include a theoretical rationale after hypotheses and question, and leave out an extended discussion about the origin and use of the theory
In a separate section	This approach clearly separates the theory from other components of the research process, and it enables a reader to better identify and to understand the theory-base for the study	The theory discussion stands in isolation from other components of the research process and, as such, a reader may not easily connect it with other components of the research process

hypotheses or questions derived from the theory. These hypotheses or questions contain variables (or constructs) that the researcher needs to define. Alternatively, an acceptable definition might be found in the literature. From here, the investigator locates an instrument to use in measuring or observing attitudes or behaviors of participants in a study. Then the investigator collects scores on these instruments to confirm or disconfirm the theory.

This deductive approach to research in the quantitative approach has implications for the *placement of a theory* in a quantitative research study (see Table 7.1). A general guide is to introduce the theory early in a plan or study. This means that the researcher presents it in the introduction, in the literature review section, immediately after hypotheses or research questions (as a rationale for the connections among the variables), or in a separate section of the study. Each placement has its advantages and disadvantages.

I prefer to write the theory into a separate section so that readers can clearly identify the theory from other components of the research process. Such a separate passage provides a complete explication of the theory section, its use, and how it relates to the study I am proposing.

A Model for Writing a Quantitative Theoretical Perspective

Using these ideas, the following presents a model for writing a quantitative theoretical perspective section into a research plan. Assume that the task is to identify a theory that explains the relationship between independent and dependent variables. The following procedure might be used:

1. Look in the discipline-based literature for a theory. If the unit of analysis for variables is individuals, look in the psychology literature; to study groups or organizations, look in the sociological literature. If the project examines individuals and groups, consider the social psychology literature. Of course, theories from other discipline theories may be useful, too (e.g., to study an economic issue, the theory may be found in economics).

2. Look also at prior studies that address the topic or a closely related topic. What theories were used by other authors? Limit the number of theories and try to identify *one overarching theory* that explains the central hypothesis or research question in the study.

3. As mentioned earlier, ask the *rainbow* question that bridges the independent and dependent variables: Why would the independent variable(s) influence the dependent variables?

4. Script out the theory section. Follow these lead sentences: "The theory that I will use will be _____ (name the theory). It was developed by _____ (identify the origin or source for the theory), and it was used to study _____ (identify the topics where one finds the theory being applied). This theory indicates that _____ (identify the propositions or hypotheses in the theory). As

applied to my study, this theory holds that I would expect my independent variable(s) _____ (state independent variables) to influence or explain the dependent variable(s) _____ (state dependent variables) because _____ (provide a rationale based on the logic of the theory)."

Thus, the topics to include in a quantitative theory discussion are the theory to be used, the central hypotheses or propositions of the theory, information about past use of the theory and its application, and statements that reflect how the theory relates to a proposed study. This model is illustrated in the example by Crutchfield (1986) below.

Example 7.1 *A Quantitative Theory Section*

Crutchfield (1986) wrote a doctoral dissertation titled *Locus of Control, Interpersonal Trust, and Scholarly Productivity*. Surveying nursing educators, her intent was to determine if locus of control and interpersonal trust affected the levels of publications of the faculty. Her dissertation included a separate section in the introductory chapter titled "Theoretical Perspective." What follows is this section, including the following points:

- The theory she planned to use
- The central hypotheses of the theory
- Information about who has used the theory and its applicability
- An adaptation of the theory to variables in her study using the "if . . . then" logic

Here is a section of her study, reproduced in its entirety. I added annotations (in bold type) to mark key passages.

Theoretical Perspective

In formulation of a theoretical perspective for studying the scholarly productivity of faculty, social learning theory provides a useful prototype. This conception of behavior attempts to achieve a balanced synthesis of cognitive psychology with the principles of behavior modification (Bower & Hilgard, 1981). Basically, this unified theoretical framework "approaches the explanation of human behavior in terms of a continuous (reciprocal) interaction between cognitive, behavioral, and environmental determinants" (Bandura, 1977, p. vii). **(Author identifies the theory for the study.)**

While social learning theory accepts the application of reinforcements such as shaping principles, it tends to see the role of rewards as both conveying information about the optimal response and providing incentive motivation for a given act because of the anticipated reward. In addition, the learning principles of this theory place special emphasis on the important roles played by vicarious, symbolic, and self-regulating processes (Bandura, 1971).

Social learning theory not only deals with learning, but seeks to describe how a group of social and personal competencies (so-called personality) could evolve out of social conditions within which the learning occurs. It also addresses techniques of personality assessment (Mischel, 1968), and behavior modification in clinical and educational settings (Bandura, 1977; Bower & Hilgard, 1981; Rotter, 1954).**(Author describes social learning theory.)**

Further, the principles of social learning theory have been applied to a wide range of social behavior such as competitiveness, aggressiveness, sex roles, deviance, and pathological behavior (Bandura & Walters, 1963; Bandura, 1977; Mischel, 1968; Miller & Dollard, 1941; Rotter, 1954; Staats, 1975). **(Author describes the use of the theory.)**

Explaining social learning theory, Rotter (1954) indicated that four classes of variables must be considered: behavior, expectancies, reinforcement, and psychological situations. A general formula for behavior was proposed which states: "the potential for a behavior to occur in any specific psychological situation is the function of the expectancy that the behavior will lead to a particular reinforcement in that situation and the value of that reinforcement" (Rotter, 1975, p. 57).

Expectancy within the formula refers to the perceived degree of certainty (or probability) that a causal relationship generally exists between behavior and rewards. This construct of generalized expectancy has been defined as *internal* locus of control when an individual believes that reinforcements are a function of specific behavior, or as *external* locus of control when the effects are attributed to luck, fate, or powerful others. The perceptions of causal relationships need not be absolute positions, but rather tend to vary in degree along a continuum depending upon previous experiences and situational complexities (Rotter, 1966). **(Author explains variables in the theory.)**

In the application of social learning theory to this study of scholarly productivity, the four classes of variables identified by Rotter (1954) will be defined in the following manner.

1. Scholarly productivity is the desired behavior or activity.

2. Locus of control is the generalized expectancy that rewards are or are not dependent upon specific behaviors.

3. Reinforcements are the rewards from scholarly work and the value attached to these rewards.

4. The educational institution is the psychological situation which furnishes many of the rewards for scholarly productivity.

With these specific variables, the formula for behavior which was developed by Rotter (1975) would be adapted to read: The potential for scholarly behavior to occur within an educational institution is a function of the expectancy that this activity will lead to specific rewards and of the value that the faculty member places on these rewards. In addition, the interaction of interpersonal trust with locus of control must be considered in relation to the expectancy of attaining rewards through behaviors as recommended in subsequent statements by Rotter (1967). Finally, certain characteristics, such as educational preparation, chronological age, post-doctoral fellowships, tenure, or full-time versus part-time employment may be associated with the scholarly productivity of nurse faculty in a manner similar to that seen within other disciplines. **(Author applied the concepts to her study.)**

The following statement represents the underlying logic for designing and conducting this study. If faculty believe that: (a) their efforts and actions in producing scholarly works will lead to rewards (locus of control), (b) others can be relied upon to follow through on their promises (interpersonal trust), (c) the rewards for scholarly activity are worthwhile (reward values), and (d) the rewards are available within their discipline or institution (institutional setting), then they will attain high levels of scholarly productivity (pp. 12-16). **(Author concluded with the "if . . . then" logic to relate the independent variables to the dependent variables.)**

Variation in Theory-Use in Qualitative Research

Qualitative inquirers use theory in their studies in several ways. They employ theory as a broad explanation, much like in *quantitative* research. This theory provides an *explanation* for behavior and attitudes, and it may be complete with variables, constructs, and hypotheses. For example, ethnographers employ cultural themes or "aspects of culture" (Wolcott, 1999, p. 113) to study in their qualitative projects. These might be themes such as social control, language, stability and change, or social organization such as kinship or families (see Wolcott's 1999 discussion about texts that address cultural topics in anthropology). Themes in this context provide a ready-made series of hypotheses to be tested from the literature. Although researchers might not refer to them as theories, they provide broad explanations that anthropologists use to study the culture-sharing behavior and attitudes of people.

Alternatively, qualitative researchers increasingly use a *theoretical lens or perspective* to guide their study and raise the questions of gender, class, and race (or some combination) they would like to address. The case could easily be made that qualitative research of the 1980s underwent a transformation to broaden its scope of inquiry to include these theoretical lenses. These are the theories mentioned earlier in this book, contained in Chapter 1. They provide a lens (even a theory) to guide the researchers as to what issues are important to examine (e.g., marginalization, empowerment) and the people that need to be studied (e.g., women, homeless, minority groups). They also indicate how the researcher positions himself or herself in the qualitative study (e.g., up front or biased from personal, cultural, and historical contexts) and how the final written accounts need to be written (e.g., without further marginalizing individuals, by collaborating with participants). In critical ethnography studies, researchers begin with a theory that informs their studies. This causal theory might be a theory of emancipation or repression (J. Thomas, 1993). Rossman and Rallis (1998) capture, in a few words, the sense of theory as critical and postmodern perspectives in qualitative inquiry:

> As the 20th century draws to a close, traditional social science has come under increasing scrutiny and attack as those espousing critical and postmodern perspectives challenge objectivist

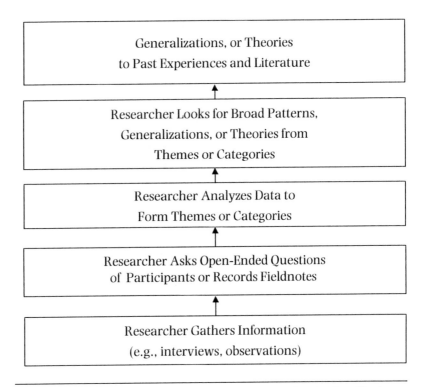

Figure 7.5 The Inductive Logic of Research in a Qualitative Study

assumptions and traditional norms for the conduct of research. Central to this attack are four interrelated notions: (a) Research fundamentally involves issues of power; (b) the research report is not transparent but rather it is authored by a raced, gendered, classed, and politically oriented individual; (c) race, class, and gender are crucial for understanding experience; and (d) historic, traditional research has silenced members of oppressed and marginalized groups. (p. 66)

Distinct from this theoretical orientation are qualitative studies i which theory (or some other broad explanation) becomes the *end poi* for a study. It is an inductive process of building from the data to broa themes to a generalized model or theory (see Punch, 1998). The log of this inductive approach is shown in Figure 7.5. The research begins by gathering detailed information from participants and forms this information into categories or themes. These themes or categories are developed into broad patterns, theories, or generalizations that are then compared with personal experiences or with existing literature on the topic.

The development of themes and categories into patterns, theories, or generalizations suggests a varied end point for qualitative studies. For example, in case study research, Stake (1995) refers to an assertion as a propositional generalization—the researcher's summary of interpretations and claims—to which is added the researcher's own personal experiences, called "naturalistic generalizations" (p. 86). As another example, grounded theory provides a different end point. Inquirers hope to discover a theory that is grounded in information from participants (Strauss & Corbin, 1998). Lincoln and Guba (1985) refer to "pattern theories" as an explanation that develops during naturalistic or qualitative research. Rather than the deductive form found in quantitative studies, these "pattern theories" or "generalizations" represent interconnected thoughts or parts linked to a whole. W. L. Neuman (1991) provides additional information about "pattern theories":

> Pattern theory does not emphasize logical deductive reasoning. Like causal theory, it contains an interconnected set of concepts and relationships, but it does not require causal statements. Instead, pattern theory uses metaphor or analogies so that relationship "makes sense." Pattern theories are systems of ideas that inform. The concepts and relations within them form a mutually reinforcing, closed system. They specify a sequence of phases or link parts to a whole. (p. 38)

Finally, some qualitative studies *do not employ any explicit theory.* However, the case can be made that no qualitative study begins from pure observation and that prior conceptual structure composed of theory and method provides the starting point for all observations (Schwandt, 1993). Still, one sees qualitative studies that contain no *explicit* theoretical orientation, such as in phenomenology, in which inquirers attempt to build the essence of experience from participants (e.g., see Riemen, 1986). In these studies, the inquirer constructs a rich, detailed description of a central phenomenon.

My advice on theory-use in a qualitative proposal is this:

- Decide if theory is to be used in the qualitative proposal.

- If it is used, then identify how the theory will be used in the study, such as an up-front explanation, as an end point, or as an advocacy lens.

- Locate the theory in the proposal in a manner consistent with its use.

Locating the Theory or Pattern in Qualitative Research

How theory is used affects its placement in a qualitative study. In those studies with a cultural theme or a theoretical lens, the theory occurs in the opening passages of the study. Consistent with the emerging design of qualitative inquiry, the theory may appear at the beginning and be modified or adjusted based on participant views. Even in the most theory-oriented qualitative design, such as critical ethnography, Lather (1986) qualifies the use of theory:

> Building empirically grounded theory requires a reciprocal relationship between data and theory. Data must be allowed to generate propositions in a dialectical manner that permits use of *a priori* theoretical frameworks, but which keeps a particular framework from becoming the container into which the data must be poured. (p. 267)

Example 7.2   *An Example of Theory-Use Early in a Qualitative Study*

Murguia, Padilla, and Pavel (1991) studied the integration of 24 Hispanic and Native American students into the social system of a college campus. They were curious about how ethnicity influenced social integration, and they began by relating the participants' experiences to a theoretical model, the Tinto model of social integration. They felt that the model had been "incompletely conceptualized and, as a consequence, only imprecisely understood and measured" (p. 433).

Thus, the model was not being tested in the study as one would find in a quantitative project, but modified in the study. At the end of the study, the authors refined Tinto's model and advanced their modification that described the rootedness and functions of ethnicity. In contrast to this approach, in qualitative studies with an end point of a theory (e.g., a grounded theory), a pattern, or a generalization, the theory emerges at the end of the study. This theory might be presented as a logic diagram, a visual representation of relationships among concepts.

Example 7.3   *A Theory at the End*
of a Qualitative Study

Using a national database of 33 interviews with academic department chairpersons, we (Creswell & Brown, 1992) developed a grounded theory interrelating variables (or categories) of chair influence on scholarly performance of faculty. The theory section came into the article as the last section, where the authors presented a visual model of the theory developed inductively from categories of information supplied by interviewees. In addition, the authors also advanced directional hypotheses that logically followed from the model. Moreover, in the section on the model and the hypotheses, the authors compared their results with findings from other studies and theoretical speculations in the literature. For example, the authors stated:

> This proposition and its sub-propositions represent unusual, even contrary evidence, to our expectations. Contrary to proposition 2.1, we expected that the career stages would be similar not in type of issue but in the range of issues. Instead we found that the issues for post-tenure faculty covered almost all the possible problems on the list. Why would this group's needs be more extensive? The research productivity literature suggests that one's research performance does not decline with the award of tenure (Holley 1977). Perhaps diffuse career goals of post-tenure faculty expand the possibilities for "types" of issues. In any case, this sub-proposition focuses attention on the understudied career group that Furniss (1981) reminds us needs to be examined in more detail. (p. 58)

As this example shows, we developed a visual model that interrelated variables, derived this model inductively from informant comments, and placed the model at the end of the study, where the central propositions in it could be contrasted with the existing theories and literature.

MIXED METHODS THEORY-USE

Mixed methods studies may include theory deductively in theory testing and verification, or inductively as in an emerging theory or pattern. In either situation, the use of theory may be directed by the emphasis on either quantitative or qualitative approaches in the mixed methods research. Another way to think about theory in mixed methods research is the use of a *theoretical lens or perspective* to guide the study. Here we have limited information about the procedures involved in using a theoretical lens to study gender, race/ethnicity/disability, sexual orientation, and other bases of diversity (Mertens, 2003). Several authors, however, have begun the discussion.

The first were Greene and Caracelli (1997), who mentioned the use of a "transformative design" as a distinct form of mixed methods research. This design gave primacy to value-based, action-oriented research such as in participatory action research and empowerment approaches. In this design, they suggest mixing the value commitments of different traditions in research (e.g., bias-free from quantitative and bias-laden from qualitative), the use of diverse methods, and a focus on action solutions in research. Unfortunately, they do not specify the procedures involved in incorporating this theoretical perspective into the practice of research.

More information on procedures has appeared in a chapter written by Creswell, Plano Clark, Gutmann, and Hanson (2003). They identify the use of theoretical perspectives such as gendered, feminist perspectives; cultural/racial/ethnic perspectives, lifestyle perspectives, critical perspectives, and class and social status perspectives. In Creswell et al.'s view, these perspectives represent one of the major decisions to be made in the selection of mixed methods strategies. They further develop visual models of these strategies for both sequential and concurrent mixed methods approaches, and they indicate some of the strengths and weaknesses (e.g., it is appealing to those interested in change despite limited discussions about procedures (also see Chapter 11 of this book).

Mertens (2003) continues the discussion. As outlined in Box 7.1, she advocates for the importance of a theory-lens in mixed methods

Box 7.1 Transformative-Emancipatory Questions for Mixed Methods Researchers Throughout the Research Process

Defining the Problem and Searching the Literature

- Did you deliberately search the literature for concerns of diverse groups and issues of discrimination and oppression?
- Did the problem definition arise from the community of concern?
- Did your mixed methods approach arise from spending quality time with these communities? (i.e., building trust? using an appropriate theoretical framework other than a deficit model? developing balanced—positive and negative—questions? developing questions that lead to transformative answers, such as questions focused on authority and relations of power in institutions and communities?)

Identifying the Research Design

- Does your research design deny treatment to any groups and respect ethical considerations of participants?

Identifying Data Sources and Selecting Participants

- Are the participants of groups associated with discrimination and oppression?
- Are the participants appropriately labeled?
- Is there a recognition of diversity within the target population?
- What can be done to improve the inclusiveness of the sample to increase the probability that traditionally marginalized groups are adequately and accurately represented?

Identifying or Constructing Data Collection Instruments and Methods

- Will the data collection process and outcomes benefit the community being studied?
- Will the research findings be credible to that community?

- Will communication with that community be effective?
- Will the data collection open up avenues for participation in the social change process?

Analyzing, Interpreting, and Reporting and Using Results

- Will the results raise new hypotheses?
- Will the research examine subgroups (i.e., multilevel analyses) to analyze the differential impact on diverse groups?
- Will the results help understand and elucidate power relationships?
- Will the results facilitate social change?

SOURCE: Adapted from D. M. Mertens (2003), "Mixed Methods and the Politics of Human Research: The Transformative-Emancipatory Perspective," in A. Tashakkori & C. Teddlie (Eds.), *Handbook of Mixed Methods in the Social and Behavioral Sciences.* Adapted with permission.

research. In detailing a "transformative/emancipatory paradigm" and specific procedures, she emphasizes the role that values play in studying feminist, ethnic/racial, and disability issues. Her "transformative theory" is an umbrella term for research that is emancipatory, anti-discriminatory, participative, Freirian, feminist, racial/ethnic, for individuals with disabilities, and for all marginalized groups.

Mertens identifies the implication of these transformative theories for mixed methods research. These involve integration of the transformative-emancipatory methodology into all phases of the research process. Reading through the questions in Box 7.1, one gains a sense of the importance of studying issues of discrimination and oppression and of recognizing diversity among study participants. These questions also address treating individuals respectfully through gathering and communicating data collection and through reporting results that lead to changes in social processes and relationships.

In using theory in a mixed methods proposal

- Determine if theory is to be used.

- Identify its use in accord with quantitative or qualitative approaches.

● If theory is used as in a transformational strategy of inquiry, define this strategy and discuss the points in the proposed study in which the emancipatory ideas will be used.

Example 7.4   *A Transformative-Emancipatory Mixed Methods Study*

Hopson, Lucas, and Peterson (2000) studied issues in a urban, predominantly African American HIV/AIDS community. Consistent with a transformative-emancipatory framework, they examined the language of participants with HIV/AIDS within the participants' social context. They first conducted 75 open-ended ethnographic interviews to identify "language themes" (p. 31), such as blame, ownership, and acceptance or non-acceptance. They also collected 40 semistructured interviews that addressed demographics, daily routine, drug use, knowledge of HIV/AIDS risks, and drug and sexual sociobehavioral characteristics. From this qualitative data, the authors used concepts and questions to refine follow-up questions, including the design of a quantitative postintervention instrument. The authors suggested that empowerment approaches in evaluation can be useful, with researchers listening to the voices of real people and acting on what program participants say.

The design in this study gave "primacy to the value-based and action-oriented dimensions of different inquiry traditions" (Greene & Caracelli, 1997, p. 24) in a mixed methods study. The authors used a theoretical lens for reconfiguring the language and dialogue of participants, and they advanced the importance of empowerment in research.

SUMMARY

Researchers use theory in a quantitative study to provide an explanation or prediction about the relationship among variables in the study. A theory explains how and why the variables are related, acting as a bridge between or among the variables. Theory may be broad or narrow in scope, and researchers state their theories in several ways, such as a series of hypotheses, "if . . . then" logic statements, or visual models. Using theories deductively, investigators advance the theories at the beginning of the study in the literature review. They also include them with the hypotheses or research questions or place them in a separate section. A script can help design the theory section for a research proposal.

In qualitative research, inquirers employ theory as a broad explanation much like in quantitative research, such as in ethnographies. It may also be a theoretical lens or perspective that raises questions related to gender, class, or race, or some combination. Theory also appears as an end point of a qualitative study, a generated theory, a pattern, or a generalization that emerges inductively from data collection and analysis. Grounded theorists, for example, generate a theory "grounded" in the views of participants and place it as the conclusion of their studies. Some qualitative studies do not include an explicit theory and present descriptive research of the central phenomenon.

Mixed methods researchers use theory either deductively (as in quantitative research) or inductively (as in qualitative research). Writers also are beginning to identify the use of theoretical lenses or perspectives (e.g., related to gender, lifestyle, race/ethnicity, and class) in their mixed methods studies. A transformational-emancipatory design incorporates this perspective, and recent developments have identified procedures for incorporating this perspective into all phases of the research process.

WRITING EXERCISES

Writing Exercises

1. Write a "theoretical perspective" section for your research plan following the script for a quantitative theory discussion presented in this chapter.

2. For a quantitative proposal you are planning, draw a visual model of the variables in the theory using the procedures for causal model design advanced in this chapter.

3. Locate qualitative journal articles that (a) use an a priori theory that is modified during the process of research, (b) generate or develop a theory at the end of the study, and (c) represent descriptive research without the use of an explicit theoretical model.

4. Locate a mixed methods study that uses a theoretical lens, such as a feminist, ethnic/racial, or class perspective. Identify specifically in the article how the lens shapes the steps taken in the research process using Box 7.1 as a guide.

ADDITIONAL READINGS

Flinders, D. J., & Mills, G. E. (Eds.). (1993). *Theory and concepts in qualitative research: Perspectives from the field.* **New York: Teachers College Press, Teachers College, Columbia University.**

> David Flinders and Geoffrey Mills have edited a book about perspectives from the field—"theory at work"—as described by different qualitative researchers. The chapters illustrate little consensus about defining theory and whether it is a vice or virtue. Further, theory operates at many levels in research, such as formal theories, epistemological theories, methodological theories, and metatheories. Given this diversity, it is best to see actual theory at work in qualitative studies, and this volume illustrates practice from critical, personal, formal, and educational criticism.

Mertens, D. M. (1998). *Research methods in education and psychology: Integrating diversity with quantitative and qualitative approaches.* **Thousand Oaks, CA: Sage.**

> Throughout this research methods text, Donna Mertens provides an integration of the "emancipatory paradigm" of research. Her brief overview of this paradigm or theoretical perspective is excellent. The paradigm, according to Mertens, places central importance on the lives of individuals who have been marginalized. It analyzes the inequities based on gender, race, ethnicity, or disability, and it is linked to social action. It uses an "emancipatory theory"—a set of beliefs about the ways a program works or why a problem occurs. It also relates theory to the questions asked and the recommenations for action.

Thomas, G. (1997). What's the use of theory? *Harvard Educational Review, 67*(1), 75-104.

> Gary Thomas presents a reasoned critique of the use of theory in educational inquiry. He notes the various definitions of theory and maps out four broad uses of theory: as thinking and reflection, as tighter or looser hypotheses, as explanations for adding to knowledge in different fields, and as formally expressed statements in science. Having noted these uses, he then embraces the thesis that theory unnecessarily structures and constrains thought. Instead, ideas should be in a constant flux, and should be "ad hocery" as characterized by Toffler.

10 Various Entries: Constructionism, Critical Theory, Epistemology, Falsification, Ontology, Paradigm, Philosophy of Social Research, Positivism, Postmodernism

MICHAEL S. LEWIS-BECK, ALAN BRYMAN and TIM F. LIAO

CONSTRUCTIONISM, SOCIAL

Social constructionism is, first of all, an account of knowledge-generating practices— both scientific and otherwise. At this level, constructionist theory offers an orientation toward knowledge making in the sciences, a standpoint at considerable variance with the empiricist tradition. At the same time, social constructionism contains the ingredients of a theory of human functioning; at this level, it offers an alternative to traditional views of individual, psychological processes. Constructionist premises have also been extended to a variety of practical domains, opening new departures in such fields as therapy, organizational management, and education. (For more complete accounts, see Gergen, 1994, 1999.) Of special relevance, they have contributed to the flourishing of many new forms of research methods in the social sciences.

SOCIAL CONSTRUCTIONIST ASSUMPTIONS

Social constructionism cannot be reduced to a fixed set of principles but is more properly considered a continuously unfolding conversation about the nature of knowledge and our understanding of the world. However, several themes are typically located in writings that identify themselves as constructionist. At the outset, it is typically assumed that our accounts of the world—scientific and otherwise—are not dictated or determined in any principled way by what there is. Rather, the terms in which the world is understood are generally held to be social artifacts, products of historically situated interchanges among people. Thus, the extent to which a given form of understanding prevails within a culture is not fundamentally dependent on the empirical validity of the perspective in question but rather on the vicissitudes of social process (e.g., communication, negotiation, communal conflict, rhetoric). This line of reasoning does not at all detract from the significance of various forms of cultural understanding, whether scientific or otherwise. People's constructions of the world and self are essential to the broader practices of a culture—justifying, sustaining, and transforming various forms of conduct. In addition, different communities of meaning making may contribute differentially to the resources available to humankind—whether it be "medical cures," "moral intelligibilities," institutions of law, or "reasons to live." However, constructionism does challenge the warrant of any group—science included—to proclaim "truth" beyond its perimeters. What is true, real, and good within one tradition may not be within another, and there are no criteria for judging among traditions that are themselves free of traditions, their values, goals, and way of life.

SOCIAL CONSTRUCTION AND SOCIAL SCIENCE

The social constructionist views favored by this composite of developments begin to furnish a replacement for traditional empiricist accounts of social science. In the process of this replacement, one may discriminate between two phases, deconstruction and reconstruction. In the former phase, pivotal assumptions of scientific rationality, along with bodies of empirically justified knowledge claims, are placed in question. This work essentially represents an elaboration and extension of the early anti-foundationalist arguments, now informed by the additional developments within the literary and critical domains. Thus, an extensive body of literature has emerged, questioning the warrant and the ideological implications of claims to truth, empirical hypothesis testing, universal rationality,

laws of human functioning, the value neutrality of science, the exportation of Western scientific practices, and so on.

Immersion in this literature alone would lead to the conclusion that social constructionism is nihilistic in its aims. However, as many believe, the deconstructive process is only a necessary prolegomenon to a reconstructive enterprise. Within the reconstructive phase, the chief focus is on ways in which scientific inquiry, informed by constructionist views, can more effectively serve the society of which it is a part. From this emerging sensibility, several developments are noteworthy. First, constructionst ideas place a strong emphasis on theoretical creativity; rather than "mapping the world as it is," the invitation is to create intelligibilities that may help us to build new futures. Theories of collaborative cognition, cyborg politics, and actor networks are illustrative. Second, constructionism has stimulated much work in cultural study, the critical and illuminating examination of everyday life practices and artifacts. Third, constructionist ideas have helped to generate a range of new practices in therapy, organizational change, and education in particular. Many scholars also find that in challenging disciplinary boundaries to knowledge, constructionist ideas invite broad-ranging dialogue. Thus, new areas of interest have been spawned, linking for example, theology and costructionism, literary theory and social movements, and personality study and ethical theory.

SOCIAL CONSTRUCTION AND RESEARCH METHODS

Although much constructionist writing is critical of traditional empirical methods in the social sciences, these criticisms are not lethal. There is nothing about constructionist ideas that demands one kind of research method as opposed to another; every method has its ways of constructing the world. Thus, although traditional empiricist methods may be viewed as limited and ideologically problematic, they do have important uses. However, the major importance of constructionist ideas in the domain of methodology has been to incite discussion of new methods of inquiry. Although these new methods tend to be viewed as "qualitative" (Denzin & Lincoln, 2000), constructionists do not subscribe to the traditional qualitative/quantitative distinction that holds the former as preliminary and inferior to the latter. Most qualitative inquiry has different aims, different values, and a different politics than those inherent in quantitative inquiry. Thus far, constructionist work has functioned, in particular, to support research methods emphasizing the following:

- *Value reflection:* Who is advantaged by the research methods and who may be discredited? Is the research subject exploited by the research or treated as a mere object?
- *Subject voice:* Is the voice of the subject of research heard or legitimated by the method or obliterated by the research procedure?
- *Collaborative participation:* Can the subjects of research participate with the researcher in the generation of knowledge? Can they share in or benefit from the outcomes?
- *Multiple standpoints:* Are multiple viewpoints and values represented in the research, or does one standpoint dominate?
- *Representational creativity:* Must the representation of research be limited to formal writing, or can more populist and richly compelling forms of representation be located?

In its research emphases, constructionist assumptions are particularly evident in PARTICIPATORY ACTION RESEARCH (Reason & Bradbury, 2000), discourse analysis (Wetherell, Taylor, & Yates, 2001), narrative inquiry (see, e.g., Josselsyn, 1996), participatory ethnography, and literary and performative approaches to representation (see, e.g., Ellis & Bochner, 1996).

—Kenneth J. Gergen

REFERENCES

Denzin, N. K., & Lincoln, Y. S. (Eds.). (2000). *Handbook of qualitative research* (2nd ed.). Thousand Oaks, CA: Sage.

Ellis, C., & Bochner, A. P. (Eds.). (1996). *Composing ethnography.* Walnut Creek, CA: AltaMira.

Gergen, K. J. (1994). *Realities and relationships.* Cambridge, MA: Harvard University Press.

Gergen, K. J. (1999). *An invitation to social construction.* London: Sage.

Josselsyn, R. (Ed.). (1996). *Ethics and process in the narrative study of lives.* Thousand Oaks, CA: Sage.

Reason, P., & Bradbury, H. (Eds.). (2000). *Handbook of action research, participative inquiry and practice.* Sage: London.

Wetherell, M., Taylor, S., & Yates, S. J. (Eds.). (2001). *Discourse theory and practice.* London: Sage.

CRITICAL THEORY

To the extent that any theorization of societal mechanisms and modes of conducting social relations does not accord with dominant ways of viewing society and social relations, it may be said to be critical. The term *critical theory,* however, is normally reserved for a particular set of ideas associated with what become known as the Frankfurt School of Social Research and its followers, who have modified and extended its original insights, aspirations, and agendas.

Under the auspices of its second director, Max Horkheimer (1895–1973), the Institute for Social Research at Frankfurt centered its interests on the following key areas: EXPLANATIONS for the absence of a unified working-class movement in Europe, an examination of the nature and consequences of capitalist crises, a consideration of the relationship between the political and the economic spheres in modern societies, an account for the rise of fascism and Nazism as political movements, the study of familial socialization, and a sustained critique of the link between POSITIVISM and science. To pursue this study, those figures who stood between Hegel, Marx, and the Frankfurt School—such as Schopenhauer and Nietzsche, who had both questioned the Enlightenment project—required systematic engagement to recover the promise of Marxism.

As noted, the changing climate shaped the work of these scholars. In Nazi Germany, the institute found itself under threat with the result that its leading members, including Theodor Adorno (1903–1969), Max Horkheimer, and Herbert Marcuse (1898–1979), emigrated to the United States (Adorno and Horkheimer returned after World War II). Here they found a self-confident bourgeois liberal-capitalism, with its apparent ability to absorb and neutralize proletarian consciousness. Here was the personification of the ideology of individualism accompanied by ideas of success and meritocracy. Analyzing these trends and their consequences necessitated a consideration of culture that, until this time, had been largely devalued in Marxist circles.

The work of these scholars was interdisciplinary (thus anticipating debates that are more prominent in contemporary times), accompanied by critiques of both positivist and interpretivist approaches to understanding human relations. On one hand, positivism had failed to examine the conditions under which capitalism develops and is sustained. On the other hand, interpretivism was held to be inadequate due to an exclusive concentration on the process of self-understanding and self-consciousness. The result was an uncritical acceptance of dominant forms of consciousness within given societies and a failure to consider the structural determinants of human actions.

Historical investigations were then undertaken into the Enlightenment project. Here we find that

> the individual is wholly devalued in relation to the economic powers, which at the same time press the control of society over nature to hitherto unsuspected heights. ... The flood of detailed information and candy-floss entertainment simultaneously instructs and stultifies mankind. (Adorno & Horkheimer, 1944/1979, pp. xiv–xv)

On this basis, studies examined the process of ideological incorporation. Herbert Marcuse (1968), in *One Dimensional Man,* thus spoke of the "technicaladministrative control" of society.

This meta-critique noted the following question: Having rejected interpretivist social theory, how can the important analysis of mental states be achieved? This is where Sigmund Freud enters as part of the whole history of the relationship between psychoanalysis and social theory. This focus moves away from an understanding of the solitary ego in the social world to the *self-misunderstanding* person who fails to see the causes of his or her own symptoms. However, issues remained. Up to the time of the Frankfurt theorists, Marxists had dismissed psychoanalysis as unworthy of attention and a distraction from the primary purpose of overthrowing an unjust economic system.

Psychoanalysis, after all, may be seen as the practice of amelioration, not resolution, let alone revolution. Conceptually speaking, it starts from the individual and tends to play down social conditions and constraints.

Therefore, if Freud's work was to serve the needs of critical theory, it required modification. At this point, Leo Lowenthal and Eric Fromm enter the scene as central to this process in the development of critical theory. Fromm, for example, examined the relationship between the individual and totalitarianism. He also held throughout his life that our capacity for love and freedom is inextricably bound up with socioeconomic conditions. The interest in Freud was also apparent in sociopsychological studies on the structure of modern personality types carried about by Adorno and his associates in 1950, as well as in the writings of Willhelm Reich on the relationship between sexuality and capitalism.

For critical theory, there is a constant interaction between THEORY and facts, and theorists seek to recognize the relationship between the constitution of their propositions and the social context in which they find themselves. REFLEXIVITY concerning the relationship between what is produced, under what circumstances, and with what effects distinguishes traditional from critical theory. In addition, the issue of research results feeding back into social life is not a "problem" for researchers. On the contrary, the adequacy of critical research lies in its value for informing political actions.

Although critical social research aligns itself with the "wishes and struggles of the age," it remains the case that critics, although recognizing the impossibility of separating values from research, regard justifications for conflating the two as untenable. After all, who is to define the values that are of importance? Furthermore, what is the basis of critique? Is it the autonomy of the free individual? The idea of autonomy becomes an abstraction because how can any individual be presumed to be separate from the social relations of whom he or she is a part? The basis of critique then becomes so far removed from reality that it appears aloof and withdrawn. These and other criticisms have been made of research practice informed by critical theory.

Of all contemporary scholars, Jürgen Habermas has continued most prolifically in this tradition and addressed the above issues through extensive modi-fication and critique. This legacy is also evident in the writings of Nancy Fraser (1997) and Axel Honneth (1996), who have contributed to debates on recognition and redistribution, as well as Pierre Bourdieu's (2000) contributions to a "realpolitik of reason." As for Michel Foucault, his own words in "Remarks on Marx" will suffice: "The Frankfurt School set problems that are still being worked on. Among others, the effects of power that are connected to a rationality that has been historically and geographically defined in the West, starting from the sixteenth century on" (Foucault, 1991, p. 117).

—Tim May

REFERENCES

Adorno, T., & Horkheimer, M. (1979). *Dialectic of enlightenment* (J. Cumming, Trans.). London: Verso. (Original work published 1944.)

Bourdieu, P. (2000). *Pascalian meditations* (R. Nice, Trans.). Cambridge, UK: Polity.

Comstock, D. E. (1994). A method for critical research. In M. Martin & L. C. McIntyre

(Eds.), *Readings in the philosophy of social science* (pp. 625–639). Cambridge: MIT Press.

Foucault, M. (1991). *Remarks on Marx: Conversations with Duccio Trombadori* (R. J. Goldstein & J. Cascaito, Trans.). New York: Semiotext(e).

Fraser, N. (1997). *Justice interruptus: Critical reflections on the 'postsocialist' condition.* London: Routledge Kegan Paul.

Honneth, A. (1996). *The struggle for recognition: The moral grammar of social conflicts* (J. Anderson, Trans.). Cambridge: MIT Press.

Marcuse, H. (1968). *One dimensional man: The ideology of industrial society.* London: Sphere.

Morrow, R. A. (with Brown, D. D.). (1994). *Critical theory and methodology.* London: Sage.

Wiggershaus, R. (1995). *The Frankfurt School: Its history, theories and political significance* (M. Robertson, Trans.). Cambridge, UK: Polity.

EPISTEMOLOGY

In philosophy, epistemology refers to a THEORY of knowledge, a theory of how human beings come to have knowledge of the world around them—of how we know what we know. Epistemology provides a philosophical grounding for establishing what kinds of knowledge are possible and for deciding how knowledge can be judged as being both adequate and legitimate. In the social sciences, the term is used in the context of deciding which scientific procedures produce reliable social scientific knowledge.

Two theories of knowledge have predominated in philosophical discourse since the scientific revolution in the 17th century: RATIONALISM (represented by René Descartes, Gottfried Leibniz, and Benedict de Spinoza) and EMPIRICISM (represented by John Locke, George Berkeley, and David Hume). The concern was to find a secure foundation for scientific knowledge and to distinguish this from belief and prejudice. Rationalism is based on the idea that reliable knowledge is derived from the use of "pure" reason, from establishing indisputable axioms and then using formal logic to arrive at conclusions. From this point of view, mathematics produces such knowledge. Empiricism, on the other hand, relies on the use of the human senses to produce reliable knowledge. This means that knowledge of the world can be obtained only through direct sense-experience.

In the context of the social sciences, these philosophical positions can be further elaborated in terms of two dominant epistemological positions and their associated ontological positions (see ONTOLOGY). In the first epistemological position, known as nominalism, the concepts that are used in description and explanation are simply regarded as convenient, collective names that are invented as summaries of the general categories of things that have been observed, such as "social actors" or "social groups." These collectivities should neither be confused with reality itself nor attributed with the capacity to act; reality is made up of events, and only individuals can act. In the second epistemological position, known as REALISM, scientific concepts are viewed as revealing something about social reality that is not necessarily observable. Such concepts are designed to penetrate beyond observable events to a reality that underlies and explains them (see also CRITICAL realism).

When nominalism and realism are combined with the two major alternative ontological positions, materialism and idealism, a four-way classification scheme is generated. Empiricism combines a materialist ontology (see IDEALISM) with a nominalist epistemology, substantialism combines a materialist ontology with a realist epistemology, subjectivism combines an idealist ontology with a nominalist epistemology, and rationalism combines an idealist ontology with a realist epistemology (Johnson, Dandeker, & Ashworth, 1984).

In empiricism, reality is viewed as being constituted of material things that can be observed by the use of the human senses. Concepts and generalizations are shorthand summaries based on many observations. Substantialism also adopts a materialist view of reality but accepts that people in different times and places can interpret reality differently. Nevertheless, the material world is seen to constrain human actions and social relations. Because subjectivism rejects the notion of a material world and views reality as being socially constructed and interpreted, knowledge of this reality is available only from the accounts that social actors can give of it. Finally, rationalism views reality as both real and general; it exists independently of people, their consciousness, and their circumstances. Because this reality is made up of ideas, knowledge of it can be obtained only by examining thought process, the innate ideas shared by human beings—in short, the structure of mind itself. These four positions must be regarded as ideal types, between which there are inherent tensions (Johnson et al., 1984). They are associated with the major PHILOSOPHIES of social-science. Empiricism is associated with POSITIVISM and FALSIFICATIONISM, substantialism is associated with CRITICAL REALISM, and subjectivism is associated with INTERPRETIVISM. Rationalism can be found in Emile Durkheim's work on suicide but is now uncommon in the social sciences.

—Norman Blaikie

REFERENCES

Blaikie, N. (1993). *Approaches to social enquiry.* Cambridge, UK: Polity.

Crotty, M. (1998). *The foundations of social research.* London: Sage.

Johnson, T., Dandeker, C., & Ashworth, C. (1984). *The structure of social theory.* London: Macmillan.

FALSIFICATIONISM

Falsificationism is a philosophy of science, also known as critical rationalism, that uses the logic of deduction to provide the foundation for the HYPOTHETICO-DEDUCTIVE METHOD. It was developed in the 1930s by Karl Popper (1959) to deal with the deficiencies of POSITIVISM. The positivist position is rejected in favor of a different logic of explanation based on a critical method of trial and error in which theories are tested against "reality." Falsificationism shares some aspects of positivism's *ontology* but rejects its EPISTEMOLOGY. It adopts the position that the natural and social sciences differ in their content but not in the logical form of their methods.

Although Popper was not a member of the Vienna circle, the group of scientists and philosophers that was responsible for developing logical positivism, he had a close intellectual contact with it. He shared with this tradition the view that scientific knowledge, imperfect though it may be, is the most certain and reliable knowledge available to human beings. However, he was critical of positivism—particularly logical positivism—and was at pains to distance himself from the circle. He rejected the idea that observations provide the foundation for scientific theories, and he recognized the important historical role played by metaphysical ideas in the formation of scientific theories.

Popper argued that observation is used in the service of deductive reasoning; theories are invented to account for observations, not derived from them, as in INDUCTION. Rather than scientists waiting for nature to reveal its regularities, they must impose regularities on the world and, by a process of trial and error, use observation to try to reject false theories (deduction). Theories that survive this critical process are provisionally accepted but never proven to be true. All knowledge is tentative and subject to ongoing critical evaluation. This critical attitude makes use of both verbal argument and observation; observation is used in the interest of argument.

The question of whether theories or observations come first was not a problem for Popper. He accepted that a hypothesis is preceded by observations, particularly those that it seeks to explain. However, these observations presuppose a frame of reference, that is, one or more theories.

In addressing the appropriate logic for the social sciences in his later work, Popper (1961) summarized what he called his main thesis. The logic of the social sciences, like that of the natural sciences, consists in trying out tentative solutions to certain problems; solutions are proposed and criticized. A solution that is not open to criticism must be excluded as unscientific. The ultimate criticism is to attempt to refute the theory. If the theory is refuted, another must be tried. However, if the theory withstands the testing, we can accept it temporarily, although it should be subjected to further discussion and criticism. Hence, the method of science is one of tentative attempts to solve problems by making conjectures that are controlled by severe criticism. The so-called objectivity of science lies in the objectivity of the critical method.

Popper argued that although science is a search for truths about the world or universe, we can never establish whether these theories are true. All that can be done is to eliminate false theories by a process of conjecture and refutation. Some theories will be rejected and some tentatively accepted (corroborated). This process allows us to get as near the truth as possible, but we never know when we have produced a true theory. Some scientist in the future may test the theory in some other circumstances and find it to be false. Therefore, theories must always be regarded as tentative—they may be refined or refuted in the future. All that we can do is get rid of theories that do not match reality. Popper believed that there is no more rational procedure than the method of conjecture and refutation. It is a process of boldly proposing theories, of trying our best to show that these are wrong, and of accepting them tentatively if our critical efforts are unsuccessful.

Criticisms made of the logic of deduction also apply to falsificationism.

—Norman Blaikie

REFERENCES

Blaikie, N. (1993). *Approaches to social enquiry.* Cambridge, UK: Polity.

Chalmers, A. F. (1982). *What is this thing called science?* St. Lucia: University of Queensland Press.

Popper, K. R. (1959). *The logic of scientific discovery.* London: Hutchinson.

Popper, K. R. (1961). *The poverty of historicism.* London: Routledge & Kegan Paul.

ONTOLOGY, ONTOLOGICAL

Ontology is a branch of philosophy that is concerned with the nature of what exists. It is the study of theories of being, theories about what makes up reality. In the context of social science: All theories and methodological positions make assumptions (either implicit or explicit) about what kinds of things do or can exist, the conditions of their existence, and the way they are related.

Theories about the nature of social reality fall into two categories: What exists is viewed either as a set of material phenomena or as a set of ideas that human beings have about their world. The materialist position assumes that, from a human viewpoint, both natural and social phenomena have an independent existence, and both types of phenomena have the potential to constrain human actions (see REALISM). Natural constraints may be in the form of gravity, climate, and our physical bodies, whereas social constraints include culture, social organization, and the productive system. Materialism is associated with the doctrine of naturalism, which claims that because there is little difference between the behavior of inanimate objects and that of human beings, the logics of enquiry appropriate in the natural sciences can also be used in the social sciences. The idealist position, on the other hand, claims that there are fundamental differences between natural and social phenomena, that humans have culture and live in a world of their shared interpretations (see IDEALISM). Social action is not mere behavior but instead involves a process of meaning giving. It is these meanings that constitute social reality (Johnson, Dandeker, & Ashworth, 1984, pp. 13–15).

Ontological assumptions underpin all social theo ries and methodological positions; they make different claims about what exists in their domain of interest. For example, POSITIVISM and FALSIFICATIONIS entail ontological assumptions of an ordered universe made up of discrete and observable events. Human activity is regarded as observable behavior taking place in observable, material circumstances. Social reality is regarded as a complex of causal relations between events that are depicted as a patchwork of relations between variables. INTERPRETIVISM, on the other hand, assumes that social reality is the product of processes by which human beings together negotiate the meanings of actions and situations. Human experience is characterized as a process of interpretation rather than direct perception of an external physical world. Hence, social reality is not some "thing" that may be interpreted in different ways; it is those interpretations (Blaikie, 1993, pp. 94, 96).

Because ontological claims are inevitably linked with epistemological claims (see EPISTEMOLOGY), it is difficult to discuss them separately (Crotty, 1998, p. 10). Assertions about what constitutes social phenomena have implications for the way in which it is possible to gain knowledge of such phenomena. Differences in the types of ontological and epistemological claims cannot be settled by empirical enquiry. Although they are open to philosophical debate, the proponents of the various positions ultimately make their claims as an act of faith.

—Norman Blaikie

REFERENCES

Blaikie, N. (1993). *Approaches to social enquiry.* Cambridge, UK: Polity Press.

Crotty, M. (1998). *The foundations of social research.* London: Sage.

Johnson, T., Dandeker, C., & Ashworth, C. (1984). *The structure of social theory.* London: Macmillan.

PARADIGM

In everyday usage, *paradigm* refers either to a model or an example to be followed or to an established system or way of doing things. The concept was introduced into the philosophy of science by Thomas Kuhn (1970) in his discussion of the nature of scientific progress.

As a reaction against philosophies of science that prescribed *the* appropriate scientific method, such as Popper's FALSI-FICATIONISM, Kuhn (1970) focused on the practices of communities of scientists. He saw such communities as sharing a paradigm or "discipline matrix" consisting of their views of the nature of the reality they study (their ontology), including the components that make it up and how they are related; the techniques that are appropriate for investigating this reality (their EPISTEMOLOGY); and accepted examples of past scientific achievements (exemplars) that provide both the foundation for further practice and models for students who wish to become members of the community. He suggested that a mature science is dominated by a single paradigm.

According to Kuhn (1970), most of the time, scientists engage in *normal science,* research that is dominated by "puzzle-solving" activities and is firmly based on the assumptions and rules of the paradigm. Normal science extends the knowledge that the paradigm provides by testing its predictions and further articulating and filling out its implications; it does not aim for unexpected novelty of fact or theory. In the course of normal science, the paradigm is not challenged or tested; failure to solve a puzzle will be seen as the failure of the scientist, not the paradigm.

Occasions arise when some puzzles cannot be solved, or gaps appear between what the paradigm would have anticipated and what is observed. These anomalies may be ignored initially, as commitment to a paradigm produces inherent resistance to their recognition. Kuhn (1970) argued that a paradigm is a prerequisite to perception itself, that what we see depends both on what we look at and also on what our previous visual-conceptual experience has taught us to see. Adherence to a paradigm is analogous to an act of faith, and to suggest that there is something wrong with it is likely to be interpreted as heresy.

Anomalies may lead to a crisis of confidence in the paradigm. There emerges a period of *extraordinary science,* accompanied by a proliferation of competing articulations, the willingness to try anything, the expression of discontent, the recourse to philosophy, and debates over fundamentals. The situation is ripe for the emergence of a new paradigm and novel theories.

Kuhn (1970) has described the process of replacing the old paradigm with a new one as a *scientific revolution.* A new paradigm may be proposed to replace an existing one—a paradigm that can solve the new puzzles raised by the anomalies and can handle the puzzles that the previous paradigm had solved. However, such revolutions occur only slowly, usually taking a generation or longer. According to Kuhn, the process by which a scientist moves from working with the old paradigm to the new is analogous to a religious conversion; it involves not just adopting a fundamentally different way of viewing the world but also living in a different world. Once a new paradigm is established, a new phase of normal science will commence. In time, new anomalies will emerge and further revolutions will occur.

Kuhn (1970) argued that rival paradigms are incommensurable. This is because the concepts and propositions of theories produced by a community of scientists depend on the assumptions and beliefs in their paradigm for their particular meaning. As paradigms embody different and incompatible world-views, it will be difficult for members of different scientific communities to communicate effectively, and it will be impossible to adjudicate between competing theories. There is no neutral language of observation, no common vocabulary, and no neutral ground from which to settle claims.

For Kuhn, scientific progress is not achieved by the accumulation of generalizations derived from observation (INDUCTION) or by the critical testing of new hypotheses (deduction/FALSIFICATIONISM)— it is achieved by scientific revolutions that change the way a scientific community views the world and defines and goes about solving puzzles (for reviews, see Blaikie, 1993, pp. 105–110; Riggs, 1992, pp. 22–59).

Kuhn's work has spawned a vast literature and has received detailed criticism by philosophers and historians of science, such as Lakatos and Laudan (for a review, see Riggs, 1992). It was used as a framework for understanding the crisis in sociology in the 1960s and 1970s (see, e.g., Friedricks, 1970), when there were vigorous disputes between competing paradigms (see, e.g., Ritzer, 1980).

—Norman Blaikie

REFERENCES

Blaikie, N. (1993). *Approaches to social enquiry.* Cambridge, UK: Polity.

Friedricks, R. (1970). *A sociology of sociology.* New York: Free Press.

Kuhn, T. S. (1970). *The structure of scientific revolutions* (2nd ed.). Chicago: University of Chicago Press.

Riggs, P. J. (1992). *Whys and ways of science.* Melbourne, Australia: Melbourne University Press.

Ritzer, G. (1980). *Sociology: A multiple paradigm science.* Boston: Allyn & Bacon.

PHILOSOPHY OF SOCIAL RESEARCH

The philosophy of social research is a branch of the PHILOSOPHY OF SOCIAL SCIENCE. It involves a critical examination of social research practice, as well as the various components of social research and their relationships.

The social researcher is confronted with a plethora of choices in the design and conduct of social research. These include the research problem; the RESEARCH QUESTION(S) to investigate this problem; the research strategies to answer these questions; the approaches to social enquiry that accompany these strategies; the concepts and theories that direct the investigation; the sources, forms, and types of data; the methods for making selections from these data sources; and the methods for collecting and analyzing the data to answer the research questions (Blaikie, 2000). At each point in the research process, philosophical issues are encountered in the evaluation of the options available and in the justification of the choices made. It is becoming increasingly difficult for social researchers to avoid these issues by simply following uncritically the practices associated with a particular *paradigm*.

PHILOSOPHICAL ISSUES

The philosophical issues that enter into these choices include types of ontological and epistemological assumptions, the nature of EXPLANATION, the types of THEORY and methods of construction, the role of language, the role of the researcher, OBJECTIVITY and truth, and generalizing results across time and space (Blaikie, 2000). As these issues are interrelated, the choice made on some issues has implications for the choice on other issues. This brief discussion of some of these issues is dependent on the more detailed discussion of related key concepts in this encyclopedia.

Ontological and Epistemological Assumptions

A key concern of philosophers of science and social science is the examination of claims that are made by theorists and researchers about the kinds of things that exist in the world and how we can gain knowledge of them. Social researchers, whether they realize it or not, have to make assumptions about both of these to proceed with their work. A range of positions can be adopted. To defend the position taken, social researchers need to have an understanding of the arguments for and against each position and be able to justify the stance taken. (See ONTOLOGY and EPISTEMOLOGY for a discussion of the range of positions.)

Theory Types and Their Construction

Philosophers have given considerable attention to the forms that theory takes and the processes by which theory is generated. In the social sciences, it is useful to distinguish between two types of theory: theoreticians' theory and researchers' theory. The former uses abstract concepts and ideas to understand social life at both the macro and micro levels. The latter is more limited in scope and is developed and/or tested in the context of social research. Although these two types of theory are related, their form and level of abstraction are different (Blaikie, 2000, pp. 142–143, 159–163). It is researchers' theory that is of concern here.

Some researchers' theories consist of general laws that are related in networks and are generated by INDUCTION from DATA. Others take the form of a set of propositions, of differing levels of generality, which form a deductive argument. Their origin is regarded as being unimportant, but their empirical testing is seen to be vital (see FALSIFICATIONISM). Some theories consist of descriptions of generative structures or mechanisms that are hypothesized to account for some phenomenon and are arrived at by the application of an informed imagination to a problem (see RETRODUCTION). Other theories consist of either rich descriptions or abstractions, perhaps in the form of ideal types of actors, courses of action, and situations. They are derived from social actors' concepts and interpretations (see ABDUCTION and INTERPRETIVISM). Philosophers of social science have put forward arguments for and criticisms of all four types of theory construction (see Blaikie, 1993).

The Nature of Explanation

One of the most vexed questions in the social sciences is how to explain social life. One controversy centers on the source of the explanation, whether it lies in social structures or in individual motives, that is, holism versus individualism. The issue is whether the source is to be found external to social actors or within them.

A related controversy is concerned with types of explanations, with the distinction between causal explanations and reason explanation. The former, which can take various forms, follows the logics of explanation used in the natural sciences, whereas the latter rejects these as being appropriate in the social sciences and replaces them with the reasons or motives social actors can give for their actions. Whether the use of reasons or motives can be regarded as explanations or just provide understanding is a matter of some debate.

Causal explanations, whether in the natural or social sciences, are of three major forms: pattern, deductive, and retroductive. In pattern explanations (see INDUCTION and POSITIVISM), a well-established generalization about regularities in social life can provide low-level explanations. For example, if it has been established that "juvenile delinquents come from broken homes," it is possible to use this to explain why some young people commit crimes—it is their family background. Deductive explanations (see FALSIFICATIONISM) start with one or more abstract theoretical premises and, by the use of deductive logic and other propositions, arrive at a conclusion that can either be treated as a hypothesis or as the answer to a "why" research question. Retroductive explanations (see RETRODUCTION and CRITICAL REALISM) rely on underlying causal structures or mechanisms to explain patterns in observed phenomena.

The Role of Language

The philosophical issue here is what relationship there should be, if any, between scientific language and objects in the world. The positions adopted on this issue are dependent on the ontological assumptions adopted. For example, in POSITIVISM, the use of a theory-neutral observation language is considered to be unproblematic, whereas in FALSIFICATIONISM, this is rejected on the grounds that all observations are theory dependent.

In positivism, language is regarded as a medium for describing the world, and it is assumed that there is an isomorphy between the structural form of language and the object-worlds to which language gives access. However, in some branches of INTERPRETIVISM, language is regarded as the medium of everyday, practical social activity. The issue here is the relationship between this lay language and social scientific language, with a number of writers advocating that the latter should be derived from the former by a process of ABDUCTION. The choice is between the imposition of technical language on the social world and the derivation of technical language from the everyday language.

The Role of the Researcher

Social researchers have adopted a range of stances toward the research process and the participants. These positions range from complete detachment to committed involvement. Philosophers of social science have critically examined these stances in terms of their achievability and their consequences for research outcomes.

Each stance is associated with the use of particular approaches to social enquiry and research strate gies. The role of *detached observer* is concerned with OBJECTIVITY and is associated with positivism and the logics of induction and deduction. The role of *faithful reporter* is concerned with social actors' points of view and is associated with some branches of interpretivism. The role of *mediator of languages* is concerned with generating understanding and is associated with some branches of HERMENEUTICS and with the logic of abduction. The role of *reflective partner* is concerned with emancipation and is associated with both critical theory and feminism. Finally, the role of *dialogic facilitator* is associated with POSTMOD-ERNISM and is concerned with reducing the researcher's authorial influence by allowing a variety of "voices" to be expressed (see Blaikie, 2000, pp. 52–56).

Objectivity

No concept associated with social research evokes both more emotion and confusion than objectivity. Researchers frequently aim to produce objective results and are often criticized when they are seen to fail. Some research methods are praised because they are seen to be objective, and others are criticized because they are assumed not to be objective. The philosophical issues are as follows: What does it mean to be "objective," and what do methods and results have to be like to be objective?

In positivism, being objective means keeping facts and values separate, that is, not allowing the researcher's values and prejudices to contaminate the data. This is a deceptively simple idea but one that turns out to be impossible to achieve. For a start, the notion of a "fact" is a complex one, and the difference between facts and values is not clear-cut. For some philosophers, keeping facts and values separate can mean not taking sides on issues involved in the research. However, some researchers favor a particular point of view (in feminism, women's points of

view). Values themselves can also be a topic for investigation.

For some philosophers, objectivity is achieved by using methods that are regarded as being appropriate by a community of scientists. This, of course, means adopting a particular set of values. Objectivity is also considered by some to entail the use of replicability. Procedures are used that other researchers can repeat, thus making possible the validation of results. Again, acceptability of particular methods is the criterion.

Some interpretive social scientists eschew concerns with objectivity and argue that researchers should be as subjective as possible. What this means is that researchers should immerse themselves completely in the life of the people they study, as this is seen to be the only way another form of life can be understood. What they aim for is an authentic account of that form of life, an account that is faithful to social actors' points of view.

Truth

Philosophers have developed a number of theories to defend their views of the nature of "truth." The *correspondence* theory of truth appeals to evidence gained from "objective" observation. It is assumed that an unprejudiced observer will be able to see the world as it really is and will be able to report these observations in a theory-neutral language. It is assumed that a theory is true because it agrees with the facts (see POSITIVISM). Of course, to achieve this, there has to be agreement about what are the facts. The *tentative* theory of truth argues that the theory-dependence of observations and the nature of the logic of falsification mean that the testing of deductively derived theory can never arrive at the truth. Although finding the truth is the aim, the results of deductive theory testing are always subject to future revision. In contrast, the *consensus* theory of truth is based on the idea of rational discussion free from all constraints and distorting influences. Although evidence may be important, it is rational argument that will determine the truth. Then there is the *pragmatic* theory of truth, which argues that something is true if it is useful, if it can be assimilated into and verified by the experiences of a community of people. In the correspondence theory, truth is seen to be established for all time. In the consensus theory, disinterested logical argument by anyone should arrive at the same truth. However, in the tentative theory, truth is seen to change as testing proceeds and, in the pragmatic theory, as experience changes. Finally, in the *relativist* theory of truth, there are many truths because it is assumed that there are multiple social realities. As no one has a privileged or neutral position from which to judge the various truths, it is impossible to determine which is the "truest." This range of positions makes the concept of truth rather less secure than common sense would suggest.

Generalizing

There seems to be a desire among practitioners of all sciences to be able to generalize their findings beyond the context in which they were produced, that their theories will apply across space and time (see GENERALIZATION). This is particularly true of positivism, in which inductive logic is used. Despite the fact that generalizations are based on finite observations, the aim is to produce universal laws, such as, "juvenile delinquents come from broken homes." Many philosophers have argued that this aim is impossible and have suggested less ambitious aspirations. Falsificationists, for example, accept the tentative nature of their theories, as well as the possibility that they may be replaced by better theories in the future. In addition, they may state some propositions in their theories in a general form but also include conditions that limit their applicability. In fact, it is the search for such conditions to which much scientific activity is devoted. For example, although the general proposition that "juvenile delinquents come from broken homes" may be included at the head of a deductive theory, limiting conditions—such as, "in some broken homes, children are inadequately socialized into the norms of society"—limit the theory to certain kinds of broken homes. The search for underlying mechanisms in CRITICAL REALISM is based on an assumption that they are real and not just the creation of scientists. However, such researchers see their task as not only finding the appropriate mechanisms but also establishing the conditions and contexts under which they operate. Mechanisms may be general, but their ability to operate is always dependent on the circumstances. Hence, these theories are always limited in time and space. Within interpretivism, it is generally accepted that any social scientific account of social life must be restricted in terms of time and space. Any understanding must be limited to the context from which it was abductively derived. Whether the same type of understanding is relevant in other social contexts will be dependent on further investigation. In any case, all understanding is time bound.

One aspect of generalizing that causes considerable confusion is the difference between the form of theoretical propositions and what happens in sample surveys (see SURVEY). If a PROBABILITY SAMPLE is drawn from a defined POPULATION, and if response rates are satisfactory, the results obtained from the sample can be statistically generalized back to the population from which the sample was drawn. Beyond that population, all generalizations have to be based on other evidence and argument, not on statistical procedures. In this regard, generalizing beyond sampled populations is essentially the same as generalizing from NONPROBABILITY SAMPLES and CASE STUDIES (Blaikie, 2000).

ASPECTS OF SOCIAL RESEARCH

A number of aspects of social research practice are associated with the issues discussed in the previous section. The ones reviewed here involve choices from among alternatives.

Approaches to Social Enquiry

At an abstract level, social research is conducted within theoretical and methodological perspectives, that is, within different approaches to social enquiry. These approaches have been characterized in various ways and usually include positivism, falsificationism (or critical rationalism), hermeneutics, interpretivism, critical theory, critical realism, structuration theory, and feminism (Blaikie, 1993). Each approach works with its own combination of ontological and epistemological assumptions (see Blaikie, 1993, pp. 94–101). The choice of approach and its associated research strategy has a major bearing on other RESEARCH DESIGN decisions and the conduct of a particular research project.

Research Strategies

Four basic strategies can be adopted in social research, based on the logics of induction, deduction, retroduction, and abduction (Blaikie, 1993, 2000). Each research strategy has a different starting point and arrives at a different outcome. The inductive strategy starts out with the collection of data, from which generalizations are made, and these can be used as elementary explanations. The deductive strategy starts out with a theory that provides a possible answer to a "why" research question. The conclusion that is logically deduced from the theory is the answer that is required. The theory is tested in the context of a research problem by the collection of relevant data. The retroductive strategy starts out with a hypothetical model of a mechanism that could explain the occurrence of the phenomenon under investigation. It is then necessary to conduct research to demonstrate the existence of such a mechanism. The abductive strategy starts out with lay concepts and meanings that are contained in social actors' ACCOUNTS of activities related to the research problem. These accounts are then redescribed in technical language, in social scientific accounts. The latter provide an understanding of the phenomenon and can be used as the basis for more elaborate theorizing.

The four research strategies work with different ontological assumptions. The inductive and deductive strategies share the same ontological assumptions (see POSITIVISM, INDUCTION, FALSIFICATIONISM, and DEDUCTION); the retroductive strategy works with a tiered notion of reality, which particularly distinguishes between the domains of the actual (what we can observe) and the real (underlying structures and mechanisms) (see CRITICAL REALISM and RETRODUCTION). The abductive strategy adopts a social constructionist view of social reality (see INTERPRETIVISM and ABDUCTION). It is important for researchers to be aware of these differences as they have implications for other choices and for the interpretation of results.

The inductive strategy is only really useful for answering "what" research questions as generalizations from data have been shown to be an inadequate basis for answering "why" questions. The deductive and retroductive strategies are exclusively used for answering "why" questions, although both require that descriptions of observed patterns first be established. The abductive strategy can be used to answer both "what" and "why" questions.

There are extensive philosophical criticisms of each strategy and debates about their relative merits. None of them is without some controversial features. In the end, the social researcher has to evaluate the arguments and then make a judgment about their suitability for the problem at hand while, at the same time, recognizing their limitations.

CONCLUSION

All this suggests that an understanding of the issues dealt with in the philosophy of social research is essential for any social scientist. The choices that have to be made in doing social research require social scientists to take sides on philosophical issues. A lack of understanding of what is involved in making these choices can lead to naive and inconsistent research practices.

—Norman Blaikie

REFERENCES

Blaikie, N. (1993). *Approaches to social enquiry.* Cambridge, UK: Polity.

Blaikie, N. (2000). *Designing social research: The logic of anticipation.* Cambridge, UK: Polity.

Hughes, J. A. (1990). *The philosophy of social research* (2nd ed.). Harlow, UK: Longman.

Williams, M., &May, T. (1996). *Introduction to the philosophy of social research.* London: UCL Press.

POSITIVISM

Positivism is a philosophy of science that rejects metaphysical speculation in favor of systematic observation using the human senses. "Positive" knowledge of the world is based on GENERALIZATIONS from such observations that, given sufficient number and consistency, are regarded as producing laws of how phenomena coexist or occur in sequences. In the 19th century, positivism was not merely a philosophy of science; it expressed a more general worldview that lauded the achievements of science.

CENTRAL TENETS

Although numerous attempts have since been made to identify the central tenets of positivism, the following are generally accepted as its main characteristics.

1. *Phenomenalism.* Knowledge must be based on experience, on what observers can perceive with their senses. This perception must be achieved without the subjective activity of cognitive processes; it must be "pure experience" with an empty consciousness.

2. *Nominalism.* Any abstract concepts used in scientific explanation must also be derived from experience; metaphysical notions about which it is not possible to make

any observations have no legitimate existence except as names or words. Hence, the language used to describe observations must be uncontaminated by any theoretical notions.

3. *Atomism.* The objects of experience, of observation, are regarded as discrete, independent atomic impressions of events, which constitute the ultimate and fundamental elements of the world. Insofar as these atomic impressions are formed into generalizations, they do not refer to abstract objects in the world, only regularities among discrete events.

4. *General laws.* Scientific theories are regarded as a set of highly general lawlike statements; establishing such general laws is the aim of science. These laws summarize observations by specifying simple relations or constant conjunctions between phenomena. EXPLANATION is achieved by subsuming individual cases under appropriate laws. These laws are general in scope, in that they cover a broad range of observations, and are universal in form, in that they apply, without exception, across time and space.

5. *Value judgments and normative statements.* "Facts" and "values" must be separated as values do not have the status of knowledge. Value statements have no empirical content that would make them susceptible to any tests of their validity based on observations.

6. *Verification.* The truth or falsity of any scientific statement can be settled with reference to an observable state of affairs. Scientific laws are verified by the accumulation of confirming evidence.

7. *Causation.* There is no CAUSALITY in nature, only regularities or constant conjunctions between events, such that events of one kind are followed by events of another kind. Therefore, if all we have are regularities between types of events, then explanation is nothing more than locating an event within a wider ranging regularity.

VARIETIES OF POSITIVISM

According to Halfpenny (1982), it is possible to identify 12 varieties of positivism. However, following Outhwaite (1987), these can be reduced to 3. The first was formulated by August Comte (1798–1857) as an alternative to theological and metaphysical ways of understanding the world. He regarded all sciences as forming a unified hierarchy of related levels, building on mathematics at the lowest level, followed by astronomy, physics, chemistry, biology, and, finally, sociology.

The second version, known as *logical positivism,* was founded in Vienna in the 1920s. The catch-cry of these philosophers was that any concept or proposition that does not correspond to some state of affairs (i.e., cannot be verified by experience) is regarded as being meaningless (*phenomenalism*). At the same time, it is argued that the concepts and propositions of the higher level sciences *can* be reduced to those of the lower ones. In other words, they adopted the reductionist position that the propositions of the social sciences could ultimately be analyzed down to those of physics.

The third version, which was derived from the {second and is sometimes referred to as the "standard view" in the philosophy of science, dominated the English-speaking world in the post–World War II period. Its fundamental tenet is that all sciences, including the social sciences, are concerned with developing explanations in the form of universal laws or generalizations. Any phenomenon is explained by demonstrating that it is a specific case of some such law. These laws refer to "constant conjunctions" between events or, in the case of the social sciences, statistical correlations or regularities ("general law").

This third version is based on the belief that there can be a *natural* scientific study of people and society, the doctrine known as the *unity of scientific method.* It is argued that despite the differences in subject matter of the various scientific disciplines, both natural and social, the same method or logic of explanation can be used, although each science must elaborate these in a way appropriate to its objects of enquiry.

> At its most general, positivism is a theory of the nature, omnicompetence and unity of science. In its most radical shape it stipulates that the only valid kind of (non-analytic) knowledge is scientific, that such knowledge consists in the description of the invariant patterns, the coexistence in space and succession over time, of observable phenomena ... Its naturalistic insistence on the unity of science and scientistic disavowal of any knowledge apart from science induce its aversion to metaphysics, insistence upon a strict value/fact dichotomy and tendency to historicist confidence in the inevitability of scientifically mediated progress. (Bhaskar, 1986, p. 226)

POSITIVISM IN THE SOCIAL SCIENCES

It was through the work of August Comte and Emile Durkheim that positivism was introduced into the social sciences. Forms of positivism have dominated sociology, particularly in the decades immediately following World War II, and continue to do so today in disciplines such as psychology and economics. However, in recent years, positivism has been subjected to devastating criticism (for reviews, see Blaikie, 1993, pp. 101–104; Bryant, 1985).

CRITICISM

Some of the main points of dispute are the claim that experience can be a sound basis for scientific knowledge, that science should deal only with observable phenomena and not with abstract or hypothetical entities, that it is possible to distinguish between an atheoretical observation language and a theoretical language, that theoretical concepts have a 1:1 correspondence with "reality" as it is observed, that scientific laws are based on constant conjunctions between events in the world, and that "facts" and "values" can be separated.

Positivism has been attacked from many perspectives, including INTERPRETIVISM, FALSIFICATIONISM, and CRITICAL REALISM. The interpretive critique has focused on positivism's inadequate view of the nature of social reality—its ONTOLOGY. Positivism takes for granted the socially constructed world that interpretivism regards as social reality. Positivists construct fictitious social worlds out of the meaning it has for *them* and neglect what it means to the social actors.

The central feature of the falsificationist critique is positivism's process for "discovering" knowledge and the basis for justifying this knowledge. First, because they regard experience as an inadequate source of knowledge, and as all observation involves interpretation, falsificationists have argued that it is not possible to distinguish between observational statements and theoretical statements; all statements about the world are theoretical, at least to some degree. Second, it is argued that experience is an inadequate basis for justifying knowledge because it leads to a circular argument. On what basis can experience be established as a justification for knowledge except by reference to experience?

Positivism's claim that reality can be perceived directly by the use of the human senses has been thoroughly discredited. Even if it is assumed that a single, unique physical world exists independently of observers—and this assumption is not universally accepted—the process of observing it involves both conscious and unconscious interpretation. Observations are "theory laden." The processes that human beings use to observe the world around them, be it in everyday life or for scientific purposes, are not analogous to taking photographs. In "reading" what impinges on our senses, we have to engage in a complex process that entails both the use of concepts peculiar to the language of a particular culture and expectations about what is "there." Furthermore, we do not observe as isolated individuals but as members of cultural or subcultural groups that provide us with ontological assumptions. Therefore, observers are active agents, not passive receptacles.

The realist solution to the theory-laden nature of observation and description is to draw the distinction between the transitive and intransitive objects of science. Although our descriptions of the *empirical* domain may be theory dependent, the structures and mechanisms of the *real* domain exist independently of our descriptions of them. Reality is not there to be observed as in positivism, nor is it just a social construction; it is just there. Therefore, according to the realists, the relative success of competing theories to represent this reality can be settled as a matter of rational judgment (see REALISM and CRITICAL REALISM).

As well as accusing positivism of having an inadequate ontology, critical realism also attacked the positivist method of explanation in terms of constant conjunctions between events. Even if two kinds of phenomena can be shown to occur regularly together, there is still the question of why this is the case. According to critical realism, establishing regularities between observed events is only the starting point in the process of scientific discovery. Constant conjunctions of events occur only in closed systems, those produced by experimental conditions. However, positivism treats the world of nature as a closed system. In open systems characteristic of both nature and society, a large number of generative mechanisms will be exercising their powers to cause effects at the same time. What is observed as an "empirical" conjunction may, therefore, not reflect the complexity of the mechanisms that are operating.

—Norman Blaikie

REFERENCES

Bhaskar, R. (1986). *Scientific realism and human emancipation.* London: Verso.

Blaikie, N. (1993). *Approaches to social enquiry.* Cambridge, UK: Polity.

Bryant, C. G. A. (1985). *Positivism in social theory and research.* London: Macmillan.

Halfpenny, P. (1982). *Positivism and sociology: Explaining social life.* London: Allen & Unwin.

Outhwaite, W. (1987). *New philosophies of social science: Realism, hermeneutics and critical theory.* London: Macmillan.

POSTMODERNISM

Postmodernism is a term used in a variety of intellectual and cultural areas in rather different ways. The use of the same word creates a confusing and misleading impression of unity and coherence in developments across societal, academic, and cultural fields. There are three broad ways of talking about postmodernism: as an orientation in architecture and art, as a way of describing contemporary (Western or possibly global) society, and as a philosophy. This article mainly focuses on postmodernism in the third sense (i.e., as a philosophy or intellectual style within the social sciences), but a brief overview of other ways of using the term is also called for, especially because they are often viewed as linked. Postmodernism is impossible to define; it even runs against its spirit to try to do so. Many people do, however, use the term to refer to a style of thinking/cultural orientation emphasizing fragmentation and instability of meaning: an unpacking of knowledge, rationality, social institutions, and language.

Postmodernism began to be used in the 1970s as a term for a traditionally and locally inspired approach in architecture, in contrast to the ahistoric and superrational functionalism. Postmodernism also involves the mixing of architectural styles. In the arts, postmodernism represents a partial continuation but also a partial break with modernism. Characterized by a rejection of the idea of representation and an emphasis on the challenge and the unfamiliar (e.g., Picasso), modernism in the arts actually has some affinity with postmodern philosophy. Nevertheless, the postmodern idea of "de-differentiation" between different spheres—such as high culture and low (mass) culture—and the break with elite ideas of a specific space and function of art make it possible to point at some overall features of postmodernism as an overall label that seems to work broadly in a diversity of fields:

the effacement of the boundary between art and everyday life; the collapse of the hierarchical distinction between high and mass/popular culture; a stylistic promiscuity favouring eclecticism and the mixing of codes; parody, pastiche, irony, playfulness and the celebration of the surface "depthlessness" of culture; the

decline of the originality/genius of the artistic producer and the assumption that art can only be repetitive. (Featherstone, 1988, p. 203)

To the extent that there is such a trend in the arts— and some skeptics say that postmodernism is a favored idea among certain art critics rather than among larger groups of artists—that is indicative of wider societal developments, it fits into the idea of postmodernism representing a new society or a period in societal development.

Postmodernism started to be used in the social sciences in the late 1970s, drawing on French and, to some extent, Anglo-Saxon philosophers and social scientists (e.g., Derrida, Foucault, Baudrillard, Lyotard, Jameson, Harvey, and Bauman). Some of these rejected the term *postmodernism*; Foucault also resisted the idea of a "postmodern society or a period." In particular, Jameson and Harvey, but also to some extent Lyotard, have been influential in forming ideas about a new period in societal development.

With references to a distinct societal period, we move postmodernism from culture to social science. Many authors then talk about *postmodernity* instead of postmodernism, and we will follow this custom here. There are various opinions about the meaning of this epoch. Some say that postmodernity signals postindustrialism as well as postcapitalism, but others suggest that postmodernity refers to cultural changes *within* capitalism. The periodization idea typically indicates some notion of sequentiality— postmodernism (postmodernity) comes after modernism (modernity), but what this means is debated: Opinions vary from postmodernism emerging from the 1920s to the time after the Second World War and to the more recent time. An influential author is Jameson (1983), who refers to

a general feeling that at some point following World War II a new kind of society begun to emerge (variously described as postindustrial society, multinational capitalism, consumer society, media society and so forth). New types of consumption, planned obsolescence; an ever more rapid rhythm of fashion and styling changes; the penetration of advertising, television and the media generally to a hitherto unparalleled degree throughout society; the replacement of the old tension between city and country, center and province, by the suburb and by universal standardization; the growth of the great networks of superhighways and the arrival of automobile culture—these are some of the features which would seem to mark a radical break with that older prewar society. (pp. 124–125)

Postmodernity presupposes modernity, an orientation associated with the Enlightenment project. The most common point of departure in describing modernity—and thus postmodernity—is to focus on rationality seen as guiding principle as well as an attainable objective for the modern project. Rationality is embodied especially in the certainty and precision of science and knowledge, as well as the far-reaching control and manipulation of nature that this knowledge makes possible. Postmodernity then often refers to the idea of a society characterized by widely dispersed cultural orientations that doubt the possibilities and blessings of this rationalizing project, manifested in science, formal organizations (bureaucracies), and social engineering. "Postmodern society" thus goes against the claimed certainty, objectivity, and progress orientation of modernity.

There are different opinions of the relationship between modernity/postmodernity in terms of sequentiality /overlap. Whether the emergence of postmodernity means replacement of modernity or the emergence of a stream existing parallel with and in opposition to it is debated. For many commentators, postmodernity is better seen as a kind of reaction or comment on modernism than a developmental phase coming after and replacing modernism. Arguably, principles and practices of modernity still seem to dominate a great deal of contemporary Western society.

Postmodernity is sometimes linked to postmodernism as a basic way of thinking about the world. It is then argued that societal developments call for sensitizing vocabularies and ideas that can say something interesting about recent developments and contemporary society. Conventional (modernist) social science and its language are viewed as outdated, incapable of representing subtle but pervasive societal developments. But opponents argue that discussions around postmodernity and postmodernism should be kept separated and confusions avoided: Matters of periodization and identification of social trends are empirical issues, whereas postmodernism is based on philosophical ideas and preferences for intellectual style uncoupled from how to describe contemporary society and social changes. One should be clear when addressing postmodernity and when being postmodernist, it is said.

Leaving postmodernity and the relationship between the period and the intellectual style and moving over to the latter, we enter frameworks and ideas in strong opposition to conventional ideas of social theory and methodology. *Postmodernism,* in this sense, strongly overlaps what is referred to as *poststructuralism,* and the two terms are frequently, when it comes to intellectual agenda and commitments, used as synonyms. There is still a tendency that postmodernism—also when separated from the post-modernity/period issues—refers to a societal/cultural context (e.g., Lyotard, 1984), whereas poststructuralism has a more strict interest in philosophy, particularly around language issues. The points of departures of the two "isms" also differ; postmodernism, in the case of Lyotard (1984), departs from changes in the conditions of knowledge production, whereas poststructuralists move away from the ideas of French structuralism (e.g., de Saussure). But increasingly in social science, postmodernism and poststructuralism are viewed as referring to the same agenda, but with *postmodernism* being the more popular term.

Very briefly, postmodernism can be described as "an assault on unity" (Power, 1990). For postmodernists, social science is a humble and subjective enterprise, characterized by tentativeness, fragmentation, and indeterminacy. Actually, many postmodernists would hesitate in labeling their work as social science. The social and the science part becomes downplayed, if not rejected, by those taking postmodernism into its more extreme positions. For postmodernists, the social, as conventionally understood—systems, structures, agents, shared meanings, a dominant social order, and so forth—is replaced by discourse (language with strong constructing effects), images, and simulations in circulation.

The label of *postmodernism* in social science often summarizes the following five assumptions and foci (Alvesson & Deetz, 2000; Smart, 2000):

• *The centrality of discourse—textuality— where the constitutive power of language is emphasized and "natural" objects are viewed as discursively produced.* This means that there are no objects or phenomena outside or independent of language. Instead, language is an active force shaping our worlds. Different discourses thus mean different social realities.

• *Fragmented identities—emphasizing subjectivity as a process and the death of the individual, autonomous, meaning-creating subject.* The discursive production of the individual replaces the conventional "essentialistic" understanding of people. Against the conventional, "modernist" view of the human being as an integrated whole—the origin of intentions, motives, and meaning—postmodernists suggest a decentered, fragmented, and discourse-driven subject. There is, for example, no true meaning or experience associated with being a "woman"—instead, dominating discourses produce different versions of "woman" (e.g., mother, worker, voter, sexual being) with different effects on temporal subjectivities.

• *The critique of the idea of representation, where the indecidabilities of language take precedence over language as a mirror of reality and a means for the transport of meaning.* It is not possible to represent an objective reality out there. Pure descriptions or a separation of documentation and analysis become impossible. We cannot control language, but must struggle with—or simply accept—the locally context-dependent, metaphorical, and constitutive nature of language. Issues around texts and authorship then become crucial in social science (as well as in other fields of cultural work).

• *The loss of foundations and the power of grand narratives, where an emphasis on multiple voices and local politics is favored over theoretical frameworks and large-scale political projects.* Against the ambition to produce valid general truths guiding long-term, broad-scaled social and scientific projects, knowledge and politics are seen as local and governed by short-term, performance-oriented criteria. Sometimes multiple voices and diversity are privileged.

• *The power-knowledge connection, where the impossibilities in separating power from knowledge are assumed and knowledge loses a sense of innocence and neutrality.*

Power and knowledge are not the same, but they are intertwined and dependent on each other. Knowledge always has power effects; it produces a particular version of reality and—through being picked up and affecting how people relate to their worlds—shapes it.

Taking these five ideas seriously leads to a drastic reconceptualization of the meaning of social studies. Some people expect and hope that "the postmodern turn," leading to a stress on "the social construction of social reality, fluid as opposite to fixed identities of the self, and the partiality of truth will simply overtake the modernist assumptions of an objective reality" (Lincoln & Guba, 2000, p. 178).

Postmodernist ideas are pushed more or less far and in somewhat different directions. A possible distinction is between skeptical and affirmative postmodernism (Rosenau, 1992). The skeptical version promotes a "negative" agenda, based on the idea of the impossibility of establishing any truth. Representation becomes a matter of imposing an arbitrary meaning on something. Research becomes a matter of deconstruction, the tearing apart of texts by showing the contradictions, repressed meanings, and thus the fragility behind a superficial level of robustness and validity. This approach strongly discourages empirical work, at least as conventionally and positively understood.

Affirmative postmodernism also questions the idea of truth and validity but has a more positive view of social research. Playfulness, irony, humor, eclecticism, and methodological pluralism are celebrated. So is local knowledge (including a preference for situated knowledge and a rejection of the search for abstract, universal truths). This version is not antithetical to empirical work and empirical claims, but issues around description, interpretation, and researcher authority become problematic. This has triggered profound methodological debates in many fields of social and behavioral science, especially in anthropology (Clifford & Marcus, 1986) and feminism (Nicholson, 1990).

Postmodernism can be seen as a key part in a broader trend in philosophy and social science, summarized as the "linguistic turn." This means a radical reconceptualization of language: It is seen *not* as a passive medium for the transport of meaning, a fairly unproblematic part of social life and institutions and carefully mastered by the competent social scientist. Instead, language (discourse) becomes a crucial constituting social force to be targeted by social researchers, who are themselves forced to struggle with basic problems around representation and authorship.

The implications for social research are substantial but, as said, may be taken more or less far and may inspire and rejuvenate rather than finish empirical social science (Alvesson, 2002). Interviews can, for example, be seen not as simple reports of reality or sites for the expression of the meanings and experiences of the interviewees but as local settings in which dominant discourses constitute subjects and their responses. Ethnographies are less viewed as the authoritative reports of other cultures based on carefully carried out fieldwork and more as fictional texts in which the authorship and the constructions of those being studied matter as much or more than the phenomena "out there" claimed to be studied. Rather than capturing meanings, finding patterns, and arriving at firm conclusions, postmodernistically inspired social research shows the indecisiveness of meaning, gives space for multiple voices, and opens up for alternative readings.

—Mats Alvesson

REFERENCES

Alvesson, M. (2002). *Postmodernism and social research.* Buckingham, UK: Open University Press.

Alvesson, M., & Deetz, S. (2000). *Doing critical management research.* London: Sage.

Clifford, J., & Marcus, G. E. (Eds.). (1986). *Writing culture.* Berkeley: University of California Press.

Featherstone, M. (1988). In pursuit of the postmodernism: An introduction. *Theory, Culture & Society, 5,* 195–215.

Jameson, F. (1983). Postmodernism and consumer society. In H. Foster (Ed.), *Postmodern culture.* London: Pluto.

Lincoln, Y., & Guba, E. (2000). Paradigmatic controversies, contradictions, and emerging confluences. In N. Denzin & Y. Lincoln (Eds.), *Handbook of qualitative research* (2nd ed., pp. 163–188). Thousand Oaks, CA: Sage.

Lyotard, J.-F. (1984). *The postmodern condition: A report on knowledge.* Minneapolis: University of Minnesota Press.

Nicholson, L. (Ed.). (1990). *Feminism/postmodernism.* New York: Routledge Kegan Paul.

Power, M. (1990). Modernism, postmodernism and organisation. In J. Hassard & D. Pym (Eds.), *The theory and philosophy of organisations.* London: Routledge Kegan Paul.

Rosenau, P.M. (1992). *Post-modernism and the social sciences: Insights, inroads and intrusions.* Princeton, NJ: Princeton University Press.

Smart, B. (2000). Postmodern social theory. In B. Turner (Ed.), *The Blackwell companion to social theory* (pp. 447–480). Oxford, UK: Blackwell.

Paradigmatic Controversies, Contradictions, and Emerging Confluences

EGON G. GUBA and YVONNA S. LINCOLN

I n our chapter for the first edition of the *Handbook of Qualitative Research,* we focused on the contention among various research paradigms for legitimacy and intellectual and paradigmatic hegemony (Guba & Lincoln, 1994). The postmodern paradigms that we discussed (postmodernist critical theory and constructivism)[1] were in contention with the received positivist and postpositivist paradigms for legitimacy, and with one another for intellectual legitimacy. In the more than 10 years that have elapsed since that chapter was published, substantial changes have occurred in the landscape of social scientific inquiry.

On the matter of legitimacy, we observe that readers familiar with the literature on methods and paradigms reflect a high interest in ontologies and epistemologies that differ sharply from those undergirding conventional social science. Second, even those established professionals trained in quantitative social science (including the two of us) want to learn more about qualitative approaches, because new young professionals being mentored in graduate schools are asking serious questions about and looking for guidance in qualitatively

oriented studies and dissertations. Third, the number of qualitative texts, research papers, workshops, and training materials has exploded. Indeed, it would be difficult to miss the distinct turn of the social sciences toward more interpretive, postmodern, and criticalist practices and theorizing (Bloland, 1989, 1995). This nonpositivist orientation has created a context (surround) in which virtually no study can go unchallenged by proponents of contending paradigms. Further, it is obvious that the number of practitioners of new-paradigm inquiry is growing daily. There can be no question that the legitimacy of postmodern paradigms is well established and at least equal to the legitimacy of received and conventional paradigms (Denzin & Lincoln, 1994).

On the matter of hegemony, or supremacy, among postmodern paradigms, it is clear that Geertz's (1988, 1993) prophecy about the "blurring of genres" is rapidly being fulfilled. Inquiry methodology can no longer be treated as a set of universally applicable rules or abstractions. Methodology is inevitably interwoven with and emerges from the nature of particular disciplines (such as sociology and psychology) and particular perspectives (such as Marxism, feminist theory, and queer theory). So, for instance, we can read feminist critical theorists such as Olesen (2000) or queer theorists such as Gamson (2000), or we can follow arguments about teachers as researchers (Kincheloe, 1991) while we understand the secondary text to be teacher empowerment and democratization of schooling practices. Indeed, the various paradigms are beginning to "interbreed" such that two theorists previously thought to be in irreconcilable conflict may now appear, under a different theoretical rubric, to be informing one another's arguments. A personal example is our own work, which has been heavily influenced by action research practitioners and postmodern critical theorists. Consequently, to argue that it is paradigms that are in contention is probably less useful than to probe where and how paradigms exhibit confluence and where and how they exhibit differences, controversies, and contradictions.

◫ MAJOR ISSUES CONFRONTING ALL PARADIGMS

In our chapter in the first edition of this *Handbook,* we presented two tables that summarized our positions, first, on the axiomatic nature of paradigms (the paradigms we considered at that time were positivism, postpositivism, critical theory, and constructivism; Guba & Lincoln, 1994, p. 109, Table 6.1); and second, on the issues we believed were most fundamental to differentiating the four paradigms (p. 112, Table 6.2). These tables are reproduced here as a way of reminding our readers of our previous statements. The axioms defined the ontological, epistemological, and methodological bases for both established and emergent paradigms; these are shown here in Table 8.1. The issues most often in contention that we examined were inquiry aim, nature of knowledge, the way knowledge is accumulated, goodness (rigor and validity) or quality criteria, values, ethics, voice, training, accommodation, and hegemony; these are shown in Table 8.2. An

examination of these two tables will reacquaint the reader with our original *Handbook* treatment; more detailed information is, of course, available in our original chapter.

Since publication of that chapter, at least one set of authors, John Heron and Peter Reason, have elaborated on our tables to include the *participatory/cooperative* paradigm (Heron, 1996; Heron & Reason, 1997, pp. 289–290). Thus, in addition to the paradigms of positivism, postpositivism, critical theory, and constructivism, we add the participatory paradigm in the present chapter (this is an excellent example, we might add, of the hermeneutic elaboration so embedded in our own view, constructivism).

Our aim here is to extend the analysis further by building on Heron and Reason's additions and by rearranging the issues to reflect current thought. The issues we have chosen include our original formulations and the additions, revisions, and amplifications made by Heron and Reason (1997), and we have also chosen what we believe to be the issues most important today. We should note that *important* means several things to us. An important topic may be one that is widely debated (or even hotly contested)—validity is one such issue. An important issue may be one that bespeaks a new awareness (an issue such as recognition of the role of values). An important issue may be one that illustrates the influence of one paradigm on another (such as the influence of feminist, action research, critical theory, and participatory models on researcher conceptions of action within and with the community in which research is carried out). Or issues may be important because new or extended theoretical and/or field-oriented treatments for them are newly available—voice and reflexivity are two such issues.

Table 8.3 reprises the original Table 6.1 but adds the axioms of the participatory paradigm proposed by Heron and Reason (1997). Table 8.4 deals with seven issues and represents an update of selected issues first presented in the old Table 6.2. "Voice" in the 1994 version of Table 6.2 has been renamed "inquirer posture," and we have inserted a redefined "voice" in the current

Table 8.1.   Basic Beliefs (Metaphysics) of Alternative Inquiry Paradigms

Item	Positivism	Postpositivism	Critical Theory et al.	Constructivism
Ontology	Naïve realism—"real" reality but apprehendible	Critical realism—"real" reality but only imperfectly and probabilistically apprehendible	Historical realism—virtual reality shaped by social, political, cultural, economic, ethnic, and gender values; crystallized over time	Relativism—local and specific constructed and co-constructed realities
Epistemology	Dualist/objectivist; findings true	Modified dualist/objectivist; critical tradition/community; findings probably true	Transactional/subjectivist; value-mediated findings	Transactional/subjectivist; created findings
Methodology	Experimental/manipulative; verification of hypotheses; chiefly quantitative methods	Modified experimental/manipulative; critical multiplism; falsification of hypotheses; may include qualitative methods	Dialogic/dialectical	Hermeneutical/dialectical

Table 8.2. Paradigm Positions on Selected Practical Issues

Item	Positivism	Postpositivism	Critical Theory et al.	Constructivism
Inquiry aim	Explanation: prediction and control		Critique and transformation; restitution and emancipation	Understanding; reconstruction
Nature of knowledge	Verified hypotheses established as facts or laws	Nonfalsified hypotheses that are probable facts or laws	Structural/historical insights	Individual or collective reconstructions coalescing around consensus
Knowledge accumulation	Accretion—"building blocks" adding to "edifice of knowledge"; generalizations and cause-effect linkages		Historical revisionism; generalization by similarity	More informed and sophisticated reconstructions; vicarious experience
Goodness or quality criteria	Conventional benchmarks of "rigor": internal and external validity, reliability, and objectivity		Historical situatedness; erosion of ignorance and misapprehension; action stimulus	Trustworthiness and authenticity, including catalyst for action
Values	Excluded—influence denied		Included—formative	Included—formative
Ethics	Extrinsic: tilt toward deception		Intrinsic: moral tilt toward revelation	Intrinsic: process tilt toward revelation; special problems
Voice	"Disinterested scientist" as informer of decision makers, policy makers, and change agents		"Transformative intellectual" as advocate and activist	"Passionate participant" as facilitator of multivoice reconstruction
Training	Technical and quantitative; substantive theories	Technical; quantitative and qualitative; substantive theories	Resocialization; qualitative and quantitative; history; values of altruism, empowerment, and liberation	
Accommodation	Commensurable		Incommensurable with previous two	
Hegemony	In control of publication, funding, promotion, and tenure		Seeking recognition and input; offering challenges to predecessor paradigms, aligned with postcolonial aspirations	

Table 8.3.   Basic Beliefs of Alternative Inquiry Paradigms—Updated

Issue	Positivism	Postpositivism	Critical Theory et al.	Constructivism	Participatory[a]
Ontology	Naïve realism—"real" reality but apprehendible	Critical realism—"real" reality but only imperfectly and probabilistically apprehendible	Historical realism—virtual reality shaped by social, political, cultural, economic, ethnic, and gender values; crystallized over time	Relativism—local and specific co-constructed realities	Participative reality—subjective-objective reality, cocreated by mind and given cosmos
Epistemology	Dualist/objectivist; findings true	Modified dualist/objectivist; critical tradition/community; findings probably true	Transactional/ subjectivist; value-mediated findings	Transactional/ subjectivist; co-created findings	Critical subjectivity in participatory transaction with cosmos; extended epistemology of experiential, propositional, and practical knowing; cocreated findings
Methodology	Experimental/ manipulative; verification of hypotheses; chiefly quantitative methods	Modified experimental/ manipulative; critical multiplism; falsification of hypotheses; may include qualitative methods	Dialogic/dialectical	Hermeneutical/ dialectical	Political participation in collaborative action inquiry; primacy of the practical; use of language grounded in shared experiential context

a. Entries in this column are based on Heron and Reason (1997).

Table 8.4. Paradigm Positions on Selected Issues—Updated

Issue	Positivism		Postpositivism	Critical Theories	Constructivism	Participatory[a]
Nature of knowledge	Verified hypotheses established as facts or laws		Nonfalsified hypotheses that are probable facts or laws	Structural/historical insights	Individual and collective reconstructions sometimes coalescing around consensus	Extended epistemology: primacy of practical knowing; critical subjectivity; living knowledge
Knowledge accumulation	Accretion—"building blocks" adding to "edifice of knowledge"; generalizations and cause-effect linkages			Historical revisionism; generalization by similarity	More informed and sophisticated reconstructions; vicarious experience	In communities of inquiry embedded in communities of practice
Goodness or quality criteria	Conventional benchmarks of "rigor": internal and external validity, reliability, and objectivity			Historical situatedness; erosion of ignorance and misapprehensions; action stimulus	Trustworthiness and authenticity including catalyst for action	Congruence of experiential, presentational, propositional, and practical knowing; leads to action to transform the world in the service of human flourishing
Values	Excluded—influence denied			Included—formative		
Ethics	Extrinsic—tilt toward deception			Intrinsic—moral tilt toward revelation	Intrinsic—process tilt toward revelation	
Inquirer posture	"Disinterested scientist" as informer of decision makers, policy makers, and change agents			"Transformative intellectual" as advocate and activist	"Passionate participant" as facilitator of multivoice reconstruction	Primary voice manifest through aware self-reflective action; secondary voices in illuminating theory, narrative, movement, song, dance, and other presentational forms
Training	Technical and quantitative; substantive theories	Technical; quantitative and qualitative; substantive theories		Resocialization; qualitative and quantitative; history; values of altruism, empowerment and liberation		Coresearchers are initiated into the inquiry process by facilitator/researcher and learn through active engagement in the process; facilitator/researcher requires emotional competence, democratic personality and skills

a. Entries in this column are based on Heron and Reason (1997), except for "ethics" and "values."

Table 8.5. In all cases except "inquirer posture," the entries for the participatory paradigm are those proposed by Heron and Reason; in the one case not covered by them, we have added a notation that we believe captures their intention.

We make no attempt here to reprise the material well discussed in our earlier *Handbook* chapter. Instead, we focus solely on the issues in Table 8.5: axiology; accommodation and commensurability; action; control; foundations of truth and knowledge; validity; and voice, reflexivity, and postmodern textual representation. We believe these seven issues to be the most important at this time.

While we believe these issues to be the most contentious, we also believe they create the intellectual, theoretical, and practical space for dialogue, consensus, and confluence to occur. There is great potential for interweaving of viewpoints, for the incorporation of multiple perspectives, and for borrowing, or *bricolage,* where borrowing seems useful, richness enhancing, or theoretically heuristic. For instance, even though we are ourselves social constructivists/constructionists, our call to action embedded in the authenticity criteria we elaborated in *Fourth Generation Evaluation* (Guba & Lincoln, 1989) reflects strongly the bent to action embodied in critical theorists' perspectives. And although Heron and Reason have elaborated a model they call the *cooperative paradigm,* careful reading of their proposal reveals a form of inquiry that is post-postpositive, postmodern, and criticalist in orientation. As a result, the reader familiar with several theoretical and paradigmatic strands of research will find that echoes of many streams of thought come together in the extended table. What this means is that the categories, as Laurel Richardson (personal communication, September 12, 1998) has pointed out, "are fluid, indeed what should be a category keeps altering, enlarging." She notes that "even as [we] write, the boundaries between the paradigms are shifting." This is the paradigmatic equivalent of the Geertzian "blurring of genres" to which we referred earlier.

Our own position is that of the constructionist camp, loosely defined. We do not believe that criteria for judging either "reality" or validity are absolutist (Bradley & Schaefer, 1998); rather, they are derived from community consensus regarding what is "real," what is useful, and what has meaning (especially meaning for action and further steps). We believe that a goodly portion of social phenomena consists of the meaning-making activities of groups and individuals around those phenomena. The meaning-making activities themselves are of central interest to social constructionists/constructivists, simply because it is the meaning-making/sense-making/attributional activities that shape action (or inaction). The meaning-making activities themselves can be changed when they are found to be incomplete, faulty (e.g., discriminatory, oppressive, or non-liberatory), or malformed (created from data that can be shown to be false).

We have tried, however, to incorporate perspectives from other major nonpositivist paradigms. This is not a complete summation; space constraints prevent that. What we hope to do in this chapter is to acquaint readers with the larger currents, arguments, dialogues, and provocative writings and theorizing, the better to see perhaps what we ourselves do not even yet see: where and when confluence is possible, where constructive rapprochement might be negotiated, where voices are beginning to achieve some harmony.

▣ AXIOLOGY

Earlier, we placed values on the table as an "issue" on which positivists or phenomenologists might have a "posture" (Guba & Lincoln, 1989, 1994; Lincoln & Guba, 1985). Fortunately, we reserved for ourselves the right to either get smarter or just change our minds. We did both. Now, we suspect (although Table 8.5 does not yet reflect it) that "axiology" should be grouped with "basic beliefs." In *Naturalistic Inquiry* (Lincoln & Guba, 1985), we covered some of the ways in which values feed into the inquiry process: choice of the problem, choice of paradigm to guide the problem, choice of theoretical framework, choice of major data-gathering and data-analytic methods, choice of context, treatment of values already resident

Table 8.5.   Critical Issues of the Time

Issue	Positivism	Postpositivism	Critical Theory et al.	Constructivism	Participatory
Axiology	Propositional knowing about the world is intrinsically valuable.		Propositional, transactional knowing is instrumentally valuable as a means to social emancipation, which is an end in itself, is intrinsically valuable.		Practical knowing about how to flourish with a balance of autonomy, cooperation, and hierarchy in a culture is an end in itself, is intrinsically valuable.
Accommodation and commensurability	Commensurable for all positivist forms		Incommensurable with positivist forms; some commensurability with constructivist, criticalist, and participatory approaches, especially as they merge in liberationist approaches outside the West		
Action	Not the responsibility of the researcher; viewed as "advocacy" or subjectivity, and therefore a threat to validity and objectivity		Found especially in the form of empowerment; emancipation anticipated and hoped for; social transformation, particularly toward more equity and justice, is end goal	Intertwined with validity; inquiry often incomplete without action on the part of participants; constructivist formulation mandates training in political action if participants do not understand political systems	
Control	Resides solely in researcher		Often resides in "transformative intellectual"; in new constructions, control returns to community	Shared between inquirer and participants	Shared to varying degrees
Relationship to foundations of truth and knowledge	Foundational	Foundational	Foundational within social critique	Antifoundational	Nonfoundational

Issue	Positivism	Postpositivism	Critical Theory et al.	Constructivism	Participatory
Extended considerations of validity (goodness criteria)	Traditional positivist constructions of validity; rigor, internal validity, external validity, reliability, objectivity		Action stimulus (see above); social transformation, equity, social justice	Extended constructions of validity: (a) crystalline validity (Richardson); (b) authenticity criteria (Guba & Lincoln); (c) catalytic, rhizomatic, voluptuous validities (Lather); (d) relational and ethics-centered criteria (Lincoln); (e) community-centered determinations of validity	See "action" above
Voice, reflexivity, postmodern textual representations	Voice of the researcher, principally; reflexivity may be considered a problem in objectivity; textual representation unproblematic and somewhat formulaic		Voices mixed between researcher and participants	Voices mixed, with participants' voices sometimes dominant; reflexivity serious and problematic; textual representation an extended issue	Voices mixed; textual representation rarely discussed but problematic; reflexivity relies on critical subjectivity and self-awareness
			Textual representation practices may be problematic—i.e., "fiction formulas" or unexamined "regimes of truth"		

within the context, and choice of format(s) for presenting findings. We believed those were strong enough reasons to argue for the inclusion of values as a major point of departure between positivist, conventional modes of inquiry and interpretive forms of inquiry.

A second "reading" of the burgeoning literature and subsequent rethinking of our own rationale have led us to conclude that the issue is much larger than we first conceived. If we had it to do all over again, we would make values or, more correctly, axiology (the branch of philosophy dealing with ethics, aesthetics, and religion) a part of the basic foundational philosophical dimensions of paradigm proposal. Doing so would, in our opinion, begin to help us see the embeddedness of ethics within, not external to, paradigms (see, for instance, Christians, 2000) and would contribute to the consideration of and dialogue about the role of spirituality in human inquiry. Arguably, axiology has been "defined out of" scientific inquiry for no larger a reason than that it also concerns "religion." But defining "religion" broadly to encompass spirituality would move constructivists closer to participative inquirers and would move critical theorists closer to both (owing to their concern with liberation from oppression and freeing of the human spirit, both profoundly spiritual concerns). The expansion of basic issues to include axiology, then, is one way of achieving greater confluence among the various interpretivist inquiry models. This is the place, for example, where Peter Reason's profound concerns with "sacred science" and human functioning find legitimacy; it is a place where Laurel Richardson's "sacred spaces" become authoritative sites for human inquiry; it is a place—or *the* place—where the spiritual meets social inquiry, as Reason (1993), and later Lincoln and Denzin (1994), proposed some years earlier.

☑ Accommodation and Commensurability

Positivists and postpositivists alike still occasionally argue that paradigms are, in some ways, commensurable; that is, they can be retrofitted to each other in ways that make the simultaneous practice of both possible. We have argued that at the paradigmatic, or philosophical, level, commensurability between positivist and postpositivist worldviews is not possible, but that within each paradigm, mixed methodologies (strategies) may make perfectly good sense (Guba & Lincoln, 1981, 1982, 1989, 1994; Lincoln & Guba, 1985). So, for instance, in *Effective Evaluation* we argued:

> The guiding inquiry paradigm most appropriate to responsive evaluation is . . . the naturalistic, phenomenological, or ethnographic paradigm. It will be seen that qualitative techniques are typically most appropriate to support this approach. There are times, however, when the issues and concerns voiced by audiences require information that is best generated by more conventional methods, especially quantitative methods. . . . In such cases, the responsive conventional evaluator will not shrink from the appropriate application. (Guba & Lincoln, 1981, p. 36)

As we tried to make clear, the "argument" arising in the social sciences was *not about method,* although many critics of the new naturalistic, ethnographic, phenomenological, and/or case study approaches assumed it was.[2] As late as 1998, Weiss could be found to claim that "some evaluation theorists, notably Guba and Lincoln (1989), hold that it is impossible to combine qualitative and quantitative approaches responsibly within an evaluation" (p. 268), even though we stated early on in *Fourth Generation Evaluation* (1989) that

> those claims, concerns, and issues that have *not* been resolved become the advance organizers for information collection by the evaluator. . . . *The information may be quantitative or qualitative.* Responsive evaluation does not rule out quantitative modes, as is mistakenly believed by many, but deals with whatever information is responsive to the unresolved claim, concern, or issue. (p. 43)

We had also strongly asserted earlier, in *Naturalistic Inquiry* (1985), that

> qualitative methods are stressed within the naturalistic paradigm not because the paradigm is antiquantitative but because qualitative methods

come more easily to the human-as-instrument. *The reader should particularly note the absence of an antiquantitative stance,* precisely because the naturalistic and conventional paradigms are so often—mistakenly—equated with the qualitative and quantitative paradigms, respectively. Indeed, *there are many opportunities for the naturalistic investigator to utilize quantitative data—probably more than are appreciated.* (pp. 198–199; emphasis added)

Having demonstrated that we were not then (and are not now) talking about an antiquantitative posture or the exclusivity of *methods,* but rather about the philosophies of which paradigms are constructed, we can ask the question again regarding commensurability: Are paradigms commensurable? Is it possible to blend elements of one paradigm into another, so that one is engaging in research that represents the best of both worldviews? The answer, from our perspective, has to be a cautious *yes.* This is especially so if the models (paradigms) share axiomatic elements that are similar, or that resonate strongly between them. So, for instance, *positivism* and *postpositivism* are clearly commensurable. In the same vein, elements of *interpretivist/postmodern* critical theory, constructivist and participative inquiry, fit comfortably together. Commensurability is an issue only when researchers want to "pick and choose" among the axioms of positivist and interpretivist models, because the axioms are contradictory and mutually exclusive.

▣ THE CALL TO ACTION

One of the clearest ways in which the paradigmatic controversies can be demonstrated is to compare the positivist and postpositivist adherents, who view action as a form of contamination of research results and processes, and the interpretivists, who see action on research results as a meaningful and important outcome of inquiry processes. Positivist adherents believe action to be either a form of advocacy or a form of subjectivity, either or both of which undermine the aim of objectivity. Critical theorists, on the other hand, have always advocated varying degrees of social

action, from the overturning of specific unjust practices to radical transformation of entire societies. The call for action—whether in terms of internal transformation, such as ridding oneself of false consciousness, or of external social transformation—differentiates between positivist and postmodern criticalist theorists (including feminist and queer theorists). The sharpest shift, however, has been in the constructivist and participatory phenomenological models, where a step beyond interpretation and *Verstehen,* or understanding, toward social action is probably one of the most conceptually interesting of the shifts (Lincoln, 1997, 1998a, 1998b). For some theorists, the shift toward action came in response to widespread nonutilization of evaluation findings and the desire to create forms of evaluation that would attract champions who might follow through on recommendations with meaningful action plans (Guba & Lincoln, 1981, 1989). For others, embracing action came as both a political and an ethical commitment (see, for instance, Carr & Kemmis, 1986; Christians, 2000; Greenwood & Levin, 2000; Schratz & Walker, 1995; Tierney, 2000).

Whatever the source of the problem to which inquirers were responding, the shift toward connecting research, policy analysis, evaluation, and/or social deconstruction (e.g., deconstruction of the patriarchal forms of oppression in social structures, which is the project informing much feminist theorizing, or deconstruction of the homophobia embedded in public policies) with action has come to characterize much new-paradigm inquiry work, both at the theoretical and at the practice and *praxis*-oriented levels. Action has become a major controversy that limns the ongoing debates among practitioners of the various paradigms. The mandate for social action, especially action designed and created by and for research participants with the aid and cooperation of researchers, can be most sharply delineated between positivist/postpositivist and new-paradigm inquirers. Many positivist and postpositivist inquirers still consider "action" the domain of communities other than researchers and research participants: those of policy personnel, legislators, and civic and political officials. Hard-line foundationalists presume that the taint of action will interfere with, or even negate, the objectivity that is a (presumed) characteristic of rigorous scientific method inquiry.

▣ CONTROL

Another controversy that has tended to become problematic centers on *control* of the study: Who initiates? Who determines salient questions? Who determines what constitutes findings? Who determines how data will be collected? Who determines in what forms the findings will be made public, if at all? Who determines what representations will be made of participants in the research? Let us be very clear: The issue of control is deeply embedded in the questions of voice, reflexivity, and issues of postmodern textual representation, which we shall take up later, *but only for new-paradigm inquirers.* For more conventional inquirers, the issue of control is effectively walled off from voice, reflexivity, and issues of textual representation, because each of those issues in some way threatens claims to rigor (particularly objectivity and validity). For new-paradigm inquirers who have seen the preeminent paradigm issues of ontology and epistemology effectively folded into one another, and who have watched as methodology and axiology logically folded into one another (Lincoln, 1995, 1997), control of an inquiry seems far less problematic, except insofar as inquirers seek to obtain participants' genuine participation (see, for instance, Guba & Lincoln, 1981, on contracting and attempts to get some stakeholding groups to do more than stand by while an evaluation is in progress).

Critical theorists, especially those who work in community organizing programs, are painfully aware of the necessity for members of the community, or research participants, to take control of their futures. Constructivists desire participants to take an increasingly active role in nominating questions of interest for any inquiry and in designing outlets for findings to be shared more widely within and outside the community. Participatory inquirers understand action controlled by the local context members to be the aim of inquiry within a community. For none of these paradigmatic adherents is control an issue of advocacy, a somewhat deceptive term usually used as a code within a larger metanarrative to attack an inquiry's rigor, objectivity, or fairness. Rather, for new-paradigm researchers control is a means of fostering emancipation, democracy, and community empowerment, and of redressing power imbalances such that those who were previously marginalized now achieve voice (Mertens, 1998) or "human flourishing" (Heron & Reason, 1997). Control as a controversy is an excellent place to observe the phenomenon that we have always termed "Catholic questions directed to a Methodist audience." We use this description—given to us by a workshop participant in the early 1980s—to refer to the ongoing problem of illegitimate questions: questions that have no meaning because the frames of reference are those for which they were never intended. (We could as well call these "Hindu questions to a Muslim," to give another sense of how paradigms, or overarching philosophies—or theologies—are incommensurable, and how questions in one framework make little, if any, sense in another.) Paradigmatic formulations interact such that control becomes inextricably intertwined with mandates for objectivity. Objectivity derives from the Enlightenment prescription for knowledge of the physical world, which is postulated to be separate and distinct from those who would know (Polkinghorne, 1989). But if knowledge of the social (as opposed to the physical) world resides in meaning-making mechanisms of the social, mental, and linguistic worlds that individuals inhabit, then knowledge cannot be separate from the knower, but rather is rooted in his or her mental or linguistic designations of that world (Polkinghorne, 1989; Salner, 1989).

▣ FOUNDATIONS OF TRUTH AND KNOWLEDGE IN PARADIGMS

Whether or not the world has a "real" existence outside of human experience of that world is an open question. For modernist (i.e., Enlightenment, scientific method, conventional, positivist) researchers, most assuredly there is a "real" reality "out there," apart from the flawed human apprehension of it. Further, that reality can be approached (approximated) only through the utilization of methods that prevent human contamination of its apprehension or comprehension. For foundationalists in the empiricist tradition, the foundations of scientific truth and knowledge about reality reside in rigorous application of testing phenomena against a template as much devoid of human bias, misperception, and other "idols" (Francis Bacon, cited in Polkinghorne, 1989) as instrumentally possible. As Polkinghorne (1989) makes clear:

> The idea that the objective realm is independent of the knower's subjective experiences of it can be found in Descartes's dual substance theory, with its distinction between the objective and subjective realms. . . . In the splitting of reality into subject and object realms, what can be known "objectively" is only the objective realm. True knowledge is limited to the objects and the relationships between them that exist in the realm of time and space. Human consciousness, which is subjective, is not accessible to science, and thus not truly knowable. (p. 23)

Now, templates of truth and knowledge can be defined in a variety of ways—as the end product of rational processes, as the result of experiential sensing, as the result of empirical observation, and others. In all cases, however, the referent is the physical or empirical world: rational engagement with it, experience of it, empirical observation of it. Realists, who work on the assumption that there is a "real" world "out there," may in individual cases also be foundationalists, taking the view that all of these ways of defining are rooted in phenomena existing outside the human mind. Although we can think about them, experience them, or observe them, they are nevertheless transcendent, referred to but beyond direct apprehension. Realism is an ontological question, whereas foundationalism is a criterial question. Some foundationalists argue that real phenomena necessarily imply certain final, ultimate criteria

for testing them as truthful (although we may have great difficulty in determining what those criteria are); nonfoundationalists tend to argue that there are no such ultimate criteria, only those that we can agree upon at a certain time and under certain conditions. Foundational criteria are discovered; nonfoundational criteria are negotiated. It is the case, however, that most realists are also foundationalists, and many nonfoundationalists or antifoundationalists are relativists.

An ontological formulation that connects realism and foundationalism within the same "collapse" of categories that characterizes the ontological-epistemological collapse is one that exhibits good fit with the other assumptions of constructivism. That state of affairs suits new-paradigm inquirers well. Critical theorists, constructivists, and participatory/cooperative inquirers take their primary field of interest to be precisely that subjective and intersubjective social knowledge and the active construction and cocreation of such knowledge by human agents that is produced by human consciousness. Further, new-paradigm inquirers take to the social knowledge field with zest, informed by a variety of social, intellectual, and theoretical explorations. These theoretical excursions include Saussurian linguistic theory, which views all relationships between words and what those words signify as the function of an internal relationship within some linguistic system; literary theory's deconstructive contributions, which seek to disconnect texts from any *essentialist* or transcendental meaning and resituate them within both author and reader historical and social contexts (Hutcheon, 1989; Leitch, 1996); feminist (Addelson, 1993; Alpern, Antler, Perry, & Scobie, 1992; Babbitt, 1993; Harding, 1993), race and ethnic (Kondo, 1990, 1997; Trinh, 1991), and queer theorizing (Gamson, 2000), which seeks to uncover and explore varieties of oppression and historical colonizing between dominant and subaltern genders, identities, races, and social worlds; the postmodern historical moment (Michael, 1996), which problematizes truth as partial, identity as fluid, language as an unclear referent system, and method and criteria as potentially coercive (Ellis & Bochner, 1996); and criticalist theories of social change (Carspecken, 1996; Schratz & Walker, 1995). The realization of the richness of the mental, social, psychological, and linguistic worlds that individuals and social groups create and constantly re-create and cocreate gives rise, in the minds of new-paradigm postmodern and poststructural inquirers, to endlessly fertile fields of inquiry rigidly walled off from conventional inquirers. Unfettered from the pursuit of transcendental scientific truth, inquirers are now free to resituate themselves within texts, to reconstruct their relationships with research participants in less constricted fashions, and to create re-presentations (Tierney & Lincoln, 1997) that grapple openly with problems of inscription, reinscription, metanarratives, and other rhetorical devices that obscure the extent to which human action is locally and temporally shaped. The processes of uncovering forms of inscription and the rhetoric of metanarratives are *genealogical*—"expos[ing] the origins of the view that have become *sedimented and accepted as truths*" (Polkinghorne, 1989, p. 42; emphasis added)—or *archaeological* (Foucault, 1971; Scheurich, 1997).

New-paradigm inquirers engage the foundational controversy in quite different ways. Critical theorists, particularly critical theorists more positivist in orientation, who lean toward Marxian interpretations, tend toward foundational perspectives, with an important difference. Rather than locating foundational truth and knowledge in some external reality "out there," such critical theorists tend to locate the foundations of truth in specific historical, economic, racial, and social infrastructures of oppression, injustice, and marginalization. Knowers are not portrayed as *separate from* some objective reality, but may be cast as unaware actors in such historical realities ("false consciousness") or as aware of historical forms of oppression, but unable or unwilling, because of conflicts, to act on those historical forms to alter specific conditions in this historical moment ("divided consciousness"). Thus the "foundation" for critical theorists is a duality: social critique tied in turn to raised consciousness of the possibility of positive and liberating social change. Social critique may exist apart from social change, but both are necessary for criticalist perspectives.

Constructivists, on the other hand, tend toward the antifoundational (Lincoln, 1995, 1998b; Schwandt, 1996). *Antifoundational* is the term used to denote a refusal to adopt any permanent, unvarying (or "foundational") standards by which truth can be universally known. As one of us has argued, truth—and any agreement regarding what is valid knowledge—arises from the relationship between members of some stakeholding community (Lincoln, 1995). Agreements about truth may be the subject of community *negotiations* regarding what will be accepted as truth (although there are difficulties with that formulation as well; Guba & Lincoln, 1989). Or agreements may eventuate as the result of a *dialogue* that moves arguments about truth claims or validity past the warring camps of objectivity and relativity toward "a communal test of validity through the argumentation of the participants in a discourse" (Bernstein, 1983; Polkinghorne, 1989; Schwandt, 1996). This "communicative and pragmatic concept" of validity (Rorty, 1979) is never fixed or unvarying. Rather, it is created by means of a community narrative, itself subject to the temporal and historical conditions that gave rise to the community. Schwandt (1989) has also argued that these discourses, or community narratives, can and should be bounded by moral considerations, a premise grounded in the emancipatory narratives of the critical theorists, the philosophical pragmatism of Rorty, the democratic focus of constructivist inquiry, and the "human flourishing" goals of participatory and cooperative inquiry.

The controversies around foundationalism (and, to a lesser extent, essentialism) are not likely to be resolved through dialogue between paradigm adherents. The likelier event is that the "postmodern turn" (Best & Kellner, 1997), with its emphasis on the social construction of social reality, fluid as opposed to fixed identities of the self, and the partiality of all truths, will simply overtake modernist assumptions of an objective reality, as indeed, to some extent, it has already done in the physical sciences. We might predict that, if not in our lifetimes, at some later time the dualist idea of an objective reality suborned by limited human subjective realities will seem as quaint as flat-earth theories do to us today.

▣ VALIDITY: AN EXTENDED AGENDA

Nowhere can the conversation about paradigm differences be more fertile than in the extended controversy about validity (Howe & Eisenhart, 1990; Kvale, 1989, 1994; Ryan, Greene, Lincoln, Mathison, & Mertens, 1998; Scheurich, 1994, 1996). Validity is not like objectivity. There are fairly strong theoretical, philosophical, and pragmatic rationales for examining the concept of objectivity and finding it wanting. Even within positivist frameworks it is viewed as conceptually flawed. But validity is a more irritating construct, one neither easily dismissed nor readily configured by new-paradigm practitioners (Enerstvedt, 1989; Tschudi, 1989). Validity cannot be dismissed simply because it points to a question that has to be answered in one way or another: Are these findings sufficiently authentic (isomorphic to some reality, trustworthy, related to the way others construct their social worlds) that I may trust myself in acting on their implications? More to the point, would I feel sufficiently secure about these findings to construct social policy or legislation based on them? At the same time, radical reconfigurations of validity leave researchers with multiple, sometimes conflicting, mandates for what constitutes rigorous research.

One of the issues around validity is the conflation between method and interpretation. The postmodern turn suggests that no method can deliver on ultimate truth, and in fact "suspects all methods," the more so the larger their claims to delivering on truth (Richardson, 1994). Thus, although one might argue that some methods are more suited than others for conducting research on human construction of social realities (Lincoln & Guba, 1985), no one would argue that a single method—or collection of methods—is the royal road to ultimate knowledge. In new-paradigm

inquiry, however, it is not merely method that promises to deliver on some set of local or context-grounded truths, it is also the processes of interpretation. Thus we have two arguments proceeding simultaneously. The first, borrowed from positivism, argues for a kind of rigor in the application of method, whereas the second argues for both a community consent and a form of rigor—defensible reasoning, plausible alongside some other reality that is known to author and reader—in ascribing salience to one interpretation over another and for framing and bounding an interpretive study itself. Prior to our understanding that there were, indeed, two forms of rigor, we assembled a set of methodological criteria, largely borrowed from an earlier generation of thoughtful anthropological and sociological methodological theorists. Those methodological criteria are still useful for a variety of reasons, not the least of which is that they ensure that such issues as prolonged engagement and persistent observation are attended to with some seriousness.

It is the second kind of rigor, however, that has received the most attention in recent writings: Are we *interpretively* rigorous? Can our cocreated constructions be trusted to provide some purchase on some important human phenomenon?

Human phenomena are themselves the subject of controversy. Classical social scientists would like to see "human phenomena" limited to those social experiences from which (scientific) generalizations may be drawn. New-paradigm inquirers, however, are increasingly concerned with the single experience, the individual crisis, the epiphany or moment of discovery, with that most powerful of all threats to conventional objectivity, feeling and emotion. Social scientists concerned with the expansion of what count as social data rely increasingly on the experiential, the embodied, the emotive qualities of human experience that contribute the narrative quality to a life. Sociologists such as Ellis and Bochner (2000) and Richardson (2000) and psychologists such as Michelle Fine (see Fine, Weis, Weseen, & Wong, 2000) concern themselves with various forms of autoethnography and personal experience methods, both to overcome the abstractions of a social science far gone with quantitative descriptions of human life and to capture those elements that make life conflictual, moving, problematic.

For purposes of this discussion, we believe the adoption of the most radical definitions of social science is appropriate, because the paradigmatic controversies are often taking place at the edges of those conversations. Those edges are where the border work is occurring, and, accordingly, they are the places that show the most promise for projecting where qualitative methods will be in the near and far future.

Whither and Whether Criteria

At those edges, several conversations are occurring around validity. The first—and most radical—is a conversation opened by Schwandt (1996), who suggests that we say "farewell to criteriology," or the "regulative norms for removing doubt and settling disputes about what is correct or incorrect, true or false" (p. 59), which have created a virtual cult around criteria. Schwandt does not, however, himself say farewell to criteria forever; rather, he resituates social inquiry, with other contemporary philosophical pragmatists, within a framework that transforms professional social inquiry into a form of practical philosophy, characterized by "aesthetic, prudential and moral considerations as well as more conventionally scientific ones" (p. 68). When social inquiry becomes the practice of a form of practical philosophy—a deep questioning about how we shall get on in the world and what we conceive to be the potentials and limits of human knowledge and functioning—then we have some preliminary understanding of what entirely different criteria might be for judging social inquiry.

Schwandt (1996) proposes three such criteria. First, he argues, we should search for a social inquiry that "generate[s] knowledge that complements or supplements rather than displac[ing] lay probing of social problems," a form of knowledge for which we do not yet have the *content,* but from which we might seek to understand the aims of practice from a variety of perspectives, or with different lenses. Second, he proposes a "social inquiry

as practical philosophy" that has as its aim "enhancing or cultivating *critical* intelligence in parties to the research encounter," critical intelligence being defined as "the capacity to engage in moral critique." And finally, he proposes a third way in which we might judge social inquiry as practical philosophy: We might make judgments about the social inquirer-as-practical-philosopher. He or she might be "evaluated on the success to which his or her reports of the inquiry enable the training or calibration of human judgment" (p. 69) or "the capacity for practical wisdom" (p. 70).

Schwandt is not alone, however, in wishing to say "farewell to criteriology," at least as it has been previously conceived. Scheurich (1997) makes a similar plea, and in the same vein, Smith (1993) also argues that validity, if it is to survive at all, must be radically reformulated if it is ever to serve phenomenological research well (see also Smith & Deemer, 2000).

At issue here is not whether we shall have criteria, or whose criteria we as a scientific community might adopt, but rather what the nature of social inquiry ought to be, whether it ought to undergo a transformation, and what might be the basis for criteria within a projected transformation. Schwandt (1989; also personal communication, August 21, 1998) is quite clear that both the transformation and the criteria are rooted in dialogic efforts. These dialogic efforts are quite clearly themselves forms of "moral discourse." Through the specific connections of the dialogic, the idea of practical wisdom, and moral discourses, much of Schwandt's work can be seen to be related to, and reflective of, critical theorist and participatory paradigms, as well as constructivism, although Schwandt specifically denies the relativity of truth. (For a more sophisticated explication and critique of forms of constructivism, hermeneutics, and interpretivism, see Schwandt, 2000. In that chapter, Schwandt spells out distinctions between realists and nonrealists, and between foundationalists and nonfoundationalists, far more clearly than it is possible for us to do in this chapter.)

To return to the central question embedded in validity: How do we know when we have specific social inquiries that are faithful enough to some human construction that we may feel safe in acting on them, or, more important, that members of the community in which the research is conducted may act on them? To that question, there is no final answer. There are, however, several discussions of what we might use to make both professional and lay judgments regarding any piece of work. It is to those versions of validity that we now turn.

Validity as Authenticity

Perhaps the first nonfoundational criteria were those we developed in response to a challenge by John K. Smith (see Smith & Deemer, 2000). In those criteria, we attempted to locate criteria for judging the *processes* and *outcomes* of naturalistic or constructivist inquiries (rather than the application of methods; see Guba & Lincoln, 1989). We described five potential outcomes of a social constructionist inquiry (evaluation is one form of disciplined inquiry; see Guba & Lincoln, 1981), each grounded in concerns specific to the paradigm we had tried to describe and construct, and apart from any concerns carried over from the positivist legacy. The criteria were instead rooted in the axioms and assumptions of the constructivist paradigm, insofar as we could extrapolate and infer them.

Those authenticity criteria—so called because we believed them to be hallmarks of authentic, trustworthy, rigorous, or "valid" constructivist or phenomenological inquiry—were fairness, ontological authenticity, educative authenticity, catalytic authenticity, and tactical authenticity (Guba & Lincoln, 1989, pp. 245–251). *Fairness* was thought to be a quality of balance; that is, all stakeholder views, perspectives, claims, concerns, and voices should be apparent in the text. Omission of stakeholder or participant voices reflects, we believe, a form of bias. This bias, however, was and is not related directly to the concerns of objectivity that flow from positivist inquiry and that are reflective of inquirer blindness or subjectivity. Rather, this fairness was defined by deliberate attempts to prevent marginalization, to act

affirmatively with respect to inclusion, and to act with energy to ensure that all voices in the inquiry effort had a chance to be represented in any texts and to have their stories treated fairly and with balance.

Ontological and educative authenticity were designated as criteria for determining a raised level of awareness, in the first instance, by individual research participants and, in the second, by individuals about those who surround them or with whom they come into contact for some social or organizational purpose. Although we failed to see it at that particular historical moment (1989), there is no reason these criteria cannot be—at this point in time, with many miles under our theoretic and practice feet—reflective also of Schwandt's (1996) "critical intelligence," or capacity to engage in moral critique. In fact, the authenticity criteria we originally proposed had strong moral and ethical overtones, a point to which we later returned (see, for instance, Lincoln, 1995, 1998a, 1998b). It was a point to which our critics strongly objected before we were sufficiently self-aware to realize the implications of what we had proposed (see, for instance, Sechrest, 1993).

Catalytic and tactical authenticities refer to the ability of a given inquiry to prompt, first, action on the part of research participants and, second, the involvement of the researcher/evaluator in training participants in specific forms of social and political action if participants desire such training. It is here that constructivist inquiry practice begins to resemble forms of critical theorist action, action research, or participative or cooperative inquiry, each of which is predicated on creating the capacity in research participants for positive social change and forms of emancipatory community action. It is also at this specific point that practitioners of positivist and postpositivist social inquiry are the most critical, because any action on the part of the inquirer is thought to destabilize objectivity and introduce subjectivity, resulting in bias. The problem of subjectivity and bias has a long theoretical history, and this chapter is simply too brief for us to enter into the various formulations that either take account of subjectivity or posit it as a positive learning experience, practical, embodied, gendered, and emotive. For purposes of this discussion, it is enough to say that we are persuaded that objectivity is a chimera: a mythological creature that never existed, save in the imaginations of those who believe that knowing can be separated from the knower.

Validity as Resistance, Validity as Poststructural Transgression

Laurel Richardson (1994, 1997) has proposed another form of validity, a deliberately "transgressive" form, the *crystalline*. In writing experimental (i.e., nonauthoritative, nonpositivist) texts, particularly poems and plays, Richardson (1997) has sought to "problematize reliability, validity and truth" (p. 165) in an effort to create new relationships: to her research participants, to her work, to other women, to herself. She says that transgressive forms permit a social scientist to "conjure a different kind of social science . . . [which] means changing one's relationship to one's work, *how* one knows and tells about the sociological" (p. 166). In order to see "how transgression looks and how it feels," it is necessary to "find and deploy methods that allow us to uncover the hidden assumptions and life-denying repressions of sociology; resee/refeel sociology. Reseeing and retelling are inseparable" (p. 167).

The way to achieve such validity is by examining the properties of a crystal in a metaphoric sense. Here we present an extended quotation to give some flavor of how such validity might be described and deployed:

I propose that the central imaginary for "validity" for postmodernist texts is not the triangle—a rigid, fixed, two-dimensional object. Rather the central imaginary is the crystal, which combines symmetry and substance with an infinite variety of shapes, substances, transmutations, multidimensionalities, and angles of approach. Crystals grow, change, alter, but are not amorphous. Crystals are prisms that reflect externalities *and* refract within themselves, creating different colors, patterns, arrays, casting off in different directions. What we see depends upon our angle of repose. Not triangulation, crystallization. In postmodernist

mixed-genre texts, we have moved from plane geometry to light theory, where light can be *both* waves *and* particles. Crystallization, without losing structure, deconstructs the traditional idea of "validity" (we feel how there is no single truth, we see how texts validate themselves); and crystallization provides us with a deepened, complex, thoroughly partial understanding of the topic. Paradoxically, we know more and doubt what we know. (Richardson, 1997, p. 92)

The metaphoric "solid object" (crystal/text), which can be turned many ways, which reflects and refracts light (light/multiple layers of meaning), through which we can see both "wave" (light wave/human currents) and "particle" (light as "chunks" of energy/elements of truth, feeling, connection, processes of the research that "flow" together) is an attractive metaphor for validity. The properties of the crystal-as-metaphor help writers and readers alike see the interweaving of processes in the research: discovery, seeing, telling, storying, re-presentation.

Other "Transgressive" Validities

Laurel Richardson is not alone in calling for forms of validity that are "transgressive" and disruptive of the status quo. Patti Lather (1993) seeks "an incitement to discourse," the purpose of which is "to rupture validity as a regime of truth, to displace its historical inscription . . . via a dispersion, circulation and proliferation of counterpractices of authority that take the crisis of representation into account" (p. 674). In addition to catalytic validity (Lather, 1986), Lather (1993) poses *validity as simulacra/ironic validity; Lyotardian paralogy/neopragmatic validity,* a form of validity that "foster[s] heterogeneity, refusing disclosure" (p. 679); *Derridean rigor/rhizomatic validity,* a form of behaving "via relay, circuit, multiple openings" (p. 680); and *voluptuous/situated validity,* which "embodies a situated, partial tentativeness" and "brings ethics and epistemology together . . . via practices of engagement and self-reflexivity" (p. 686). Together, these form a way of interrupting, disrupting, and transforming "pure" presence into a disturbing, fluid, partial, and problematic presence—a poststructural and decidedly postmodern form of discourse theory, hence textual revelation.

Validity as an Ethical Relationship

As Lather (1993) points out, poststructural forms for validities "bring ethics and epistemology together" (p. 686); indeed, as Parker Palmer (1987) also notes, "every way of knowing contains its own moral trajectory" (p. 24). Peshkin reflects on Noddings's (1984) observation that "the search for justification often carries us farther and farther from the heart of morality" (p. 105; quoted in Peshkin, 1993, p. 24). The *way* in which we know is most assuredly tied up with both *what* we know and our *relationships with our research participants.* Accordingly, one of us worked on trying to understand the ways in which the ethical intersects both the interpersonal and the epistemological (as a form of authentic or valid knowing; Lincoln, 1995). The result was the first set of understandings about emerging criteria for quality that were also rooted in the epistemology/ethics nexus. Seven new standards were derived from that search: positionality, or standpoint, judgments; specific discourse communities and research sites as arbiters of quality; voice, or the extent to which a text has the quality of polyvocality; critical subjectivity (or what might be termed intense self-reflexivity); reciprocity, or the extent to which the research relationship becomes reciprocal rather than hierarchical; sacredness, or the profound regard for how science can (and does) contribute to human flourishing; and sharing the perquisites of privilege that accrue to our positions as academics with university positions. Each of these standards was extracted from a body of research, often from disciplines as disparate as management, philosophy, and women's studies (Lincoln, 1995).

▣ Voice, Reflexivity, and Postmodern Textual Representation

Texts have to do a lot more work these days than they used to. Even as they are charged by poststructuralists and postmodernists to reflect upon their representational practices, representational practices themselves become more problematic. Three of the most engaging, but painful, issues are the problem of voice, the status of reflexivity, and the problematics of postmodern/poststructural textual representation, especially as those problematics are displayed in the shift toward narrative and literary forms that directly and openly deal with human emotion.

Voice

Voice is a multilayered problem, simply because it has come to mean many things to different researchers. In former eras, the only appropriate "voice" was the "voice from nowhere"—the "pure presence" of representation, as Lather terms it. As researchers became more conscious of the abstracted realities their texts created, they became simultaneously more conscious of having readers "hear" their informants—permitting readers to hear the exact words (and, occasionally, the paralinguistic cues, the lapses, pauses, stops, starts, reformulations) of the informants. Today voice can mean, especially in more participatory forms of research, not only having a real researcher—and a researcher's voice—in the text, but also letting research participants speak for themselves, either in text form or through plays, forums, "town meetings," or other oral and performance-oriented media or communication forms designed by research participants themselves. Performance texts, in particular, give an emotional immediacy to the voices of researchers and research participants far beyond their own sites and locales (see McCall, 2000). Rosanna Hertz (1997) describes voice as

> a struggle to figure out how to present the author's self while simultaneously writing the respondents' accounts and representing their selves. Voice has multiple dimensions: First, there is the voice of the author. Second, there is the presentation of the voices of one's respondents within the text. A third dimension appears when the self is the subject of the inquiry. . . . Voice is how authors express themselves within an ethnography. (pp. xi–xii)

But knowing how to express ourselves goes far beyond the commonsense understanding of "expressing ourselves." Generations of ethnographers trained in the "cooled-out, stripped-down rhetoric" of positivist inquiry (Firestone, 1987) find it difficult, if not nearly impossible, to "locate" themselves deliberately and squarely within their texts (even though, as Geertz [1988] has demonstrated finally and without doubt, the authorial voice is rarely genuinely absent, or even hidden).[3] Specific textual experimentation can help; that is, composing ethnographic work into various literary forms—the poetry and plays of Laurel Richardson are good examples—can help a researcher to overcome the tendency to write in the distanced and abstracted voice of the disembodied "I." But such writing exercises are hard work. This is also work that is embedded in the practices of reflexivity and narrativity, without which achieving a voice of (partial) truth is impossible.

Reflexivity

Reflexivity is the process of reflecting critically on the self as researcher, the "human as instrument" (Guba & Lincoln, 1981). It is, we would assert, the critical subjectivity discussed early on in Reason and Rowan's edited volume *Human Inquiry* (1981). It is a conscious experiencing of the self as both inquirer and respondent, as teacher and learner, as the one coming to know the self within the processes of research itself.

Reflexivity forces us to come to terms not only with our choice of research problem and with those with whom we engage in the research process, but with our selves and with the multiple identities that represent the fluid self in the research setting (Alcoff & Potter, 1993). Shulamit Reinharz (1997), for example, argues that we not only "*bring* the self to the field . . . [we also] *create* the self in the field" (p. 3). She suggests that although we all have many selves we bring with us, those selves fall into three categories: research-based selves, brought selves (the selves that historically, socially, and personally create our standpoints), and situationally created selves

(p. 5). Each of those selves comes into play in the research setting and consequently has a distinctive voice. Reflexivity—as well as the poststructural and postmodern sensibilities concerning quality in qualitative research—demands that we interrogate each of our selves regarding the ways in which research efforts are shaped and staged around the binaries, contradictions, and paradoxes that form our own lives. We must question our selves, too, regarding how those binaries and paradoxes shape not only the identities called forth in the field and later in the discovery processes of writing, but also our interactions with respondents, in who we become to them in the process of *becoming* to ourselves. Someone once characterized qualitative research as the twin processes of "writing up" (field notes) and "writing down" (the narrative). But Clandinin and Connelly (1994) have made clear that this bitextual reading of the processes of qualitative research is far too simplistic. In fact, many texts are created in the process of engaging in fieldwork. As Richardson (1994, 1997, 2000; see also Richardson & St. Pierre, Chapter 38, this volume) makes clear, writing is not merely the transcribing of some reality. Rather, writing—of all the texts, notes, presentations, and possibilities—is also a process of discovery: discovery of the subject (and sometimes of the problem itself) and discovery of the self.

There is good news and bad news with the most contemporary of formulations. The good news is that the multiple selves—ourselves and our respondents—of postmodern inquiries may give rise to more dynamic, problematic, open-ended, and complex forms of writing and representation. The bad news is that the multiple selves we create and encounter give rise to more dynamic, problematic, open-ended, and complex forms of writing and representation.

Postmodern Textual Representations

There are two dangers inherent in the conventional texts of scientific method: that they may lead us to believe the world is rather simpler than it is, and that they may reinscribe enduring forms of historical oppression. Put another way, we are confronted with a crisis of authority (which tells us the world is "this way" when perhaps it is some other way, or many other ways) and a crisis of representation (which serves to silence those whose lives we appropriate for our social sciences, and which may also serve subtly to re-create *this* world, rather than some other, perhaps more complex, but just one). Catherine Stimpson (1988) has observed:

> Like every great word, "representation/s" is a stew. A scrambled menu, it serves up several meanings at once. For a representation can be an image—visual, verbal, or aural.... A representation can also be a narrative, a sequence of images and ideas.... Or, a representation can be the product of ideology, that vast scheme for showing forth the world and justifying its dealings. (p. 223)

One way to confront the dangerous illusions (and their underlying ideologies) that texts may foster is through the creation of new texts that break boundaries; that move from the center to the margins to comment on and decenter the center; that forgo closed, bounded worlds for those more open-ended and less conveniently encompassed; that transgress the boundaries of conventional social science; and that seek to create a social science about human life rather than *on* subjects.

Experiments with how to do this have produced "messy texts" (Marcus & Fischer, 1986). Messy texts are not typographic nightmares (although they may be typographically nonlinear); rather, they are texts that seek to break the binary between science and literature, to portray the contradiction and truth of human experience, to break the rules in the service of showing, even partially, how real human beings cope with both the eternal verities of human existence and the daily irritations and tragedies of living that existence. Postmodern representations search out and experiment with narratives that expand the range of understanding, voice, and storied variations in human experience. As much as they are social scientists, inquirers also become storytellers, poets, and playwrights, experimenting with personal narratives, first-person accounts, reflexive interrogations, and deconstruction of the forms of tyranny embedded in representational practices (see Richardson, 2000; Tierney & Lincoln, 1997).

Representation may be arguably the most open-ended of the controversies surrounding phenomenological research today, for no other reasons than that the ideas of what constitutes legitimate inquiry are expanding and, at the same time, the forms of narrative, dramatic, and rhetorical structure are far from being either explored or exploited fully. Because, too, each inquiry, each inquirer, brings a unique perspective to our understanding, the possibilities for variation and exploration are limited only by the number of those engaged in inquiry and the realms of social and intrapersonal life that become interesting to researchers. The only thing that can be said for certain about postmodern representational practices is that they will proliferate as forms and they will seek, and demand much of, audiences, many of whom may be outside the scholarly and academic world. In fact, some forms of inquiry may never show up in the academic world, because their purpose will be use in the immediate context, for the consumption, reflection, and use of indigenous audiences. Those that are produced for scholarly audiences will, however, continue to be untidy, experimental, and driven by the need to communicate social worlds that have remained private and "nonscientific" until now.

🔲 A GLIMPSE OF THE FUTURE

The issues raised in this chapter are by no means the only ones under discussion for the near and far future. But they are some of the critical ones, and discussion, dialogue, and even controversies are bound to continue as practitioners of the various new and emergent paradigms continue either to look for common ground or to find ways in which to distinguish their forms of inquiry from others.

Some time ago, we expressed our hope that practitioners of both positivist and new-paradigm forms of inquiry might find some way of resolving their differences, such that all social scientists could work within a common discourse—and perhaps even several traditions—once again. In retrospect, such a resolution appears highly unlikely and would probably even be less than useful. This is not, however, because neither positivists nor phenomenologists will budge an inch (although that, too, is unlikely). Rather, it is because, in the postmodern moment, and in the wake of poststructuralism, the assumption that there is no single "truth"—that all truths are but partial truths; that the slippage between signifier and signified in linguistic and textual terms creates re-presentations that are only and always shadows of the actual people, events, and places; that identities are fluid rather than fixed—leads us ineluctably toward the insight that there will be no single "conventional" paradigm to which all social scientists might ascribe in some common terms and with mutual understanding. Rather, we stand at the threshold of a history marked by multivocality, contested meanings, paradigmatic controversies, and new textual forms. At some distance down this conjectural path, when its history is written, we will find that this has been the era of emancipation: emancipation from what Hannah Arendt calls "the coerciveness of Truth," emancipation from hearing only the voices of Western Europe, emancipation from generations of silence, and emancipation from seeing the world in one color.

We may also be entering an age of greater spirituality within research efforts. The emphasis on inquiry that reflects ecological values, on inquiry that respects communal forms of living that are not Western, on inquiry involving intense reflexivity regarding how our inquiries are shaped by our own historical and gendered locations, and on inquiry into "human flourishing," as Heron and Reason (1997) call it, may yet reintegrate the sacred with the secular in ways that promote freedom and self-determination. Egon Brunswik, the organizational theorist, wrote of "tied" and "untied" variables—variables that are linked, or clearly not linked, with other variables—when studying human forms of organization. We may be in a period of exploring the ways in which our inquiries are both tied and untied, as a means of finding where our interests cross and where we can both be and promote others' being, as whole human beings.

◙ NOTES

1. There are several versions of critical theory, including classical critical theory, which is most closely related to neo-Marxist theory; postpositivist formulations, which divorce themselves from Marxist theory but are positivist in their insistence on conventional rigor criteria; and postmodernist, poststructuralist, or constructivist-oriented varieties. See, for instance, Fay (1987), Carr and Kemmis (1986), and Lather (1991). See also Kemmis and McTaggart (2000) and Kincheloe and McLaren (2000).

2. For a clearer understanding of how methods came to stand in for paradigms, or how our initial (and, we thought, quite clear) positions came to be misconstrued, see Lancy (1993) or, even more currently, Weiss (1998, esp. p. 268).

3. For example, compare this chapter with, say, the work of Richardson (2000) and Ellis and Bochner (2000), where the authorial voices are clear, personal, vocal, and interior, interacting subjectivities. Although some colleagues have surprised us by correctly identifying which chapters each of us has written in given books, nevertheless, the style of this chapter more closely approximates the more distanced forms of "realist" writing than it does the intimate, personal "feeling tone" (to borrow a phrase from Studs Terkel) of other chapters. Voices also arise as a function of the material being covered. The material we chose as most important for this chapter seemed to demand a less personal tone, probably because there appears to be much more "contention" than calm dialogue concerning these issues. The "cool" tone likely stems from our psychological response to trying to create a quieter space for discussion around controversial issues. What can we say?

◙ REFERENCES

Addelson, K. P. (1993). Knowers/doers and their moral problems. In L. Alcoff & E. Potter (Eds.), *Feminist epistemologies* (pp. 265–294). New York: Routledge.

Alcoff, L., & Potter, E. (Eds.). (1993). *Feminist epistemologies*. New York: Routledge.

Alpern, S., Antler, J., Perry, E. I., & Scobie, I. W. (Eds.). (1992). *The challenge of feminist biography: Writing the lives of modern American women.* Urbana: University of Illinois Press.

Babbitt, S. (1993). Feminism and objective interests: The role of transformation experiences in rational deliberation. In L. Alcoff & E. Potter (Eds.), *Feminist epistemologies* (pp. 245–264). New York: Routledge.

Bernstein, R. J. (1983). *Beyond objectivism and relativism: Science, hermeneutics, and praxis.* Oxford: Blackwell.

Best, S., & Kellner, D. (1997). *The postmodern turn.* New York: Guilford.

Bloland, H. (1989). Higher education and high anxiety: Objectivism, relativism, and irony. *Journal of Higher Education, 60,* 519–543.

Bloland, H. (1995). Postmodernism and higher education. *Journal of Higher Education, 66,* 521–559.

Bradley, J., & Schaefer, K. (1998). *The uses and misuses of data and models.* Thousand Oaks, CA: Sage.

Carr, W. L., & Kemmis, S. (1986). *Becoming critical: Education, knowledge and action research.* London: Falmer.

Carspecken, P. F. (1996). *Critical ethnography in educational research: A theoretical and practical guide.* New York: Routledge.

Christians, C. G. (2000). Ethics and politics in qualitative research. In N. K. Denzin & Y. S. Lincoln (Eds.), *Handbook of qualitative research* (2nd ed., pp. 133–155). Thousand Oaks, CA: Sage.

Clandinin, D. J., & Connelly, F. M. (1994). Personal experience methods. In N. K. Denzin & Y. S. Lincoln (Eds.), *Handbook of qualitative research* (pp. 413–427). Thousand Oaks, CA: Sage.

Denzin, N. K., & Lincoln, Y. S. (Eds.). (1994). *Handbook of qualitative research.* Thousand Oaks, CA: Sage.

Ellis, C., & Bochner, A. P. (Eds.). (1996). *Composing ethnography: Alternative forms of qualitative writing.* Walnut Creek, CA: AltaMira.

Ellis, C., & Bochner, A. P. (2000). Autoethnography, personal narrative, reflexivity: Researcher as subject. In N. K. Denzin & Y. S. Lincoln (Eds.), *Handbook of qualitative research* (2nd ed., pp. 733–768). Thousand Oaks, CA: Sage.

Enerstvedt, R. (1989). The problem of validity in social science. In S. Kvale (Ed.), *Issues of validity in qualitative research* (pp. 135–173). Lund, Sweden: Studentlitteratur.

Fay, B. (1987). *Critical social science.* Ithaca, NY: Cornell University Press.

Fine, M., Weis, L., Weseen, S., & Wong, L. (2000). For whom? Qualitative research, representations, and social responsibilities. In N. K. Denzin & Y. S. Lincoln (Eds.), *Handbook of qualitative research* (2nd ed., pp. 107–131). Thousand Oaks, CA: Sage.

Firestone, W. (1987). Meaning in method: The rhetoric of quantitative and qualitative research. *Educational Researcher, 16*(7), 16–21.

Foucault, M. (1971). *The order of things: An archaeology of the human sciences.* New York: Pantheon.

Gamson, J. (2000). Sexualities, queer theory, and qualitative research. In N. K. Denzin & Y. S. Lincoln (Eds.), *Handbook of qualitative research* (2nd ed., pp. 347–365). Thousand Oaks, CA: Sage.

Geertz, C. (1988). *Works and lives: The anthropologist as author.* Cambridge: Polity.

Geertz, C. (1993). *Local knowledge: Further essays in interpretive anthropology.* London: Fontana.

Greenwood, D. J., & Levin, M. (2000). Reconstructing the relationships between universities and society through action research. In N. K. Denzin & Y. S. Lincoln (Eds.), *Handbook of qualitative research* (2nd ed., pp. 85–106). Thousand Oaks, CA: Sage.

Guba, E. G., & Lincoln, Y. S. (1981). *Effective evaluation: Improving the usefulness of evaluation results through responsive and naturalistic approaches.* San Francisco: Jossey-Bass.

Guba, E. G., & Lincoln, Y. S. (1982). Epistemological and methodological bases for naturalistic inquiry. *Educational Communications and Technology Journal, 31,* 233–252.

Guba, E. G., & Lincoln, Y. S. (1989). *Fourth generation evaluation.* Newbury Park, CA: Sage.

Guba, E. G., & Lincoln, Y. S. (1994). Competing paradigms in qualitative research. In N. K. Denzin & Y. S. Lincoln (Eds.), *Handbook of qualitative research* (pp. 105–117). Thousand Oaks, CA: Sage.

Harding, S. (1993). Rethinking standpoint epistemology: What is "strong objectivity"? In L. Alcoff & E. Potter (Eds.), *Feminist epistemologies* (pp. 49–82). New York: Routledge.

Heron, J. (1996). *Cooperative inquiry: Research into the human condition.* London: Sage.

Heron, J., & Reason, P. (1997). A participatory inquiry paradigm. *Qualitative Inquiry, 3,* 274–294.

Hertz, R. (1997). Introduction: Reflexivity and voice. In R. Hertz (Ed.), *Reflexivity and voice.* Thousand Oaks, CA: Sage.

Howe, K., & Eisenhart, M. (1990). Standards for qualitative (and quantitative) research: A prolegomenon. *Educational Researcher, 19*(4), 2–9.

Hutcheon, L. (1989). *The politics of postmodernism.* New York: Routledge.

Kemmis, S., & McTaggart, R. (2000). Participatory action research. In N. K. Denzin & Y. S. Lincoln (Eds.), *Handbook of qualitative research* (2nd ed., pp. 567–605). Thousand Oaks, CA: Sage.

Kincheloe, J. L. (1991). *Teachers as researchers: Qualitative inquiry as a path to empowerment.* London: Falmer.

Kincheloe, J. L., & McLaren, P. (2000). Rethinking critical theory and qualitative research. In N. K. Denzin & Y. S. Lincoln (Eds.), *Handbook of qualitative research* (2nd ed., pp. 279–313). Thousand Oaks, CA: Sage.

Kondo, D. K. (1990). *Crafting selves: Power, gender, and discourses of identity in a Japanese workplace.* Chicago: University of Chicago Press.

Kondo, D. K. (1997). *About face: Performing race in fashion and theater.* New York: Routledge.

Kvale, S. (Ed.). (1989). *Issues of validity in qualitative research.* Lund, Sweden: Studentlitteratur.

Kvale, S. (1994, April). *Validation as communication and action.* Paper presented at the annual meeting of the American Educational Research Association, New Orleans.

Lancy, D. F. (1993). *Qualitative research in education: An introduction to the major traditions.* New York: Longman.

Lather, P. (1986). Issues of validity in openly ideological research: Between a rock and a soft place. *Interchange, 17*(4), 63–84.

Lather, P. (1991). *Getting smart: Feminist research and pedagogy with/in the postmodern.* New York: Routledge.

Lather, P. (1993). Fertile obsession: Validity after poststructuralism. *Sociological Quarterly, 34,* 673–693.

Leitch, V. B. (1996). *Postmodern: Local effects, global flows.* Albany: State University of New York Press.

Lincoln, Y. S. (1995). Emerging criteria for quality in qualitative and interpretive research. *Qualitative Inquiry, 1,* 275–289.

Lincoln, Y. S. (1997). What constitutes quality in interpretive research? In C. K. Kinzer, K. A. Hinchman, & D. J. Leu (Eds.), *Inquiries in literacy: Theory and practice* (pp. 54–68). Chicago: National Reading Conference.

Lincoln, Y. S. (1998a). The ethics of teaching qualitative research. *Qualitative Inquiry, 4,* 305–317.

Lincoln, Y. S. (1998b). From understanding to action: New imperatives, new criteria, new methods for interpretive researchers. *Theory and Research in Social Education, 26*(1), 12–29.

Lincoln, Y. S., & Denzin, N. K. (1994). The fifth moment. In N. K. Denzin & Y. S. Lincoln (Eds.), *Handbook of qualitative research* (pp. 575–586). Thousand Oaks, CA: Sage.

Lincoln, Y. S., & Guba, E. G. (1985). *Naturalistic inquiry.* Beverly Hills, CA: Sage.

Marcus, G. E., & Fischer, M. M. J. (1986). *Anthropology as cultural critique: An experimental moment in the human sciences.* Chicago: University of Chicago Press.

McCall, M. M. (2000). Performance ethnography: A brief history and some advice. In N. K. Denzin & Y. S. Lincoln (Eds.), *Handbook of qualitative research* (2nd ed., pp. 421–433). Thousand Oaks, CA: Sage.

Mertens, D. (1998). *Research methods in education and psychology: Integrating diversity with quantitative and qualitative methods.* Thousand Oaks, CA: Sage.

Michael, M. C. (1996). *Feminism and the postmodern impulse: Post–World War II fiction.* Albany: State University of New York Press.

Noddings, N. (1984). *Caring: A feminine approach to ethics and moral education.* Berkeley: University of California Press.

Olesen, V. L. (2000). Feminisms and qualitative research at and into the millennium. In N. K. Denzin & Y. S. Lincoln (Eds.), *Handbook of qualitative research* (2nd ed., pp. 215–255). Thousand Oaks, CA: Sage.

Palmer, P. J. (1987, September-October). Community, conflict, and ways of knowing. *Change, 19,* 20–25.

Peshkin, A. (1993). The goodness of qualitative research. *Educational Researcher, 22*(2), 24–30.

Polkinghorne, D. E. (1989). Changing conversations about human science. In S. Kvale (Ed.), *Issues of validity in qualitative research* (pp. 13–46). Lund, Sweden: Studentlitteratur.

Reason, P. (1993). Sacred experience and sacred science. *Journal of Management Inquiry, 2,* 10–27.

Reason, P., & Rowan, J. (Eds.). (1981). *Human inquiry.* London: John Wiley.

Reinharz, S. (1997). Who am I? The need for a variety of selves in the field. In R. Hertz (Ed.), *Reflexivity and voice* (pp. 3–20). Thousand Oaks, CA: Sage.

Richardson, L. (1994). Writing: A method of inquiry. In N. K. Denzin & Y. S. Lincoln (Eds.), *Handbook of qualitative research* (pp. 516–529). Thousand Oaks, CA: Sage.

Richardson, L. (1997). *Fields of play: Constructing an academic life.* New Brunswick, NJ: Rutgers University Press.

Richardson, L. (2000). Writing: A method of inquiry. In N. K. Denzin & Y. S. Lincoln (Eds.), *Handbook of qualitative research* (2nd ed., pp. 923–948). Thousand Oaks, CA: Sage.

Rorty, R. (1979). *Philosophy and the mirror of nature.* Princeton, NJ: Princeton University Press.

Ryan, K. E., Greene, J. C., Lincoln, Y. S., Mathison, S., & Mertens, D. (1998). Advantages and challenges of using inclusive evaluation approaches in evaluation practice. *American Journal of Evaluation, 19,* 101–122.

Salner, M. (1989). Validity in human science research. In S. Kvale (Ed.), *Issues of validity in qualitative research* (pp. 47–72). Lund, Sweden: Studentlitteratur.

Scheurich, J. J. (1994). Policy archaeology. *Journal of Educational Policy, 9,* 297–316.

Scheurich, J. J. (1996). Validity. *International Journal of Qualitative Studies in Education, 9,* 49–60.

Scheurich, J. J. (1997). *Research method in the postmodern.* London: Falmer.

Schratz, M., & Walker, R. (1995). *Research as social change: New opportunities for qualitative research.* New York: Routledge.

Schwandt, T. A. (1989). Recapturing moral discourse in evaluation. *Educational Researcher, 18*(8), 11–16, 34.

Schwandt, T. A. (1996). Farewell to criteriology. *Qualitative Inquiry, 2,* 58–72.

Schwandt, T. A. (2000). Three epistemological stances for qualitative inquiry: Interpretivism, hermeneutics, and social constructionism. In N. K. Denzin & Y. S. Lincoln (Eds.), *Handbook of qualitative research* (2nd ed., pp. 189–213). Thousand Oaks, CA: Sage.

Sechrest, L. (1993). *Program evaluation: A pluralistic enterprise.* San Francisco: Jossey-Bass.

Smith, J. K. (1993). *After the demise of empiricism: The problem of judging social and educational inquiry.* Norwood, NJ: Ablex.

Smith, J. K., & Deemer, D. K. (2000). The problem of criteria in the age of relativism. In N. K. Denzin & Y. S. Lincoln (Eds.), *Handbook of qualitative research* (2nd ed., pp. 877–896). Thousand Oaks, CA: Sage.

Stimpson, C. R. (1988). Nancy Reagan wears a hat: Feminism and its cultural consensus. *Critical Inquiry, 14,* 223–243.

Tierney, W. G. (2000). Undaunted courage: Life history and the postmodern challenge. In N. K. Denzin & Y. S. Lincoln (Eds.), *Handbook of qualitative research* (2nd ed., pp. 537–553). Thousand Oaks, CA: Sage.

Tierney, W. G., & Lincoln, Y. S. (Eds.). (1997). *Representation and the text: Re-framing the narrative voice.* Albany: State University of New York Press.

Trinh, T. M. (1991). *When the moon waxes red: Representation, gender and cultural politics.* New York: Routledge.

Tschudi, F. (1989). Do qualitative and quantitative methods require different approaches to validity? In S. Kvale (Ed.), *Issues of validity in qualitative research* (pp. 109–134). Lund, Sweden: Studentlitteratur.

Weiss, C. H. (1998). *Evaluation* (2nd ed.). Upper Saddle River, NJ: Prentice Hall.

12

Various Snapshots

H. WILLMOTT; J.M. BARTUNEK; J. PFEFFER; C.M. FIOL
and E.J. O'CONNOR; T. WATSON; O. SORENSON;
A.M. GRANT; J.E. DUTTON and B.D. ROSSO;
A.S. DENISI; G. NORTHCRAFT

For Informed Pluralism, Broad Relevance and Critical Reflexivity

Hugh Willmott

The future of management and organization studies (MOS) will be sealed by developments in the wider social, political and intellectual milieu in which it evolves, and to which it contributes. Whatever the course of its future development, however, it seems likely that MOS will continue to be buffeted by demands for academic rigour and applicability to practice. When subjected to these pressures, the recurrent risk is not that the field will buckle or disintegrate, but rather that it will bring about a reactionary return to some mythical, apparently authoritative notion of rigour and a narrow sense of relevance in which the particular demands of privileged groups, such as managers, policy makers and academics, are represented as universally valued.

My hope is that this reactionary scenario will not unfold, and that, instead, a flourishing of informed pluralism will characterize the future development of the field. Pluralism is a powerful antidote to the prospect of a regressive trajectory. Pluralism is 'healthy' not just because it fosters diversity but because, in principle, it helps to problematize and temper knowledges that claim sole authority, and thereby underwrite dogma and tyranny. Informed pluralism is distinguished by an incorporation within each knowledge claim, or contribution, of a critical awareness of its own limits. The basis of this awareness is an in-depth appreciation of, and not just a passing acquaintance with, the nature and value of alternative methodological strategies for constructing our studies, and associated knowledges, of management and organization.

Informed pluralism is also 'healthy' when it challenges an easy, repressively tolerant, assumption that each contribution to, or 'image' of, organization and management provides a unique and necessary part of a larger picture. What might be termed the jigsaw concept of MOS slides past a close examination of how approaches may be in opposition, rather than complementary, to each other. Some pieces may fit together but others form parts of very different puzzles. The jigsaw notion of pluralism simply ignores the divergent epistemological and ontological assumptions upon which the distinctiveness of the different puzzles and associated 'pieces' is founded. And it also slides past consideration of the practical outcome, or relevance, of giving much greater attention to some of these puzzles and pieces than to others.

So, I would hope to see the flourishing of an informed, radical pluralism where there is an inquisitiveness about, and reflection upon, the value-basis and the likely outcomes, intended and unanticipated, of different ways of constructing knowledges of management and organization. Associated with this hope for the future is a balancing of knowledge being evaluated in relation to conceptions of epistemological correctness or ontological credibility by giving greater weight to an assessment of its practical effects. This emphasis is informed by a belief that the value of knowledge ultimately resides in its broad relevance notably, its capacity to enrich collective self-understanding and thereby provide the basis for sustaining and improving the quality of life – ecologically as well as socially – for all sensuous beings. It seems to me that many different kinds of power-knowledge – from the instrumental to the meditative – can contribute to this capability; and hence my emphasis upon pluralism in order to counter contemporary vulnerabilities to the effects of a monist conception of scientific enquiry which is corrosive of collective self-determination.

With this, we require critical reflexivity. By this, I mean a capacity to recognize the inescapably partial and constructed foundation of all knowledge claims about management and/or organization. It involves an awareness of the contingencies of knowledge production, embedded as knowledge inescapably is in particular traditions, disciplines, methodological protocols, temporal contexts, etc. In addition to reminding us particularity of what counts as knowledge – for example, in its dependence upon the privileging of particular epistemological and ontological assumptions – critical reflexivity heightens attentiveness to its (unavoidable) ethical significance with regard to the consequences of taking knowledge claims to be true. So, when practising an informed pluralism, critical reflexivity would be incorporated in assessing the value and validity of diverse forms of analyses in relation to ethical criteria, and not predominantly in relation to its degree of compliance or correspondence with a projected ontology, whether 'realist' or 'constructionist' in formulation; or its adherence to a favoured set of methodological protocols, whether 'quantitative' or 'qualitative' in attribution. Of course, ethical criteria are themselves diverse, contested and open to debate; and it is in the explication of currently unacknowledged ethical implications of knowledge production as well as in the debating of relevant ethical criteria that MOS, guided by informed pluralism, can make a useful contribution.

The interrelationship of informed pluralism, broad relevance and critical reflexivity is at the core of my hopes for the future of MOS. A key resource and inspiration for this possible future has been, and is likely to continue to be, the strands of knowledge production that comprise the rich and contested traditions of critical thinking as applied to, and developed within, MOS: critical hermeneutics, Critical Theory, radical feminism, poststructuralism, critical realism, post-Marxism, postcolonialism, etc. Such critical thinking has taken MOS in a pluralist direction that is more informed about the differences and limitations of varied forms of analysis; it has promoted a broader conception of relevance; and it has stimulated a critical reflexivity about knowledge-claims. By valuing and nurturing a plurality of traditions, MOS is more likely to interrogate topics and to engage with diverse audiences in ways that are attentive to its broader social and ecological relevance and consequences. But, to return to the historical embeddedness of MOS, the extent to which such a future is realized will depend, above all else, upon the conduciveness and receptivity of the broader milieu in which MOS develops; and, more specifically, the extent to which this milieu is supportive of an informed pluralism wherein the diverse strands of critical management studies can be expected to play a key role.

REFERENCES

Alvesson, M. and Willmott, H.C. (1996) *Making Sense of Management: A Critical Introduction*. London: Sage.

Willmott, H.C. (2003) 'Organizational theory as critical science: The case of 'New Organizational Forms', in C. Knudsen and H. Tsoukas (eds), *Organization Theory as Science: Prospects and Limitations*. Oxford: Oxford University Press. pp. 88–112.

Willmott, H.C. (2005) 'Theorizing contemporary control: Some poststructuralist responses to some critical realist questions', *Organization*, 12 (5): 747–780.

The Nature of Research Practice

Jean M. Bartunek

Please conduct a thought experiment.

Imagine someone who has a doctorate in management or organization studies and substantial research training in both quantitative and qualitative methods. Imagine that she has been working in a corporate setting and conducting research there.

Now imagine that, for a diversion from her normal fast-paced and time-pressured work, she is studying you, an academic, as you go about researching and writing a scholarly article. She might watch you plan the article carefully in advance or she might see that you initiate it because of a kind of serendipity (a book falls off your bookshelf). She might see you working in a very messy office, and see that you are interrupted regularly while you work. She might interview you about why you take breaks to surf the Internet or eat snacks while you're working. She might see you go through drafts and drafts, first of a proposal, and then, eventually, of the whole paper. She might see you collect data and watch the complications you encounter as you do so. She might talk with you about all your other activities, the teaching, the committee work, and your family life, that provide the context in which your research takes place. She might see your happiness when you are finally ready to 'get the article off your desk' by submitting it. She might hear your anger when your article is rejected or gets an unfair review. She might, if she has sufficient patience, observe what happens to you and your article for several years until it (hopefully) appears in print.

These particular events are, of course, only a small part of what someone studying you would see, only a small part of what goes into carrying out a research project from beginning to end. What would be the value of such a thought experiment?

When we as academics conduct studies, especially those that rely on observation or an equivalent methodology, the processes of the people and/or organizational units we study are open to view. We explore their cognitive maps, their aims and how they hope to accomplish these aims. We see them struggle to reach decisions. We see differences and disagreements among members of an organizational group or between groups. We see wrong paths they go down, ways they get back on track (or not), and factors that affect their success. Features like these are often key to understanding organizations and the actions within them.

But what about our own research processes as academics? Our own cognitive maps about our work, or, as Argyris and Schön (1974) more properly refer to them, our theories of action, play central roles in the conduct of our research. Our initial and evolving aims for our work, the ways we expect to achieve these aims, and the processes through which organizational research takes place are important in determining how our initial ideas become expanded, modified, and/or discarded all together and eventually lead to a scholarly product. But, as Weick (1989) notes, they are not often salient to us as academics.

For example, I began to write the first draft of this short essay while I was sitting in an airplane as we flew over the Midwest U.S. I chose that setting because I was having difficulty getting started, and I figured that sitting in a plane would provide relatively few distractions.

This is not the kind of description that is typically included in depictions of how scholarly products are presented. But it helps to make explicit two important pieces of information.

The first is my theory of action. Argyris and Schön (1974) argued that all human beings, researchers included, have theories of action about how to behave effectively with others, to accomplish particular intended consequences. These may not be fully explicit and may not look like the types of propositions or hypotheses that are easily assessed by structural equation modelling, but they are hypotheses nonetheless.

My hypothesis, implicit at the time, was something like the following: I'm much more likely to begin a somewhat ambiguous task that I'm interested in but don't quite know how to do if I can play with it in a setting where I will have very few other options for behaviour and where I have a finite amount of time, so I won't feel as if I have to complete anything. An airplane might provide such a setting. I tested the hypothesis by bringing the invitation letter and a small laptop computer with me and by typing whatever came to my mind. Fortunately, my hypothesis was supported; I did get started with this article.

The second piece of information this description contributes is observation of what I actually did. More than three decades ago Henry Mintzberg (1973) conducted an observational study and then wrote a book that detailed how managers actually acted. This book showed that the functions of managers that had been assumed by classical management theorists bore only sketchy correspondence with the ways that managers actually spend their time. His work opened up completely new understandings of and approaches to studying management.

What did I actually do? I thought a bit. I typed on a laptop sitting on a plane. I looked no different from the other passengers typing on their laptops. My 'practice' appeared to be very ordinary activity, just as the other passengers' typing appeared to be.

There are an increasing number of occasions being provided in which a select group of accomplished management scholars have been invited to write about how they work. Peter Frost co-edited multiple volumes in which scholars were invited to reflect on this. Arthur Bedeian has edited an autobiography series. Hari Tsoukas, as editor of *Organization Studies*, has begun a new section of that journal called 'Vita Contemplativa' in which he has invited some scholars to describe their intellectual careers. Kenneth Smith and Michael Hitt edited a book in which scholars told how their influential theories came to be developed.

But on the whole, little is known, in any systematic way, about how individual scholarly works on organizational behaviour and management are actually produced, the ways through which articles (the ones with high impact and the ones without any impact) are conceived, designed, carried to fruition and then published. Or not.

But this is very important. This is the practice of research, the way that causal models, questionnaire numbers, interviews, observations, archival data, and so forth get imagined, carried out, collected, conducted, written about, and translated into scholarly contributions. Similar to what Mintzberg found about managing, these processes are likely best described in different categories than those typically used in teaching research methods. Attention to these processes may help develop much greater understanding of what scholarly work really entails than do standard emphases on what theorizing and research processes ought to be. Weick (1989: 519) noted, for example, that most discussions of theory building are mechanistic, with 'little appreciation of the often intuitive, blind, wasteful, serendipitous, creative quality of the process'.

Continued

Why might it be best to have a practitioner, albeit one trained in social science research methods, conduct such a study? It is unlikely that if Mintzberg's managers had studied themselves they would have seen anywhere near what Mintzberg did; too many of their actions would not stand out for them as worthy of attention. It seems likely that people who work in settings other than academia, who bring different norms, concerns and questions with them than academics do, would be more likely to view what we are doing from different frameworks than our standard ones, and thus help to make much that is tacit about scholarly processes much more explicit.

For example, a manager told me recently that in his job having two months to write a paper was a luxury; he was used to a few days at most. For me, and for many academics, two months to write a paper is barely enough time to start thinking about it. This conversation made me aware of a norm about time in academia that I had not thought of before. There are undoubtedly many other norms that we are unaware of, but that might be obvious to others.

In addition, those in other occupations might help surface our theories of action more effectively. What are our aims when we are writing a scholarly article? Contribute to theory? Get an 'A' hit? Get tenure? Help our doctoral students get jobs? Get into print faster than a competitor? How do both the macro (developing elegant theory) and micro (waiting to write until we're on an airplane) processes of our working on the article contribute to these explicit and implicit aims?

Perhaps joint insider-outsider studies (Bartunek and Louis, 1996) in which both the researchers (those who work outside academia) and research participants (academic researchers) attend to processes and work together to interpret what's going on might be valuable. Outsiders can help to surface our aims, practices and norms, while academics can help explore cognitions and feelings about them. Such joint work and reflection are likely to lead to more heterogeneous conjectures, and thus more creative understandings (Weick, 1989) of what doing scholarly research is and means in practice for academics than reflections carried out solely by academics.

Regardless of whether an experiment such as I have described remains in our thoughts or is actually conducted, it might heighten academic researchers' attention to the theories that guide our action, to our practice, to the norms of our profession, and how integral these are for our research practice.

REFERENCES

Argyris, C. and Schön, D. (1974) *Theory in Practice.* San Francisco: Jossey-Bass.
Bartunek, J.M. and Louis, M.R. (1996) *Insider-Outsider Team Research.* Thousand Oaks, CA: Sage.
Mintzberg, H. (1973) *The Nature of Managerial Work.* New York: Harper and Row.
Weick, K.E. (1989) 'Theory construction as disciplined imagination', *Academy of Management Review*, 14: 516–531.

Organization Studies is (and should be) Different from Economics

Jeffrey Pfeffer

Organization studies suffers from economics envy. In subfields ranging from the study of organizational strategy, where transaction costs and industrial organization economics hold sway to the study of managing people where, in the domain of human resource management, the only outcomes that seem to matter are some version of productivity, quality, profitability, or stock market return, to the exploration of individual decision making and motivation where the assumptions of individual rationality and the pursuit of self-interest tend to dominate, and in many other topic domains as well, organization studies not only cites the economics literature at an increasing rate but has bought in many of the behavioral assumptions that underlie economics. This economics dominance is the case even though, as Ghoshal (2005) has argued, many of these economic assumptions are harmful for our students and for practice, and even though, as Bazerman (2005) has noted, many of these economic assumptions and theories have been shown to be wrong.

There are numerous problems with the fascination with economics logic, language, and assumptions. The first is that, as documented in many places, this interest is not reciprocated – economics is almost exclusively a field that cites itself and where there seems to be little interest in incorporating the insights or ideas of related fields, such as organization studies (e.g. Ferraro et al., 2005). Second, it is not the case that in the end, 'truth triumphs'. As has been shown, there are many mechanisms that make theories become self-fulfilling (Ferraro et al., 2005), so that the theories that are believed and advocated most strongly may win in the marketplace of ideas, regardless of either their utility or empirical validity.

Third, and perhaps most importantly, organization studies runs the risk of leaving some important questions unasked, and some important insights unexplored to the extent it becomes too much a step-cousin of economics. As the critical theorists note, much of organization theory is written from the point of view of the interests of those in power. Performance, for the most part, is company profitability or return to shareholders, not how many people have a comfortable retirement or the levels of alienation and distrust in the workplace. Strategy is about achieving sustainable competitive advantage, not whether or not such competitive advantage has any implication for sustainability (in terms of resource use) or for the production or diminution of inequality in a society. The various control regimes and strategies to which people are subjected, ranging from strong cultures to financial incentives, are seldom investigated in terms of their effects on the people themselves as contrasted with their effects on compliance with organizational requests. Many more examples, I am sure, come to your mind.

Because economics and its methodology is primarily premised on individual rationality and methodological individualism, many important topics fade into the background to the extent organization studies adopts economics thinking. For instance, as my colleague James March has often lamented, seeing organizations and institutions as simply a nexus of contracts or as a place where individual preferences come together denies a lot of the fundamental reality and explanatory power that derives from seeing organizations as having a life and an existence and power of their own, separate from their members and different from the idea that 'the people make the place.' Organizations not only reflect individual deals and inducements-contributions calculations and the preferences that people bring to the workplace, but they also are powerful shapers of attitudes and preference, what people believe to be fair and just, how people see their work and even their time, and how people make sense of the world in which they exist. Emotions is another topic that fades into the background with too much emphasis on rational choice. Moreover, even the very phrase 'decision biases', used to describe phenomena such as the availability heuristic or anchoring and adjustment, presumes a normative correctness to some forms of decision logic over others, with little consideration of their relative frequency or of their consequences for people. The 'norms' are set against a theoretical conception of judgment and choice, not against a base rate of what people actually do, nor against some standards of appropriateness derived from alternative theoretical conceptions.

'Interdisciplinary' is a term that seems to evoke unquestioned positive approval, and the idea that organization studies should borrow from economics has assumed a taken-for-granted quality. But there is much to be gained from proposing incompatible theoretical views and then confronting alternative predictions and explanations with data. As Thomas Kuhn reminded us, that is how scientific progress occurs. So, 'paradigm wars' may actually be healthy for the organization sciences, and not being coopted by economics is crucial for maintaining a set of topics, assumptions, and methods that otherwise will be lost.

REFERENCES

Bazerman, Max, H. (2005) 'Conducting influential research: The need for prescriptive implications', *Academy of Management Review*, 30 (1), January: 25–31.

Ferraro, Fabrizio, Pfeffer, Jeffrey and Sutlon, Robert, I. (2005) 'Economics language and assumptions: How theories can become self-fulfilling', *Academy of Management Review*, 30 (1), January: 8–24.

Ghoshal, Sumantra (2005) Bad management theories are destroying good management practices', *Academy of Management Learning and Education*, 4 (1), March: 75–91.

Nurturing the Divide: Toward Maximizing the Value of Management Research from both Sides of the Atlantic

C. Marlena Fiol and Edward J. O'Connor

THE DIVIDE

The push-pull dynamic that seems to characterize the relations between N. American and European management scholars is fascinating – and dysfunctional. The Academy of Management (AoM) has attempted to be inclusive of non-N. American (e.g. European, the focus of this note) traditions by claiming to 'internationalize', while simultaneously holding tightly onto N. American research standards and norms. Europeans have responded on the one hand by increasing their membership in the AoM and linking their associations to the AoM, and on the other hand, by increasingly emphasizing in their associations all of the ways that their research is *not* like N. American research. On both sides, there is both a pull toward integration and a push for separation. We seem to be enmeshed in a no-win situation.

The Pull to internationalize the AoM and the Push against changing standards and norms

In his 1998 Presidential address to the AoM, Bill Starbuck projected (based on trends at the time) that more than half of the Academy's members would be living outside the United States within just a few years. To address this trend, the AoM leadership has attempted to become a global society by broadening participation in governance and editorial processes and by expanding its family of associations. For example, it belongs to the International Federation of Scholarly Associations of Management (IFSAM), a global organization explicitly aimed at fostering international cooperation. And the European Group for Organizational Studies (EGOS) and the European Academy of Management (EURAM) are a part of the AoM's 'family' of Associated Societies.

At its core, however, few doubt that the AoM remains solidly North American. The officers and the power structure of the academy and its journals are decidedly N. American. Twelve of the 15 Board members, all editors of the AoM's journals, and 72 of the 79 AoM Fellows are N. American! Many N. Americans view European management research as 'sloppy' café conversations, based on very little systematic data of any kind, which provides a strong motivation to push to keep United States standards firmly in place. Here's an example: Members of one of the divisions of the AoM recently received a questionnaire on the quality of journals that did not even include a European journal on the list!

It is hardly surprising that the number of new international members has not reached the 50% level Starbuck predicted in his 1998 address; out of the 16,151 AoM members in April of 2006, only about one-third live outside the United States. According to one informant, many members of the associated European conferences 'hate the AoM', but the AoM doesn't seem to notice, continuing to believe that it is, in fact, successfully 'internationalizing'.

Continued

The Push to differentiate European research and the Pull to legitimize it through N. American affiliations

At the same time, European scholars are pushing to differentiate their work from N. American research. According to informants, Europe's largest management associations were explicitly formed as a counterbalance to the AoM. As early as 1973, EGOS was founded as an intellectual antidote to N. American management theory and research, regarded by one EGOSian as 'second rate, managerialist, highly reductionist and with little grounding in the social sciences'.

More recently (2000), EURAM was formed, again explicitly to counter AoM's positivist perspective, and to foster a more eclectic European approach to research. Its journal, the *European Management Review*, has the ambition of being the journal of first choice for management scholars, especially drawing on untapped intellectual resources from outside of N.A. The *EMR-AMR* ('*European*' rather than what is often referred to as the '*American*' *Management Review*) contrarian symbolism is hard to miss!

The push for European differentiation has been as schizophrenic as AoM's pull for internationalization, however. There is no doubt that many would like Europe to develop its own distinctive orientation and research products – e.g. a distinct accreditation standard. At the same time, however, the European accreditation organization has recently negotiated a cooperative agreement with the N. American accreditation board (AACSB). And despite the desire to be different than the AoM and its standards, many seem pleased with the legitimacy that European associations may gain by attracting N. American participants.

ALL OF THIS IS NOT SURPRISING

In his research on the deep-rooted Israeli-Palestinian conflicts, Kelman (2001) described a negative interdependence between the identities of the groups, such that asserting one group's identity requires opposing the identity of the other. We have found a similar pattern of negative interdependence in other arenas of conflict (Fiol et al., 2006): In many cases each group's identity is actually defined by the fact that they are *not* the 'other'. Does this sound familiar?

Attempting to integrate conflicting groups into a single transcendent whole without first developing within each group a respected and secure sense of separateness will have predictable consequences: (1) Each group's own identity will be too threatened to acknowledge the value of the 'other', and (2) the potentially valuable unique contributions of each group are watered down through necessary compromises. In other words, premature integration will violate the core of both sides, leading to the schizophrenic push-pull dynamics we have described.

MUTUAL EXCHANGE AND COOPERATION RATHER THAN INTEGRATION

Integration is an over-rated concept that is not likely to get us what we want even if European and N. American associations were to become much more 'international'. Not surprisingly, dual-identity researchers (e.g. Gaertner et al., 1999) are beginning to provide empirical evidence that relations among groups with conflicting identities are likely to be more cooperative when each group maintains a strong and distinctive sense of its differentiated self along with a feeling of togetherness with the 'other', than when only the togetherness is emphasized.

This implies a way out of our push-pull dynamic that entails nurturing the distinctive differences of each group. It implies a celebration of what is uniquely American about the AoM, and a celebration of what is uniquely European about European associations. Most important, it requires a shift from a group identity based on 'who we are *not*', to a deep appreciation within each group of 'who we are' to successfully move down this path. European associations, such as EURAM, which were originally formed partially in opposition to the AoM, are beginning to establish their identity as unique and distinctive societies. From the perspective of dual identity theory, it is important for them to continue to nurture their own separateness and to fulfill their own distinctive needs before attempting to associate too closely with other groups.

We were told that when EGOS began, it was expressly intended to be an upscale management association for Europeans. N. Americans were allowed to present, but not to chair their sessions/tracks. According to some EGOSians, it is becoming more AoM-like with more Americans running tracks. From the perspective of dual identity theory, this is an unfortunate trend that does not nurture the differences that make each group unique.

Complete and lasting separation among the scholarly groups from both sides of the Atlantic is certainly not the desired end. However, to bring incompatible groups such as these together, they must first be pulled apart and strengthened separately. Steps leading to the needed separation and strengthening include:

1 Identify and loosen the schizophrenic connections that keep each group negatively tethered to the other (e.g. discourage self-definitions based on *not* being like 'them').
2 Promote and nourish the differentiated identity of each separate group (e.g. communicate and celebrate the impact on the field of the group's work; develop a clear and relevant measurement system for documenting the value of the work).
3 Promote a sense of belonging within each group (e.g. instill pride in belonging to one's own group; establish frequent meaningful contact among ingroup members; make membership in the group highly visible).

The ultimate objective is for European and N. American (as well as other) research communities to feel strength in their separate and distinct identities in order to then, simultaneously, feel a bond of commitment to a common research cause. To attempt integration and commonality before separating and strengthening is only likely to lead to more schizophrenic and highly dysfunctional behaviors. Only after finding our own separate and unique sources of strength can we honestly ask what it is that we can accomplish as a global research community that we cannot accomplish separately, and how those outcomes may be valuable for both (all) groups.

REFERENCES

Fiol, C.M., Pratt, M.G. and O'Connor, E.J. (2006) 'Towards a model of managing entrenched identity conflicts'. Working paper, University of Colorado-Denver.

Continued

Gaertner, S.L., Dovidio, J.F., Nier, J.A., Ward, C.M. and Banker, B.S. (1999) 'Across cultural divides: The value of a superordinate identity', in D.A. Prentice and D.T. Miller (eds) *Cultural Divides: Understanding and Overcoming Group Conflict*, New York: Russell Sage Foundation. pp. 173–212.

Kelman, H.C. (2001) 'The role of national identity in conflict resolution', in R.D. Ashmore, L. Jussim and D. Wilder (eds), *Social Identity, Intergroup Conflict, and Conflict Reduction* New York: Oxford University Press. pp. 187–212.

Organization and Management Studies: An End in Itself or a Means Towards a Better Social and Economic life?

Tony Watson

Coming to terms with the unintended consequences of human actions and initiatives is one of the greatest recurring challenges that the human species has faced since it first invented societies. And handling the ways in which *means* tend to subvert *ends* has been a particular issue for the species since it invented bureaucracies. Taking its lead from Max Weber, organization theory has been especially concerned with the issue of means failing to lead to the ends which they were devised to achieve – most notoriously with bureaucracy coming to exist for bureaucracy's sake.

Organization and management studies provide us with powerful resources for understanding the processes whereby means become ends in themselves. They have the potential to inform choices and organizational practices which might lead to more effective links between intentions and effects. But is the potential being realised? Might not organization and management studies be in danger of becoming ends in themselves? I suggest that there is a real danger of this happening. There are several ways in which this might be happening in the business and management schools, the organizations where, for better or worse, organization and management studies have their home.

The very organization of organization and management studies is at the heart of the problem here. There is a complex division of labour at work. This too readily functions more as an end in itself than as a route towards something else. There are divisions of labour which reflect divisions in organizations themselves (marketing, operations management, human resource management, for example). On top of this are divisions which reflect the varying scholarly or disciplinary backgrounds and commitments of teachers and researchers (economics, engineering, psychology, sociology, mathematics). Making all this even more complicated, there are divisions between those who give their work a critical social scientific emphasis and those who give it a more 'applied' emphasis.

At the risk of being accused of intellectual imperialism, I would suggest that organization theory has considerable unrealized potential as a *means* of pulling things together in the application of social science to business and managerial issues. Unfortunately, however, organization theory has tended to become an *end* in itself. The 'academic subject' has become more important to many of its practitioners than its 'subject matter'. After a close examination of a series of recently published books in organization studies (Watson, 2006), I observed what might be characterized as a highly dysfunctional level of dissension among scholars and suggested that these authors might be 'condemning organization studies to a life at the margins of both the academy and the world of practice'. Surely, I suggested in my pain, 'organizational studies can ... aspire to be something more than the plaything of disengaged intellectuals disputing with each other over their theories and paradigms in the privacy of their academic playground'.

There are no simple prescriptions that can be offered to bring intellectual means more into line with social ends in the organizational sphere. Some bold suggestions can be ventured, however. At the level of business schools in general, thought needs to be given

Continued

to identifying a common task that can be shared across the divisions and departments. This, I suggest, should be one of *improving our understanding of the organizing and managing of the invention, production and distribution of goods, services, and the administration of public life*. And if organization theory is going to offer itself as a key means towards achieving this end, serious attention needs to be given to calming down the methodological disputes which cripple it. This does not mean developing a bland unified organization theory but working, instead, in a spirit of *pragmatic pluralism*. This would prioritize the analysis of organizational patterns and processes occurring outside the academy, with much greater direct interaction between organizational actors and academic researchers. Theoretical texts and concepts would be treated as means to understanding the organizational world and not as ends in themselves. As long as they are deployed within an epistemologically and ontologically consistent manner within each separate study, concepts from across the social sciences would be drawn upon. But the key criterion for judging the studies which emerge from this activity would be that of how effectively they inform the practices of those who study them in our business schools or read them elsewhere – be those people managers, workers, policy makers or social commentators. Organization and management studies cannot directly improve social and economic life but it can do a great deal more than it currently does to inform the choices that members of society make with regard to organizations and their management.

REFERENCE

Watson, Tony J. (2006) 'The organization and disorganization of organization studies' (review essay), *Journal of Management Studies*, 43 (2): 367–382.

The Tyranny of Theory

Olav Sorenson

What do I currently see as the biggest impediment to the advancement of a science of management and organizations? Theory – or at least what I will call the 'tyranny of theory'.

The tyranny of theory manifests itself in many forms. It is the editor who rejects a manuscript for its lack of theoretical novelty or for its expected – often referred to as 'obvious' – empirical findings. It is the reviewer who complains that a paper does not have explicit, or (more absurdly) a large enough number of, hypotheses. It is the author who assigns new terminology to existing ideas. It is the reader denigrating a paper for its lack of a 'big idea'.

One can most easily see the consequence of this oppression in what does *not* appear in print in the most influential journals in the field. One rarely sees articles identifying important but unexplained empirical regularities, bringing higher quality or more detailed data to bear on ideas proposed in earlier papers, re-examining the magnitude of effects using more appropriate and sophisticated estimation techniques or identification strategies, or replicating the results of prior studies in new settings or on different data sets. Yet the advancement of any science relies on all of these types of papers.

Where did we go astray? The problem resides not with theory itself. Any improvement in our understanding of the world requires that we iterate between observing, developing models (theory) to explain what we observe, and then scrutinizing their ability to predict behavior in new settings. The problem instead stems from the fact that students of management and organizations have come to worship 'theory' as an idol – somehow superior to the empirical observation and theory testing stages of the scientific endeavor. Though I cannot say when exactly this belief emerged, one can easily see how it persists. Young scholars feel obliged to acquiesce to accumulate the publications necessary to gain tenure, and through the feedback they receive on their own submissions, future reviewers and editors become indoctrinated into the religion that all papers must propose new theory.

In this fetish, we are not alone. To some extent, the idolization of theory pervades the social sciences. So many economists have engaged in model building that in many subfields at least one causal story exists to explain any conceivable empirical observation. And, as in the management literature, sociologists have a penchant for developing new theory tailored to each specific empirical setting. Though one might reprove their relative frequency, theory testing and other forms of more purely empirical research are nonetheless alive and well in both of these disciplines. In the field of management and organizations, however, this imbalance has reached a level verging on monotheism.

As a consequence, knowledge does not accrete. With few notable exceptions – such as organizational ecology or the research on 'structural holes' – we do not engage in research programs. Rather, nearly every paper develops 'novel' theory and uses different measures. We cannot compare results across studies. We cannot say whether most theories apply outside the very narrow contexts in which they have been developed. Trying to understand whether the vast majority of the literature amounts to anything beyond idiosyncratic rationalizations of empirical regularities in specific settings amounts to a Sisyphean task.

Continued

The irony then is that the tyranny of theory has actually stonewalled advancement; despite hundreds of papers detailing thousands of person-years of research, our understanding of management and organizations has advanced surprising little in the last two decades.

A remedy exists. Together we can end this tyranny through individual acts of heresy. Authors can write purely empirical papers – replicating existing results in new settings, re-estimating previous models with new techniques, and simply describing interesting phenomena. Reviewers and editors can evaluate papers on the basis of the quality of their data and analysis rather than on their theoretical novelty and importance. Those intent on engaging in theory can allocate their efforts to reducing the existing menagerie of ideas by identifying equivalencies, redundancies, and special cases.

Ten years down the road, we may have – indeed I hope we will have – matured and look back at the current state of the field with a somewhat fond reminiscence of the foolishness of our floundering. Or we may instead find ourselves facing a field-level mid-life crisis – futilely attempting to relive an adolescence when scholars roamed virgin intellectual territory and thought big thoughts.

That's Important!
Making a Difference with Organizational Research

Adam M. Grant, Jane E. Dutton, and Brent D. Rosso

Organizational scholars care about doing interesting research that captures attention, engages readers, and generates novel insights (Davis, 1971; Bartunek et al., 2006). There is growing concern in our field, however, that interesting research is not necessarily important research. Some have suggested that our research is irrelevant and may even harm managerial practice (Ghoshal, 2005). In response, attention has begun to shift toward conducting research that truly matters, has impact, and makes a social contribution. Despite energy in the field around conducting research that makes a difference, there is little agreement about what 'making a difference' actually means – is it enriching theory, educating students, offering clear direction for managers, or improving public policy and human well-being? Our objective here is to invite deeper consideration of what scholars can do, individually and collectively, to conduct organizational research that makes a difference.

As we examine calls for organizational research that has impact, two questions come to the forefront. First, *for whom* do we want to make a difference (i.e., who are our beneficiaries)? Second, *how* do we want to make a difference (i.e., what forms of impact can we have)? The different audiences we target as beneficiaries of our efforts shape the form that our impact takes. For example, defining fellow academics as beneficiaries implies making a difference primarily by advancing knowledge, while defining students as beneficiaries implies making a difference by sharing this knowledge and making it relevant to students' lives. Defining managers as beneficiaries implies making a difference by making this knowledge practical, while defining communities and societies as beneficiaries implies making a difference by linking the knowledge to policy. Whom do we want to impact? How do we want to make a difference? We propose that deliberate reflection upon these questions is a critical step in enabling difference-making. However, personal reflection alone is not sufficient; we also need to consider the institutional practices that support or undermine our efforts to make a difference. Although many of us are attracted to the field by the prospect of making a difference, achieving these aspirations is much more challenging. We consider three changes in institutional practices that may enable organizational scholars to more effectively make a difference.

First, we propose changes in doctoral education practices. Every organizational scholar faces two charges: producing knowledge and communicating knowledge. Our doctoral training, however, focuses disproportionately on producing knowledge at the expense of communicating it. Suppose we took the communication dimension of scholarship seriously, redefining writing as an art form and public speaking as a performance. We might design courses to provide training in writing, presentation, and public speaking skills to teach doctoral students to communicate their ideas with greater impact and to a broader range of beneficiaries. Such training might better equip scholars to be public intellectuals, with greater access and impact through effective use of a broader range of media. Such training might also aid in capturing the attention of managers and other organizational

Continued

knowledge users, as scholars might be better equipped to make transparent the relevance of organizational research to managers' daily activities.

Second, we suggest changes in academic incentive systems. Current incentive systems reward us for narrowing our questions and can thwart attempts to make a difference beyond our classrooms. Until we reach tenure, we are discouraged from writing books, consulting for organizations, and speaking to public policy. If our aim is to motivate more organizational scholars to seek and create opportunities to make a difference, we need more incentives and rewards for doing so.

Third, we believe that new forms of academic-practitioner dialogues need to be introduced. In current conversations, academics and practitioners often do not occupy the same dialogical or physical space. Designing conferences at which academics and practitioners can share knowledge and ideas on equal ground is one step toward traversing these boundaries. We might also champion and cultivate new communication forums such as interactive websites and blogs for scholars, practitioners, and policymakers to discuss key problems, challenges, and opportunities in organizational life.

These are just a few ideas for how organizational scholars can have a broader and more lasting impact. We encourage organizational scholars to identify other ways to make a difference and reflect on the particular beneficiaries and forms of impact that matter to them – *for whom* and *how* do we want to make a difference? We also encourage organizational scholars to collaborate and innovate in improving doctoral education, incentive systems, and academic-practitioner dialogues. We hope this brief discussion of difference-making will make a difference in how organizational scholars conduct and communicate research, as well as how we structure the institutional practices that undergird our scholarly endeavors.

REFERENCES

Bartunek, J.M., Rynes, S.L. and Ireland, R.D. (2006) 'What makes management research interesting, and why does it matter?', *Academy of Management Journal*, 49: 9–15.

Davis, M.S. (1971) 'That's interesting!: Toward a phenomenology of sociology and a sociology of phenomenology', *Philosophy of Social Science*, 1: 309–344.

Ghoshal, S. (2005) 'Bad management theories are destroying good management practices', *Academy of Management Learning & Education*, 4: 75–91.

Some Thoughts About Trade-Offs

Angelo S. DeNisi

A few years ago, I was asked to participate on a panel that dealt with the trade-offs between relevance and rigor. I thought it would be fun (and it was), but I remembered asking why anyone would consciously choose one over the other. I still wonder why someone would make such a choice, but I realize that much of our research involves some type of trade-off, even if not quite as dramatic as the one discussed at that panel. Yet, I believe that there are some trade-offs we cannot afford to make as a field if we hope to progress. I thought I'd comment on some of these 'non-negotiables'.

I am old enough that, when I was completing my graduate program, most studies employed relatively simple analytical methods. These did not necessarily make these studies better, but it was easier to understand what was actually going on in the study. Statistical techniques have become much more sophisticated and complex. There are many issues, stemming from problems of levels of analysis, that can be addressed by using hierarchical linear modeling, and that would otherwise be difficult to address. Path models help us understand issues of potential causality better than simple regression. Yet, I am concerned that some authors are willing to trade-off clarity for statistical sophistication, and this makes it more difficult for our research to have the impact it should. I am not suggesting that we should abandon more sophisticated statistical techniques, but I do feel that we need to make extra effort to make sure that all our readers understand what we are really saying in our papers.

Another trade-of involving measurement and analysis that we cannot afford to make is between measurement and theory. We use more sophisticated statistical and measurement techniques because they are useful tools to help us address important issues. They are not an end unto themselves, and they cannot replace or compensate for good theory. I often read papers that seem to be more about applying a new technique rather than about answering an important question. Empirical studies still need to be driven by strong theory and construct-valid measures.

The globalization of business has led to a globalization of our field and our research, and this has resulted in another potential trade-off that I don't believe we can afford to make. Some authors seem to believe that unique samples are a good substitute for good theory. Although I see fewer papers that seem to accept this trade-off, the problem persists. Multi-national studies require theory as well as do studies employing single samples. The fact that no one ever compared the levels of job commitment among workers in France and those in Nigeria, for example, is not sufficient justification for conducting a study comparing the two. There needs to be some reason why we would expect there to be such differences and some theory for why these differences might be important.

When I participated in that panel, I think I came down hard on the side of rigor. I guess I still would, but I have come to believe that good theory is at least as important as rigor, and therefore, I think our field is harmed by any trade-off involving strong theory. I believe it was Kurt Lewin who said there is nothing so practical as a good theory. I want to close by echoing that sentiment and adding that there is also no substitute for good theory – if we expect to progress as a field.

Shifting Sands in Communities of Scholars

Greg Northcraft

The landscape of academic research and publishing in business schools has endured a subtle but fundamental transformation in the last few decades. It's no longer *authors* who are competing for space in the top journals. Instead, the entity of academic competition is now the authorship *team*. When the top academic business schools first opened their doors, virtually all submissions were single-authored; today the single-authored publication is a rare feat.

And no wonder – the average article length seems to be continually increasing as are the number of citations and the length of methods sections (Schminke and Mitchell, 2003). In other words, it takes a more complex contribution to get published in a top journal today than it used to. A more complex contribution requires more creativity and innovation, and perhaps a more stunning array of skills and expertise. It should not be terribly surprising, then, that the growth of co-authorship has coincided with a technological shrinking of the *de facto* distance among potential collaborators – first by overnight document delivery, then fax, and finally the ubiquitous e-mail. Today e-mail is the vehicle that enables far-flung collaborations, and in doing so may be fueling an escalating 'arms race' of idea complexity in research.

This sounds good for the field, doesn't it? But there is a cloud to this silver lining. Technology that makes it easier to connect with those far away also makes it less necessary to connect with those close by. When I first started my own academic career 25 years ago, we had a *local* community of scholars because that was really the only community that was possible. Long-distance telephones calls were prohibitively expensive, travel budgets were limited, fax machines were a twinkle in someone's eye, and the idea of e-mail – well, that was inconceivable. So I worked with the diverse scholars around me – diverse because most schools can't afford to hire people who do the same thing – and our collaborations provided the glue that held our community of scholars together. A brief read through management journals 25 years ago confirms that at the time, local collaborations were the rule.

Today, e-mail has redefined the reference community of scholars for many of my colleagues. Distant collaborations – certainly cross-country but even cross-national – are now as much the rule as the exception. This raises questions for the future of the local community of scholars, for research, and perhaps for the definition of what it means to be a university faculty member. If your department hires a new addition to its local community of scholars who arrives on the local scene but continues (via technology) to work primary with prior collaborators elsewhere, what have you actually added to the local scholarly community? Technology may make it easy to collaborate with a diverse co-authorship team, but the attractiveness and comfort of similar others (and the start-up costs of working with dissimilar others) suggests that technology may lead scholars to invest primarily in relationships with those like them. Thus, while technology may make it possible to reach a more diverse set of collaborators, in fact it can also be used to maintain contact with a very similar set of collaborators, rather than (without technology) braving local collaboration with dissimilar others.

In a related vein, a few years ago my university began to think that distributed learning models might provide an effective vehicle to fulfill the outreach obligations entailed in its land-grant heritage. Distributed learning allows students who can't be physically present to nevertheless participate, for example by e-commuting into a classroom via the internet. Of course, the perfection of this technology will mean that not only students can e-commute into the classroom – so can their professors! Its one sort of problem if the students are never on campus, but it seems something else together if the faculty aren't. Is that really what the university of the future is supposed to look like? Perhaps I'm a bit 'old school,' but I think a lot of my best collaborations were born of the informal contact of regular social interaction with colleagues – coffee, lunch, 'happy hour' – the kind of informal contact that can't happen over e-mail.

The technological 'shrinking' of the world accomplishes a lot of good – like the possibility of working from home or collaborating with friends overseas – so it's a genie we can't put back in the bottle. What we can do is try to acknowledge, understand, and manage the subtle effects of technological advances. For a local community of scholars, those effects include substituting all those great new things we can do now for all the things we used to have to do – like being at work and talking to the person in the office next door.

REFERENCE

Schminke, M. and Mitchell, M. (2003) 'From the Editors: In the beginning…' *Academy of Management Journal*, 46 (3): 279–282.

Multiparadigm Inquiry: Exploring Organizational Pluralism and Paradox

MARIANNE W. LEWIS and MIHAELA L. KELEMEN

ABSTRACT   Organization studies is a robust field, replete with diverse, often contentious perspectives that may enrich understandings of pluralism and paradox. Yet polarization of modern paradigms and ruptures between modern and postmodern stances may inhibit researchers from tapping this potential. In response, this article delves into a provocative alternative – multiparadigm inquiry. First, we juxtapose modern, postmodern and multiparadigm approaches to contrast their underlying assumptions. We then review three multiparadigm strategies, exploring their objectives, exemplars and limitations. Our conclusion addresses how multiparadigm inquiry fosters greater reflexivity, while posing considerable challenges.

KEYWORDS   multiparadigm ▪ paradigm ▪ paradox ▪ pluralism ▪ reflexivity

Pluralism and paradox are inherent features of contemporary life. Dramatic technological and cultural changes continue to blur traditional boundaries – occupational, institutional and national – and complicate the social milieu. Organizations, for instance, face seemingly contradictory demands for control *and* autonomy, coordination *and* individuality, expansion *and* contraction (Bouchikhi, 1998). Meanwhile, to comprehend such tensions, researchers increasingly veer from the dominant positivist paradigm, exploring interpretivist, critical and postmodern perspectives.

Awareness of the uncertainty and flexibility of knowledge is energizing the social sciences (Holland, 1999). This energy is evident in the evolving 'paradigm debate.' Despite his varied definitions, Kuhn (1970) stressed that a paradigm provides a worldview. As such, a paradigm offers coherent assumptions regarding how the world should be studied – assumptions that attract an enduring community of scholars, yet remain sufficiently open-ended to encompass diverse research problems. Subsequent scholars (e.g. Burrell & Morgan, 1979) specified sets of assumptions to distinguish multiple and co-existing paradigms, fuelling arguments over paradigm dominance (e.g. Donaldson, 1998) and commensurability (e.g. Jackson & Carter, 1991). Postmodernists deepen the discussion, critiquing paradigm constraints in favor of eclectic and fluid discourses (e.g. Chia, 1996).

As the paradigm debate continues, the social sciences appear increasingly fragmented and reflexive. Organization studies offers a case in point. The field has become marked by numerous, deep-seated divisions, illustrated by conflicts over the roles of structure versus agency and causation versus meaning in research (Weaver & Gioia, 1994). Such tensions intensified in Europe during the 1980s and early 1990s, and recently gained relevance in North America. Despite their differences, most researchers on both sides of the Atlantic now recognize that a single paradigm is necessarily limiting, helping expose certain facets of organizations, while obscuring others (Burrell, 1996; Weick, 1999). This recognition has fostered growing interest in a provocative alternative – multiparadigm inquiry. Multiparadigm advocates use divergent paradigm lenses to contrast their varied representations and explore plurality and paradox (e.g. Lewis & Grimes, 1999; Schultz & Hatch, 1996; Ybema, 1996). Indeed Mingers (1997) praised organization studies for exemplifying reflexivity and encouraging multiparadigm interests in the 'hard sciences' (e.g. physics, biology, operations research).

Nevertheless, multiparadigm inquiry remains under-utilized for three primary reasons. First, exemplars have yet to articulate an explicit philosophical framework for this approach (Mingers, 1997). Scherer (1998) claimed that multiparadigm inquiry offers a midpoint between the extremes of modern dogmatism and postmodern relativism, but questioned the assumptions on which it is based. For if all approaches rely on an underlying ideology, ontology, and/or epistemology, then what are the foundations of a multiparadigm perspective? Second, researchers need further guidance regarding multiparadigm strategies. Recent works examine specific strategies (e.g. Lewis & Grimes, 1999; Schultz & Hatch, 1996), but researchers lack a deeper appreciation of their value and challenges (Mingers, 1997). Third, discussions of research implications have stopped short. Scholars need to engage in more 'disciplined reflexivity' (Weick, 1999), questioning the impact of multiparadigm inquiry on researchers' perceptions of organizational life and their own work.

This article addresses each of these issues in turn, thereby extending understandings of multiparadigm inquiry. We begin by building a framework that contrasts multiparadigm assumptions with those of modern and post-modern stances. We then discuss three multiparadigm strategies, extending Lewis and Grimes' (1999) recent review by further examining their merits and limitations. Selected and highly diverse exemplars illustrate how researchers have applied each strategy to explore plurality and paradox. Our conclusion delves into the implications of multiparadigm inquiry, its value as well as its philosophical, cognitive, and cultural challenges.

Toward a multiparadigm framework

The fate of our times, one might think, would be such as to encourage a profound pluralism with respect to interpretation . . . Yet pluralism need not mean nihilism; that anything is as good as anything else, that any interpretation will do.

(Clegg, 1990: 16)

Seeking to comprehend rising organizational tensions, researchers have produced an explosion of varied, often contentious approaches. Modern and postmodern stances, for example, offer contrasting positions in the paradigm debate. Modern paradigms multiply, aiding construction of distinct and static representations (c.f. Burrell & Morgan, 1979; Morgan, 1997), as post-modernists question paradigm constraints, applying eclectic methods to expose contradictions and fluidity (c.f. Hassard & Parker, 1994; Kilduff & Mehra, 1997). Such theoretical diversity may enrich understandings of pluralism and paradox. Yet polarization of modern paradigms and ruptures between modern and postmodern stances inhibit researchers from tapping this potential.

In light of this challenge, Clegg (1990) claimed that role of researchers becomes that of 'interpreters,' translating, penetrating and investigating different *modes of rationality*. Multiparadigm inquiry facilitates this role, linking modern desires for order and stability with postmodern emphases on flux and fragmentation (Scherer, 1998). To clarify its philosophical underpinnings, we contrast multiparadigm inquiry with modern and postmodern stances. Our framework, summarized in Table 1, operates at a particularly high level of abstraction. For instance, while paradigms promote *specific epistemological assumptions*, modern and postmodern stances offer varied views of the *nature of epistemology*. Given their fictitious distinctions, however, modern, post-modern and paradigmatic labels are clearly problematic. We juxtapose these

Table 1 Alternative approaches to inquiry

	Modern	Multiparadigm	Postmodern
Ideology	**Centering**	**Accommodating**	**De-centering**
	Focus on authorship, promote chosen voices, beliefs and issues	Value divergent paradigm lenses	Stress fluctuating and fragmented discourses
	Sharpen selective focus	Explore paradox and plurality	Accentuate difference and uncertainty
Ontology	**Strong**	**Stratified**	**Weak**
	States of being	Multiple dimensions	Processes of becoming
	Entities are distinct, determinant and comprehensible	Expose interplay of entities and processes	Meanings are indeterminant, in constant flux and transformation
Epistemology	**Restricted**	**Pluralist**	**Eclectic**
	Employ paradigm prescriptions systematically	Apply divergent paradigm lenses	Use varied methods freely
	Construct cohesive representations to advance paradigm development	Reflect organizational tensions and encourage greater reflexivity	Deconstruct organizational contexts and processes to produce small stories or modest narratives

'ideal types' not to enforce social conventions, but to stress differences and interconnections relevant to multiparadigm inquiry. Furthermore, modern and postmodern distinctions are not meant to canvas all possible approaches to organization studies, but to accentuate opposing positions in the evolving paradigm debate.

Modern paradigms: Cohesive and static representations

For decades scholars have mapped paradigms, examining distinct sets of assumptions and their impacts on researcher' worldviews. Burrell and Morgan (1979), for example, parsed four paradigms by delineating disparate ontological and epistemological assumptions. Others review extant studies to depict how empirically derived and socially constructed ideologies differentiate paradigm perspectives (e.g. Alvesson, 1987; Zey-Ferrell & Aiken, 1981). Despite many variations, such maps polarize paradigms into seemingly incommensurable sets of ideologies, ontologies and/or epistemologies. From postmodern stances, however, paradigms exhibit philosophical similarities based

on their common modernity. Modern paradigms share beliefs in Enlightenment notions of 'progress' and 'reason,' stressing the ability to logically discriminate among alternatives and construct cohesive and static representations
of organizational life (Cooper & Burrell, 1988).

Ideology signifies assumptions regarding the focal point of research;
assumptions that necessarily privilege some voices, beliefs and issues over
others. From modernist stances, ideologies appear *centered* on the subject.
The author assumes omnipotence, detailing certain facets of the subject, and
ignoring others, to reduce uncertainty and deepen understandings. Some
paradigms promote a selective focus because they are certain of its 'truth
claims' (e.g. positivism as posed by Donaldson, 1998), others because such
privileging is deemed a moral responsibility (e.g. critical theory as advocated
by Parker, 1995). By sharpening researchers' perspectives, modern paradigms may foster insights into particular organizational tensions. For
example, a positivist lens helps address issues pertinent to managers. To
enhance organizational performance, researchers may examine means of
coping with the paradoxical need to divide and coordinate work. Yet
modernism is not confined to a managerialist center, also encompassing
paradigms that amplify typically silenced voices in hopes of igniting the
emancipation potential of the Enlightenment (Hassard, 1994). A critical
lens, for instance, may expose how labor interests oppose managerial pre-
rogatives, highlighting the unintended consequences of power asymmetries
in organizations.

Ontology denotes assumptions about the nature of reality. Modern
paradigms promote *strong* ontologies, seeking to represent the essence of
entities – e.g. structures, meanings, and myths – within discrete 'states of
being' (Chia, 1995). This is not to say that modernists do not examine processes, for ideographic modernists certainly do. However, such processes as
structuring, sense-making and mystifying are viewed as patterned interactions, and thereby are rendered abstract and static. From this position,
phenomena appear as self-contained and comprehensible entities (e.g. social
relations, cultural symbols, control mechanisms).

Epistemological assumptions address how researchers attempt to
understand phenomena of interest, and what forms of knowledge are
considered 'scientific' (Burrell & Morgan, 1979). Adhering to a 'paradigm
mentality,' modernists presume that epistemology is necessarily *restricted* –
and restrictive – prescribing a way of knowing (i.e. research objectives,
methods) appropriate for the respective subject of study and fitting the
conventions espoused by a given research community (Grimes & Rood,
1995). By rigorously applying epistemological prescriptions, modernists
construct internally consistent representations of organizational life. In this

way, research contributes insights that refute, support or extend extant knowledge, continuously advancing paradigm development.

Yet modern stances are under increasing fire. Critics argue that paradigms have lost their value in light of on-going cultural and technological changes. Whitehead (1985), for one, questioned modernist tendencies to reify objects of inquiry, naively mistaking research abstractions for reality, and producing biased and simplistic representations (Chia, 1995). To quell pluralism or resolve paradoxes, modernists often over-rationalize or separate contradictions. In contrast, postmodernists oppose dualistic thinking (e.g. discipline/empowerment, labor/management distinctions), which may privilege one side of a duality and marginalize the other (Knights, 1997).

Postmodernism: Fragmented and fluctuating discourses

Postmodernism spans numerous, often conflicting stances including French structuralism, romanticism, phenomenology, nihilism, existentialism, and hermeneutics (Strathern, 1987 in Rosenau, 1992). Its more skeptical proponents offer pessimistic assessments of the human condition and proclaim the impossibility of truth. In contrast, affirmative stances are oriented toward process and either open to political action (i.e. resistance) or content with the recognition of visionary, non-dogmatic projects, ranging from New Age religion to New Wave life styles (Rosenau, 1992). Given its diverse strands, postmodernism remains one of the most ambiguous approaches in academia. Yet recently researchers have attempted to sketch postmodern assumptions regarding ideology (Cooper & Burrell, 1988), ontology (Chia, 1995) and epistemology (Kilduff & Mehra, 1997). Applying their insights, we broadly depict postmodernism as a challenge to existing social science knowledge that stresses fluctuating and fragmented discourses. Its advocates draw on irony, parody and allusion, seeking to refine our sensitivity to differences and our ability to tolerate the paradoxical (Lyotard, 1984).

Postmodernism advocates *de-centering* stances toward ideology. Proponents reject the notion that the human subject is the center of meaning and proclaim the 'death of the author' (Derrida, 1978). Assumptions guiding research do not simply stem from rational and autonomous choices made by the researcher, but are constituted in the interplay of discourses in which the research subjects and the researcher participate. According to Lyotard (1984), subjects struggle with an infinite number of discourses (i.e. language games) as they attempt to bolster their identity in a tenuous environment. Thus postmodernists do not pursue knowledge to reduce uncertainty, as this is an inherent feature of contemporary life. Rather they 'call attention to the margins and away from some mythical center' to expose irony, conflict and diversity (Kilduff & Mehra, 1997: 461).

Postmodern stances apply *weak* ontologies that assume an ephemeral and indeterminate reality. According to Cooper and Law (1995), modernism's 'ontology of being' emphasizes outcomes, whereas postmodernism favors an 'ontology of becoming' that views reality as a process in continuous making. Commitment to an ontology of becoming implies that researchers treat 'actions, relationships and processes as primary and therefore more "real" than social entities such as "individuals" or "organizations"' (Chia, 1995: 601). '*Reality* is in perpetual flux and transformation and hence unrepresentable through any *static* conceptual framework or paradigm of thought' (Chia, 1996: 46, italics in original). Representations are always mediated by the perceptions of the observer and the conventions of the extant knowledge systems (Calas & Smircich, 1999).

Postmodernists reject the possibility of neutral language, overarching metanarratives and a final representation of reality. Advocates assume epistemology is *eclectic*, freeing researchers to apply whatever methods they deem useful (Kilduff & Mehra, 1997). Questioning modernist claims to authority, postmodern stances encourage attempts to deconstruct taken-for-granted meanings by exploring contradictions in scientific texts and amplifying a cacophony of voices. Research helps expose the intricate cultural, historical and political contexts of organizational life, and the impacts of researchers' identities and assumptions on their findings. In sum, postmodernists recognize that 'knowledge can only be produced in "small stories" or "modest narratives," mindful of their locality in space and time and capable of adapting or disappearing as needed' (Calas & Smircich, 1999: 651).

Yet critics, typically targeting skeptical extremes, view postmodernism as a relativist quagmire, sparking jeers of irrelevance and purposeless critique. As Clegg and Hardy jest, by preferring the safety of esoteric theorizing, postmodernists may 'not only free themselves from the chore of rendering their theories intelligible to individuals who might find it difficult to decipher the words of a postmodern text, let alone derive any meaning from it; they also absolve themselves of the responsibility for doing so' (1996: 692). Likewise, Parker (1995) argued that by eschewing notions of 'reason' and 'progress,' postmodernists may disable the emancipatory project of modern critical theory. Furthermore, the collapse of distinctions debilitates the explanatory power of theory. Postmodern approaches to paradox and pluralism may foster ambivalence, losing the vitality of theoretical contradictions in praise of non-committed freedom (Koot et al., 1996).

Multiparadigm inquiry: A provocative alternative

Multiparadigm inquiry arose with early attempts to differentiate between modern paradigms and their worldviews (e.g. Alvesson, 1987; Smircich, 1983). Over time, however, multiparadigm strategies have become more varied, also seeking to employ and link divergent paradigm perspectives (see Lewis & Grimes, 1999). To clarify its underlying assumptions, we now contrast multiparadigm inquiry with modern and postmodern stances (see Table 1). This provocative alternative seeks to explore contrasting representations, which may offer 'insights into the characteristic contradictions and tensions embodied in contemporary organizations' (Reed, 1985: 201). In sum, the primary goals of a multiparadigm approach are twofold: (1) to encourage greater awareness of theoretical alternatives and thereby facilitate discourse and/or inquiry across paradigms, and (2) to foster greater understandings of organizational plurality and paradox.

Multiparadigm researchers apply an *accommodating* ideology, valuing paradigm perspectives for their potential to inform each other toward more encompassing theories. All modes of thought expose certain facets of organizational life by ignoring others: 'The (postmodern) philosophers ignore everyone; the functionalists ignore workers; critical theorists ignore managers (even oppressed managers because, in the view of many of these theorists, there is no such thing). Even ethnographers distance themselves . . . ignoring the power structures that created not only the subject but also themselves' (Clegg & Hardy, 1996: 693, parentheses in original). Multiparadigm inquiry strives to respect opposing approaches and juxtapose the partial understandings they inspire. Paradigm lenses may reveal seemingly disparate, but interdependent facets of complex phenomena.

Multiparadigm inquiry promotes a *stratified* ontology, assuming multiple dimensions of reality. Reality is at once 'made' and 'in the making' as advocates examine both entities and processes, rather than collapsing these dimensions. Social entities (e.g. structure, culture) denote contextualized heuristics, co-existing with the processes through which actors use, reproduce and transform these heuristics (Spender, 1998). According to Reed, entities and processes 'operate at different levels of abstraction that tie into each other within a stratified, multilevel, and relational model of society' (1997: 31). From this ontological foundation, organizations appear as social spaces torn in multiple directions (Bouchikhi, 1998); for despite the rise in (often subtle) entities for control, organizational actors increasingly pursue numerous, diverse, even contradictory goals.

In multiparadigm inquiry, a *pluralist* epistemology 'rejects the notion of a single reference system in which we can establish truth' as bounded rationality binds us within our own learning processes, while allowing us to explore alternatives (Spender, 1998: 235). Advocates assume that paradigm lenses help construct alternative representations, exposing different dimensions of organizational life. As each lens offers a selective focus, researchers seek multiple perspectives of particularly complex and ambiguous phenomena. Contrasting modern representations may enable more insightful understandings – e.g. revealing forces pulling toward compliance *and* resistance, empowerment *and* discipline. Yet researchers also may tap postmodern sensibilities to critique socially constructed paradigm boundaries and encourage self-reflection on the research process (e.g. Hassard, 1993; Martin, 1992). Hence, exemplars use multiple perspectives to highlight the plurality and paradoxes of organizational life, as well as the uncertainties of knowledge.

Multiparadigm inquiry values the prescriptions offered by modern paradigms, yet simultaneously disavows the claim to a singular truth. This does not imply some idyllic, 'best-of-both-worlds' approach. On the contrary, multiparadigm researchers live in a glasshouse open to attack from modernists and postmodernists alike. Some modernists would strongly refute the notion that paradigms are sense-making heuristics, rather than 'truth bearing' (e.g. Donaldson, 1998); others would critique their use as fostering fictitious research (e.g. Parker & McHugh, 1991). Meanwhile, postmodernists stress that applying paradigmatic conventions may reify their hegemony and oversimplify, or worse homogenize, their disparate understandings (Burrell, 1996). The following sections explore multiparadigm inquiry further. We review three research strategies, then come full circle to reiterate the contributions and challenges of this provocative alternative.

A guide to multiparadigm strategies

Multiparadigm inquiry celebrates paradigm proliferation for providing theoretical richness, choice and opportunity. Yet strategies for applying multiple paradigms are varied and poorly understood, limiting their accessibility to researchers (Mingers, 1997). Recently, however, Lewis and Grimes (1999) distinguished three multiparadigm strategies: multiparadigm reviews, multiparadigm research, and metaparadigm theory building. They broadly described the strategies as follows:

> Multiparadigm reviews involve recognition of divides and bridges in existing theory (e.g. characterizing paradigms X and Y), whereas multiparadigm research involves using paradigm lenses (X and Y) empirically to collect and analyze data and cultivate their diverse

representations of organizational phenomena. Lastly, in metaparadigm theory building, theorists strive to juxtapose and link conflicting paradigm insights (X and Y) within a novel understanding (Z).

(Lewis & Grimes, 1999: 673)

Building from our previous framework, this section extends Lewis and Grimes (1999) by detailing the underlying assumptions, objectives and limitations of these strategies and reviewing highly diverse exemplars (see Table 2). Although we discuss each strategy separately, Lewis and Grimes (1999) stressed their complementarity. Indeed, we view the strategies as fitting Brocklesby's (1997) depiction of multiparadigm transformation: a process through which researchers learn to recognize, use, then accommodate diverse perspectives. Multiparadigm reviews first help raise researchers' paradigm consciousness to foster greater awareness of the insights and blinders enabled by divergent lenses. Multiparadigm research then entails immersion within alternative paradigm cultures to learn experientially their languages and norms. Lastly, metaparadigm theory building helps researchers consider opposing views simultaneously, and thereby develop more accommodating understandings that reflect organizational plurality and paradox.

Multiparadigm reviews: Raising paradigm consciousness

Multiparadigm reviews examine existing literature to expose researchers' underlying and typically taken-for-granted assumptions (Lewis & Grimes, 1999). The primary goal of this strategy is to raise researchers' paradigm consciousness. According to Brocklesby (1997), most researchers operate within a single paradigm, but lack an acute sense of their theoretical predilections. Yet such awareness is critical as 'what we know of as "reality" is an active projection of our own cognitive structure . . . we see the world in terms of ourselves' (1997: 195). Multiparadigm reviews help address such questions as: What sets of assumptions do researchers apply when investigating an organizational phenomenon? And how do paradigm lenses influence what is seen/not seen? By making paradigm assumptions explicit, multiparadigm reviews may distinguish the value and limits of divergent perspectives, and foster greater self- and social reflection on the research process.

Multiparadigm reviews seek to explore the *pluralism and paradoxes of social theory*, highlighting tensions between varied theoretical viewpoints (Poole & Van de Ven, 1989). Reviewers depict paradigms as modern academic constructions that privilege – and, in turn, suppress or neglect – certain organizational voices and interests. By categorizing extant literature within a paradigm framework, reviewers distinguish the selective focus of different

Table 2   Multiparadigm strategies

	Multiparadigm reviews	Multiparadigm research	Metaparadigm theory building
Objective	Raise paradigm consciousness by distinguishing the insights and blinders of alternative lenses	Cultivate disparate representations via immersion within alternative paradigm cultures	Build more accommodating understandings by juxtaposing and linking disparate paradigm representations
Challenges	Potential for reinforcing a 'paradigm mentality'; need to avoid promoting certain lenses over others	Likelihood of contaminating representations with pre-existing assumptions; trials of learning different cultural norms	Potential for resulting theory to appear as a closed and authoritative metanarrative; difficulty of attaining a metaparadigm perspective
Exemplars	Organizations (Morgan, 1997); organizational culture (Smircich, 1983); work (Alvesson, 1987); work and technology design (Grint, 1991); structure (Gioia & Pitre, 1990); total quality management (Kelemen, 1995)	Work organization (Hassard, 1993), small-firm strategy (Graham-Hill, 1996), organization politics (Bradshaw-Camball & Murray, 1991), organizational culture (Martin, 1992)	Organizational culture (Daymon, 2000; Shultz & Hatch, 1996; Ybema, 1996), power (Gaventa, 1980), multidivisional organizations (Clegg, 1990), advanced manufacturing technology (Lewis & Grimes, 1999)

lenses. Highlighting paradigm diversity serves to open theoretical choice. As Morgan (1983) explained, research is necessarily a choice-making process, because all lenses are inherently exclusionary and parochial. By clarifying paradigm alternatives, researchers may compare their work to a wider realm of literature, recognize their theoretical predilections, and appreciate insights enabled by opposing viewpoints.

Phenomena amenable to review are open to myriad interpretations, typically demonstrated by a highly contested, fragmented and vast research domain (illustrated by the exemplars in Table 2). Reviewers examine the understandings contributed by different paradigm lenses, and critique the anomalies ignored or facets distorted at the periphery of each lens. To categorize literature within paradigms, reviewers scrutinize researchers' language. Cannella and Paetzold explained, that 'a person's position regarding a paradigm becomes most clear when he or she uses terms, such as knowledge, as though all readers will implicitly hold shared meanings of them'

(1994: 333). Some reviewers also analyze the metaphors researchers employ. Smircich (1983) and Morgan (1997) detailed diverse organizational metaphors and the images they promote – e.g. organizations as machines, organisms, brains, political systems, *and* psychic prisons.

Several reviews model this multiparadigm strategy. Alvesson (1987), for instance, sought to explore conflicting views of contemporary work. He grouped extant research within three paradigms – consensus, control and critique – that emphasize work methods, power implications and value rationality, respectively. His work exposed how each lens relies on a different point of departure, impacting researchers' depictions of the quality, degradation and self-regulation of work. Yet, in conjunction, these frames of reference help reveal the intricacies of organizational life. Similarly, Grint (1991) analyzed disparate assumptions regarding the design of work and technology. Positioning theories along a political continuum, he differentiated between technocratic and critical orientations and their resulting optimistic (i.e. skill upgrading) versus pessimistic (i.e. deskilling) representations, respectively. Along a determinist–interpretivist continuum, he distinguished paradigms according to the roles actors play in the design process, from passive observers at the mercy of inertia or macro socio-economic forces to active participants in social construction.

Gioia and Pitre (1990) reviewed alternative theory-building approaches, illustrating how opposing paradigms offer unique insights into organizational structure. Applying Burrell and Morgan's (1979) typology, they described how a functionalist deductive focus highlights stable characteristics of structure; a radical stucturalist dialectical analysis uncovers historically and politically embedded structural contradictions; interpretivist induction reveals structuring processes through which actors construct social meanings and roles; and radical humanist critiques expose reified deep structures and communicative distortions. Likewise, Kelemen (1995) explored tensions in the vast literature of total quality management (TQM). From a positivist perspective TQM is seen to be an objective phenomenon, which can be comprehended and therefore quantified and improved upon. She described TQM gurus (e.g. Juran, Deming, Peters) as applying positivist conventions to prescribe 'best practices' for implementing TQM and highlight its potential for empowerment and continuous organizational improvements. In contrast, a constructivist lens helps reveal the role of power and language in the social construction of TQM meanings and practices and the consequences these may have upon the identity making of managers and employees alike.

Critics, however, note two primary challenges of multiparadigm reviews. First, reviewers are placed in a tenuous position, seeking to accentuate paradigm diversity, but avoid reifying paradigmatic distinctions.

Ackroyd (1992) warned that multiparadigm reviews may reinforce a 'paradigm mentality' that fosters further polarization and fragmentation. Second, reviewers need to avoid promoting any particular paradigm, yet are always examining literature through their own lens. Donaldson (1998) claimed that multiparadigm reviews are simply another form of critique, whereby the reviewers bolster their favored radical approach and downplay more mainstream views. Yet 'its skill lies in the way it seems to offer an authoritative master framework that gives the impression of independence' (1998: 271). These limitations require reviewers to stress that paradigm distinctions serve as sense-making heuristics – useful guides for identifying alternative viewpoints (Lewis & Grimes, 1999). Reviewers also must remain acutely aware of their own predilections, stating their frame of reference up front and stressing the insights and biases enabled by *each* paradigm lens. These responses help balance the limits of multiparadigm reviews with their potential. For raising paradigm consciousness may help researchers 'question, possibly for the first time, the veracity of the claim that the social consensus surrounding a paradigm's body of knowledge somehow represents proof of the truth' (Brocklesby, 1997: 200). Such awareness opens space for researchers to question, appreciate and even embrace alternative perspectives.

Multiparadigm research: Cultivating diverse representations

Paradigms aid construction of distinct explanations of phenomena; contestable and provisional representations dependent upon a researcher's choice of lens (Knights, 1997). Multiparadigm research seeks to cultivate diverse representations, detailing the images highlighted by varied lenses. Applying the conventions prescribed by alternative paradigms, researchers develop contrasting or multi-sided accounts that may depict the ambiguity and complexity of organizational life. Morgan (1983) described the resulting representations as similar to Allison's (1971) case studies of the Cuban Missile Crisis, but grounded in more disparate assumptions.

Multiparadigm research entails exploring paradigms from *within*, applying divergent lenses empirically to collect and analyze data. Using an anthropological metaphor, Hassard (1993) explained that researchers immerse themselves within varied paradigm cultures, familiarizing themselves with their differing linguistic and methodological norms. According to Brocklesby (1997), such immersion enables experiential learning that further elevates paradigm consciousness. By recognizing the viability of each representation, researchers may experience first-hand the tensions of theoretical pluralism and paradox. Ideally, this strategy engages researchers more fully in a quest for understanding – an understanding that encourages tolerance, preserves theoretical diversity, and fosters non-obsessive uses of paradigm lenses (Flood & Romm, 1997).

Multiparadigm researchers immerse themselves within each chosen paradigm in turn. Keeping lenses and emerging representations separate helps respect the integrity of their disparate assumptions (Martin, 1992). Resulting representations seek to depict the organizational voices, concerns and interests magnified by opposing lenses. However, analyses of a common phenomenon may demonstrate that paradigm images need not operate at the extremes, but may overlap and foster counterintuitive insights. During the analytical process, researchers often comment that paradigm distinctions appear increasingly ambiguous and fluid, revealing their focus on interwoven dimensions of organizational life (Lewis & Grimes, 1999).

Illustrating this strategy, Hassard (1993) examined a work organization – a British Fire Service – using Burrell and Morgan's four 'analytic cameras.' To apply seemingly incommensurable lenses, he approached construction of multiple representations as an exploration into 'the language-games of everyday life.' Employing Wittgenstein's notions, paradigms appeared to accent diverse and equal discourses predicated upon their distinct cultural rules, yet sharing an overarching metalanguage. Whereas Hassard paired each lens with a different, paradigm-appropriate issue of work organization, Graham-Hill (1996) examined a common issue, small-firm strategy, across these paradigms. To write four stories of a family business, he conducted a series of free-flowing, stream-of-conscious interviews with its CEO, which he then analyzed using case study methods indicative of each lens. Similarly, Bradshaw-Camball and Murray (1991) used functionalist, interpretivist, and critical paradigms to investigate organizational politics. Using naturalist methods, they conducted an extensive study of hospital administration. They then analyzed the collected data using each lens, spinning three contrasting accounts of budgeting games and illusion making.

Martin (1992) applied an alternative set of lenses, avoiding Burrell and Morgan's (1979) strict emphasis on ontological and epistemological assumptions. By reviewing extant studies of culture, she identified three perspectives – integration, differentiation and fragmentation – grounded in disparate theoretical assumptions and focused on different facets of organizational culture. Using these perspectives, she sought to amplify the voices each privileged and explore their sensitivities to varied observations and explanations. Martin relied extensively on actors' quotations to represent each viewpoint, permitting each perspective to 'speak' without interruption and in its own words. The result was a paradoxical image of organizational culture as a source of harmony, a product of inherent conflicts of interest, *and* a reflection of contemporary ambiguities.

Not surprisingly, critiques of multiparadigm research abound. Parker and McHugh (1991) and Deetz (1996), for example, claimed that researchers' 'home' paradigms contaminate their use of alternative perspectives. According to Jackson and Carter (1991), true immersion within different paradigms would require a quasi-religious conversion. Weaver and Gioia (1994) responded by noting how such criticisms rely on the incommensurability thesis, which posits that meaningful communication across paradigms is impossible. Using a common analogy, they argue that cross-cultural experiences are trying for anthropologists and ordinary persons alike, but this does not negate the possibility of learning foreign languages and practices. Advocates stress that journeys to other paradigms must be approached via a desire to learn new sets of explicit and implicit research premises (i.e. techniques and values). According to Hassard (1993), multiparadigm research demands an intense suspicion of personal assumptions. Researchers must question their roles in perpetuating self-fulfilling prophecies, as findings may reproduce pre-existing views. Yet sincere attempts may prove profoundly enlightening. Martin, for instance, described applying multiple lenses, particularly those farthest from your 'home,' as therapeutic, capable of shocking researchers out of their comfort zone and aiding examination of deeply repressed explanations (1992: 177).

Metaparadigm theory building: Accommodating paradigm diversity

Metaparadigm theory building strives to enhance theorists' abilities to think paradoxically – to entertain conflicting knowledges simultaneously. According to Lewis and Grimes (1999), this strategy fosters more accommodating understandings by juxtaposing paradigm representations. Such accommodation does not imply integration, but a portrayal of theoretical tensions that reflects organizational plurality and paradox. Hence, theorists seek a higher level of abstraction from which they may explore paradigm disparity *and* complementarity (Gioia & Pitre, 1990).

Metaparadigm theory is comprised of second-order constructs, which provide a reference system for linking disparate representations (Gioia & Pitre, 1990). Second-order constructs are more abstract than typical research variables, remaining open to interpretation from varied perspectives (Reed, 1997). The result is a theory of paradigm interplay. As Schultz and Hatch (1996) explained, interplay accentuates interconnections and differences among paradigm representations, fostering an appreciation of how paradigm insights and limitations are most apparent from an opposing view. Preserving opposition invokes a creative tension that may inspire theorists to break free of traditional dualities and explore tensions, exemplified by their depict-ing culture as general *and* contextual, clear *and* ambiguous, stable *and* unstable.

Metatheorizing techniques help theorists juxtapose paradigm represen-tations in search of conflicts and patterns. For instance, conjecture inversion entails reframing broad research questions within different paradigms to identify gaps and overlaps in understandings (Gioia & Pitre, 1990). Grimes and Rood (1995) suggested using conversation techniques, viewing paradigms as debating 'voices,' presenting their views, reacting to others, elaborating dis-agreements and possibly finding shared ground. Particularly heated debates, such as those between Marxist and functionalist views, may highlight con-trasting interests. Theorists may then iterate between paradigms that provide the most *relevant* viewpoint, using switching rules based on Habermas's (1971) knowledge–interest scheme. For instance, examining a new technology, a Marxist lens may expose concerns over labor control and skills, while a func-tionalist lens highlights issues of system reliability and performance.

Alternatively, Poole and Van de Ven (1989) proposed examining para-digm representations as revealing varied spatial and/or temporal dimensions. For instance, Bradshaw-Camball and Murray (1991) suggested that their lenses expose organizational politics at different *depths*. The functionalist lens may draw attention to the surface, revealing more conscious conflicts and bases of power. An interpretivist viewpoint may then accent more sub-conscious processes of structuring reality that maintain illusions of power. Lastly, the radical lens accentuates the deep structure of politics embedded in a larger social and ideological context of asymmetrical power relations. Simi-larly, Daymon (2000) applied Martin's (1992) three perspectives, seeking to explore their interplay. She theorized that the viewpoints operate continu-ously, but their relative salience differs at certain *times*. In her study, inte-gration took precedence during the start-up of a new television station while managerial activities emphasized cohesion; fragmentation then assumed primacy as conflicts intensified over the art versus science of broadcasting; while differentiation gradually gained salience as cultural ambiguity increas-ingly appeared inherent in daily organizational life.

Further exemplars illustrate diverse approaches to metaparadigm theory building. For instance, Gaventa's (1980) metaparadigm theory of quiescence and rebellion in an Appalachian coal mine knits together con-trasting accounts based on Lukes' three dimensions of power. Similarly, Clegg (1990) used varied 'modes of rationality' to examine multidivisional organiz-ations across national cultures. Seeking a theory of postmodern organiz-ations, rather than a postmodern theory, he linked power and institutional perspectives to explore anomalies in organizational forms ignored by contingency theory. Likewise, Ybema (1996) sought to extend Martin's (1992) either/or representations, juxtaposing her cultural lenses to depict their interplay in a Dutch amusement park. He found that such conflicting views reveal shifting cultural and social relationships among workgroups, 'paradoxical patterns of unity and disunity in organizations. Boundaries between people appear and disappear: they are marked or ignored depending on the ideas, interests, and identities that are at stake, and the setting in which the interactions take place' (1996: 43).

Lewis and Grimes (1999) provided a particularly detailed example of metaparadigm theory building, which applies all three multiparadigm strategies. They first reviewed existing technology literature using Burrell and Morgan's (1979) framework. They then applied the four paradigm lenses to analyze existing case studies, written from differing paradigm orientations, and construct alternative accounts of the design of advanced manufacturing technology (AMT). Using conjecture inversion and conversation techniques, they then juxtaposed the perspectives to highlight multiple dimensions of the design process. Accenting different spatial dimensions, regulation lenses voiced managerial interests in operational effectiveness, while radical change paradigms promoted labor concerns over potential domination and control. Exposing alternative temporal dimensions, objective paradigms highlighted stable institutional properties such as design specifications, while subjective lenses helped depict dynamic, underlying processes of their social construction. In conjunction, AMT design appeared as a disruptive and paradoxical social process that is simultaneously empowering and deskilling, determined and chosen.

Metaparadigm theory building is arguably the most provocative of multiparadigm strategies for two reasons. First, from postmodern stances, theorists open themselves to the criticism of having replaced paradigm representations with simply another, albeit more inclusive, metanarrative. In response, theorists often conclude by encouraging further inquiry, stressing that results are open to future critique, reinterpretation and elaboration (e.g. Lewis & Grimes, 1999; Ybema, 1996). Second, critics question where theorists 'stand' when applying a metaparadigm view (e.g. Scherer, 1998). According to Gioia and Pitre (1990: 596), a metavantage point exists 'above the plane of paradigms.' Yet they stress that the viewer typically is grounded in the assumptions of a particular paradigm. Theorists cannot shed their predisposition, but can contrast their favored representations with those of other paradigms. The goal is an expanded purview, which allows alternatives to co-exist and engage in potentially more insightful and creative interactions. As Morgan (1983) explained, theorists may learn to view (and depict) paradigms as detailing different layers of meanings. In this light, critical self-reflection, again, becomes vital. For the theory-building process will likely invoke a deep sense of humility as theorists 'become aware of the precarious quality of their knowledge' (Brocklesby, 1997: 214).

Implications of multiparadigm inquiry

To render multiparadigm inquiry more appealing to organizational researchers, it is not enough to address its rationale (i.e. developing a philosophical framework) and workings (i.e. identifying specific multiparadigm strategies). It also requires identifying its deeper implications. We now unpack the potential contributions of multiparadigm inquiry, as well as its philosophical, cognitive, and cultural challenges.

Potential contributions: Fostering greater relevance and reflexivity

> Reflexivity . . . the deepening of the self's capacity to recognise that it views certain information as hostile, to recognise the various dodges that it uses to deny, ignore, or camouflage information that is hostile to it, and to strengthen its capacity to accept and to use hostile information. In short, what Reflexive Sociology seeks is not an insulation, but a transformation of the sociologist's self, and hence, of his [sic] praxis in the world.
>
> (Gouldner, 1973: 495)

The potential contributions of multiparadigm inquiry accrue on varied levels. On a *pragmatic* level, this approach aids the exploration of pluralism and paradox, facilitating the development of understandings more in tune with the diversity, complexity and ambiguity of organizational life. On a *philosophical* level, multiparadigm inquiry encourages greater reflexivity in research. Yet such benefits are intertwined: to capture organizational intricacies one must reflect on one's own research practices and their potential impact upon the object of inquiry. Conversely, reflexivity may be fuelled as the researcher recognizes inherent tensions surrounding the phenomenon of inquiry.

Use of a single modern paradigm produces a potentially valuable, but narrow view, incapable of exposing the multi-faceted nature of organizational reality. Multiparadigm inquiry, in contrast, may foster 'more comprehensive portraits of complex organizational phenomena' (Gioia & Pitre, 1990: 587) by helping researchers confront and explore contradictions. By applying varied lenses, researchers are better equipped to shed light on tensions of organizational life – e.g. exposing conflicting demands as complementary, and opposing interests as interwoven.

Moreover, engagement in multiparadigm inquiry fosters greater reflexivity. Holland (1999) identified four levels of reflexivity. 'Reflexivity 1' is a low-level version that downplays – or more likely, ignores – the role of paradigmatic assumptions in shaping scholarly practice. Rather, researchers question whether they have rigorously applied appropriate techniques to get closer to the 'truth' or to capture meaning within a certain context. Researchers do not question their underlying assumptions or their impacts. Yet, as Brocklesby noted, 'it is only by constantly re-examining and questioning the foundational assumptions of various theories and practices that the discipline can avoid becoming trapped within a limited range of conceptual possibilities' (1997: 192).

The subsequent three levels are promoted by each of the multiparadigm strategies in turn. 'Reflexivity 2' corresponds to multiparadigm reviews. Researchers learn to identify their own and others' viewpoints, scrutinizing their underpinnings and influence on research (Flood & Romm, 1997). 'Reflexivity 2' rests on the belief that we can never expand our understandings unless we constantly examine our own assumptions in light of insights made available by other paradigms. Multiparadigm research extends this thinking by encouraging 'reflexivity 3.' Researchers travel across paradigms to appreciate different languages and methodologies (Holland, 1999). At this level, research appears as a continuous process of self-discovery, and reflexivity arises out of experimentation with new research practices. Lastly, 'reflexivity 4' relates to metaparadigm theory building. This level of reflexivity is not bound by paradigmatic constraints (Holland, 1999). Rather, it transcends personal and political concerns, as researchers explore intricate differences in identity between researchers, the subjects of research and the audiences for the text (Herts, 1997).

Multiparadigm inquiry fosters intense reflexivity (i.e. levels 2, 3 and 4), helping researchers examine their work and selves at new depths. This is not to say that reflexivity is the ultimate goal, as it may, if taken to its extreme, encourage the formation of 'navel-gazing' scholarly communities – excessively introspective and egotistical. Given such precautions, however, one of the greatest values of multiparadigm inquiry is the potential for personal learning, even enlightenment. From our own, first-hand experiences as well as the writings of other multiparadigm researchers, we believe that the exploration of alternative worldviews opens powerful doors of perception. Researchers often note that multiparadigm inquiry forever altered their perspective, impacting their future research even when attempting to return to more single-paradigm concerns (e.g. Lewis & Grimes, 1999; Martin, 1992).

As Reed (1997: 22) noted: 'A retreat back into a golden ago of philosophical innocence and/or empirical pragmatism is unlikely to be an attractive or viable option when the "genie" of ontological and epistemological reflection has been let out of the bottle and there is no chance of forcing or coaxing it back in.'

Challenges of multiparadigm inquiry

> A successful multi-paradigm perspective, in short, must explain how different theoretical approaches might be related, but must do so (a) while preserving genuine multiplicity (e.g. the relatedness does not involve the reduction of one approach to another) and (b) without uncritically embracing the disunifying 'paradigms' paradigm (i.e. the increasingly entrenched view of organizational inquiry which – by appealing to the incommensurability thesis – purports unalterably to divide the field into mutually exclusive, contradictory metatheoretical camps).
>
> (Weaver & Gioia, 1994: 566)

Multiparadigm inquiry raises considerable philosophical, cognitive, and cultural challenges. Advocates, for instance, face *philosophical challenges* as they must weigh the claims for and against paradigm incommensurability. Some commentators depict paradigms as competing intellectual lenses (Burrell & Morgan, 1979; Jackson & Carter, 1991). Accordingly, there can be no linguistic or analytical bridges between them, as each takes recourse to particular ontological, epistemological or ideological presumptions. In contrast, multiparadigm researchers question incommensurability (e.g. Gioia & Pitre, 1990; Morgan, 1997), seeking to contrast paradigm perspectives. Following Parker's (1995) stones analogy, rather than apply extreme relativism, refuting the existence of stones, multiparadigm inquiry explores ways of describing their feel, appearance and uses depending upon one's point of view. Taking an obvious creative leap, organizational phenomena may exhibit varied qualities of 'solidity' to varied actors, depending upon their roles, political interests, cultural backgrounds, etc. Hence, multiparadigm researchers may argue the undesirability of choosing one view *over* another, but do not negate the possibility of juxtaposing such views. Distinguishing disparate lenses may prove inspiring, extending researchers' peripheral vision dramatically, yet never completely.

Multiparadigm inquiry also provokes considerable *cognitive challenges* as researchers strive to learn not only the language of different paradigms, but also their social and political practices. According to Brocklesby (1997), researchers must form propositional (i.e. methodological) and common sense (i.e. intuitive) knowledges of each paradigm. Yet researchers' socialization within their home paradigm – and the understandings and comfort it provides – make it difficult to acknowledge other ways of viewing the world. Researchers must leave behind (temporarily) their old paradigm to engage an alternative. Such empirical engagement can be a painful exercise. As Lincoln explained, 'fooling around with a new paradigm is an intensely personal process, evolving from not only intellectual but also personal, social, and possibly political transformation' (1990: 67). Such challenges help explain why many multiparadigm exemplars stem from doctoral experiences, prior to researchers' entrenchment in a single paradigm (e.g. Graham-Hill, 1996; Hassard, 1985; Kelemen, 1995; Lewis, 1996). Yet, regardless of academic tenure, exploring multiple paradigms offers a potentially frame-breaking experience. Once researchers become immersed in different cultures, their mindsets are forever changed. They may attempt to 'return home,' applying their once favored conventions, but their participation alters for they can no longer pretend that their paradigm is complete (Brocklesby, 1997).

Cultural challenges arise as multiparadigm inquiry threatens the traditional conventions of varied research communities. According to McCloskey (1994), researchers gain acclaim, legitimacy and visibility for their work by following a specific set of established procedures. Yet, if research conventions dictate what counts as quality or knowledge, our research itself plays a significant role in perpetuating or questioning these conventions. Multiparadigm inquiry may encourage research choices to become more conscious and informed. By developing cross-paradigm sensitivity, researchers may engage in provocative and enlightening work that extends their peripheral vision and awakens their self-reflective capabilities. Theory that considers, even accommodates, divergent perspectives, may contribute intricate understandings – understandings that mute objectivity/subjectivity debates and offer insights for more diverse organizational actors. Although multiparadigm inquiry is yet to be regarded as legitimate by the entire field, it has found resonance with a growing cadre of researchers, who are prepared to put to trial their academic credibility in order to explore pluralism and paradox inherent within organizations and organizational studies.

Concluding note

By tapping modern and postmodern insights, multiparadigm inquiry adheres to Kilduff and Mehra's conviction that 'the practice of research should never be a timid adventure' (1997: 476). Yet, simultaneously, multiparadigm exemplars question modern claims of incommensurability and the extremes of postmodern relativism. Researchers value multiple paradigm lenses, while recognizing their blinders. Such divergent lenses may enable insights into varied facets of organizations, potentially enhancing understandings of how dramatic transformations are intensifying ambiguity, complexity and conflict. Multiparadigm strategies may guide explorations of pluralism and paradox, fostering development of more relevant and comprehensive theory. For the challenges of contemporary academia necessarily reflect those of organizational life:

> The same paradoxical demands are made of researchers of complex social and cultural processes. They cannot simply adopt existing, standardized approaches. The whimsicality of reality can only be grasped with a multi-perspective approach that combines various methods of data collection, multi-level analysis and the in-built view of paradoxes in the research plan. This calls for creativity, for serendipity-proness, for not being afraid to walk on thin ice, for an attitude of fundamental scepticism about fixed models and solutions and for a critical reflection on one's own actions.
>
> (Koot et al., 1996: 211)

References

Ackroyd, S. Paradigms lost: Paradise regained? In M. Reed and M. Hughes (Eds), *Rethinking organization*. London: Sage, 1992.

Allison, G.T. *Essence of decision: Explaining the Cuban Missile Crisis*. Boston, MA: Little Brown, 1971.

Alvesson, M. *Consensus, control, and critique*. Brookfield, VT: Avebury, 1987.

Bouchikhi, H. Living with and building on complexity: A constructivist perspective on organizations. *Organization*, 1998, 5(2), 217–32.

Bradshaw-Camball, P. & Murray, V.V. Illusions and other games: A trifocal view of organizational politics. *Organization Science*, 1991, 2, 379–98.

Brocklesby, J. Becoming multimethodology literate: An assessment of the cognitive difficulties of working across paradigms. In J. Mingers and A. Gills (Eds), *Multimethodology*. New York: Wiley, 1997.

Burrell, G. Paradigms, metaphors, discourses, genealogies. In S. Clegg, C. Hardy and W. Nord (Eds), *Handbook of organization studies*. Thousand Oaks, CA: Sage, 1996.

Burrell, G. & Morgan, G. *Sociological paradigms and organizational analysis*. Portsmouth, NH: Heinemann, 1979.

Calas, M.B. & Smircich, L. Past postmodernism? Reflections and tentative directions. *Academy of Management Review*, 1999, 24, 649–71.

Cannella, A.A., Jr. & Paetzold, R.L. Pfeffer's barriers to the advance of organizational science: A rejoinder. *Academy of Management Review*, 1994, 19, 331–42.

Chia, R. From modern to postmodern organizational analysis. *Organization Studies*, 1995, 16(4), 579–605.

Chia, R. *Organizational analysis as deconstructive practice*. New Yorki: Walter de Gruyter, 1996.

Clegg, S. *Modern organizations*. Thousand Oaks, CA: Sage, 1990.

Clegg, S. & Hardy, C. Conclusion: Representations. In S. Clegg, C. Hardy and W. Nord (Eds), *Handbook of organization studies*. Thousand Oaks, CA: Sage, 1996.

Cooper, R. & Burrell, G. Modernism, postmodernism and organizational analysis: An introduction. *Organization Studies*, 1988, 9(1), 91–112.

Cooper, R. & Law, J. Organization: Distal and proximal views. *Research in the Sociology of Organizations*, 1995, 13, 237–74.

Daymon, C. Culture formation in a new television station: A multi-perspective analysis. *British Journal of Management*, 2000, 11, 121–35.

Deetz, S. Describing differences in approaches to organization science: Rethinking Burrell and Morgan and their legacy. *Organization Science*, 1996, 7, 191–207.

Derrida, J. *Writing and difference*. (Translated by A. Bass.) London: Routledge, 1978.

Donaldson, L. The myth of paradigm incommensurability in management studies: Comments by an integrationist. *Organization*, 1998, 5(2), 267–72.

Flood, R. & Romm, N. From metatheory to 'multimethodology'. In J. Mingers and A. Gills (Eds), *Multimethodology*. New York: Wiley, 1997.

Gaventa, J. *Power and powerlessness: Quiescence and rebellion in an Appalachian valley*. Urbana: University of Illinois Press, 1980.

Gioia, D.A. & Pitre, E. Multiparadigm perspectives on theory building. *Academy of Management Review*, 1990, 15, 584–602.

Gouldner, A.W. *The coming crisis of western sociology*. London: Heinemann, 1973.

Graham-Hill, S. Small business strategy: A multiparadigm perspective, unpublished dissertation, University of Kentucky, 1996.

Grimes, A.J. & Rood, D.L. Beyond objectivism and relativism: Descriptive epistemologies. In J.P. Jones III, W. Natter and T.R. Schatzki (Eds), *Objectivity and its other*. New York: Guilford, 1995.

Grint, K. *The sociology of work: An introduction*. London: Polity Press, 1991.

Habermas, J. *Towards rational society*. London: Heinemann, 1971.

Hassard, J. Multiple paradigms and organisational research: An analysis of work behaviour in the Fire Service, unpublished PhD thesis, University of Aston, Birmingham, 1985.

Hassard, J. *Sociology and organization theory*. Cambridge: Cambridge University Press, 1993.

Hassard, J. Postmodern organizational analysis: Toward a conceptual framework. *Journal of Management Studies*, 1994, 31, 303–24.

Hassard, J. & Parker, M. (Eds) *Postmodernism and organization*. Newbury Park, CA: Sage, 1994.

Herts, R. (Ed.) *Reflexivity and voice*. Thousand Oaks, CA: Sage, 1997.

Holland, R. Reflexivity. *Human Relations*, 1999, 52(4), 463–84.

Jackson, N. & Carter, P. In defense of paradigm commensurability. *Organization Studies* 1991, 12(1), 109–27.

Kelemen, M. The role of leadership in achieving TQM in the UK service sector: A multiparadigm study, unpublished PhD thesis, University of Oxford, 1995.

Kilduff, M. & Mehra, A. Postmodernism and organizational research. *Academy of Management Review*, 1997, 22, 453–81.

Knights, D. Deconstruction: Dualism, gender, and postmodernism revisited. *Organization Studies*, 1997, 18(1), 1–19.

Koot, W., Sabelis, I. & Ybema, S. Global identity–local oddity? Paradoxical processes in contemporary organizations. In W. Koot, I. Sabelis and S. Ybema (Eds), *Contradictions in context*. Amsterdam: VU University Press, 1996.

Kuhn, T.S. *The structure of scientific revolutions*. Chicago, IL: University of Chicago Press, 1970.

Lewis, M.W. Advanced manufacturing technology design: A multiparadigm study, unpublished dissertation, University of Kentucky, 1996.

Lewis, M.W. & Grimes, A.J. Metatriangulation: Building theory from multiple paradigms. *Academy of Management Review*, 1999, 24, 672–90.

Lincoln, Y. The making of a constructivist: A remembrance of transformations past. In E.G. Guba (Ed.), *The paradigm dialog*. Newbury Park, CA: Sage, 1990.

Lyotard, J.F. *The post-modern condition: A report on knowledge.* (Translated by G. Bennington & B. Marsuni.) Manchester: Manchester University Press, 1984.

McCloskey, D.N. *Knowledge and persuasion in economics*. Cambridge: Cambridge University Press, 1994.

Martin, J. *Cultures in organizations: Three perspectives*. New York: Oxford University Press, 1992.

Mingers, J. Multi-paradigm methodology. In J. Mingers and A. Gills (Eds), *Multimethodology*. New York: Wiley, 1997.

Morgan, G. *Beyond method*. Newbury Park, CA: Sage, 1983.

Morgan, G. *Images of organization*. Thousand Oaks, CA: Sage, 1997.

Parker, M. Critique in the name of what? Postmodernism and critical approaches to organization. *Organization Studies*, 1995, 16(4), 553–65.

Parker, M. & McHugh, G. Five texts in search of an author: A response to John Hassard's multiple paradigms and organizational analysis. *Organization Studies*, 1991, 12(3), 451–6.

Poole, M.S. & Van de Ven, A.H. Using paradox to build management and organization theories. *Academy of Management Review*, 1989, 14, 562–78.

Reed, M. *Redirections in organizational analysis*. London: Tavistock, 1985.

Reed, M. In praise of duality and dualism: Rethinking agency and structure in organizational analysis. *Organization Studies*, 1997, 18(1), 21–42.

Rosenau, P.M. *Postmodernism and the social sciences: Insights, inroads and intrusions*. Princeton, NJ: Princeton University Press, 1992.

Scherer, A.G. Pluralism and incommensurability in strategic management and organization theory: A problem in search of a solution. *Organization*, 1998, 5(2), 147–68.

Schultz, M. & Hatch, M.J. Living within multiple paradigms: The case of paradigm interplay in organizational culture studies. *Academy of Management Review*, 1996, 21, 529–57.

Smircich, L. Concepts of culture and organizational analysis. *Administrative Science Quarterly*, 1983, 28, 339–58.

Spender, J.-C. Pluralist epistemology and the knowledge-based theory of the firm. *Organization*, 1998, 5(2), 233–56.

Weaver, G.R. & Gioia, D.A. Paradigms lost: Incommensurability vs structurationist inquiry. *Organization Studies*, 1994, 15(4), 565–90.

Weick, K.E. Theory construction as disciplined reflexivity: Tradeoffs of the 90s. *Academy of Management Review*, 1999, 24, 797–807.

Whitehead, A.N. *Science and the modern world*. London: Free Association Books, 1985.

Ybema, S. A duck-billed platypus in the theory and analysis of organizations: Combinations of consensus and dissensus. In W. Koot, I. Sabelis and S. Ybema (Eds), *Contradictions in context*. Amsterdam: VU University Press, 1996.

Zey-Ferrell, M. & Aiken, M. *Complex organizations: Critical perspectives*. Glenview, IL: Foresman, 1981.

Marianne W. Lewis is an assistant professor of Management at University of Cincinnati. Her research explores tensions, conflicts, and paradoxes that both impede and enable innovation. In particular, her work addresses the challenges of implementing advanced manufacturing technology, developing new products, and building organization theory. Representative articles appear in the *Academy of Management Review, Academy of Management Journal, Journal of Operations Management,* and *Journal of Management Education.* She earned her PhD in Management from the University of Kentucky, and MBA from Indiana University.
[E-mail: Marianne.lewis@uc.edu]

Mihaela Kelemen is lecturer in Quality Management at the Department of Management, Keele University, UK. Her research covers topics such as Total Quality Management, Business Process Re-engineering, gender and organizations, economies in transition, postmodern theories of organizations, and has been published in journals such as: *Journal of Management Studies, British Journal of Management, Scandinavian Journal of Management, Gender, Work, Organisation* and *Studies in Cultures, Organisations and Societies.* Her book on critical approaches to the management of quality will be published by Sage in 2002.
[E-mail: m.l.kelemen@mngt.keele.ac.uk]

Production and Consumption in Organizational Knowledge: The Case of 'the Paradigms Debate'

JOHN S. HASSARD and MIHAELA L. KELEMEN

UMIST and Keele University, UK

Abstract. *Recent debates on the production of knowledge in organizational analysis are interpreted from a largely postmodernist, 'sociology of consumption' perspective. Drawing upon the work of Jean-François Lyotard, Michel de Certeau and Stanley Deetz in particular, the analysis rejects both positivist and conventionalist theses on knowledge production in favour of a deconstructionist approach that embraces acts of production and consumption in a reflexive way. The argument is developed by way of a case study of production and consumption in organizational analysis. Through an assessment of scientific status and institutional control—centrally in relation to the 'paradigm incommensurability' debate—a taxonomy of styles of knowledge production and consumption is proposed. Five main 'camps' comprise this taxonomy— non-consumers, integrationists, protectionists, pluralists and postmodernists. We describe the basic knowledge philosophies of the camps and subject them to evaluation and critique. This analysis sees, inter alia, Jeffrey Pfeffer's proposals for producing an integrated knowledge paradigm for organizational analysis—the so-called 'Pfefferdigm' thesis—confounded by the indeterminate rationalities and networks of signification of postmodern analysis. For explaining processes of knowledge production and consumption, it is argued ultimately that the notion of 'discourse' should replace that of 'paradigm'.* **Key words.** *discourse; organization theory; paradigms; production*

This paper concerns debates surrounding the nature of knowledge within academic social science. In particular, it concerns the production and consumption of knowledge in that branch of sociology concerned with the study of organizations.

Since the mid-1960s, one of the key debates within this field has centred upon whether organizational knowledge is best accrued from the theories and empirical practices of a single research paradigm or a number of competing ones. During the 1970s and 1980s, a crude interpretation of this debate pictured an ongoing struggle between monoparadigm absolutism, largely favouring coherence around the axioms of traditional social systems theory, and pluri-paradigm relativism, under whose auspices a number of theory communities proliferate within a volatile, contested terrain of 'anything goes' (Feyerabend, 1975). A popular shorthand for this debate has been the dispute between 'contingency theory' and 'the critics' (see Donaldson, 1985, 1996).

Since the mid-1990s, the debate has been vitalized by views expressed by the influential American administrative scientist Jeffrey Pfeffer (1993, 1997). Notable here is his suggestion that in order to achieve academic respectability organizational analysis should concern itself with producing a discrete paradigm of clearly articulated practices and standards. Pfeffer offers the example of political science as a sub-discipline of social science that has achieved this aim. The 'Pfefferdigm debate', as it has become known, is predicated on the view that the theoretical variety and epistemological relativism advocated by 'the critics' will lead ultimately to the nascent discipline of organizational analysis committing professional suicide. It is Pfeffer's belief that paradigm plurality will ultimately ring the death knell for organizational analysis, because the type of knowledge it offers is insufficient to enlist the support of influential institutions, especially research funding agencies.

The present paper questions the logic of much of Pfeffer's thesis. We take issue with his largely 'integrationist' view, one that apparently wishes to 'settle' the paradigm incommensurability debate, for we doubt that the production of such community consensus is achievable given the current status of knowledge practices. Such practices are not stable and coherent, but continuously in the making. They are shaped by (and shape) power relations and competing discourses (Foucault, 1980). They infer a process in which knowledge is at the same time produced and consumed. Typically referred to as 'the postmodern condition of knowledge' (Lyotard, 1984/1997), this scenario views knowledge as a set of cultural practices situated in and inextricably linked to the material and social circumstances in which it is produced and consumed. As sociomaterial practice, knowledge is processual and provisional: its production relies on resources disembodied from their original content and made available through their transformation, legitimization and institutionalization (Gherardi and Nicolini, 2000). Its consumption is ensured through processes of social participation in a community of practice—a means of 'being in the world', not simply 'knowing the world' (Bourdieu, 1990).

In this paper, therefore, it is our view that even de facto codification of community standards is something that is beyond our analytical grasp. Our reason is simply that the largely unbridled nature of knowledge production and consumption in contemporary organizational analysis serves to make such integrationism mere wishful thinking. In short, we believe that consumption practices will continue to confound any 'bounding' of organizational knowledge in the foreseeable future.

This argument is developed in three main phases. First, we review, briefly, the relationship between theory communities and the production of knowledge in organization theory. This analysis, which takes recourse to debates on the nature of scientific status and institutional control, rejects linear explanations of research practice in favour of a politically infused perspective in which knowledge production takes place in and reflects a highly contested terrain (Reed, 1992). We note how the fashion, since the mid-1960s, for establishing clear community demarcations has reflected the development of a strong 'productivist' orientation in organizational analysis. We argue, however, that this perspective should be employed with caution. At best, it should be used as a heuristic device to allow researchers to identify and subsequently question their own intellectual practices and those of hypothetical academic 'others' (Cooper, 1983).

The second phase of the argument begins by confirming this emphasis on the production of knowledge in traditional commentaries on scientific progress. We argue that any analysis of knowledge production must engender an appreciation of acts of consumption. The consumption of knowledge fuels the creation of new knowledge while new knowledge acquires its status as 'knowledge' only when selected for consumption by important players. We believe that all producers of knowledge are also consumers, although one does not have to produce knowledge simply because of the act of consumption. In debating such processes, we take recourse to the work of de Certeau (1984) and Lyotard (1984/1997) to explore the various 'forms of manoeuvre' available to consumers of organizational knowledge. Consumers of organizational knowledge range from academic peers to students, managers, workers, government administrators and the public at large. We focus mainly on academic peers who, by sitting on research panels and journal boards, acting as conference organizers, journal and book reviewers or as mere readers of published and unpublished work, have the institutional power to decide what forms of organizational knowledge are to be accorded the status of 'knowledge'. This section discusses how the consumption of knowledge is a process characterized by instability, fragmentation and heterogeneity. Above all, it is a process that is difficult to control 'at a distance' (Law, 1987). Our argument ultimately revolves around a postmodern position under which attempts at the codification of scientific practice are subverted by researchers' 'tactics of consumption' (de Certeau, 1984). This

sees the knowledge space of social science characterized as a heterogeneous network of shifting research identities, with knowledge
'constructed' at the intersection of processes of production and consumption.

The third phase of the article then attempts to place some (temporary)
structure on this shifting space by offering a modernist interpretation of
current styles of knowledge production and consumption in organizational analysis. In so doing, we offer a taxonomy of characteristic responses to the paradigm incommensurability debate—a debate that has
become central to understanding the state of knowledge practices in the
field (see, for example, Jackson and Carter, 1991; Hassard, 1993; Pfeffer,
1993; Schultz and Hatch, 1996; Scherer 1998). This taxonomy classifies
responses to the debate in terms of five main styles or 'camps' of
production and consumption—non-consumers, integrationists, protectionists, pluralists and postmodernists—and literature representative of
each is reviewed and discussed. We suggest that such multifaceted, and
sometimes contradictory, responses are not only natural but also actually
desirable in light of a sociology of consumption that reflects the fragmented nature of social science and society. Given the substantive
content and epistemological stance of the article, the analysis emphasizes
the explanatory power of postmodernism, and in particular the role of
research 'discourses', in making sense of production and consumption
processes.

Finally, in conclusion, we offer some implications for future research
and analysis. We argue that in the light of new empirical 'realities'
(especially the rise of consumerism in post-industrial society) discussions of community practice in organizational analysis should embrace
acts of consumption as well as production. In so doing, we promote the
explanatory power of discourse, above that of paradigm, in the analysis of
the disciplinary matrices of social science in general and organizational
analysis in particular.

Part One: The Production of Knowledge

The traditional emphasis in analyses of the nature of scientific knowledge is on a phenomenon that is relentlessly 'produced' through either
inductive or deductive means. In this view, the products of scientific
enterprise are frequently consumed through cause-and-effect type relationships. Knowledge is produced in order to be consumed at a later
stage, commonly following dissemination through appropriate academic
and/or professional channels. A strong sense of linearity and positivist
logic underpins the process.

Often associated with this essentially positivist and unilinear view is
the metaphor of the so-called 'hierarchy of sciences' (Cole, 1983). The
dominant image here is of natural science, through its success in adopt-

ing cold and factual methodologies, being somehow located at the top of the scientific hierarchy, with other, less 'pure' sciences—commonly the human and social—situated below. One implication is that the modern, western natural science model can or should provide a methodological exemplar for the social sciences, given that the latter struggles to achieve academic and social legitimacy. Natural science, underpinned by experimental methods and positivist philosophies, is deemed to be scientifically 'superior' to social science in that it appears to offer an 'objective' way of looking at the world. Scientific progress, a 'rational' enterprise, is equated with the 'cumulative growth in knowledge' (Reed, 1985: 201) whereby 'knowledge grows linearly as new data are added to the existing stock of research findings' (Astley, 1985: 479). The natural sciences are deemed successful in that they progressively add more dust to the dust pile of knowledge.

In contrast, conventionalist philosophy, and in particular the writings of Thomas Kuhn (1962/1970) and his followers (see Lakatos and Musgrave, 1970), take exception to such rationalist historicism. Under conventionalism, the process of knowledge production and accumulation is not such a linear, incremental accomplishment. Instead, it is the result of scientific 'wars' in which 'Old Guards' are recurrently overthrown by bands of 'Young Turks'. Here, rather than take recourse to the dictates of rational or formal logic, science practice reflects the irrational forces of consensus, dogma and belief, essentially mirroring the culture of the political community (Shapere, 1971). The production of knowledge concerns the (re)solving of 'puzzles' rather than 'problems', for answers already reside within the dominant scientific 'exemplar' (Kuhn, 1970). This process involves sociological consensus as much as scientific experimentation. Knowledge progresses through recurrent phases of 'normal' and 'revolutionary' activity, rather than by (scientific) giants standing on one another's shoulders.

In the present article, we wish to question the efficacy of both of these 'progress' narratives—positivism and conventionalism—as frameworks for defining the status of knowledge in organizational analysis. Instead, we will turn to postmodernism and consider the notion of *discourse* as a metaphor for conceptualizing knowledge production and consumption in the field. In so doing, we attempt to depart from a linguistically naive version of postmodernism and discourse theory—one that privileges language as constitutive of social phenomena at the expense of non-linguistic, material practices. Instead, we emphasize the material and heterogeneous nature of discourse. We are concerned, in Foucauldian fashion, to highlight the institutional bases of discourse, the positions from which people speak and the power relations that make this possible or restrain it. In particular, we see scientific discourse as a practice, or rather a set of practices, that allows institutions to privilege particular forms of knowledge and the conditions that make them possible.

Paradigms and Production

Of the two progress narratives outlined above, it can be argued that an adapted version of Kuhnian conventionalism has become normative in explanations of knowledge development and community practice in organizational analysis. This version sees the theoretical and empirical cake sliced into various sociological 'paradigms', the number and composition of which vary according to the metatheoretical recipe being used. From a production of knowledge perspective, such paradigms represent sets of assumptions and convictions that are held in common by communities of researchers.[1]

In organizational studies, the debate on paradigms and their role in the research process was given momentum by the publication of Burrell and Morgan's (1979) *Sociological Paradigms and Organizational Analysis*. This book outlined a number of key debates concerning the production of knowledge in the field. One of their main arguments was that in order to place knowledge production in context we must first possess a structuralist understanding of the scientific and political assumptions that underpin major intellectual traditions. Burrell and Morgan 'produce' this context though specifying the philosophical and methodological (meta)-theories that serve to define the intellectual character of well-known research approaches. Both 'mainsteam' and 'alternative' schools and movements are situated in terms of their relative position on a map of intellectual terrain produced through relating 'theories of social science' to 'theories of society'. A two-by-two matrix provides the technology for this map, whereby four 'sociological paradigms' are produced to represent the major 'belief systems' of academics and others who practise organizational analysis.

One of the more contentious aspects of this thesis, however, was that, instead of such paradigms being arenas for open, scholarly debate, they represent, instead, hermetically sealed intellectual compartments. In Burrell and Morgan's analysis, an extremely strong version of the conventionalist notion of paradigm incommensurability is applied. Here, such paradigm incommensurability presupposes that:

> ... a synthesis [between paradigms] is not possible, since in their pure form [paradigms] are contradictory, being based on at least one set of meta-theoretical assumptions. They represent alternatives, in the sense that one can operate in different paradigms sequentially over time, but mutually exclusive, in the sense that one cannot operate in more than one paradigm at any given point in time, since in accepting the assumptions of one, we defy the assumptions of all the others. (Burrell and Morgan, 1979: 25)

As these four incommensurable sociological paradigms—functionalism, interpretivism, radical humanism and radical structuralism—are found to coexist at one time, it is argued that benchmarking between paradigms is impossible, for proponents live in different life-worlds and speak different technical languages. Scientific communication is not so much difficult as logically impossible (Burrell and Morgan, 1979).[2] It is to this form of 'hyper-relativism' that Pfeffer (1993) so strongly objects in his article on 'Barriers to the Advance of Organizational Science'. Although Pfeffer's meta-narrative, like that of Burrell and Morgan, is largely 'productivist', it is one directed at entirely different ends.

We wish to argue, however, that such ends are impossible to achieve because of the heterogeneity, fragmentation and dynamic nature of knowledge practices brought about by the so-called 'postmodern condition' (Lyotard, 1984/1997). For Lyotard, the 'postmodern condition' is one characterized by increased cultural fragmentation, new modes of experience, subjectivity and culture triggered by the development of new types of information, knowledge and technology. These new modes of experience and subjectivity foreground the power of consumption acts in constructing difference, playfulness, inclusion and exclusion.

Part Two: The Consumption of Knowledge

While it can be argued that knowledge is produced through the interaction of institutional materials and symbolic conditions, it can be argued also that it is 'reproduced' only when singled out for attention by those who find it 'meaningful' (Knights, 1997). According to Munro (1998), for example, knowledge is never meaningful in its own right: to become meaningful, it has to 'exteriorize' itself. Knowledge is usually mediated/exteriorized through linguistic and non-linguistic practices in which actions and interactions are made accountable to oneself and to the other (Gherardi and Nicolini, 2000). Such practices are in fact acts of consumption, serving purposes as diverse as expressing one's identity, marking attachment to social groups, exhibiting social distinction or ensuring social participation in various activities (Edgell et al., 1996).

The consumption of knowledge, however, has generally played a secondary role in the (grand) narrative explanations of scientific progress, for, in terms of the use of material and symbolic resources, the focus has been placed primarily on the strategic and operational actions of producers and the attributes of their theories. McKinley et al. (1999), for example, argue that evolving schools of thought must display a combination of novelty, continuity and scope to achieve legitimacy and therefore 'paradigm' status. The consumption of knowledge is seen to be directly correlated with and resulting from such attributes, in that 'the more that both novelty and continuity are displayed by a developing organization theory school of thought, the more likely detection and assimilation of the school's intellectual products by organizational scholars will be' (McKinley et al., 1999: 639) and 'the greater the scope of a developing school and its intellectual products, the greater the detection and assimilation of those products will be' (McKinley et al., 1999: 641).

According to de Certeau (1984), however, the consumption of knowledge should not be limited to such a secondary role, for its social and intellectual significance is profound. It can be argued that a more thoroughgoing understanding of processes of paradigm proliferation and regulation would involve exploration of those forms of manoeuvre available to the consumers of knowledge in the simultaneous spaces created by the producers. The propagation and consumption of knowledge depends, to a large extent, on what the individuals or communities do with it. Each of these individuals or communities may behave in different ways: they may ignore it, alter it, traduce it, supplement it or appropriate it (Gherardi and Nicolini, 2000). Thus, the consumption of knowledge is a process characterized by instability, fragmentation and heterogeneity (de Certeau, 1984). To repeat, it is a process that is difficult to 'control at a distance' (see Law, 1987). From this point of view, the project of producing a universalistic, ubiquitous and centralized paradigm for any social science discipline or field appears akin to the proverbial search for the 'holy grail', given for example the analytical elusiveness of social reality, the political character of the social scientific enterprise, and the heterogeneous nature of acts of consumption.[3] Put simply, de Certeau feels that responses to the strategy of knowledge production cannot be predicted, anticipated, or indeed managed according to any 'grand plan'. Such responses, which he terms 'tactics of consumption', cannot be articulated by producers of knowledge, individually or collectively, nor can they be fixed by the system in which they are found to proliferate.[4]

It can be argued therefore that, in the sphere of organizational analysis, the concept or project of producing a 'dominant' analytical paradigm is one that is likely to trigger a set of heterogeneous and shifting responses from researchers. Some may reject it, others internalize it, and still others subvert it. While some authors suggest ways in which a dominant paradigm *could* or even *should* be 'produced'—notably Pfeffer (1993) who as we know illustrates the apparently comparable and commendable case of political science—we will argue that the nature and logic of such heterogeneous 'acts of consumption' serve to confound such an enterprise.

Further, it is our view that consumption is a far more elusive concept analytically, given that there are few mechanisms for boundary setting, or for ensuring 'control at a distance'. From a predominantly consumption-of-knowledge perspective, the dynamic of paradigms is not one exclusive to documenting static sets of structuralist assumptions about science and the determined role of scientists. Instead, after Lyotard (1984/1997), it is our view that dependence on such presuppositions as the basis for sociological explanation may lead ultimately to an internal erosion of the 'legitimacy principle'. In processes of deconstruction, there are simply no ways to justify situating science and scientists metatheoretically within such spatial and temporal concrete.[5]

Our view is that, primarily, it is the *language* conventions, techniques and representational practices—recognized as scientifically legitimate and which are regularly mustered by members of a particular scientific community—that serve in practice to establish paradigm 'identity'. Allegiance to a paradigm is allegiance to a heterogeneous and shifting collection of language conventions embedded in the practice of a particular context—in other words, allegiance primarily to a set of *discourses*.

Consumption, Discourse and the Petits Récits

Since the early 1970s, much attention has focused on the view that social science (and in particular that branch concerned with the study of organizations) is in the midst of a 'knowledge crisis' (see Grint, 1991; Hassard, 1993; Reed, 1996). From Gouldner (1970) and Friedrichs (1970) onwards, writers have claimed that the traditional grand narratives of social science no longer offer robust explanations of the increasingly complex and elusive structures and processes of social and cultural phenomena.

In recent years, similar arguments have been advanced by writers who talk of a 'postmodern condition' in philosophy, social science and the humanities (see Harvey, 1990; Lyotard, 1984/1997). For many, postmodernism represents an 'alternative' explanatory medium for social theory and affairs, one founded on the recognition and importance of 'local' rather than 'grand' *genres* of intellectual discourse. As noted, one of the main exponents of this form of analysis has been Jean-François Lyotard, especially in his book *The Postmodern Condition: A Report on Knowledge* (1997/1984). In a key passage, Lyotard (1984/1997: 27) discusses the role of the *petit récit* (or 'little narrative') as the 'quintessential form of imaginative invention, particularly in science' (1984/1997: 60). For Lyotard, the *petit récit*, like Wittgenstein's (1953) 'technical language-games' (see Phillips, 1977), thrives in linguistic life-worlds that are altogether different to those of 'grand' narratives, whose habitats, it is claimed, are now under threat.

For Lyotard, each 'little narrative' possesses its own specific way of representing the world. As such, conflicts between them are difficult if not impossible to resolve, given the lack of a 'judgement rule' applicable to both. Lyotard, in fact introduces the notion of *differand* to account for such processes, a term he employs to reflect the maintenance of a state of 'continuous difference', and to account for the difficulty in making judgements about linguistic conflicts. For Lyotard, there is no way in which a scientific discourse can dominate all others through invoking a source of meta-narrative authority to ensure legitimacy.

Lyotard (1984/1997) suggests that the 'postmodern condition' is also one of conflict. In order to understand scientific relations, Lyotard insists we require not only a theory of linguistic 'communication' but also a theory of language 'games'—which accepts conflict, or 'agonistics', as a fundamental principle.[6] Most theories of scientific communication, however, appear wedded to a production of knowledge perspective, which claims to have access to what is right or wrong by upholding the 'scientific method' as the supreme arbiter. Lyotard's stance is different. He argues that, although the *appearance* of communication between 'little narratives' is a necessary function of scientific action, it is also a contingent one.[7] As there are no meta-narratives to regulate such linkages, this is an area where a researcher has to be 'active', i.e. by taking on the job of the 'philosopher', not just that of the 'scientist'. In so doing, the researcher will, among others, attempt to seek out new idioms which can 'speak for the silent', guarantee the conditions for 'participating in idioms', 'witness *differands*', and by and large write about the world 'in the service of the unknown' (Lyotard, 1984/1997). Writing from this position, we locate the moral responsibility of the researcher who cannot claim innocence from the representational force that he or she brings to theory (Calás and Smircich, 1999).

Lyotard develops this argument further to suggest that a theory of games, based on agonistics, represents a case of move-and-countermove on the part of researchers and their narratives. This is accomplished to the extent that the research game remains continuously open and heterogeneous. New moves provide opportunities for establishing new *petits récits*, which remain outside of the narrative domain of those in positions of institutional authority. Agonistics therefore emphasizes processes of knowledge consumption, the 'new moves' representing 'tactics of consumption', which function actively in response to strategies of knowledge production.

In Lyotard's philosophy, therefore, explanations of community and institution in social science take recourse not to the absolutism of positivism or the relativism of conventionalism but to the deconstructive reflexivity of postmodernism. Lyotard offers a critique of the production perspective on knowledge, which is predicated on the existence of paradigms and their aspiration to be based on 'inherent' emancipatory qualities. The postmodern notion of discourse, on the other hand, reflects a process of scientific interaction that includes not only the production of knowledge and the products of knowledge, but also, more importantly, the act of consumption.

From a postmodernist perspective on knowledge, therefore, what one should fear is the 'naturalization' of discourse(s); that is, the closure of potential meanings when a particular discourse is elevated into a 'standard' language and heralded as the 'key' to knowledge and scientific progress. Naturalization does not affect only the meanings of words used by researchers, but also their interactional routines and identities (Fairclough, 1996). Naturalization, however, is a process that is constantly resisted and subverted through tactics of consumption—the points of resistance that attempt to manipulate, subvert, oppose or delegitimize the standard language. As we have stressed, these points of resistance are irregularly distributed across the knowledge space. They form a heterogeneous network of shifting and decentred identities which researchers may take on at various points in time. In what follows, we offer a tangible expression of our argument through discussing some of these 'tactics' in relation to the 'Pfefferdigm' debate on paradigm commensurability and incommensurability.

Part Three: Case Study—Responses to the 'Paradigms Debate'

Based on this reading of the sociology of consumption, and in particular the view of the knowledge space as consisting of a heterogeneous network of shifting research identities, we now wish—for the purpose of case explanation—to place some (temporary) structure on this space through identifying contemporary responses to knowledge production. In so doing, we offer an essentially modernist 'taxonomy' of the forms or styles of knowledge production and consumption witnessed in relation to the paradigm incommensurability debate in organizational analysis. Although elements of this taxonomy may possibly be deemed to be employed largely as productivist 'straw men', innocently awaiting post-modern deconstruction (and whilst indeed a postmodern position is favoured in the analysis: see below) our intention primarily is to develop such a classification for pedagogical reasons of case explanation. The aim is for the taxonomy to be of explanatory value to students/researchers seeking to make sense of the 'paradigms debate' in terms of the distinctive discourses of production and consumption at work. In the event, this taxonomic assessment forms the basis for a discourse-analytic case study of the debate, and inter alia a critique of Jeffrey Pfeffer's (1993) proposals for paradigm integration. Finally, it should be noted that this taxonomy is essentially the personal or social construction of the authors, who are themselves seeking to consume the debate in a particular way (although it is hoped that the substance of the argument may have wider resonance).

Paradigms and Pfefferdigms: A Taxonomy of Responses

For explanatory purposes, it is our view that responses to the 'paradigms debate' in organizational analysis can usefully be typified, classified and clustered into five main 'camps'. First, those researchers who may not be aware of the debate on paradigms, and/or do not make it explicit in their writings, we call 'non-consumers'. Second, to Pfeffer (1993) and his followers, who advocate the production of an overarching integrated paradigm, we give the appellation 'integrationists'. Third, those who support a strong version of the relativist thesis of paradigm incommensurability we name 'protectionists'. Fourth, those who would jettison the paradigm incommensurability thesis by urging us to engage in multiparadigm research we term 'pluralists'. And finally, those who advocate the need to challenge the essentially 'productivist' discourse of the paradigms debate we call the 'postmodernists'.

We now offer a description and analysis of each camp. Although this analysis is offered primarily as a case study of tactics of consumption, in keeping with our desire to remain reflexive, we seek to acknowledge openly—by way of critique and deconstruction—the 'camp' in which our own intellectual sympathies reside—that of the postmodernists. As such, case explanation is developed at two levels—one taxonomic and descriptive, the other critical and partisan.

The Non-consumers. The *non-consumers* form a vast camp and fall, we feel, into three main categories. First, there are those who are simply unaware of debates relating to paradigm assumptions, proliferation and incommensurability. These researchers are oblivious to arguments that suggest the power of paradigmatic assumptions to shape perceptual orientation in their professional activities.[8] Second, there are those who are perhaps cognisant of the debate but find its level of abstraction less than useful in the pursuit of their everyday research duties. Such researchers may not be convinced of the practical value of the debate for empirical or experimental purposes and thus choose not to engage with it. Third, there are those who, although possibly at ease with the terminology of the debate, may simply refuse to engage with its arguments in order to strengthen the position of mainstream management studies, as portrayed in 'functionalist' paradigms.

This non-consumers taxonomy is of course largely hypothetical and impressionistic. It is also probably by no means exhaustive or definitive and should at best be regarded as heuristic. The boundaries between these groupings are in any case not clearly definable and it would be indeed very difficult to judge if someone does not engage with the debate because of its level of abstraction or because of a wish to propagate mainstream practice. Although an empirical study may shed some light on the makings and motivations of the non-consumer camp, the non-consumers group is one we need spend relatively little time on in our analysis of production and consumption practices.

The Integrationists. The second camp, the *integrationist*, we feel subscribes to the view that organizational analysis is in a 'pre-paradigmatic' state, meaning that it has yet to achieve scientific maturity (at which time one paradigm dominates for a considerable period). While we accept that 'organization studies is a subject area that, since its development as a discrete academic specialism has suffered considerably from a crisis of identity' (Knights, 1997: 7), we do not believe that the 'crisis' can be resolved via an integrationist project. Although the integrationist project posits a need to combine paradigms into a newly integrated field, it often appears to suggest (somewhat unreflexively perhaps) that a version of a positivist paradigm will provide most of the necessary foundations for this integration (see Donaldson, 1985, 1998; Pfeffer, 1993).

As noted, Pfeffer (1993) basically argues that there is no future for organizational analysis—strictly speaking 'organizational science'—unless the academic community reaches consensus over the nature of a dominant paradigm. He states that 'consensus itself, however achieved, is a vital component for the advancement of knowledge in a field. Without some minimal level of consensus about research questions and methods, fields can scarcely expect to produce knowledge in a cumulative, developmental process' (Pfeffer, 1993: 611). Pfeffer's views thus appear deeply rooted in productionist assumptions. In particular, he appears to support a 'hierarchy of the sciences' thesis. The field of organizational science is apparently characterized by a considerably low level of paradigm development, particularly when compared with adjacent sciences such as psychology, economics and (especially) political science. Pfeffer contends that at present there is not only disagreement over which of the nascent paradigms available to organizational analysis is more 'useful', but also crucially over the process by which this can be decided.[9]

Pfeffer's analysis therefore appears grounded primarily in a production of knowledge perspective, one which takes organizational analysis's 'anything goes' (Feyerabend, 1975) attitude to be a reflection of the pre-paradigmatic state in which the field finds itself. On a pessimistic note, Pfeffer contends that this current state of affairs will lead to disastrous consequences as academic disciplines compete for less and less resources from key institutions, for disciplines in a more developed state paradigmatically will be favoured. Consequently, his advice is to produce a strong, unified discipline of organization studies, one that is to be consumed by researchers in ways dictated and directed by a professional intellectual academy.

We have argued that a more reflexive production/consumption perspective on knowledge may challenge such proposals on several counts. First of all, it can be argued that it is not only difficult but also in fact impossible to 'manage' acts of consumption 'at a distance'. This argument would suggest that it is beyond the power of institutions to appropriate intellectual coordinates and fix them according to some grand plan. Furthermore, heterogeneous acts of consumption challenge the so-called objectivity of the knowledge practices espoused by social scientific institutions. Such institutions are viewed merely as self-validating gatherings that attempt politically to decide upon criteria that will permit access to a 'profession', one controlled predominantly by themselves!

Pfeffer's suggestion, whilst perhaps well intended in its pragmatism, can thus be viewed as hegemonic, or even elitist. He basically suggests that organizational analysis should become more institutional, and that consensus should be enforced by professional bodies whose legitimacy is derived from 'expert' knowledge and whose main task is to decide on sets of methodological standards to be followed by the community. Diversity is welcome only to the extent that it is inscribed in an institutional way of seeing the world. To quote Pfeffer (1993: 617), 'disagreement in theoretical approaches and even in methodology will not prove detrimental ... as long as there are some agreed upon ways of resolving theoretical and methodological disputes'. Such resolution, however, is not so much a by-product of democracy, where both producers *and* consumers determine standards, but rather that of producers of knowledge expecting consumers to respond passively and in ways that are strategically anticipated. The integrationist meta-narrative thus largely ignores human agency and the political nature of acts of consumption.

The Protectionists. For us, the *protectionists* suggest that paradigms, as discrete intellectual lenses, are not so much complementary as competing, each enshrining a particular world-view. Silverman (1969), for example, suggested that the attempt to blur the boundaries between paradigms is a major obstacle to the growth of organizational analysis. Rather than promote pseudo-linkages between paradigms, we should, according to Silverman, instead address questions concerning their fundamental differences. According to the protectionist camp, there can be no linguistic or analytical bridges between paradigms, as each takes recourse to particular ontological, epistemological and methodological presuppositions. These advocates of paradigm incommensurability therefore reject any form of communication that suggests the inter-paradigmatic or dialectical synthesis of ideas.

Jackson and Carter (1991) are typical of writers who argue strongly for the logic and practice of paradigm incommensurability. They suggest that incommensurability, as a concept, has emancipatory value, for it serves to protect 'alternative' modes of organizational inquiry from the imperialistic tentacles of 'functionalist orthodoxy'. They vehemently criticize those who would oppose or decry paradigm incommensurability by suggesting that such writers have misunderstood the conventionalist message, especially of the Burrell and Morgan kind, which invites difference not synthesis. Jackson and Carter (1991: 123) argue that abandoning paradigm incommensurability can lead us 'inexorably' towards 'epistemological authoritarianism'. They advocate that paradigms should be developed on their own terms, for each presupposes a unique perspective from which concepts are defined and theories emerge. As each paradigm serves to preserve and re-enforce its academic practices and cultural characteristics: 'competing paradigms constitute for each other an otherness which gives each paradigm its specific identity' (Jackson and Carter, 1991: 123). In their view, denial of paradigm incommensurability is symptomatic of fears for epistemological heterogeneity and will eventually lead to sterility and the failure to produce any significant new perspectives for the field.

It can be argued, however, that Jackson and Carter's position is also rooted primarily in a production of knowledge meta-narrative. Whereas they suggest that the process of knowledge production is characterized by incommensurability and diversity, and indeed by incommensurable products, they avoid discussion of the diversity and heterogeneity present similarly in processes of knowledge consumption. In other words, they overlook the fact that their response to the paradigm crisis is but one of the many 'tactics of consumption' deployed in the space of knowledge production. For Jackson and Carter, like Burrell and Morgan before, it is meta-theory that determines identity. 'Otherness' is essentially the otherness of alternative paradigms, whose practices and discourses are to all intents and purposes located in other intellectual worlds.

The Pluralists. An increasing number of researchers have questioned the paradigm incommensurability thesis by advocating degrees of commensurability between paradigms, communication across paradigms, the need to engage in multiparadigm research, or by suggesting the need to move beyond paradigms by adopting a 'pragmatic' perspective. These researchers we call the *pluralists*.

A core proposition of the pluralists is that scientific paradigms can hold a range of concepts, constructs and practices in common. Gioia and Pitre (1989), for example, argue that logically paradigms must entertain common concepts, entities or 'transition zones', for otherwise there would be no basis from which a new theory could refute or amend a previous one. Similarly, Weaver and Gioia (1994) suggest that dialogue between paradigms is not only possible but also essential. Building on Giddens' theory of structuration, they argue that the mere idea that one does multiparadigm research presumes that paradigms hold certain factors in common and that various paradigms reflect upon the individual facets of a complex social phenomenon. The denial of this principle would mean that one is faced with *different* phenomena rather than multifaceted ones.

Schultz and Hatch (1996: 55) also advocate the need for multiparadigm research, suggesting that 'multi-paradigm thinking is both likely and desirable, in light of predictions about diversity in post-industrial society'. They advocate a strategy for moving between paradigms, called 'interplay', which recognizes both contrasts and connections between paradigms. In interplay, the researcher moves back and forth between paradigms, thus allowing multiple views to be held in tension. More recently, Lewis and Grimes (1999) have similarly provided a step-by-step guide to building theory from multiple paradigms, a process they label meta-triangulation.

In the UK, multiparadigm thinking and research has been advocated by Hassard (1985, 1988, 1991). His work is concerned not only with the theoretical underpinnings of paradigm commensurability (1988), but also with producing empirical accounts of a multiparadigmatic nature. Hassard's (1991, 1993) four-fold account of the work behaviour of firefighters is an illustration of how researchers can write multifaceted accounts of organizational phenomena. Although the importance of language conventions in representing the organizational world is made clear, for Hassard, paradigms also remain distinct, if negotiable, language games whose dynamic lies primarily in the production, rather than the consumption, of knowledge spaces.

While the above authors attempt to preserve the internal logic and identity of paradigms, others suggest that boundaries might in fact need to dissolve, at least on a temporary basis, in order to ensure the creation of common reference systems. McKinley (1995) and McKinley and Mone (1998), for example, recommend the creation of a 'dictionary' that would include democratically produced definitions of key organization studies constructs. This dictionary could serve as a common reference system by which paradigms can be reconciled and evaluated. In contrast, Scherer and Dowling (1995) suggest that the problem of incommensurability should not be addressed through yet another search for the 'right' criteria to evaluate systems of orientation from an observer's perspective. They argue instead that researchers with incommensurable positions should seek methods for discovering how to interact and communicate with each other in order to improve practice. Thus, the 'resolution of incommensurable theories will only be possible through a process of dialogue among the participants' (Scherer and Dowling, 1995: 231), with such a resolution having a potentially significant impact on improving managerial and organizational competence.

This appeal to pragmatism has been also discussed by Wicks and Freeman (1998), who urge researchers to move beyond epistemological distinctions between paradigms by making room for 'ethics', thus increasing, they suggest, the potential 'relevance' of research. Pragmatism is promoted as a useful intellectual tool in that it sheds light on the moral dimension of organizing. Wicks and Freeman (1998) do not think it possible simply to combine various paradigms or reconcile them in order to create a compelling alternative to the current situation. Instead, building on Rorty (1985), they advocate a method of 'pragmatic experimentation', whereby researchers construct a vision of organizational analysis that subscribes to 'usefulness', defined from the point of view of the wider community.

The pluralists discussed above present us with various approaches to attaining a sense of paradigm commensurability in organizational theory and research. Their views, however, again subscribe primarily to a productionist meta-narrative in that they variously champion the development of a field of studies that is consensually multiparadigmatic. Consumption issues are rarely discussed in their work, as is any reflexive philosophy that would include simultaneous assessments of production and consumption. Instead, a strategy of multiple paradigm research is thrown onto the world as a demonstrably 'good thing' methodologically.

The Postmodernists. Finally, the camp we term the *postmodernists*, for us, adopts a more reflexive perspective on knowledge production and consumption. Although the label postmodernism makes room for a wide pallet of competing positions, postmodernists usually champion and call for new types of knowledge, modes of writing, values and politics to overcome the deficiencies of modern discourses and practices (Best and Kellner, 1991). It is beyond the purpose of this paper to chart the murky territory of postmodern thought (see, for example, Rosenau, 1992); suffice to say that postmodernists typically rebuke the notion of paradigm as being fundamentally rooted in a production perspective on knowledge. In so doing, they call attention to acts of consumption in two major ways: first, by inquiring into the ways in which researchers consume existing knowledge in order to construct new knowledge and, second, by questioning the nature of research practices and their relation to prevailing organizational and societal discourses.

Deetz (1996) was among the first organization theorists to advocate this line of analysis. By shifting attention away from paradigmatic assumptions, he located research differences not in the ontological and epistemological assumptions of the individual researcher and the procedures or methodologies used, but in the modalities by which research concepts emerge, and the relation of research practices to the dominant discourses prevailing in organizations, the research community, and the wider community. In pursuing this case, it can be argued that researchers promote a move from meta-narrative to *petit récit*, or, in other words, from 'grand' strategies of knowledge production to 'local' tactics of consumption.

Deetz (1996) argues that there are in fact four discourses available to organizational researchers, namely the normative, interpretive, critical and dialogic. Put briefly, the *normative* discourse relies on a priori research concepts and emphasizes consensus; the *interpretive* discourse, while stressing consensus, adopts an emergent perspective on the origin of concepts and problems; the *critical* discourse adheres to dissensus and a priori modes of conceptualization; and the *dialogic* discourse embraces an emergent and dissentive logic of research (see Figure 1).

Deetz's classification calls attention to acts of consumption in two distinct ways. First, by questioning the processes by which research concepts emerge, Deetz calls into question the sort of knowledge researchers consume in order to produce their new categories. For Deetz, research concepts may be developed in relation to organizational members' day-to-day practices, as local and *emergent* concepts, or they may exist a priori, being brought to the research setting by researchers themselves. While, in the first case, concept development is the result of numerous and heterogeneous acts of consumption that operate as bridges between the researcher and his/her subjects, in the later case, the researcher takes on board (consumes) the definition embraced by the scientific community.

Emergent research thrives on a multiplicity of language games. Theoretical vocabulary as established by the scientific community is considered only a starting point, and is constantly challenged and redefined by ulterior acts of consumption which involve the interplay between the researcher's and the field members' language games. Knowledge is

Figure 1. Postmodernist Discourses

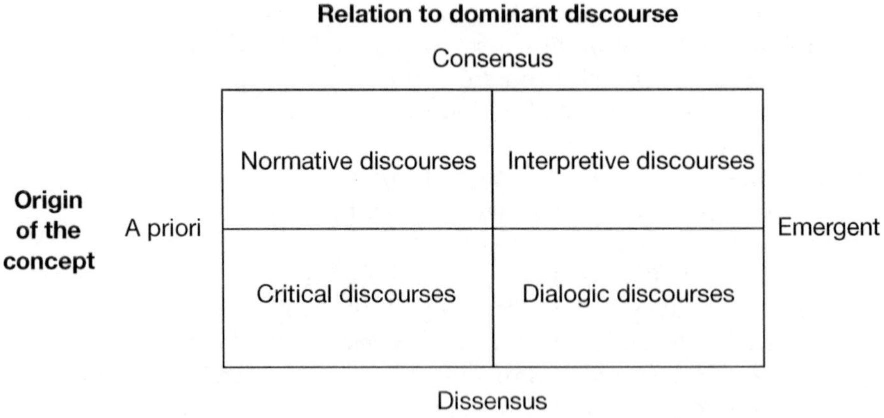

Relation to dominant discourse

Consensus

	Normative discourses	Interpretive discourses
	Critical discourses	Dialogic discourses

Origin of the concept   A priori   Emergent

Dissensus

Source Adapted from Deetz (1996).

equated with insight rather than truth; with the temporal and contextual—with that which cannot be generalized.

A priori research, on the other hand, privileges the language game of the scientific community and tends to be theory-driven, with careful attention being paid to consuming definitions prior to the research process. There is a tendency to universalize while decoding the experiences of the 'objects' of research into the language game of the researcher. The knowledge produced is considered politically free and thus not bound by prevailing power relations and discourses.

Deetz's second point regarding acts of consumption concerns the relation between the knowledge produced and the prevailing social and scientific orders. If knowledge is consumed in such a way that it supports and reinforces an existing order, it is held to be of a *consensus* type. If the opposite is the case, that is, consumption helps to problematize an existing order, it is held to be of a *dissensus* type.

Consensual knowledge is typically characterized by a search for order, integration and harmony. It focuses on representing existing order through a 'neutral' language that allows the researcher to mirror the present and the consumer of knowledge to grasp its reality.[10] On the other hand, dissensus knowledge views order as historicized and politicized, attempting to deconstruct its pillars inasmuch as they suppress conflict and struggle. Language is not seen to be a neutral instrument at the disposal of researchers but a means of reconstructing reality. The consumption of such knowledge is aimed at challenging taken-for-granted assumptions and social practices.[11]

While the normative and interpretive discourses may appeal to the dominant logic for purposes of legitimization, the remaining discourses 'witness *differands*' and thus (in Lyotard's 1984/1997 sense) speak in the name of the 'unknown, unheard and absent'. As *petits récits*, such discourses are concerned with moves and countermoves which serve to limit processes of naturalization. They may be regarded as tactics of consumption, calculated actions determined by the absence of a 'proper' locus (de Certeau, 1984). Thus, from a postmodern perspective, consensus has become an outmoded and suspect value (Lyotard, 1984/1997) and there is no reason to limit enquiry to a few paths marked by a particular elite (Kilduff and Mehra, 1997).

Conclusions and Implications for Future Research

This paper has advocated the need to move away from a primarily productionist perspective on knowledge to one which embraces acts of production and consumption in a more reflexive way. In its strongest sense, the former emphasizes a hierarchy of sciences and bemoans the pre-paradigmatic state in which organizational studies finds itself. The latter, in contrast, points to the language game character of science, the heterogeneous and slippery nature of knowledge, and rejects any hypothetical science hierarchy.

We advocate the need for a more reflexive approach on ontological and epistemological grounds. From an ontological point of view, it can be argued that the explanadum of organizational analysis has changed dramatically in the last few decades (Burrell, 1996). Organizations are now seen to inhabit a so-called post-industrial world where new forms of production and consumption have come into being. The bureaucratic organization, for example, is undermined by the network organization, the process-driven organization, or the virtual organization. Fordist mass production has given way to post-Fordist technologies that allow for flexible specialization and niche marketing (Piore and Sabel, 1984; Clegg, 1990; Casey, 1995). These new organizational realities point to the importance of the consumer in organizing both production and distribution (Bauman, 1998).

But it is not just the nature of the organizational reality that has shifted, for new forms of knowing, or new 'explanans', have accompanied the move from the industrial to post-industrial. The move from modernist to postmodernist epistemologies has allowed researchers to question not only the efficacy of 'strong' productive forms, but also the conditions that make them possible and the role they have in (re)producing social and economic relations (Hassard and Parker, 1993; White and Jaques, 1995). In this view, knowledge and power are seen as intertwined. Knowledge cannot escape the regime of power that made it visible in the first place (Foucault, 1980). Rather than ultimate and objective, knowledge is tentative and slippery, located in a space populated by both its producers and consumers.

The paper argues that most responses to the paradigm 'crisis' are grounded primarily in a productionist meta-narrative on knowledge. For example, the non-consumers produce accounts of the organizational world without paying explicit attention to paradigmatic inclinations or language conventions in use. The protectionists insist that boundaries around paradigms must be protected and respected as they serve as mechanisms for protecting paradigm identity and legitimacy. In so doing, they vehemently oppose the dominant positivist discourse without acknowledging that their own response is a 'tactic of consumption' aimed at undermining the 'mainstream'. The pluralists praise communication between paradigms and the importance of undertaking multiparadigm research. They do not believe in an inherent paradigmatic hierarchy but view each paradigm as a collection of shared, static assumptions rather than as a collection of dynamic language conventions. And the much-vaunted integrationist camp suggests that the scientific community needs to agree on a consensus paradigm in order to rescue the field from the pre-paradigmatic state in which it finds itself. In so doing, it elevates the process of knowledge production to a supreme status and down-plays the role of researchers as consumers of knowledge

The present paper, however, not only questions the aims served by this latter scenario but also engages in a postmodern project to undermine it. We agree with Burrell's (1996: 645) argument that:

> . . . the idea that one voice could drown out the rest is an attractive one . . . but it is a dream which can never be realized fully. There will, thank goodness, always be the voices of dissent and the clamour of alternatives vying for aural space.

Furthermore, we suggest that the production of a unique organizational paradigm is improbable given the existence of heterogeneous 'tactics of consumption', that is, *petits récits* which speak about the 'silent' and the 'invisible'. The consumption of knowledge cannot be systematically managed and regulated by institutions irrespective of the community motives and agendas that prevail.

Notes

We would like to thank Valérie Fournier, Martin Kilduff, Martin Parker and three anonymous reviewers for their insightful comments.

1　Guba and Lincoln (1994) suggest that paradigms are predicated on the interaction of three types of assumptions: *ontological*—concerning the nature of reality; *epistemological*—concerning the process of knowing; and *methodological*—concerning the research techniques and strategies available to researchers.

2　While, for some authors, the notion of paradigm incommensurability is 'crucial', as it raises fundamental questions about the 'reality' of phenomena under investigation (McKinley and Mone, 1998), for others, the concept 'may be one of the greatest intellectual myths of the 20th century' (Donaldson, 1998: 269).

3　In the theory of the field of cultural production, for example, Bourdieu (1993) accounts similarly for not only the product of science itself but also the producers of symbolic goods, their position in the field, publishers (as intermediates between producers and consumers) and consumers of symbolic goods.

4   Whilst tactics of consumption are never fixed, they are nevertheless spatially constrained. However, researchers can temporarily 'transform' knowledge into something quite different from that originally intended. In so doing, they may take the opportunity to resist normative practices, albeit that such a 'victory' will only be cadmean, for such researchers do not possess a knowledge space of their own, being constrained by the limits of traditional knowledge production.

5   The 'hard' sciences, however, would possibly refuse to acknowledge this fact in order to maintain cultural hegemony (see, for example, Astley and Zammuto, 1992; Lyotard, 1984/1997; Mauws and Phillips, 1995).

6   Lyotard derives his use of the concept of agonistics largely from Nietzsche's (1911/1974) 'Homer's Conquest'. In the process, he outlines how it is also 'the basis of Heraclitus's ontology and of the Sophists' dialectic, not to mention the early tragedians. A good part of Aristotle's reflections in the *Topics* and the *Sophistici Elenchi* is devoted to it' (1974: 88).

7   For Lyotard, it is important that little narratives do not in fact seek 'mutual encroachment' via linkages constructed with ideological ends in view.

8   However, as Schultz and Hatch (1996: 530) argue, 'regardless of whether organizational researchers acknowledge paradigmatic assumptions, they make and use them when they develop and apply theory'.

9   This integrationist argument has both intellectual and political dimensions. According to Donaldson (1998) the integration of paradigms is an achievable task, although 'there are real difficulties as to whether scholars will reach agreement' (1998: 267). In his view, in North America, new paradigmatic views are intertwined with a drive for intellectual 'novelty' and the personal career advancement that this may promote. In contrast, in Europe he feels paradigm debate is viewed as the means to continue the tradition of radical critique.

10 It could be argued that much research published in leading journals in management studies and organizational analysis is of this nature. This is perhaps not surprising given that potential contributors to the *Academy of Management Review* (AMR), for example, are informed that 'the management and organization theory contributions present in AMR are grounded in the "normal science disciplines" of economics, psychology, sociology, or social psychology' (Information for Contributors). The Notice to Contributors of the *Administrative Science Quarterly* suggests similarly that the aim of the journal is to 'build a coherent, cumulative body of knowledge'. In so doing, the journal has traditionally welcomed research of a consensual kind. A seeming concern for 'coherence' in knowledge is emphasized also in the Notice for Contributors of a leading UK journal, the *Journal of Management Studies*, which states 'our ultimate criterion for a paper's acceptability is that an informed reader is likely to learn something new from it that contributes to the development of coherent bodies of knowledge'.

11 Certain leading journals in management and organization studies regularly publish research that challenges dominant discourses. For example, *Organization* and the *Journal of Management Inquiry* aim to promote 'dialogue and innovation in studies of organization' (*Organization*, Aims and Scope) and

'alternative modes of expression as play, fiction, speeches, movies, new events, and scholarly work outside the common boundaries of the field' (*Journal of Management Inquiry*, Submission Guidelines). These journals are replete with postmodernist and feminist critiques of management, work and organization.

References

Astley, W.G. (1985) 'Administrative Science as Socially Constructed Truth', *Administrative Science Quarterly* 30: 497–513.

Astley, W.G. and Zammuto, R.F. (1992) 'Organization Science, Managers and Language Games', *Organization Science* 3(4): 443–60.

Bauman, Z. (1998) *Work, Consumerism and the New Poor.* Buckingham: Open University Press.

Best, S. and Kellner, D. (1991) *Postmodern Theory.* New York: The Guilford Press.

Bourdieu, P. (1990) *The Logic of Practice.* Cambridge: Polity Press.

Bourdieu, P. (1993) *The Field of Cultural Production.* Cambridge: Polity Press.

Burrell, G. (1996) 'Normal Science, Paradigms, Metaphors, Discourses and Genealogies of Analysis', in S.R. Clegg, C. Hardy and W.R. Nord (eds) *Handbook of Organization Studies*, pp. 31–56. London: Sage.

Burrell, G. and Morgan, M. (1979) *Sociological Paradigms and Organizational Analysis.* London: Heinemann.

Calás, M.B. and Smircich, L. (1999) 'Past Postmodernism? Reflections and Tentative Directions', *Academy of Management Review* 24(4): 649–71.

Casey, C. (1995) *Work, Self and Society: After Industrialism.* London: Routledge.

Clegg, S. (1990) *Modern Organizations: Organization Studies in the Postmodern World.* London: Sage.

Cole, S. (1983) 'The Hierarchy of Sciences', *American Journal of Sociology* 89: 111–39.

Cooper, R. (1983) 'The Other: A Model of Human Structuring', in G. Morgan (ed.) *Beyond Method.* London: Sage.

de Certeau, M. (1984) *The Practice of Everyday Life.* Los Angeles: University of California Press.

Deetz, S. (1996) 'Describing Differences in Approaches to Organization Science: Rethinking Burrell and Morgan and Their Legacy', *Organization Science* 7(2): 191–207.

Donaldson, L. (1985) *In Defence of Organization Theory.* Cambridge: Cambridge University Press.

Donaldson, L. (1996) *For Positivist Organization Theory: Proving the Hard Core.* London: Sage

Donaldson, L. (1998) 'The Myth of Paradigm Incommensurability in Management Studies: Comments by an Integrationist', *Organization* 5(2): 267–72.

Edgell, S., Hetherington, K. and Warde, A. (1996) *Consumption Matters.* Oxford: Blackwell/The Sociological Review.

Fairclough, N. (1996) *Language and Power.* Harlow: Addison Wesley Longman.

Feyerabend, P. (1975) *Against Method.* London: New Left Books.

Foucault, M. (1980) *Power/Knowledge.* New York: Pantheon.

Friedrichs, R. (1970) *A Sociology of Sociology.* New York: Free Press.

Gherardi, S. and Nicolini, D. (2000) 'To Transfer is to Transform: The Circulation of Safety Knowledge', *Organization* 7(2): 329–48.

Gioia, D. and Pitre, E. (1989) 'Multi-paradigm Perspectives on Theory Building', *Academy of Management Review* 5(4): 584–602.

Gouldner, A. (1970) *The Coming Crisis of Western Sociology*. London: Heinemann.

Grint, K. (1991) *The Sociology of Work: An Introduction*. Cambridge: Polity Press.

Guba, E.G. and Lincoln, Y.S. (1994) 'Competing Paradigms in Qualitative Research', in N.K. Denzin and Y.S. Lincoln (eds) *Handbook of Qualitative Research*. London: Sage.

Harvey, D. (1990) *The Condition of Postmodernity*. Oxford: Blackwell.

Hassard, J. (1985) 'Multiple Paradigms and Organizational Research: An Analysis of Work Behaviour in the Fire Service', unpublished doctoral dissertation, University of Aston, UK.

Hassard, J. (1988) 'Overcoming Hermeticism in Organization Theory: An Alternative to Paradigm Incommensurability', *Human Relations* 41(3): 247–59.

Hassard, J. (1991) 'Multiple Paradigms and Organizational Analysis: A Case Study', *Organization Studies* 12(2): 279–99.

Hassard, J. (1993) *Sociology and Organization Theory: Positivism, Paradigms and Postmodernity*. Cambridge: Cambridge University Press.

Hassard, J. and Parker, M. (1993) *Postmodernism and Organizations*. London: Sage.

Jackson, N. and Carter, P. (1991) 'In Defence of Paradigm Commensurability', *Organization Studies* 12(1): 109–27.

Kilduff, M. and Mehra, A. (1997) 'Postmodernism and Organisational Research', *Academy of Management Review* 22(2): 453–81.

Knights, D. (1997) 'Organization Theory in the Age of Deconstruction: Dualism, Gender and Postmodernism Revisited', *Organization Studies* 18(1): 1–19.

Kuhn, T.S. (1962/1970) *The Structure of Scientific Revolutions*. Chicago: The University of Chicago Press.

Lakatos, I. and Musgrave, A., eds (1970) *Criticism and the Growth of Knowledge*. Cambridge: Cambridge University Press.

Law, J. (1987) 'Technology and Heterogeneous Engineering: The Case of Portuguese Expansion', in W. Bijker, T. Hughes and T. Pinch (eds) *The Social Construction of Technological Systems: New Directions in the Sociology of Knowledge*. Cambridge, MA: MIT Press.

Lewis, M.W. and Grimes, A.J. (1999) 'Metatriangulation: Building Theory from Multiple Paradigms', *Academy of Management Review* 24(4): 672–90.

Lyotard, J.-F. (1984/1997) *The Postmodern Condition: A Report on Knowledge*. Manchester: Manchester University Press.

McKinley, W. (1995) 'Commentary: Towards a Reconciliation of the Theory—Pluralism in Strategic Management—Incommensurability and the Constructivist Approach of the Erlangen School', *Advances in Strategic Management* 12A: 249–60.

McKinley, W. and Mone, M.A. (1998) 'The Re-construction of Organization Studies: Wrestling with Incommensurability', *Organization* 5(2): 169–89.

McKinley, W., Mone, M.A. and Moon, G. (1999) 'Determinants and Development of Schools in Organization Theory', *Academy of Management Review* 24(4): 634–48.

Mauws, M.K. and Phillips, N. (1995) 'Understanding Language Games', *Organization Science* 6(3): 322–34.

Munro, R. (1999) 'After Knowledge: The Language of Information', in S. Linstead and R. Westwood (eds) *The Language of Organization*. London: Sage.

Nietzsche, F. (1911/1974) 'Homer's Contest', in M. Mugge *Complete Works*. New York: Gordon Press.

Pfeffer, J. (1993) 'Barriers to the Advance of Organizational Science: Paradigm Development as a Dependent Variable', *Academy of Management Review* 18(4): 599–620.

Pfeffer, J. (1997) 'Mortality, Reproducibility, and the Persistence of Styles of Theory', *Organization Science* 6(4): 681–6.

Phillips, D. (1977) *Wittgenstein and Scientific Knowledge*. London: Macmillan.

Piore, M.J. and Sabel, C.F. (1984) *The Second Industrial Divide: Possibilities for Prosperity*. New York: Basic Books.

Reed, M. (1985) *Redirections in Organizational Analysis*. London: Tavistock.

Reed, M. (1992) *The Sociology of Organizations: Themes, Perspectives and Prospects*. New York: Harvester Weatsheaf.

Reed, M. (1996) 'Organizational Theorising: A Historical Contested Terrain', in S.R. Clegg, C. Hardy and W.R. Nord (eds) *Handbook of Organization Studies*, pp: 31–56. London: Sage.

Rosenau, P.M. (1992) *Post-modernism and the Social Sciences: Insights, Inroads and Intrusions*. Princeton, NJ: Princeton University Press.

Rorty, R. (1985) 'Texts and Lumps', *New Literary History* 17: 1–15.

Scherer, A.G. and Dowling, M.J. (1995) 'Towards a Reconciliation of the Theory—Pluralism in Strategic Management—Incommensurability and the Constructivist Approach of the Erlangen School', *Advances in Strategic Management* 12A: 195–247.

Scherer, A.G. (1998) 'Pluralism and Incommensurability in Strategic Management and Organization Theory: A Problem in Search of a Solution', *Organization* 5(2): 147–69.

Schultz, M. and Hatch, M.J. (1996) 'Living with Multiple Paradigms: The Case of Paradigm Interplay in Organization Culture Studies', *Academy of Management Review* 1(2): 529–57.

Shapere, D. (1971) 'The Paradigm Concept', *Science* 17: 706–9.

Silverman, D. (1969) 'Correspondence: Organization: A Rejoinder', *Sociology* 3(3): 420–1.

Weaver, G.R. and Gioia, D.A. (1994) 'Paradigms Lost: Incommensurability vs. Structurationist Inquiry', *Organization Studies* 15(4): 565–90.

White, R.F. and Jaques, R. (1995) 'Operationalizing the Postmodernity Construct for Efficient Organizational Change Management', *Journal of Organizational Change Management* 8(2): 45–71.

Wicks, A.C. and Freeman, R.E. (1998) 'Organization Studies and the New Pragmatism: Positivism, Anti-positivism and the Search for Ethics', *Organization Science* 9(2): 123–40.

Wittgenstein, L. (1953) *Philosophical Investigations*. Oxford: Basil Blackwell.

John Hassard is Professor of Organizational Analysis at the University of Manchester Institute of Science and Technology and Senior Research Associate at the Judge Institute of Management Studies, Cambridge University. He previously taught at the London Business School and universities of Cardiff and Keele. He has published 10 books including *Time, Work and Organization* (1989), *Sociology and Organizational Theory* (1993), *Postmodernism and Organization* (1994), *Organization/Representation* (1999) and *Body and Organization* (2000). His research interests lie in organization theory and empirical studies of enterprise reform (with special reference to transitional economies). **Address**: UMIST, P.O. Box 88, Manchester M60 1QD, UK. [email: john.hassard@umist.ac.uk]

Mihaela Kelemen is Lecturer in quaity management and organization theory at Keele University. Her research focuses on critical approaches to quality management, economies in transition and postmodern theories of organizations. Her book on quality management is due to be published by Sage in 2002, while an edited collection on *Eastern European Management* (jointly with Monika Kostera) will be published by Palgrave shortly. **Address**: Department of Management, Keele University, Staffs ST5 5BG, UK. [email: mna05@keele.ac.uk]

The Case Against "Practicality" and "Relevance" as Gauges of Business Schools

Responding to Challenges Posed by Criticisms of Business School Research

MICHAEL A. GOLDBERG
University of British Columbia

PROLOGUE AND SETTING

The Issues

Universities are increasingly being asked to be accountable and responsive public institutions. Business schools especially, given their professional focus and powerful set of business stakeholders, have received unique criticism. Critiques span fragmented undergraduate and MBA core curricula, to a perceived excessive focus on theory and mathematical and statistical analytic methods. Important and serious issues have arisen about business school teaching and subject matter and about the value of graduates to the business community, citing high levels of technical skills, and much lower levels of interpersonal, communication, leadership, and team skills. Above all, graduates are seen as weak in integrating informa-

tion from diverse business sources and perspectives (Elfring & van Raaij, 1995).

An additional dimension of business school culture that has attracted public attention recently is research. Censure here usually focuses on the theoretical stance of much of the research efforts of elite business schools, on the use of powerful quantitative methods, and on catering to international academic peers with less apparent concern being given to the current problems and issues confronting the business community. The resulting cry for practicality is loud and often shrill.

Some Responses From the Business School Community

Business schools have been quite quick and innovative in responding in a diversity of ways to these

AUTHOR'S NOTE: This article benefits greatly from insights of two of my colleagues, Professors Gerald Gorn and Maurice D. Levi. Gerald Gorn read numerous early drafts and added important new directions for the article while helping eliminate errors and inconsistencies. Maurice Levi extended the article into a number of areas that I had missed initially. His wisdom is evident throughout. Last, editor Alan Glassman and a *JMI* reviewer provided very helpful ideas to bolster the article considerably. To all, my sincere thanks and gratitude. Residual errors of course are mine and mine alone.

criticisms and issues. At the macro level, the American Assembly of Collegiate Schools of Business (AACSB) completely overhauled its accreditation standards and accreditation processes to accommodate a broader range of MBA programs that were capable of responding directly to the calls for change coming from the business community.

At the micro or school level, an integrated array of responses has been set in motion across North America. First, schools of all sizes have been engaged in a varied assortment of strategic planning activities. These planning exercises help schools scan and understand their changing environments, assess their strategic strengths and weaknesses, and develop strategic goals for coping with and prospering in these radically changed circumstances. In most instances, existing or newly formed business advisory councils are directly involved in the planning process. An interesting side benefit of such planning activities is that they have also helped to demonstrate that business schools themselves can be much more business-like, can be much more focused, can set priorities, and can bring planned or envisioned futures into concordance with expected resources.

One recurrent response theme that is emerging is the need to privatize business schools and to think of them very much as stand-alone businesses in their own right, where they charge market levels of tuition, keep the lion's share of these tuition revenues, and use their enhanced financial resources to refocus and reposition their programs in the increasingly competitive MBA marketplace. This trend is in evidence at both public and private institutions. In some cases, the push for privatization arose from the strategic plan, whereas in other cases it led to the inauguration of the planning process. A key part of most privatization thinking is the development of a robust executive education program within the business school to visibly serve the business community and, at the same time, to earn some added income to help pay for the growing costs associated with competing in the business of being a business school.

An Overview of the Argument That Follows

The primary premise of this article, as the title suggests, is that immediate utility and practical application to business problems are very poor criteria to impose on judging either the quality or the usefulness of university-based research. As I argue subsequently, imposing such criteria is likely to be counterproductive and contrary to the actual long-term interests and needs of business.

To support the argument, I begin by examining the remarkably complementary differences between the worldviews and actions of the business and academic communities. These differences afford unique opportunities for cooperation, not just conflict. The complementarity between business and academic thinking and doing can enrich both sectors enormously if meaningful and authentic two-way conversations can be established.

Having situated the importance of these differences, I want to move on to outline the central role that traditional research and research values can play in teaching, curriculum development, and service to the business community. Therefore, I next detail the ways in which the research tradition at universities underpins and nourishes the development of the entire array of degree and nondegree courses that modern, leading business schools must offer. In this vein, it is helpful to stress that traditional research values lie at the core of all good research, even that aimed at or conducted by a professional business group.

Given this prologue, I move to discuss practicality and relevance and the pivotal importance of the core academic values of independence, academic freedom, open inquiry and debate, and research excellence. These core values lie at the heart of the basic virtues and strengths of universities. They render the university truly useful and give it meaningful and important things to say to the business community, and a sound footing for conducting conversations with business for significant mutual long-run benefit. This holds not just for business schools but for engineering, medicine, forestry, and agriculture as well; indeed, any professional school in a university in which there is a need to develop two-way information flows and conversations between practicing professionals and the academic community providers of the basic knowledge sustaining the profession.

TWO PREVIOUS SOLITUDES: BUSINESS AND ACADEMIA

Keeping the dangers of stereotyping and generalizing in mind, it is useful to sketch out the differences between the way typical business people and typical academics think and structure reality. This kind of depiction can yield useful insights about these differences and the ways in which they can be structured as powerful complements.

Business Thinking Typified

Facing daily the demands of the marketplace and of quarterly scrutiny, business people understandably take rather short-term views measured in weeks, months, and quarters. They are also operationally focused to support the smooth and profitable performance of their firms. The learning mode is rooted in the specific or particularistic and is highly experiential and inductive. When businesses do research, it is issue driven, not curiosity driven, and usually leads to proprietary and private knowledge. Research excellence or quality is a means to an end to ensure usability and reliability.

The business approach has shortcomings. It is frequently unable to step back from day-to-day problems and issues to generalize and frame them in a manner that is capable of being analyzed and treated rigorously. The short-term focus of business often precludes gaining perspective on longer-term, broader strategic and environmental issues. Such thinking could place their organization in an appropriate larger context and allow powerful and innovative insights about operating issues. Also, the concern with practical, particularistic questions often hampers the development of useful theories and generalizations, which could be applied in analogous situations that might arise. This severely limits the ability to see new opportunities and approaches to existing practices.

Academic Thinking Typified

Practical thinking and learning contrast strikingly with the usual academic approach. Without operating pressures, academics generally take a long-term view and work on problems for many years. Their route usually starts at the conceptual/theoretical level, even if the work is applied and empirical. Academics are not generally interested in particularistic problems, but rather focus on generalizable findings and constructs. The style is highly deductive and analytic, moving analytically from theory to conclusions. For most, research is curiosity driven, not propelled by societal demands or short-term needs, especially in the almost unconstrained funding era of the 1970s and 1980s. Last, research is aimed at

international academic colleagues and not at nonacademic audiences.

That their work is published and in the public domain is a source of pride for academics. As a result, their work is available to all who might be interested via traditional, refereed academic journals and now through the Internet. Academic research also holds quality and excellence as ends in themselves, being seen as fundamental parts of the research and learning tradition.

Academic thinking is powerful and usable over long time frames. However, it often lacks the institutional and situational context and content needed to make it truly rich and insightful. All too frequently, academic work is founded on untenable assumptions and abstractions, so that conclusions are often quite sterile and limited in insights about the functioning of firms and markets.

Turning the Differences to Mutually Beneficial Ends

Academics and business people clearly think and do things differently, and these differences are significant and extensive. The typical business person and academic described above are obviously caricatures defining endpoints of a continuum. Few business people or academics reside at the poles of these comparative dimensions. It is useful though to sketch out the antithetical nature of these basic belief systems as it highlights just how different are the worldviews of the two communities. More important, these striking differences provide the foundation on which a powerful dialogue can be erected that will allow businesses and academic institutions to cooperate and learn from each other.

Returning to our theme, academic management research can contribute meaningfully to business precisely because it has a very different intellectual base. Accordingly, these differences need to be fully understood and appreciated by both communities, so that the benefits can be reaped of the almost perfect complementarity of these divergent ways of thinking, learning, and doing.

The finance field provides the plainest examples of the ways in which cutting-edge research finds its way into cutting-edge practice. For example, the explosive growth of derivatives and other new financial instruments, investment products, and the rapid securitization of a vast array of real and financial assets all rest on a host of advances in finance theory and highly quantitative technical applications of the theory. Traditional academic research has also directly influenced management practice in marketing, in operations management, in managerial and financial accounting and auditing, and even in more applied areas like corporate governance, executive compensation, and retail sales and inventory management. In all of these instances, very traditional academic research continues to influence day-to-day operations in straightforward and sometimes surprising ways as later examples show.

Information and ideas have not flowed unidirectionally from the academy to business. Academia very much needs to draw on the operational focus and problem-solving experience of business to tap exciting and rich sources of new problems and puzzles. The business community is also a mother lode of data and experiential knowledge that can be productively mined by the academic community to test new (and old) theories and to probe attitudes and views on important business, organizational, and societal issues. Traditional curiosity-driven research, in which knowledge creation is an end in itself, can usefully be shaped by the experiences and insights of the nonacademic community as stakeholders in the research. Thus academic research and its resulting methods, theories, and knowledge need to increasingly be a means to broader societal ends and as the basis for fertile and diverse conversations with stakeholders outside the academic world.

Consequently, I want to sketch now, in somewhat greater detail, the several styles of academic research and the ways in which the research enterprise underpins university-based management education. I also want to suggest the ways in which better dialogue between the business and academic communities can enhance the productivity of both.

MANAGEMENT EDUCATION ERECTED ON A RESEARCH BASE

Two Divergent Styles of Management Research and Education

Two divergent styles of management education have evolved in North America. For expository purposes, I have overdrawn the differences and stereotyped these two styles to make the distinctions clearer and to provide sharply contrasting backdrops for the discussion that follows. Drawing these dissimilar educational and research philosophies as virtually polar opposites provides a ready means for comprehending better the unique aspects of the traditional academic approach and its underlying values. This understanding can then be used to bridge the business and academic solitudes.

The first style is typified by the Harvard Business School (HBS). The famed case method of management teaching and learning originated there. Its inductive approach to learning is reinforced broadly at the HBS, where the research culture is rooted in professional research, professional research outlets, and consulting activities all with a spotlight on relevance.

The contrasting style of the Sloan School of Management at the Massachusetts Institute of Technology (MIT) differs markedly from its neighbor across the Charles River, a scant few miles away.[1] In the MIT/Chicago model, the primary audience is the international scholarly community, where research originates more from the curiosity of the researcher than from the needs and demands of the business community. Learning is also highly theoretical, analytic, and deductive, in keeping with the legacy of the academic research tradition.

The HBS approach is widely admired by the business community and its relevance and practical value well established. It continues to be favored and accepted, and its graduates continue to be among the most highly paid and influential anywhere.

However, in my view, its weaknesses are significant. First, there is considerable artificiality in the use of cases. They are stories about actual business issues, but they are not real in the sense that they are ongoing and alive or that the students can actually make a difference in the outcome or circumstances of the case. Second, the heavy reliance on inductive learning is also troublesome, as is the corresponding lack of strong theoretical and analytical training. More on this shortly.

Notwithstanding the flaws of the case approach, I do see great utility in using cases selectively, although I am less certain about the case method in its entirety. I see real value in using cases as capstones and as adjuncts to theory-based analytical learning. Cases do provide valuable context for learning and for application of theories and methods, and their use should complement well the growing move to direct experiential learning through course-based business projects and through internships. As a form of experiential and inductive learning, cases can nicely expand these direct learning approaches. However, I am skeptical about the future growth and success of the traditional "pure" case method, and the applied research that goes with it, when it is used to the virtual exclusion of the theoretical and analytical approaches discussed next.

Despite, or perhaps because of, the great success of the HBS approach, I want to argue strenuously here, and in the rest of this article, for the very dissimilar MIT/Chicago style of management research, as it derives much more from conventional academic values and perspectives stereotyped earlier. Moreover, the MIT mode is most different from the business learning model, and thus understanding it can yield the greatest potential value to the business community as suggested previously. Therefore, it is helpful to outline how and why the traditional research model is so useful and relevant for the conduct and progress of both management education and practice now and in the future.

The Case for an Academic Research-Based Model of Management Education and Practice: The Giga-Volt Electricity Transmission Line As an Analogy

Research creates new knowledge. It can take numerous forms and stem from widely varying research traditions. In a research-based business school, it supports the entire educational superstructure.

In the absence of new knowledge, courses, curricula, and teaching are unlikely to be of the highest standard. In a research-based business school, we can envision academic research as the energy that drives the whole enterprise. Seen this way, high-powered academic research can be likened to a giga-volt power line and high-voltage power generation. More applied and professional research, being derivative in nature, can be likened to lower-voltage house current.

From an educational perspective, the virtue of a high-voltage line and of generating power at high voltages is that it can be stepped down to a variety of lower voltages and powers and thus is extremely flexible and adaptable. Lower voltages and wattages, however, are vastly less flexible and usable.

Applying the analogy to a business school suggests that high-powered traditional academic research provides a more useful (i.e., practical) intellectual base as it can be "stepped down" or transformed into a diversity of degree and nondegree teaching programs and a similar diversity of research applications, ranging from the most theoretical and technical to the most

applied and immediately usable. For example, doctoral programs represent a very modest transformation of this knowledge, whereas executive development programs constitute a major stepping down and transformation of this knowledge so that it is accessible to, and usable by, management professionals and practitioners. Bachelor's and master's degrees would lie somewhere in the middle.

Knowledge supplies the substantive content on which degree and nondegree courses and curricula are founded. The greater the intellectual power (back to our giga-volt analogy) available to course and program designers and instructors, the greater the content available to students and executive-development course participants. Research not only creates new knowledge; it compels researchers to be current on the rapidly expanding frontiers in their own and closely related fields. As a result, building degree and nondegree management and executive-development courses on the research tradition provides access to researchers and their state-of-the-art knowledge. Teachers with a strong research background have the unique ability to present to students and business participants the whole panoply of what is known in their field—all the way from the cutting edge to much more applied and derivative knowledge. Nonresearcher teachers are much less likely to be conversant with the state of knowledge in their area, and thus have a much more limited range of content available to them to share with their classes, whatever their level.

To summarize the point, if the only knowledge available to business schools was that derived from highly applied, demand-driven, and situationally based research, then there would be a much more limited range of teaching programs possible and available to such business schools and to their student and business stakeholders. If, however, the school's knowledge base were of a more traditional academic nature (e.g., high-powered research in our analogy), then the school has open to it the full range of academic programs—from the most advanced doctoral training and research through to the most applied and professional executive training and development programs and courses.

The giga-volt analogy applies on the service front also whether serving governments or businesses. For governments, having access to state-of-the-art research theories, methods, and findings allows a research-based business school to serve government more effectively. By drawing on the latest research findings and methods, research-based business schools can contribute to the highest levels of long- and short-term policy formulation and analysis, and to more immediate and specific policy and program research because of the intellectual rigor, power, and generalizability of the academic approach.

As for businesses, by being able to offer them the whole array of research capability from the most abstract to the most applied, a traditional, research-based business school can be of much greater relevance than it could be were it to have only an applied and professional research capacity. One has only to look at the pivotal usefulness of the most theoretical business schools to the world of modern finance to assess this argument. Indeed, the University of Chicago Graduate School of Business (GSB) transformed much of the modern financial industry through its theoretical breakthroughs in the theory and pricing of options, which led, in turn, to the boom in derivatives, futures, and options instruments offered initially by the Chicago Board of Trade and the Mercantile Exchange and subsequently by exchanges around the world. The practicality of the GSB approach is evidenced by much of the modern financial sector in Chicago, the United States more generally, and globally, too, where tens of thousands of jobs now derive from and rely on advances in academic finance.

Many of the techniques and theories used routinely by business today were developed in the academy years or even decades ago. The modern, portfolio-management industry traces its roots back to a seminal paper by Harry Markowitz in 1952, some 44 years ago (and for which he received a Nobel Prize in economics in 1990). It took the investment-management sector some two decades before it was able to use Markowitz's path-breaking ideas, yet today they are commonplace and their academic origins probably long forgotten. Similarly, it is commonplace today among public-property, tax-assessment agencies to use multivariate statistical techniques to estimate house prices at much greater levels of accuracy and at lower costs than was possible previously using labor-intensive, manual-assessment procedures. Yet these techniques also go back many decades to work by Franklin Fisher, Zvi Griliches, Carl Kaysen (1962), and Sherwin Rosen (1974) for their theoretical and methodological foundations. Of the tens of thousands of people working in the assessment and real estate appraisal fields today, few would know the work of Rosen and Fisher, Griliches, and Kaysen, which, at the time, was viewed

as unnecessarily theoretical and academic by practicing appraisal and assessment professionals.

Last, current retailing and distribution would simply not be possible were it not for the extraordinary strides that have been made in two fields. First, advances since World War II in queuing theory and in mathematical programming and optimization methods have allowed the development and implementation of very efficient, low-cost inventory control and ordering systems, such as those used by industry leaders Wal-Mart and Sears (in the United States), Sainsbury's and Marks and Spencer (in the United Kingdom), and the Hudson's Bay Company (in Canada). Second, modern retailing and advertising would be difficult to imagine without the enormous academic literature that grew out of social and experimental psychology, which is used to assess both consumer satisfaction and to analyze and predict consumer behavior.

The key underpinnings in the fields above were developed, tested, vetted, criticized, and perfected in research-intensive universities. Numerous other compelling examples could have been given as well to support the point being made here that solid, curiosity-driven academic research has not been irrelevant at all, and has paved the way and made possible exceptional advances in all facets of business—from finance to marketing, to production and distribution, to management information systems, and beyond.

Ongoing Learning and the Restocking of Knowledge Via Research: Yet Another Electrical Analogy—A Battery

Knowledge and information are quickly outdated and lose their value in our era of rapid change. In electrical terms, we have a rechargeable battery that runs down rapidly and must be recharged often.

Academic researchers continually recharge their intellectual batteries and, in the process, restock and replenish society's inventory of useful knowledge. Thus there is an invaluable and powerful future orientation built into academic research, because it seeks, in diverse ways and at diverse levels, to prepare us continuously for the future by replacing, replenishing, and advancing old and aging knowledge with new findings on which to build a robust future. Academic research also functions as a repository for much of the business practice of each era through the development of business cases, business history, and research into business practice.

A business-oriented, shorter-term approach to research, because of its operational focus, would necessarily fail to restock our knowledge warehouses with long-term, durable theories, empirical findings, and research methods. It also would not provide the solid and enduring conceptual and methodological base on which we can build a solid operating future, focused as it is on short-term, immediate operational needs and not on the future at all.

Testing Batteries and Closing the Loop Between the Academic Researchers and Business Research Users

Academic research has a large community of scholars who constantly put existing theoretical and empirical knowledge to the test. Where knowledge is found wanting, new research activities are quickly set in motion to update, revise, and replace these waning ideas and research findings. In terms of our battery analogy, the academic research community is recharging its intellectual batteries in an unrelenting way through an immense array of research projects, classroom assignments, peer reviews, and learned conferences. Without this sort of nonstop renewal, our intellectual batteries would most assuredly run down. Unfortunately, the business community is an enormous consumer of stored knowledge. It draws heavily on the findings of university and industry researchers. In its short-term demands for operational knowledge, it has little or no budget for replenishing its store of knowledge and depends on others to keep the "knowledge batteries" fully charged and continually replenished. Thus there is an enormous role for university business research to keep our knowledge batteries charged and to add new batteries with new kinds of needed energy (ideas) constantly available for use by business and government.

Looked at differently, given the conventional academic's emphasis on the durable, the generalizable, and the long term, we seldom ask how (and if) the last generation of ideas is working in practice. We also fail to ask which ideas are lacking that could help business function better. The academic world addresses this issue by continuously subjecting ideas and research findings to scrutiny, challenge, and revision. Unfortunately, no similar mechanism exists for reviewing applications and the knowledge used by the business community. Thus we must establish continuous two-way communication to provide researchers with ongoing feedback on what does not work and where current problems lie.

An illustration can help clarify the point. For years, businesses relied on an amazing assortment of rules of thumb for everything from maintaining inventories and developing seasonal marketing plans to establishing offers for income-producing businesses or properties. These rules, however, all implicitly assumed stability in underlying business practices and conditions. As we moved from an economy characterized by persistent inflation in the 1970s and 1980s to one of great price stability in the 1990s, these rules of thumb became outmoded because the implicit assumptions built into them were changing quickly and were no longer valid. These rules of thumb in many cases were the embodiment of the entire stock of operating knowledge, and this knowledge was aging rapidly and losing its utility.

In such a setting, we see that theoretical and empirical advances, such as modern inventory theory and breakthroughs in our understanding of human consumer behavior, have greatly eased the burden of businesses in coping with rapid change. The examples provided here, and countless others we could offer, depict ways in which academic research has restocked the storehouse of operating knowledge to permit businesses to cope and prosper in our volatile global economy.

PRACTICALITY AGAIN: THE FREQUENT IMPRACTICALITY OF BEING PRACTICAL

With this prologue, we can address the question of management research practicality raised in the title. Academic research culture has a great deal to offer business communities because of the ways it is different and complements business. The usual question of practicality or relevance, implying similarity to, not differences from, business practice, must be questioned at the outset as a result.

Being practical only can have meaning if it can be specified across a number of key dimensions. Specifically, *to whom* is the research, its ideas, and findings aimed. If it is aimed at a low-level operating person in a business, relevance will be defined by immediate applicability and utility. CEOs and boards of directors, however, will not find such situationally tied findings and ideas very useful given their longer-term and broader foci and responsibilities. Similarly, research concepts and results must be seen as having utility *over a particular time frame.* Very specific results have limited temporal utility and relevance in a rapidly changing world. Here, too, relevance is just as likely to be defined by durability and usefulness over a decade as it is over weeks and months. Very practical research would therefore only truly be practical (i.e., usable) over a very short time frame. Where research findings and ideas must be usable over a longer time period, a less relevant and more general set of constructs is needed.

Last, one needs to know *in which settings* the conclusions are useful. Research done in the context of narrow or unique settings is not likely to be applicable and relevant in other contexts. For research to be useful in a variety of settings requires it to be based on more general and abstract constructs, in opposition to the conventional view of relevance.

Seen differently, traditional academic thinking, with its emphasis on theory and rigorous testing, is highly practical and relevant. In a fast changing world that demands both long- and short-term solutions, good theory and academic research *is* very practical and highly relevant. Borrowing loosely from renowned sociologist Kurt Lewin, "nothing is so practical as a good theory."

Business will need to be more flexible and adaptive to compete in the next century. It will require access to, and use of, better ideas, analytical methods, and sound theoretical and empirical knowledge about the world in which it operates. In a global business setting, management research can shed powerful light on many of the issues facing business, with huge potential payoffs to those businesses that can use and benefit from this research and its underlying conceptual frame and empirical findings.

The finance sector again supports this point, and such global industry leaders as Salomon Brothers and Goldman, Sachs rely on the most recent and powerful findings from the academic finance community for their continued competitiveness. The rapidly growing investment management industry is similarly dependent on both fundamental and applied research output from leading research business schools. Finally, corporate finance and treasury functions simply cannot operate without basic and applied research from universities in such fields as hedging and risk management and international treasury management.

The North American business community, in particular, can learn much from its academic peers in other ways as well. Businesses, as we have noted, tend to overly discount the future with their short-term operating orientation. Thus they often shun investments in people and condemn their employees to live off their human capital (their experiential and school learned knowledge) and fail to recharge the knowledge batteries of the most important productive input: their people. One of the factors leading to the huge success of Korean, Japanese, and ethnic Chinese businesses is an extraordinary investment in children and employees. This human capital investment is directly tied to the very long-term view in these societies. Thus investments with very long (and continuing) paybacks, like education and learning, are valued in all of East Asia, with dramatic economic and globally competitive outcomes that all can see.

In the West, business people delude themselves when they think that Asian nations have succeeded so strikingly due to vast supplies of cheap labor and minimal labor legislation. An almost obsessive focus on human capital creation and maintenance is a much more salient explanation and one that the West would be well-advised to grasp. Business schools and their research and teaching knowledge can contribute centrally to the longer-term viability and success of Western business through the academy's bent to continuously restock the shelves of their knowledge warehouses (e.g., our knowledge batteries) and its ability to communicate the new and existing knowledge to present and future business leaders.

The academic community can help domestic businesses stay ahead by developing broad and solid understanding of the ways in which business is conducted in other cultures. The vast academic literature on Japanese business practices has been very helpful to Western business strategists to formulate effective means for competing with Japanese enterprises. Also, academic links with overseas colleagues provide extremely rich networks into overseas business communities, which can facilitate mutual understanding and international trade to the benefit of all. The "honest broker" functions that can be provided by academic research networks have scarcely been explored to date, yet holds great promise for the future.[2]

As business tackles global challenges, it continues to benefit fundamentally from basic research at universities. For example, leadership was an academic and professional curiosity to all only a few years ago. In the past few years, however, leadership has emerged as a critically important dimension of competitive organizations as well. Basic and applied research in business schools is providing insights essential to fostering and enhancing leadership in public and private organizations.

Market imperatives and developments in theory and sophisticated experimental findings have drawn consumer behavior and basic psychological theories and methods into the planning and operations of many of the most dynamic firms. Modern mass retailing would simply be impossible without the theoretical and applied advances in transportation and logistics and in operations research.

Businesses that embrace these academic approaches and incorporate academic findings into their corporate cultures and operations have succeeded against intense competition. Wal-Mart, McDonald's, Salomon Brothers, Goldman, Sachs, and General Electric (GE) are all exemplary users of the whole range of academic research—from the most theoretical to the most applied. Businesses today, and more so tomorrow, must be true learning organizations to be ahead of their global competitors or else fall behind them and risk disappearing (Senge, 1990). They require evermore knowledge and innovation to stay even with the competition—let alone to best it. Those who fail to follow the lead of the knowledge-based innovators, like Goldman, Sachs and GE, do so at their extreme peril.

ON THE PRACTICAL NECESSITY FOR ACADEMIC FREEDOM AND INTELLECTUAL INDEPENDENCE

The foregoing argues very strongly for building ties between academia and business. It also argues that academics must see research as a means, not an end in itself. It is a means by which important and exciting conversation can be started and sustained with external stakeholders in the business, government, and nonprofit sectors, and with the general public more broadly through the media.

Research activities that build on, and go beyond, purely curiosity-driven work and that are responsive to societal and public needs are clearly necessary, and I want to return to this issue subsequently. However, at this point, some cautionary flags must be raised to some of the dangers that lurk potentially as academic business researchers take on more demand-driven research.

These dangers derive from the potential loss of independence and the credibility that now is associated with academic research. In part, this credibility derives from the culture of peer review, open discussion and criticism, and public access to academic work. Independence, the tradition of academic excellence and openness, and the resulting credibility of work done in university settings are ultimately the greatest value of university-based research to society. It is vastly more important and valuable to society than making research practical and applicable in the short term (Trigger, 1992). Credibility and integrity are at the absolute core of the academic research tradition and it cannot, and indeed must not, be sacrificed or weakened for any reason whatsoever. Without this integrity, universities and university researchers have nothing special to offer society, businesses, and governments (Boyer, 1990).

Lamentably, as pressure grows for business schools to do more applied and professional research and to move academic research into broader public fora, actual and potential threats exist to the integrity and credibility of the academic research tradition. I want to argue strongly here that these core academic values must be protected if academic business researchers are to serve business well.

Tenure: Its Meaning and Its Burdens

Let us begin with perhaps the most contentious of all issues in academia: the institution of tenure. In a world of growing complexity, change, and uncertainty, high-quality and dependable knowledge is increasingly seen and appreciated as the key to successfully competing in the global economy. Accordingly, having an independent and reliable source of research knowledge is indispensable.

Protecting academic freedom, free inquiry, and open debate is absolutely central to generating the requisite knowledge for being globally competitive. In a knowledge-based global economy, free and active competition among ideas is as important as it is among firms. Only through such active and open debate can we sort out the truly compelling and powerful ideas and empirical findings from the trivial. There is a very important caveat that needs to be stressed here—one that seems to be increasingly lost and forgotten in the debates inside academia on tenure. Academic freedom is not academic license. Tenure does not confer the right to do nothing. It protects the right to inquire, and therefore establishes an implicit contract: in return for this precious right of free inquiry comes the weighty responsibility to inquire actively and, in the process, to add broadly to the stock of human knowledge and understanding and to the civility and discernment needed to enjoy and sustain a democratic society.

Therefore, tenure and the protection of academic freedom come at a significant cost. First, at leading research business schools it is awarded only to those with demonstrated research and teaching expertise. Also, there is a very strong expectation that the beneficiaries of tenure, the professoriate and its students, will perform a crucial gadfly function, questioning all manners of truths and facts—be they in the basic and applied sciences or in the humanities and social sciences. Without such an independent critic continuously questioning the status quo in all fields, human advancement and just and productive societies and organizations are not likely to long endure. The freedom to pursue new knowledge through independent, excellent, peer-reviewed, and accessible research is what tenure is all about. It is crucial that societies and businesses have academic institutions where free debate and inquiry flourish, whether or not the research and its results are immediately usable. Tenure provides the milieu within which such inquiry can be nurtured and flourish. Academics and their institutions must increasingly acknowledge and accept the pressing responsibility that comes with the traditions and conventions of tenure.

Profit-Making Universities and Research Institutes: A Misdirected but Highly Germane Controversy in an Era of Growing Privatization of Business Schools

Today's fiscal environment puts growing pressure on universities to demonstrate their value to society by earning their keep through market competition and client satisfaction. There are many appealing and valuable aspects of these calls for privatizing universities and their research functions and for making them more financially self-sufficient and less dependent on public funds. It must be pointed out, though, that universities that are truly profit-making ventures (as was Bond University in Australia) should not be confused with the superb private universities of the United States, which do charge full-cost, market-based tuition levels, but which are nonprofit and vigorously independent institutions.

Universities that set out to earn a return for their backers would be very badly conflicted and subject to serious concerns about credibility and independence. The need to earn a profit can all too easily degenerate into doing research for vested corporate and political interests, which reaches conclusions sought by these firms and interest groups. Such research is neither excellent nor unbiased nor credible. Public and private nonprofit universities are credible because their research and teaching activities occur in a climate of openness and independence, where truth in its diverse forms is sought, not short-term profits and investor returns. The independence of thought and action is the most valuable feature of universities and their research enterprises. This holds for elite, research-based business schools. Only by being independent and able to inquire freely, even when conducting contract research for governments and businesses, can a university and business school maintain its credibility and that of the knowledge it generates and communicates, and the credibility of its research and teaching programs. This credibility is what ensures the relevance and utility of its research and the credibility and relevance of its graduates.

Having sounded the foregoing warning with respect to profit-making business schools, private, privatized, or soon-to-be privatized business schools should take heed of the salient features of the foregoing discussion. Clearly, moving closer to the business and government communities, in efforts to be responsive and serve them better, places at risk the core academic values of research independence and excellence. As noted repeatedly, these core values are the only real sources of value of business school research and thinking. To sacrifice them in the name of short-term expedience will be to lose the ultimate competitive advantage possessed by business schools. Bond rating firms like Standard and Poors and Moody's provide a useful parallel here. Neither firm would be in business very long were its independence and research excellence and thoroughness to come into question. In the end, independence and research quality are really what they are selling.

Research Independence, Diversity, and Excellence Are the True Guarantors of Long-Term Societal Relevance and Practicality

The value of independent research is thus essential. There is within this independent research tradition a parallel tradition of excellence that is equally critical to relevance and utility. There has been a failure previously by academics of the need to apply these traditions of independence and excellence across a diversity of research areas and styles, spanning conceptual, methodological, and applied (or professional) approaches to obtaining knowledge. Of particular importance here is professional research that is designed explicitly and at the outset to move traditional research findings into the professional business realm to help address pressing and looming problems. Business schools, in particular, must take up the challenge of encouraging and fostering greater diversity in intellectual pursuits. Traditional scholarly research in the core functional areas of management must continue, as must the attention paid to peer review and publication in scholarly journals and books. But they are only starting points for a solid business school research portfolio.

To this invaluable and irreplaceable traditional research culture must be added research that spans functional areas and indeed other disciplines found outside business schools in engineering, the sciences, social science, and the humanities. It must be based on a fundamental shift in university research culture, which was founded almost exclusively on the curiosity of the individual researcher or research team. Research has been an end in its own right; it has been supply-driven, not demand-driven. In the future, all work, even the most theoretical and abstract, will need to be positioned better as a means to satisfy important societal ends. Thus traditional pure and fundamental academic research in the future must be, at the minimum, a means for explaining to the broad public what we are doing in universities today and how these pure research results might affect our lives long into the future. Traditional research must also serve our teaching needs and must be seen as the most critical knowledge input to the development of new and more powerful courses for graduate and undergraduate students, for the professional business and government communities, and perhaps for the general public and mass media as well.

Much greater attention must be paid to research work that moves basic scholarship into the world of business and government. Applying our basic research findings to the professional management communities that can use the research lies at the heart of the cultural shift argued for above, in which research can no longer only satisfy the curiosity of the researcher and her or his international peers.

Professional research done by academics is likely to provide very different insights from similar work undertaken by the consultant and management community. This derives directly from the academic focus on technical and conceptual excellence—a tradition that provides academically based professional research

with the power to develop more robust, substantial, and durable research output than would normally be available to less academically qualified practitioners. It is very unlikely that practitioners could have framed the commodity-linked bond problem outlined next in a way that would have yielded the powerful and usable results that Schwartz's work did. Using our high-voltage analogy, if one starts with a giga-volt, there is much more power available to step down (i.e., apply) to all lower-voltage needs.

Much greater consideration needs to be given to sharing traditional and professional research work with a wider public than just the international scholarly community. The media can be of enormous help here and should increasingly be seen as educational colleagues with special skills who are capable of bringing academic and professional findings to broader professional and public audiences.

To highlight the points made previously, consider the following examples. A forest company in British Columbia needed to raise debt to finance renewal of its capital base. It feared, however, that a traditional debt instrument with its constant monthly payment would be poorly suited to its highly cyclical cash flows. One of my former colleagues, Professor Eduardo Schwartz, was asked to tackle the problem. Its novel and complex nature required his analytic and conceptual abilities. From this very quantitative work, Schwartz (1982) developed the first commodity-linked bonds, which are now a common feature of the financial marketplace for resource-based companies.

The Province of British Columbia was concerned about the failure of a number of deposit-taking institutions in the mid-1980s. It approached our faculty to see if we could develop a more economically efficient and theoretically sound approach to deposit insurance than the flat rate that was in use. By returning to first principles and drawing on recent advances in corporate finance, several of my colleagues devised a rigorous and sophisticated method for pricing risk-adjusted deposit insurance premiums, which came directly from modern, option-pricing theory in finance (Giammarino, Zechner, & Schwartz, 1989).

These applications were all built on sound, theoretical, academic "first" principles. All addressed a very thorny, current, practical problem by going back to general academic principles and working back down to the specifics. All provided fundamental, new, and highly usable results, which would not likely have come from the professional or business community. All demonstrate that earlier academic work provided the wherewithal to tackle successfully and powerfully a difficult practical problem facing the business community in a way that consultants and staff would not likely be able to do.

CONCLUSION: THE NEED FOR BALANCE IN UNIVERSITY-BASED MANAGEMENT RESEARCH

The Virtues of Cooperation Between Academia and the Business Community

Returning to where we started, the short-term utility and application to immediate problems facing business are very poor criteria to use when judging the quality and long-term worth of management research. To argue against such criteria, however, should not be construed as arguing in favor of the status quo in the research cultures of business schools, where narrow foci, technical elegance, and disciplinary rigor have prevailed for far too long.

Arguing either for demand-driven research, which has instantaneous applicability (relevance), or for curiosity-driven scholarly research misses the realpolitik of the issue. Adherents to these two views needlessly define them in mutually exclusive terms. Instead of staking out extreme points, or debating the purity and rights of each, we need to move to a much more synthetic ground for discussion where the virtue of both positions is acknowledged and appreciated, and a healthy balance sought between the curiosity-driven (supply) and client-driven (demand) approaches to management research.

Both views are enormously important and both must be based on excellence, sound theory, and sound method. Of particular importance here is the necessity to develop two-way dialogue, in which each community learns from the other. Thus, for example, the academic community could use the knowledge, principles, and perplexing problems or questions of the business community to form the next generation of questions on which academic research agendas, in part, might be built.

The utility of such an ongoing and active conversation derives in large measure from the differences in modes of thinking and acting in the two communities, as noted earlier. The key differentiating features of management research in a university are the premia attached to creativity, long-term view, abstraction and generalizability, and the demands for excellence and

analytic power. These differentiating features provide the means by which the university-based management researcher can generalize, analyze, and provide potentially powerful insights to the unsolved (and often unframed or poorly framed) questions that face the business community. Thus, as stated often here, it is our differences that are our collective and cooperative strengths.

An Illustration of the Virtues of Cooperation and Two-Way Conversation

Over the past decade, a colleague, who is a highly published and respected researcher in finance, has developed close ties with the financial community through his teaching and administrative responsibilities. He is very much from the classic academic mold, with few business contacts early in his career. However, due to his frequent interactions with financial people, on several occasions he encountered interesting theoretical and empirical problems that led to interesting research projects, often jointly with graduate students, and to working articles and publications in respected academic journals.

His experience is instructive because it shows that two-way conversations not only allow academics to get their findings into the business community, where they can be used, but they also provide the opportunity for academics to gain insights into current business problems, which lead directly to interesting academic research. Such give and take can expand the perspectives of both communities enormously and enrich them greatly in the process.

Some Illustrative and Exemplary Two-Way Conversation Starters and Sustainers

Business and business schools have already developed a number of solid communication vehicles that have started diverse and important conversations. Virtually all business schools have business advisory councils.[3] Research centers and institutes publish wide-circulating newsletters aimed at the business as well as the academic community. Great use of adjunct professors is being made to bring business experience into the classroom, and executive development courses are designed to bring academic knowledge to the community in readily understood formats. Schools are also experimenting with executives-in-residence, whereby senior (and often retired) executives spend

1 or more days per week in the business school as resources for students and faculty working on business problems and issues and in need of practical experiential knowledge. Some schools use executive interchange programs, where faculty members spend time working and often doing research in business or government, or business executives spend an equivalent time teaching and researching in the business school. Schools increasingly are providing (and requiring)[4] student internships and actual business projects as a means to get workplace experience and knowledge to students while they are still in school. Internships and business projects also allow business schools to transfer research findings to the business community more quickly via the students. Last, site visits are also being tried where small groups of faculty visit a firm and meet with its leaders to understand the problems faced by the firm and explore how academic knowledge might help the firm deal successfully with the problems. In all cases, the flow of information is in both directions, and both the academic and the business community benefit accordingly.

Closing Comments

The global business community can and must learn from its academic colleagues, and from its Asian business competitors, the value of taking a longer-term view, seeing problems in a broader and more general context, and investing in its personal and corporate human capital (e.g., recharge the batteries). Academic behavior here presents an excellent model, and greater conversation and collaboration between the two communities could significantly enhance the ability of business to think longer term and to make needed investments in people and knowledge.

The academy must also change its ways and engage in research with a shorter-term payoff and directed toward more situationally specific issues and problems. The academic community must also appreciate, more than it does today, that its work cannot be solely curiosity driven and that there is a pressing need to respond as well to current concerns and problems facing business. Traditional curiosity-driven work needs to be shared with, and explained to, the business and government sectors in readily accessible, nontechnical language so that these external stakeholders can access the actual and potential value that traditional academic research might hold for them. The old monastic model of scholarship, where the academic community is cloistered and apart from the external world, must be replaced by a new inclusionary model, in which the academy maintains its independence but is very much a part of society.

Stated somewhat differently, academic researchers can no longer view their research as solely curiosity driven. Rather, even the most abstract and theoretical academic research needs to be seen as a means toward one of two ends. First, it needs to be seen as a means for enhancing our knowledge base, serving as input for a continuum of courses and programs running the entire gamut from research and doctoral seminars down through 1- and 2-day management short courses. Second, research needs to be seen as a powerful means for engaging in conversations with stakeholder groups, both internal and external, so that ultimately, researchers are accountable in principle to the general public using the simplest and most intuitive forms of language. Thus research should be viewed as providing the means by which interesting and enriching conversations can be held between the research community and the nonresearch community, sharing the excitement and potential of research with the broader community.

In this vein, the HBS approach has had, and continues to have, significant strengths. Traditional academic business school researchers of the MIT model might well learn from their Charles River neighbors. The two approaches not only help stake out endpoints for the Charles River but they identify useful endpoints on an academic continuum as well. And, as argued earlier, viewing the world in dichotomous terms is not helpful. We can anticipate that a diversity of elements from both approaches will be combined to create ever greater choice of business school experiences to help meet the growing demands from prospective students, alumni, and employers. Both approaches yield valuable insights and building blocks for the diversity of successful business school programs of the future, and we can expect to see innovations in management education and learning draw heavily from both.

The challenges are great, but so are the potential gains to both the academic and the business communities. There is a great incentive to take up these challenges, and realize the gains made possible by being impractical, irrelevant, and irreverent:

1. by asking often unpopular (but necessary) questions;
2. by taking our time until we are satisfied with the value of our questions and answers;

3. by asking questions and seeking answers over a longer time frame than that provided by quarterly and annual reports; and

4. by asking questions of a broader and more conceptual nature than those demanded by specific situational circumstances facing businesses.

In sum, the academic community can, and indeed must, contribute what we really have: perspective, analytical power, and integrity. In the end, our independence of opinion and findings is our greatest, most relevant and practical contribution to business, government, and society. We must accept simultaneously, however, the significant responsibilities that go hand in hand with the freedom to inquire that we academics prize so highly.

NOTES

1. The MIT model is based on the traditional economic research model pioneered at the University of Chicago Graduate School of Business nearly a century ago. I have used MIT in the text rather than the University of Chicago Graduate School of Business because of MIT's physical proximity, yet striking intellectual distance, from the HBS.

2. For example, my own Faculty of Commerce and Business Administration at the University of British Columbia has had very strong contacts for some 16 years with Shanghai Jiao Tong University, one of the leading business schools in the People's Republic of China. Increasingly, joint activities between us include the business communities in both countries with an eye toward expanding trade and business opportunities.

3. For example, in our school we not only have a Faculty Advisory Council but a number of our academic divisions, our executive development groups, and our research centers also have their own advisory groups—all which greatly assist us in bringing operating knowledge into our faculty for the benefit of students and faculty members alike. They also have the benefit of starting the process of sharing our research and teaching innovations with our business stakeholders.

4. Our new 15-month MBA program, for example, requires all students to do an internship of up to 12 weeks or to take on an in-depth business project of an equivalent duration.

REFERENCES

Boyer, E. L. (1990). *Scholarship reconsidered: Priorities for the professoriate.* Princeton, NJ: Carnegie Foundation for the Advancement of Teaching.

Elfring, T., & van Raaij, F. (1995). Research in management science: The challenge of double integration. In P. J. van Baalen (Ed.), *New challenges for the business schools* (pp. 27-37). Rotterdam: Rotterdam School of Management, Erasmus University.

Fisher, F., Griliches, Z., & Kaysen, C. (1962). The costs of automobile model changes since 1949. *Journal of Political Economy, 70,* 433-451.

Giammarino, R. M., Zechner, J., & Schwartz, E. (1989). Market valuation of bank assets and deposit insurance. *Canadian Journal of Economics, 22,* 106-127.

Markowitz, H. M. (1952). Portfolio selection. *Journal of Finance, 7,* 77-91.

Rosen, S. (1974). Hedonic price and implicit markets: Product differentiation in pure competition. *Journal of Political Economy, 82,* 34-55.

Schwartz, E. (1982). The pricing of commodity linked bonds. *Journal of Finance, 37,* 525-539.

Senge, P. (1990). *The fifth discipline: The art and practice of the learning organization.* New York: Doubleday-Currency.

Trigger, B. G. (1992). The university and the "long durée." *Transactions of the Royal Society of Canada, 3*(Series 6), 57-67.

The Future of the Business School: Knowledge Challenges and Opportunities

KEN STARKEY and SUE TEMPEST

ABSTRACT   Despite its importance, there is relatively little serious academic research into the business school. This article sets out to stimulate debate that will fill this gap. We review the origins and evolution of the business school and debates about management research and teaching in terms of ideals and practice. Increasingly, the role of the business school is being questioned but much of this debate looks at the business school in isolation from changes in the wider university sector. We situate our analysis within the broader context of debates about the university as a privileged knowledge space. We conclude by suggesting that the future of the business school can best be discussed in terms of changes in knowledge production and that the business school has the opportunity to position itself as a unique site of knowledge generation and diffusion.

KEYWORDS   business school ▪ knowledge ▪ learning ▪ management research ▪ university

There is relatively little serious academic research into the business school itself. This article sets out to stimulate debate that will fill this gap. It also confronts the irony that as the business school has become more dominant as a global institution, its role is increasingly questioned, most notably by Pfeffer and Fong (2002). Their argument is stark. The future of the business school is in doubt because its research and teaching missions are compromised, perhaps fatally.

The business school stands at the interface of a variety of conflicting forces, economic, social and cultural. We examine the emergence of the business school, its origins and evolution, and debates about business school research and teaching in terms of ideology and practice. Although recognizing the concerns that give rise to the notion of decline of the business school and even its 'end', we are less pessimistic. Although the business school faces major challenges, we identify opportunities in the engagement with the changing role of the university as a privileged knowledge space (Nowotny et al., 2001) and in developing research that is more relevant and less introverted. Space constraints dictate that we cannot consider the full range of history in our discussion or the variety of 'types' of business school or university. We gloss over differences to focus upon what we perceive as key trends and tensions in the development of contemporary debates about the role of the business school and the university.

Challenges to the business school and the university

In this section, we consider debates about the possible demise of the business school and contextualize these debates in two ways: first, by considering them in their historical context, and second, by considering them in the context of debates about the idea and purpose of the university. We recognize that management education is not confined to business schools. Antony (1986) notes that management education can be divided into three: formal management education as provided by business schools in university contexts, management training that focuses work-based skills, and management development that is focused on self-development. Formal management education constitutes the tip of 'a learning iceberg' for managers (Fox, 1997). However, we are explicitly concerned herein with the future of the business school in a university context. During the 1990s business schools (as part of the broadening role of universities) have extended their scope beyond 'intellectual/academic respectability' into the domains of vocational skills and professional development, thereby widening their role in management education.

The business school

Pfeffer and Fong's (2002) recent critique of the business school focuses on the two main functions of research and education. It rests on their evaluation of the impact of business schools on their graduates, in particular MBAs, and on the profession of management. The business school is judged wanting in both of these aspects. The MBA degree does not correlate with career success, which raises questions about this mode of education and the nature of what is being taught. There is little evidence that business and management research emanating from business schools has had any significant impact upon management practice.

There is an irony here. In the period post-World War II, business schools were criticized for their lack of a strong scientific foundation, for the weakness of their research and for being too like 'trade schools'. This criticism and funding from the Ford Foundation and the Carnegie Council set the business schools on a more mainstream academic trajectory. The irony is that this search for academic legitimation has created a distance between the concerns of the business school academic and the practice field of business:

> adopting the ways of other academic social science departments has produced a new set of problems including concerns about the relevance and centrality of business schools and business education to the world of management [and led] to an overemphasis on analysis at the expense of both integration and developing wisdom as well as leadership and interpersonal skills, or teaching the wrong things in the wrong ways to the wrong people or at least at the wrong time in their careers.
>
> (Pfeffer & Fong, 2002: 79–80)

This is a criticism repeated by Mintzberg (2004).

One strong criticism of the business school is that the focus on research has led to an academic enclave that is increasingly hermetically and hermeneutically divorced from the concerns of the 'real' world: 'business schools appeal to one another as scholarly communities through a plethora of academic journals that are utterly divorced from the challenge of everyday management' (Bailey & Ford, 1996: 8). In this process research has, to those inside the business school, come to be regarded as the primary activity and research output the prime expression of the school's identity and the mark of its prestige (Armstrong, 1995) while becoming increasingly divorced from practice.

This focus on research at the expense of practice has led to the criticism of irrelevance. A former president of the Academy of Management asked 'What if we really mattered?' and described the workings of the annual academic cycle of activity that makes it difficult for mattering to matter: 'Each August we come to talk with each other, during the rest of the year we read each others' papers in our journals and write our own papers so that we may, in turn have an audience the following August: an incestuous closed loop' (Hambrick, 1993: 13). This focus on research builds on what is perceived to be the central university role in knowledge production.

However, irony gives way to paradox when business schools attempt to shift their focus because they then run the risk of being criticized for becoming *too* revenue-driven, *too* customer-focused and, as a result, compromising their academic integrity. It is in the market for MBAs and in the highly competitive market for executive education that these criticisms are most valid. The business school emphasis on the customer has been driven by the business press and is embodied in comparative rankings of business school performance. The major players here have been *Business Week* and the *Financial Times* with surveys based upon the rankings of corporate recruiters, the evaluation of schools by their MBA graduates and research reputation.

Arguably, this development has raised the bar of business school performance in at least some of its dimensions, for example, in becoming customer-focused. In the words of one business school professor,

> we became a bit too esoteric and lost touch a little. Fortunately, our audience, which is basically corporate America, told us through the *Business Week* surveys, by punishing those who only do esoteric material and don't teach a really good managerial program. So now we're being held accountable to two audiences. We have to be academically rigorous, but we also have to be relevant.
>
> (Zell, 2001: 324)

Others think this is a step too far: 'some faculty members acknowledge that the rankings have had some positive effects, among them forcing professors to improve quality of teaching and the relevancy of business courses, most feel that the changes have gone too far and have come at too high a cost' (Zell, 2001: 324).

There is another twist to this tale of the business school's shortcomings. Pfeffer and Fong's argument tends to dis-aggregate teaching and research roles. Another way of looking at this is to ask how research informs teaching and how the teaching informs the practice of management. The knowledge embedded in the MBA curriculum has been judged negatively on a number of counts. The very structure of the MBA degree has received increasing criticism for what Leavitt (1989: 39) describes as its 'weird, almost unimaginable design'. Its effects on students' abilities to think and feel have also been criticized, perhaps most vividly by Leavitt again, for creating only narrowly focused graduates, 'critters with lopsided brains, icy hearts, and shrunken souls' (Leavitt, 1989: 39).

In the search for rankings, the schools have been charged with 'dumbing down' knowledge. Consumer voice has given too much power to consumer choice and the role of the academic as arbiter of knowledge and the curriculum that is its mediator has been undermined in the need to serve and service the customer so as to receive the good evaluations necessary to individual career advancement and to the prestige of the school. The casualties in this customer-focused process, according to its critics, are theory, research and rigour – knowledge generation and dissemination. Too much faculty time is spent in the self-serving consideration of how to play the ratings game. Antony (1986) contends that in business schools you have the inversion of the traditional academic hierarchy that marks progressive specialization from undergraduate to masters study. 'The conclusion is hard to avoid that postgraduate courses in management are designed for beginners rather than masters' (Antony, 1986: 119).

This criticism has been taken further in terms of the perceived negative impacts of business school education. The charge here is that the business school has championed an approach to business that has led to the management practices that characterize the dysfunctional aspects of contemporary capitalism. This has been demonstrated, for example, in the failure of the dot.coms, for a short period the organizations of career choice for new MBAs. The other main career choice for the MBA has been management consultancy. Management consultancies and business schools professors played a significant role in lauding the pioneering new management practices of firms such as Enron. Indeed, one of Enron's most praised management practices, before its fall from grace, was the recruitment of top MBAs from the elite business schools (Fusaro & Miller, 2002).

Business schools have been charged with complicity on a number of counts in the Enron disaster, most notably in being an active party in promoting the feeding frenzy of fast-track corporate growth without educating the executives involved in any broader perspective on the social implications of their financial and economic practices. The business school is charged with teaching in a moral and cultural vacuum. 'Too often we turn out ambitious, intelligent, driven, skilled over-achievers with one underdeveloped aptitude. Too many of the business leaders we graduate are hitting the ground running, but we have forgotten to help them to build their moral muscles' (Salbu, 2002: xiv). It seems to us too extreme to wholly agree with the view that the Enron legacy is the revelation of business as 'a terrifying enterprise only lightly tethered to morality and decency' (Salbu, 2002: xiv). However, there is some truth in the view that Enron is a symptom of a broader business and education malaise, the lack of success of the business school in training business leaders to be 'true professionals with true character' (Salbu, 2002: xiv).

In his much discussed, and best-selling, critique of the contemporary conditions of work in advanced economies, Sennett (1998) eloquently portrays the consequences of a new management culture and management practices that promote permanent restructuring, acute downsizing and new flexible ways of working as the holy grails of effective organization. The business school is complicit in the development of this new management ethos, its dissemination through business school graduates and its effects on the corrosion of character.

The university

Debates about the role and the future of the university replay those we have considered in relation to the business school. Underlying these debates is the question of the university's educational role (providing for society's human and cultural capital needs) and the university's research role (the creation of the right kinds of knowledge). The university is a key institution of modernity, perhaps the major site in which knowledge, culture and society interconnect. The modern idea of the university emerged at the end of the eighteenth century. According to this emergent idea, the university was seen as 'a knowledge producer' that provided nations with professional elites and supported the development of culture (Delanty, 2001). The university, in the founding vision of Humboldt, was seen as the producer and custodian of culture and as a source of cultural and even spiritual leadership in an increasingly industrial age.

What was new in the university at this time was the emphasis upon the university's paramount role of new knowledge creation. Previously, the university had been the privileged site for the diffusion of perceived and received wisdom, founded in religion, according to which the world was known. New ways of knowing the world ran the risk of being perceived as heresy and punished accordingly. Isaac Newton, for example, conducted secret science to avoid the risks of the latter. In the modern, enlightened vision of the university, knowledge production and diffusion were focused in the integrative academic role of research and teaching, the legacy of humanist tradition. Crucial to Humboldt's idea of the university was that the university was seen as an autonomous actor, which, through this very autonomy, was better able to serve the state's and society's long-term needs. According to this view, the university was seen as 'more than the mere training ground of civil servants but has a spiritual role to play in the cultivation of the character of the nation' (Delanty, 2001: 33).

Readings describes the reorganization of the university associated with Humboldt as follows:

> The plan outlined by Humboldt for the University of Berlin synthesized the fundamental reorganization of the discourse on knowledge by which the University took on an indirect or cultural function for the state: that of simultaneous search for its objective cultural meaning as a historical entity and the subjective moral training of its subjects as potential bearers of that identity.
>
> (Readings, 1996: 68–9)

Crucial to this discourse on knowledge was the autonomous work of philosophical reflection, which was differentiated from an emphasis upon subservience to practical utility. There was to be, in Humboldt's grand scheme, an interplay between research and teaching, united in the notion of the educational mission. The legitimation of the university here is philosophical and arises from the dual role envisaged in Humboldt's project 'which consists not only in the acquisition of learning by individuals, but also in the training of a fully legitimated subject of knowledge and society' (Lyotard, 1984: 33).

The university's relation to knowledge is articulated by a meta-narrative of 'the realization of the life of the spirit or the emancipation of humanity' (Lyotard, 1984: 52) and its 'unifying idea' and ideal of aligning culture and society (Readings, 1996: 121). There have been less grand visions. Watson (1993: 26) reminds us that research has not always enjoyed the central role in universities that it holds today. He cites Jowett, the Master of Balliol College during the late nineteenth century to highlight the focus of universities at the time on knowledge dissemination rather than production ' "Research" "Research" A mere excuse for idleness; it has never achieved, and will never achieve any results of the slightest value'. Newman's idea of the university did not include the idea of the university as a site of knowledge production either. Rather it was to serve as disseminator of the knowledge found in religious (Christian) tradition.

In the twentieth century, an era characterized by growing emphasis upon expertise and professionalization, universities were increasingly identified with servicing the economic needs of society through the production of technological expertise and the training of professional elites. The roles of the university became more various. Kerr's (2001) classic study talks about the development of the 'multiversity' to meet a growing complex of stakeholders. But these various roles were not necessarily at odds with previous iterations of the modern university's mission, in that the role of the university is still rooted in the autonomy to define what its knowledge base is and should be. As long as the university performed its fiduciary functions (Parsons & Platt, 1973) – research, professional training, general education and cultural development – then its legitimacy to define the bases for claims to knowledge, and, therefore, its research practice, was not challenged.

However, in this evolving knowledge arena, tensions were developing. According to Parsons and Platt (1973: 148),

> [t]he academic profession is that group primarily concerned with the cognitive complex that is institutionalized in the graduate schools and research activities of the university. It deals with the advancement, perpetuation and transmission of knowledge. However, the university is too multifunctional to be merely a place where universal knowledge is pursued but is nevertheless more fiduciary than technocratic or instrumental in that it differs from the corporation in being primarily a place of learning and research.

Multi-functionality increases the range of stakeholders in university practice and makes the sense of an over-arching mission harder to define. As universities defended themselves as privileged knowledge sites, a schism has slowly developed between the ideals of research and of professional training, which is increasingly desired by student and society but seen as increasingly divorced from the core university function, the transmission of knowledge based upon research that seeks as its main function to advance knowledge rather than practice. Nisbet (1971), for example, writes of the decline of the university because its notion of community based upon scholarship is in danger from the demands of professionalism, a view that is in part supported by a reading of Kerr (2001) as an apologia for the *uses* of the university rather than *the idea* of *the* university.

The calling into question has gone further. In the final 'postmodern' perspective we consider, the argument is that the university has reached the end of one particular road, that '[i]ts founding cognitive ideas – the universality of knowledge, the quest for truth, the unity of culture – are becoming irrelevant and the social and economic reality has instrumentalized the university to a point that has made its autonomy neither possible nor desirable' (Delanty, 2001: 5–6). In Readings' graphic phrase, the university is a '*ruined*' institution, one that has lost its historical *raison d'être*' (1996: 19, emphasis in original). The university has, according to this perspective, lost its cultural function. It is everywhere enmeshed in the 'corporate bureaucratization that underlies the strong homogenization of the University as an institution' (Readings, 1996: 12), a bureaucratization whose distinguishing features are an emphasis upon accountability and the aspiration to excellence, which Readings links to a philosophy of total quality management guiding the university in its relations with its 'customers'.

The search for excellence – an idea with significant management antecedents – introduces new pressures on the university's freedom to define how knowledge is to be defined, generated and diffused because the search demands that universities are judged and ranked in terms of a variety of measures of excellence, for example, make-up of the student body, class size, library resources, research grants, research outputs and a variety of other performance indicators, linked to an appeal to the salutary discipline of market forces. In the words of a Director General of UNESCO: 'It is impossible to guarantee the quality of education without having the aim of excellence resting on the domain of research, teaching, preparation, and learning' (Readings, 1996: 31).

The search for excellence downgrades the appeal to the traditional university role as defender of culture. It also runs the risk of orienting the university system too much towards practical utility rather than 'pure' knowledge.

> Excellence is clearly a purely internal unit of value that effectively brackets all questions of reference or function, thus creating an internal market. Henceforth, the question of the University is only the question of relative value-for-money, the question posed to a student who is situated entirely as a *consumer*, rather than as someone who wants to think.
>
> (Readings, 1996: 27, emphasis in original)

The question raised by this reading of the evolution of the university is whether the university, stripped of its broader knowledge mission, can be anything other than 'a bureaucratic arm of the . . . capitalist system' (Readings, 1996: 46).

Here critiques of the business school and of the university come together. Part of Pfeffer and Fong's (2002) critique of the business school is that it is failing, not least because investment in an MBA does not lead to the income returns predicted and because investment in research is not producing useful knowledge, for business, and, by implication, for society. Some have argued that the business school is both cause and symptom of the university's decline. One notable example is the humanist critic, Allan Bloom (1987), who charges the university and higher education as a whole with having betrayed its cultural and democratic heritage and with having impoverished the souls of today's students and, thus, damaged the sociocultural fabric of the nation. In doing so, he specifically identifies the MBA degree as a major factor in this impoverishment, 'a great disaster . . . a diploma that is not a mark of scholarly achievement' (Bloom, 1987: 369–70)!

The business school and the new production of knowledge

Criticism of the business school, then, has focused upon the following factors: (i) that the business school was little more than a trade school; (ii) that in transforming itself into not being a trade school business school research has become divorced from the real concerns of business; (iii) that business school education and training does not have positive effects on the careers of its graduate; (iv) that the knowledge produced by business schools is self-referential and irrelevant; (v) that in responding to customer needs the business school has become too market-driven and, in the process, knowledge has been dumbed down; and (vi) that the business school has not only failed to deliver knowledge that enhances firm and national competitiveness, but has also been a major source of the wrong sorts of knowledge for management, fostering a short-term, risk-averse orientation (Cheit, 1985) and even new management thinking and practices that have led to contemporary business and social crises.

These criticisms reflect the fact that the business school has been at the forefront of trends that now confront the university as a whole in issues of knowledge creation and diffusion. Criticisms of the business school as knowledge generator reflect debates about the kinds of knowledge modern society needs. Criticisms of its 'customer' focus – either as too close to or divorced from customer concerns – reflect debates about the university's role in providing for society's knowledge and skills needs.

It is our contention that the long-term viability of the business school will depend upon the vigorous defence of its identity and its justification in terms of its contribution to knowledge. In brief, the business school has to reflect upon its history and its future mission to arrive at a new definition of its purpose, particularly with respect to knowledge production and diffusion, that commands the respect of those it serves in ways that they themselves are perhaps only dimly aware of. We support the view that, in this new knowledge environment, a key task of the business school should focus upon 'maximizing public benefit . . . while also promoting a broader and more inclusive conception of knowledge than credentialing systems and corporate organizations typically allow' (Kleinman & Vallas, 2001: 454).

This defence of the business school implies, in part, a restatement of the traditional knowledge generation of the university, but in a context in which the nature of knowledge production has become a major social issue. The modern university has played a crucial social role – the production of knowledge and the transmission of knowledge to a growing proportion of the population (Kerr, 2001). The university was for a long time at the centre of the nation's knowledge work. This is no longer the case (Kerr, 2001). The days of the university's 'unquestioned pre-eminence' as knowledge producer have now gone (Wittrock, 1993). Gibbons et al. (1994), in an influential study, argue that a new model of knowledge is replacing the old view of knowledge in which universities played a central role.

The new production of knowledge takes place in a growing variety of sites outside the university and has as a prime characteristic the co-production of knowledge by many knowledge workers addressing problems in the context of application and in a manner that transcends disciplines. As a result the university is, at least in part, de-legitimized as a privileged, elite site of knowledge production. The shift is from Mode 1 to Mode 2 forms of knowledge production:

> Mode 2 knowledge production transcends disciplinary boundaries. It reaches beyond interdisciplinarity to transdisciplinarity. As a result the processes of cognitive insitutionalization, which typically have taken place in and through elite universities, are weakened. Scientific communities become diffused and, consequently, the university structures of faculties, departments, institutes and centres that create and sustain these communities become less relevant.
>
> (Gibbons et al., 1994: 89)

This has proceeded in parallel with the growing contestation of the knowledge claims of existing knowledge elites, which reflects a growing awareness of the risks and the unintended consequences of the application of knowledge, manifested in what has come to be called 'the risk society' in which the culture of expertise and scientific legitimacy are challenged by growing public calls for the accountability of science and technology (Beck, 1992). In business and management, the contestation of management's accountability for its business decisions is part of a similar process.

The growing concern with the nature of knowledge and changes in its mode of production has led to debates about the very identity of the university (Readings, 1996; Scott, 1998). Universities can no longer make uncontested claims to knowledge supremacy. 'The feeling of a deep crisis of purpose, administrative–managerial structure and budgeting is pervasive in many universities today. The boundaries between the university . . . and other parts of the R&D system have been steadily eroded' (Nowotny et al., 2001: 80; Kleinman & Vallas, 2001).

What is at play here is a complex re-organization and re-thinking of how science works in which

> [t]he architecture of modernist science becomes a postmodern archi-
> tecture of data flows and ethernets . . . centralization gives way to a
> dispersal of production among multiple authors at multiple sites . . .
> experiments are dispersed social–technical entities in which meaning is
> constructed at several peripheries and no single center can hold . . .
> laboratories, factories . . . disperse and recombine in ways unimagin-
> able half a century ago.
>
> (Galison & Jones, 1999: 497–8)

The result is 'a decloistering of science as the formerly separate worlds of
applied and pure research merge' and the managerial task is to come to terms
with 'new spatial and authorial complexities . . . simultaneously dispersed
and collective identities' (Galison & Jones, 1999: 526, 532–3).

Science is exposed to an unprecedented degree of 'contextualization' –
'The increasing emphasis on the contribution of science to wealth creation
(and social improvement), the growing deference to so-called "user" perspectives, the great weight now attached to ethical and environmental considerations, are all examples of the intensification of what we call
contextualization' (Nowotny et al., 2001: 166). This is not necessarily a bad
thing. Indeed there is now evidence that those scientific fields which have
tried to remain insulated from the forces of contextualization, which have
tried to maintain their own private, 'sterile space' in which scientists can do
as they please, have become less creative and productive. Some commentators suggest that contextualization is the key to improving the quantity and
quality of the knowledge developed in universities (Nowotny et al., 2001).
One example of the call for more contextualization in management
education comes from Locke (1996) who contends that management as a
cultural expression varies from country to country but this is not reflected in
syllabuses that rely on the US model of management that he contrasts to the
European tradition of industry.

Environmental science provides a positive image of the consequences
of contextualization. What has been created at the confluence of a variety of
different branches of science is a knowledge space in which the scientific and
policy debate about environmental issues has taken place. This space is populated not only by scientists, but also by politicians, company and industry
representatives, non-governmental agencies and pressure groups, as well as
the media and others. Interaction in this space has generated a body of
knowledge that has had an impact upon both research practice and public
opinion resulting in a more responsive and accessible body of knowledge.
Contextualization has supported the development of a flourishing interdisciplinary field (environmental sciences) in which new knowledge alliances,

between pre-existing disciplines such as economics and ecology, have developed.

It is in these new knowledge spaces that we can collectively address the challenges of the 'risk society' and come to terms with the impact of new knowledge and the new technologies. A growing sense of risk – physical, environmental, intellectual, ethical – undermines our sense of security in the world. This scenario is most compellingly developed by Beck (1992) who identifies physical risks, for example, of environmental impacts of science via its business applications, and intellectual risks, in that knowledge claims are increasingly complex, disputed and challenged. For example, claims of environmental degradation are themselves disputed (Starkey & Crane, 2003). This gives rise to a dual need. Consumers of knowledge and those affected by its application feel the need to become more involved in debates about knowledge's origins and implications. Producers of knowledge – scientists in both the university and corporate worlds – are challenged to reflect more on what they are doing.

In Beck's terms, '[r]eflexive modernisation means that scepticism is extended to the foundations and hazards of scientific work' (1992: 163), and the challenge of reflexivity means that 'the question of system formations that are multivalent, permitting and making possible ambivalences and transcending borders is now becoming central' (1994: 29). The sense of risk manifests itself in growing dissonance about how to manage resources of both nature and of culture. As a result, Beck perceives the growth of 'a multiple-voiced self-criticism of society . . . risk society is by tendency also a self-critical society' in which we see a process of a 'self-opening of the monopoly on truth' (Beck, 1994: 10–11, 25). This self-opening, if accepted, leads to reflexivity on the part of knowledge creators. Reflexivity requires reflection on what we know and how we know in a spirit of 'self-confrontation'.

This self-opening requires changes in the role of the university and of the business school in knowledge production and communication. A key role of the university is to make sense of a changing world. A key contribution of the university is to linkages between the potentially opposing domains of technology and culture. Galison (1997), in his study of physics, talks about 'trading zones'. The university has long served society by codifying national culture and providing for the accreditation of the professional classes. The university remains the institution in society most capable of linking the requirements of industry, technology and market forces with the demands of citizenship (Delanty, 2001: 158). And the business school has the potential to be at the heart of this task.

One problem here is the role of research in the business school, as noted by Locke (1989: 223):

> ... academia needs business co-operation in order to discover what goes on managerially in the firm, for academic research is not about the creation of knowledge that is of value to practitioners as much as about the dissemination of knowledge of the academicians. From the academic's perspective this activity smacks more of teaching than the research function.

This reliance on the cooperation of management for access and research stories makes the establishment of a more reflexive, critical approach to research and thus management education challenging.

Antony (1986) advocates the way ahead for university-based management education as courses based on rigour and intellectual excellence but warns that numeric analysis has come to be seen as a proxy for intellectual rigour. He advocates that management education should be about criticism of the social role of managers, improved performance and individual development. Watson (1993) contends that management education should lead to three distinct characteristics: first, skills of intellectual analysis as associated with a liberal education, interpersonal skills and a body of knowledge about organizations and their analysis.

This leads us to management education in business schools that is concerned with the development of the critical reflective practitioner who has a wider understanding of the social, power and ethical implications of business practice and actively challenges our existing models of management. For example, Antony (1986) advocates that greater attention should be given to the development of political skills and understanding the philosophy of government in management education. From this perspective: 'The authority of management must rest upon a moral base, secure in a concern for the integrity and the good of the community that it governs' (Antony, 1986: 198). This returns us to a pre-industrial logic of the responsibilities of leaders for the care of their community. Watson (1993) asks us to consider what extra value universities can bring to management education. He concludes that it is in the areas of disseminating knowledge and developing the intellectual skills of criticism, analysis and synthesis that universities can add value. The way forward is for universities to encourage challenge in the way management is conducted rather than reinforcement of the status quo, an argument repeated by Grey (2004).

Lack of contextualization and criticality are key issues raised by several commentators (Burgoyne & Jackson, 1997; Grey & French, 1996; Jeffcutt, 2000; Locke, 1989, 1996). The theme of contextualization in the literature builds on the need to widen the participants and contributors to management knowledge to re-engineer trust into business practice and its interface with society (Antony, 1986; Burgoyne & Jackson, 1997; Locke, 1996). This calls for plurality and diversity in the communities of discourse that shape the development of management knowledge in business schools. Burgoyne and Jackson (1997) advocate an 'arena thesis', whereby management learning would emphasize the conflicting interests of key stakeholders in business practice.

It has been noted, by Beck (1994: 29) among others, that there is a growing need for forms and forums of consensus-building cooperation among industry, politics, science, management, society and individuals and social groups (employees and consumers). Locke (1996) sees the university as potentially a key venue for such activity, owing to its ability to draw on the knowledge located in other departments and faculties beyond the business school (cultural, linguistic, sociology, etc.). Thus the role of faculty advocated by Locke (1996) is more one of facilitator in a knowledge exchange than knowledge disseminator. He also highlights the central role of business education in promoting a more inclusive syllabus that, for example, would explore issues not merely through a management lens but also through a worker or customer perspective.

As well as knowledge, Locke also sees trust as a key issue to more effective business practice to motivate workers, managers and customers to enhanced levels of interaction. Is the answer more courses in business ethics? Not according to Locke (1996: 233): 'Drawing non-managerial as well as managerial people into the education process rather than teaching courses on business ethics is the principal way to increase trust.'

The business school has a major role to play in knowledge generation and reconfiguration by providing a meeting place in which the different discourses of business and society can confront each other. To achieve this goal requires conceiving of the role of the business school in terms of the interconnectivity of different modes of knowledge and a range of different social actors to produce the new models we need to navigate the risk society. This requires greater engagement with this society – greater contextualization – and contestation of 'the Enlightenment model of knowledge produced for its own ends in the splendid isolation of the academy' (Delanty, 2001: 154).

Discussion

We are witnessing a transformation of the public sphere (Habermas, 1989) in which the future of knowledge, the university and the business school are key factors. We agree with Reich (1991) that, in this context, there is an opportunity and a need for us to redefine who we are, why we have joined together and what holds us together. This opportunity has to be addressed in a context in which the idea of the university, premised on values of neutrality, universality, detachment and objectivity, needs re-definition, as it is challenged by demands for increased relevance. Before we retreat into defensiveness or defeatism, it is worth reminding ourselves that the need to redefine itself is something which the university has done a number of times, most notably at the end of the eighteenth century when the university was on the brink of extinction. Then, the university was able to re-invent itself and to become the 'embodiment of modernity, science and democracy' (Scott, 1998: 455). We are faced with similar challenges today and the business school is uniquely positioned to benefit.

We suggest that one way of construing the response to this challenge is around the need to develop new 'narratives of expertise' (Nowotny et al., 2001). The business school, like the university, will have to redefine the legitimacy upon which it grounds its privileged knowledge claims and which form the basis of its appeal to management and to society. Here, Pfeffer and Fong (2002) are right. The business school has been found wanting as far as its role as an important site of knowledge production is concerned. Because of its retreat into itself and a knowledge production process that favours self-referentiality and a closed, some would say, 'incestuous' (Hambrick, 1993), circle of research training and publication, it has lost the right to claim any major role in the generation of knowledge. As a result, it runs the risk of being marginalized and, to the extent that its knowledge claims become less and less relevant to any other organizations but itself, also the risk of finding its claims as a privileged site for teaching increasingly contested.

What, then, is the way forward? The business school has to confront the issues concerning knowledge generation, for in the changing contours of the spaces in which knowledge is now being produced lie major opportunities in knowledge production and as knowledge arbiter and broker in a more complex and differentiated knowledge production process. What is at stake here is a redefinition of purpose in the light of the emerging reconfiguration of knowledge production.

Today, knowledge has become more important and at the same time no longer emanates from any particular source. This restructuring in the mode of knowledge implies not the end of the university but its reconfiguration. The great significance of the institution of the university today is that it can be the most important site of interconnectivity in what is now a knowledge society. There is a proliferation of so many kinds of knowledge that no particular one can unify all the others. The university cannot re-establish the broken unity of knowledge but it can open up avenues of communication between these different kinds of knowledge, in particular knowledge as science and knowledge as culture (Delanty, 2001).

The business school seems to us a potential site par excellence for this kind of interconnectivity, sitting at the interface of theory and practice, of social science and business, and with the capability to manage a knowledge-brokering role, for example, between science faculties and business.

One hurdle to cross here is to involve end-users of business school research and teaching in a more serious consideration of the business school's knowledge role. Research has become de-coupled from the business context (Starkey & Madan, 2001; Tranfield & Starkey, 1998). 'With so little countervailing pressure from the profession, faculties have felt free to pursue the rewards of academic prestige by emphasizing the teaching and scholarship favored by their parent disciplines with scant regard for their relevance to the real world of business' (Bok, 1990: 113). This also requires changes in the practices of end-users. Companies, in the main, have been more interested in business schools as credentialing bodies than in the knowledge they produce, 'treating business schools more as sorting devices to classify talent than as institutions with an important educational mission' (Bok, 1990: 113).

There are also factors internal to the business school and the university at work. The different discipline groups in the business school struggle to protect their world-view, like other academic tribes, with their own particular customs and practices which 'represent the boundary-consciousness of an hermetic community threatened on all sides with social absorption' (Geertz, 1993: 151). But the energy put into defending the frames of thinking whose roots lie in the distant past does not create an enterprise at the cutting edge of creating a new future in a world where the old certainties are increasingly contested. We agree with Delanty (2001: 7) that '[i]t is the task of the university to open up sites of communication in society rather than, as it is currently in danger of doing, becoming a self-referential bureaucratic organization'. The business school is far from immune from this danger and the increasing irrelevance it might entail.

We have covered some of the perceived failings of the business school. One that is particularly topical is the lack of success of the business school in training business leaders to be professionals with character (Salbu, 2002). This raises important questions about the business school's mission in a society in which individualism, consumerism and a particular variant of corporatism are rampant. Is the business school, in part, responsible for these qualities, a key engine of a particular *zeitgeist,* or is it merely enmeshed in the spirit of its times? This question raises important questions about the business school's educational role. Bloom (1987: 20) defines the role of university teaching in traditional and liberal terms: 'No real teacher can doubt that his task is to assist his pupil to fulfil human nature against all the deforming forces of convention and prejudice'.

The criticism of the MBA is that it is precisely an instrument of convention and possibly prejudice, in that it is based upon a particular historical view of management and managers. Sennett charts the consequences of the new capitalism in the corrosion of trust, loyalty and mutual commitment. It destroys identity.

> How can long-term purposes be pursued in a short-term society? How can durable social relations be sustained? How can a human being develop a narrative of identity and life history in a society composed of episodes and fragments? The conditions of the new economy feed instead on experience which drifts in time, from place to place, from job to job. . . . short-term capitalism threatens to corrode . . . those qualities of character which bind human beings to one another and furnishes each with a sense of sustainable self.
>
> (Sennett, 1998: 26–7)

To what extent did the business school help to create and reflect these values?

The quintessential philosophical question is: what is a good life? This links to Readings' (1996) challenge, that universities need to rethink their contribution to the reshaping of 'the social bond' in a society faced with significant pressures towards fragmentation. Business has a crucial role to play in determining the parameters of the good life available to us. Business schools too have a crucial role to play in addressing this question and in clarifying their purpose and the kinds of knowledge we need as we face the uncertainties of the new millennium. The issue here is about how to deal with what Delanty (2001) describes as the need for a new social bond and the perception that this exists in new approaches to knowledge and communication.

This suggests that the university will only survive as a central institution if it can give expression to the new social bond that is emerging of which reflexive communication is a core principle. The task here is a rethinking of the link between knowledge and human interest (Habermas, 1971). If this is to proceed it will require at least three kinds of communicative interconnecting: (i) new links between the business school and society; (ii) new links between research and practice; (iii) and changing relations between the business school and business itself to provide knowledge for and about managers that captures the new social bond that will need to exist between university, business school, and business that will allow us to cope with the increasingly complex demands of a society facing multiple challenges.

New links between business school and society could take a number of forms. One particularly rich avenue for exploration might be to involve a broader range of stakeholders in the co-production of knowledge. Rather than focus on the interplay among faculty, students and managers it may be insightful to more actively engage with customers, workers, and wider communities including social and political groups in both teaching and research contexts. Such interactions may provide insights into more sustainable and transparent methods of business practice and corporate relationships.

In searching for new links between research and practice a useful starting point may be a move away from the predominant management research method that charts changes in business practice that managers have already witnessed, making the academic's contribution little more than that of the scribe charting the latest trends. Rather than the academic as scribe and the manager as storyteller, a more contextualized approach to research would be to engage business people and the other stakeholders previously outlined in defining the problems, questions and methods that would enable genuine knowledge co-production (Adler et al., 2004). This of course requires considerable involvement for business practitioners in the research process and on a longitudinal rather than the all too frequent snap-shot basis.

Finally, this brings us to the relationship between business and business schools. The relevance debate implies closer relationships between business and business schools. Yet the more fundamental philosophical challenges facing business schools urge caution in making the ties between schools and firms too tight. It could be argued that by allowing business to fund research, faculty and real estate, academic autonomy and diversity have been challenged at the expense of developing a more holistic understanding of business practice for the longer term good life of all the key constituents of society. We identify a key future role for the business school as a forum *par excellence* for promoting constituent interplay and debate.

If business schools can encourage reflexive communication between the wider constituents of the risk society they will be better placed to help inform a vision of sustainable business practice rather than merely describing the history of past business performance. The future of the business school rests on academics developing the role of sage rather than scribe and their host universities supporting them in their quest for innovative research and teaching methods that can confront the wider challenges and opportunities of managing in our perplexing and perplexed world.

Acknowledgements

We acknowledge support for the research on which this article is based from the Economic and Social Research Council – Award Reference RES–334–25–0009.

References

Adler, N., Shani, A.B. & Styhre, A. *Collaborative research in organizations*. Thousand Oaks, CA: Sage, 2004.

Antony, P.D. *The foundation of management*. London: Tavistock, 1986.

Armstrong, J.S. The devil's advocate responds to an MBA student's claim that research harms learning. *Journal of Marketing*, 1995, 59, 101–6.

Bailey, J. & Ford, C. Management as science versus management as practice in post-graduate business education. *Business Strategy Review*, 1996, 7(4), 7–12.

Beck, U. *The risk society*. London: Sage, 1992.

Beck, U. The reinvention of politics: Towards a theory of reflexive modernization. In U. Beck, A. Giddens & S. Lash (Eds), *Reflexive modernization. Politics, tradition and aesthetics in the modern social order*. Cambridge: Polity Press, 1994.

Bloom, A. *The closing of the American mind: How higher education has failed democracy and impoverished the souls of today's students*. New York: Simon & Schuster, 1987.

Bok, D. *Universities and the future of America*. Durham, NC: Duke University Press, 1990.

Burgoyne, J. & Jackson, B. The arena thesis: Management development as a pluralistic meeting point. In J. Burgoyne & M. Reynolds (Eds), *Management learning: Integrating perspectives in theory and practice*. London: Sage, 1997.

Cheit, E.F. Business schools and their critics. *California Management Review*, 1985, 37(3), 43–63.

Delanty, G. *Challenging knowledge. The university in the knowledge society*. Buckingham: Society for Research into Higher Education/Open University Press, 2001.

Fox, S. From management education and development to the study of management learning. In J. Burgoyne & M. Reynolds (Eds), *Management learning: Integrating perspectives in theory and practice*. London: Sage, 1997.

Fusaro, P.C. & Miller, R.M. *What went wrong at Enron?* Hoboken, NJ: Wiley, 2002.

Galison, P. *Image and logic*. Chicago: Chicago University Press, 1997.

Galison, P. & Jones, C.A. Factory, laboratory, studio: Dispersing sites of production. In P. Galison & E. Thompson (Eds), *The architecture of science*. Cambridge, MA: MIT Press, 1999.

Geertz, C. *Local knowledge*. London: Fontana Press, 1993.

Gibbons, M., Limoges, C., Nowotny, H., Schwartzmann, S., Scott, P. & Trow, M. *The new production of knowledge*. London: Sage, 1994.

Grey, C. Rethinking business schools: The contribution of critical management education. *Academy of Management Learning & Education*, 2004, 3, 178–86.

Grey, C. & French, R. Rethinking management education. In R. French & C. Grey (Eds), *Rethinking management education*. London: Sage, 1996.

Habermas, J. *Knowledge and human interests*. Boston: Beacon Press, 1971.

Habermas, J. *The structural transformation of the public sphere*. Cambridge, MA: MIT Press, 1989.

Hambrick, D. What if the Academy actually mattered? *Academy of Management Review*, 1993, 19, 11–16.

Jeffcutt, P. (Ed.). *The foundation of management knowledge*. London: Routledge, 2000.

Kerr, C. *The uses of the university*, 5th edn. Cambridge, MA: Harvard University Press, 2001.

Kleinman, D.L. & Vallas, S.P. Science, capitalism, and the rise of the 'knowledge worker': The changing structure of knowledge production in the United States. *Theory and Society*, 2001, *30*, 451–92.

Leavitt, H.J. Educating our MBAs: On teaching what we haven't taught. *California Management Review*, 1989, *31*(3), 38–50.

Locke, R. *Management and higher education since 1940: The influence of America and Japan on West Germany, Great Britain and France.* New York: Cambridge University Press, 1989.

Locke, R. *The collapse of the American management mystique.* New York: Oxford University Press, 1996.

Lyotard, J.F. *The postmodern condition: A report on knowledge.* Manchester: Manchester University Press, 1984.

Mintzberg, H. *Developing managers not MBAs.* London: FT Prentice Hall, 2004.

Nisbet, R. *The degradation of the academic dogma: The university in America 1945–70.* London: Heinemann, 1971.

Nowotny, H., Scott, P. & Gibbons, M. *Re-thinking science. Knowledge and the public in an age of uncertainty.* Cambridge: Polity Press, 2001.

Parsons, T. & Platt, G. *The American university.* Cambridge, MA: Harvard University Press, 1973.

Pfeffer, J. & Fong, C.T. The end of business schools? Less success than meets the eye. *Academy of Management Learning and Education*, 2002, *1*, 78–95.

Readings, B. *The university in ruins.* Cambridge, MA: Harvard University Press 1996.

Reich, R. *The work of nations: Preparing ourselves for 21st century capitalism.* New York: Knopf, 1991.

Salbu, S. Foreword. In B. Cruver *Anatomy of greed. The unshredded truth from an Enron insider.* London: Hutchinson, 2002.

Scott, P. The end of the European university. *European Review*, 1998, *6*, 410–57.

Sennett, R. *The corrosion of character. The personal consequences of work in the new capitalism.* New York: W.W. Norton, 1998.

Starkey, K. & Crane, A. Toward green narrative: Management and the evolutionary ethic. *Academy of Management Review*, 2003, *28*, 220–37.

Starkey, K. & Madan, P. Bridging the relevance gap: Aligning stakeholders in the future of management research. *British Journal of Management*, 2001, *12*, S3–S26.

Tranfield, D. & Starkey, K. The nature, social organization and promotion of management research: Towards policy. *British Journal of Management*, 1998, *9*, 341–53.

Watson, S.R. The place for universities in management education. *Journal of General Management*, 1993, *19*(2), 14–42.

Wittrock, B. The modern university: The three transformations. In S. Rothblatt & B. Wittrock (Eds), *The European and American university since 1800.* Cambridge: Cambridge University Press, 1993.

Zell, D. The market-driven business school: Has the pendulum swung too far? *Journal of Management Inquiry*, 2001, *10*, 324–38.

Ken Starkey (BA, BSc, PhD) is Professor of Management at Nottingham University Business School. He previously held positions at Aston and St. Andrews universities. His research interests include the management of strategic change, individual and organizational learning, knowledge management, futures thinking and organization development. He is author/co-author of 10 books, including *How organizations learn* (International Thomson Press) and *Foucault, management and organization theory* (Sage), and approximately 80 articles in books and journals. He teaches mainly on MBA programmes in the areas of strategic management and organizational learning. He is author of a number of reports on the future of management research and management education and is currently principal investigator on a UK Economic and Social Research Council project on the role of the business school in knowledge production. [E-mail: kenneth.starkey@nottingham.ac.uk]

Sue Tempest (BA, MBA, PhD) is Senior Lecturer in Strategic Management at Nottingham University Business School. Her research interests include organizational learning, new forms of organization, management education and the impact of demographic ageing on strategic management. She has published in journals such as *Organization Studies, Organization Science, Management Learning, Long Range Planning* and *Human Relations*. She co-authored *The world-class business school. A UK perspective* (prepared for the Council for Excellence in Management and Leadership). [E-mail: sue.tempest@nottingham.ac.uk]